# HUNGARIAN FOLKTALES

*World Folktale Library*

The World Folktale Library presents the oral art of the greatest and most representative storytellers from diverse folk traditions. Each volume, assembled by a leading expert in the field, features authentically collected and painstakingly transcribed texts designed to capture the personal styles of the oral artists. Introductory materials offer historical background on the folk community, describe the contexts for taletelling, and provide biographical information on the storytellers. Each book is annotated with comparative notes that help place the tales in relation to international oral traditions. The series is designed both to meet the highest scholarly standards and to reach all readers who take delight in the limitlessly rich art of oral storytelling.

*General editor*
Carl Lindahl, University of Houston


*Cajun and Creole Folktales: The French Oral Tradition of South Louisiana*. Collected, transcribed, translated, annotated, and introduced by Barry Jean Ancelet.


*Hungarian Folktales: The Art of Zsuzsanna Palkó*. Collected, transcribed, annotated, and introduced by Linda Dégh. Translated by Vera Kalm.

# HUNGARIAN FOLKTALES

*The Art of Zsuzsanna Palkó*

Collected, transcribed, annotated,
and introduced by Linda Dégh
Translated by Vera Kalm

University Press of Mississippi   Jackson

Manufactured in the United States of America

99  98  97  96      4  3  2  1

The paper in this book meets the guidelines for permanence and durability of the
Committee on Production Guidelines for Book Longevity of the Council on Library
Resources.


Library of Congress Cataloging-in-Publication Data

Palkó, Zsuzsanna.
    Hungarian folktales : the art of Zsuzsanna Palkó / collected, transcribed, annota-
ted, and introduced by Linda Dégh ; translated by Vera Kalm.
    p.       cm. — (The world folktale library)
    Originally published: New York : Garland Pub., c1995, in series: The world folk-
tale library ; vol. 2, and Garland reference library of the humanities ; vol. 1736.
    Includes bibliographical references (p. ) and index.
    ISBN 0-87805-912-1
    1. Tales—Hungary—Karkasd—History and criticism. 2. Storytelling—Hungary—
Karkasd. 3. Szeklers—Hungary—Karkasd—Folklore. 4. Palkó, Zsuzsanna. I. Dégh,
Linda. II. Title. III. Series: World folktale library (Jackson, Miss.)
    [GR154.7.K39P35 1996]
    398.2'09439—dc20                                           96-28121
                                                               CIP


British Cataloging-in-Publication data available

# CONTENTS

## Glossary

# Series Editor's Preface

There has been no more important relationship between folk artist and folklorist than that between Zsuzsanna Palkó and Linda Dégh. Extraordinarily humble and modest, Mrs. Palkó would probably have concealed her great narrative gifts from all but her village circle—if it had not been for Linda Dégh, whose years of fieldwork in Mrs. Palkó's village nurtured both a consummate body of scholarship and a very special friendship. Dégh's painstaking collection of Mrs. Palkó's tales attracted the admiration of the Hungarian-speaking world. In 1954 Mrs. Palkó was named Master of Folklore by the Hungarian government and summoned to Budapest to receive ceremonial recognition. The unlettered 74-year-old woman from Kakasd had become "Aunt Zsuzsi" to Linda Dégh—and was about to become one of the world's best known storytellers, through Dégh's work.

Mrs. Palkó would tell stories literally from sundown to sunup to wide-eyed listeners, but she had never yet visited a place where thousands fell asleep each night listening to radios. She had performed magical healing rituals (Dégh 1989:126-28), but she had never experienced the underground marvels of a subway ride. In her tales she had shown her listeners castles that stood on roosters' feet, but she herself had never seen a full-length mirror: "First she thought that her neighbor was coming to meet her, and then slowly she recognized herself" (Dégh 1989: 188).

Although her words had conjured up countless enchanted castles, Mrs. Palkó had never seen a modern city. Just as she would take an unfamiliar story like "Prince Sándor" (tale no. 12 in this collection) and transform it into her own personal masterpiece, she took on Budapest and remade it as a magic world. As a judge of character, Mrs. Palkó was acutely realistic (Dégh 1989: 204); she could make the most improbable incident seem real in a personal way. With similar artistry, she made Budapest an enchanted city in order to make it real. In Linda Dégh's unforgettable account of the peasant woman's entry into Budapest, a great artist calls upon her own verbal magic to make sense of a place she has never been before:

> Her fantasy, which knew so well how to infuse life into a world never seen, was revived by reality. She arrived by night, by car, seeing the lights of the city ("It was as if the stars had come down from heaven to light my way; there must have been hundreds of thousands"). . . . Whenever a new view opened before her, she identified it with the concept she had of it in her mind: "This is the palace of the king;

in just such a one *King Lajos* lived." "Just such a flower garden was the one owned by the King who cast out *I Don't Know*." "What a beautiful equestrian statue! Such a beautiful horse! Maybe the little prince owned such a one." "You have a telephone like in the King's Palace?" (Dégh 1989: 187-88)

Without Linda Dégh, Zsuzsanna Palkó probably would not have had the opportunity to turn Budapest into a magic kingdom. Vladimir Propp would recognize Linda Dégh as the donor who helped Mrs. Palkó cross the threshold to another world.

Yet, somehow, like the Man Who Had No Story (AT 2412B), Mrs. Palkó sent everything except her Székely tales to the world beyond Hungary. One of the greatest ironies conceivable to folklorists is a great storyteller known only through the words of others. Yet, beyond the Hungarian-speaking world, we know nearly everything about Mrs. Palkó but her stories. Linda Dégh's loving and meticulous studies acquainted readers with Mrs. Palkó's personal history, family relationships, work in and out of the house, moral and religious philosophy, traditional medical practices, reputation as a village wisewoman, and status as a master storyteller. Dégh's *Folktales and Society* (1989), the most important study of traditional narrative yet published, devoted far more attention to Mrs. Palkó than to any other storyteller and made her a familiar figure among folklorists worldwide.

Yet Mrs. Palkó's growing fame did not make it any easier for Linda Dégh to make the tales known. Through Dégh's insistence, four of Mrs. Palkó's tales were translated from Hungarian to German to accompany her study *Märchen, Erzähler, und Erzählgemeinschaft* (1962). When that landmark work was translated into English as *Folktales and Society* (1969a)—much to the disappointment of Linda Dégh and the thousands who have read the book—not one of Mrs. Palkó's tales appeared with the text. The revised English-language edition of 1989 also lacked Mrs. Palkó's stories.[1]

The present collection, published more than forty years after Zsuzsanna Palkó was named Master of Folklore and more than thirty years after her death, bears unimpeachable testimony for the central importance of story and presents compelling evidence that even folklorists must continually remind themselves of story's worth.

Dégh's research into Mrs. Palkó's Székely community—which viewed storytelling as responding to and expressing a full range of village life, performance settings, and individual personalities—radically refigured the ways in which folklorists view traditional taletelling. American contextual studies of the late 1960s and the 1970s followed Dégh's lead in emphasizing the circumstances of narration and the social roles of the tellers within their communities.

Yet, like folklore publishers, many of the narrative scholars who followed Dégh stressed the notion of context to the exclusion of the text, producing a number of articles and monographs that never threatened a theory with a tale. Folklorists seemed to want to know everything about storytelling except the stories.

In contrast, Linda Dégh's scholarship has never allowed its readership to forget either the texts or their social properties and potentials. On two continents, she has performed at least two lifetimes worth of work dedicated to demonstrating the interdependence of the tale and its surroundings. Whenever she has found theory straying too far from the facts, she has gently led us back to the stories, reminding us that they are a narrative scholar's reason for being.

A case in point occurred when Linda Dégh first came to the United States from her native Hungary to accept a professorship in folklore at Indiana University. She could well have consolidated her career as the world's leading expert in the contextual study of European traditional narrative, but instead she embarked on a new career as a specialist in American belief legend. When Dégh arrived at Indiana, the standard folklorist's judgment on American legendry was that, like American culture in general, it was rationalistic, shorn of supernatural traits, rooted in realism, distinctly nonmagical. Rather than simply accepting that opinion, Linda Dégh tested it at length. She and her students undertook one of the most intensive narrative fieldwork enterprises in the history of American folklore, documenting thousands of versions of numerous legend types focused on the supernatural. The incontrovertible evidence, published in the early volumes of the journal *Indiana Folklore*, refuted the scholarly stereotype of a fully rational American folk (see, for example, Dégh 1968, Dégh 1969b, Dégh 1980). Delight in, fear of, fascination with the supernatural pervade these texts and the explanations and attitudes of the tellers: American society is no stranger to nonrational attitudes. For those who would doubt, Linda Dégh listened to, collected, and published the stories, the ultimate proof of her claims.[2]

Since redefining American folk legend (see particularly Dégh 1971), Linda Dégh has produced a series of explorations into new and old manifestations of folklore, always focusing closely on the effects of a changing world upon folktales. Among her most recent works is a book titled *American Folklore and the Mass Media,* which examines märchen and legends in advertising as well as the ways in which oral folktales, storybook fairy tales, and the contemporary media represent women's careers (Dégh 1994). A late twentieth-century folklorist's texts are no longer exclusively oral, and Linda Dégh's most recent research finds folktale texts in the midst of television commercials and news items from *Time* Magazine—contexts far removed from the Székely village where Linda Dégh first met Zsuzsanna Palkó in 1948 and, lacking even the most primitive taperecorder, first set down Mrs. Palkó's words with pencil and paper, in shorthand.

But in 1994, as in 1948, Linda Dégh's greatest work comes not from the "texts" that she reads on TV screens and magazines, but from her intensive fieldwork, her skill as a listener and observer of storytellers. One of the chapters in her recent book examines the stories of an Indiana woman named Lisa Wells—a member of a Pentecostalist church community who recounts tales affirming her beliefs. Lisa Wells may at first seem to live a world apart from Mrs. Palkó. Yet it is interesting to note the similarities between the two—both are deeply religious women with great oral gifts; both became not merely the "informants," but rather the long-time friends of Linda Dégh. In both cases,

Linda Dégh spent years listening to her narrator friends before publishing their stories and her studies of them.

As far as Linda Dégh and world technology have come since her first fieldwork in Kakasd, she continues to return to the Hungarian village where she first met Zsuzsanna Palkó. There, she has found powerful affirmation of the value of her work as a folklorist: the two volumes of tales she collected there have become a village treasure, "widely read in Kakasd, not so much because of Mrs. Palkó, but because she was the voice of the storytelling tradition of the Andrásfalva Székelys" (1989: 292). If, until now, Linda Dégh has been unsuccessful in getting the world at large to hear Mrs. Palkó's tales, she has succeeded brilliantly in a task of even greater importance: she has helped keep these tales alive for those who love them best and need them most, the community that created them. One of the happiest ironies in folklore studies is that of Linda Dégh's role in Kakasd. She began by studying Mrs. Palkó, the guardian of a great oral tradition; but she has now succeeded Mrs. Palkó as guardian. Story remains central in Linda Dégh's life, as she continues to influence the world as much with tales themselves as with her studies of them.

A major premise in Mrs. Palkó's tales, as in Linda Dégh's scholarship, is that tales do not lie. Some of the magnificent tales that follow end with a story within a story: after many dangerous adventures, a woman—like Fairy Ilona (tale no. 20)—returns home incognito, disguising her identity because she has been wrongly accused of crimes. A storytelling session begins, and the woman is invited to tell a tale; in the guise of fiction, she presents her own, true story. In growing astonishment, the listeners slowly recognize that this "made up" story is real; the truth is recognized and the long-suffering heroine is rewarded. Like these heroines, Mrs. Palkó put her most important life experiences into her stories—leaving no clear or useful distinction between autobiography and story, truth and fiction.[3]

Mrs. Palkó's tales do not lie: they are everything that Linda Dégh told us they were, decades ago. Those who find them first here, retold in a new language, will ask themselves why they have had to wait so long. This remarkable collection, a gift to every English-speaking lover of stories, is also the long overdue reward of Zsuzsanna Palkó and her most avid listener.[4]

Carl Lindahl,
General Editor,
World Folktale Library

## Notes

1. Aside from an earlier translation of "The Serpent Prince" (Ortutay 1956), tale no.7 in this collection, the only tale of Mrs. Palkó's available in English has been "Lazybones," first published in Linda Dégh's *Folktales of Hungary* (1965: 142-47, 319-20) and reprinted in Dorson's *Folktales Told around the World* (1975:114–18).

2.   Further information on Linda Dégh's career and scholarship can be found in the introduction to Burlakoff and Lindahl (1980: i-iii) and in the contributions of Grider (1979), Kish (1980), and Voigt (1980).

3.   For discussions of the autobiographical nature of Mrs. Palkó's tales, see particularly Linda Dégh's introductory notes to tales no. 8, 19, and 35, below.

4.   I thank the University of Houston for awarding me a Limited Grant in Aid to support editorial work on this series, and Katherine Oldmixon for her expert editing. Special thanks are due as well to Vera Kalm, whose extraordinary diligence and skills as a translator have brought these tales from one world to another with great vividness and power.

## Works Cited

Burlakoff, Nikolai, and Carl Lindahl. 1980. *Folklore on Two Continents: Essays in Honor of Linda Dégh*. Bloomington, IN: Trickster Press.

Dégh, Linda. 1955, 1960. *Kakasdi népmesék* [Folktales of Kakasd]. 2 volumes. Budapest: Akadémiai Kiadó.

———. 1962. *Märchen, Erzähler, und Erzählgemeinschaft: dargestellt an der ungarischen Volksüberlieferung*. Berlin: Akademie-Verlag. Veröffentlichungen des Instituts für Deutsche Volkskunde, vol. 23.

———. 1965. *Folktales of Hungary*. Trans. Judit Halász. Chicago: University of Chicago Press.

———. 1968. "The Negro in Concrete." *Indiana Folklore* 1:1: 61-67.

———. 1969a. *Folktales and Society: Story-Telling in a Hungarian Peasant Community*. Trans. Emily M. Schossberger. Bloomington: Indiana University Press.

———. 1969b. "The House of Blue Lights Revisited." *Indiana Folklore* 2:2:11-28.

———. 1971. "The Belief Legend in Modern Society." In *American Folk Legend: A Symposium*. Ed. Wayland D. Hand. Berkeley and Los Angeles: University of California Press, pp. 55-68.

———. 1980. *Indiana Folklore: A Reader*. Bloomington: Indiana University Press.

———. 1989. *Folktales and Society*. Expanded Edition with a New Afterword by the Author.

———. 1994. *American Folklore and the Mass Media*. Bloomington: Indiana University Press.

Grider, Sylvia. "Linda Dégh." In *American Women Writers*. Ed. Lina Mainiero. New York: Frederick Ungar, pp. 483-85.

Kish, Eva. 1980. "A Select Bibliography of the Works of Linda Dégh." In Burlakoff and Lindahl, pp. 383-88.

Ortutay, Gyula. 1956. *Hungarian Folktales*. Budapest: Corvina.

Photograph by Andrew Vázsonyi

Zsuzsanna Palkó

# Foreword

The thirty-five tales in this collection represent a selection from the repertoire of Mrs. Zsuzsanna Palkó, a Hungarian peasant woman from Kakasd, a village in the county of Tolna, not far from the Austrian and Slovenian borders. But this village was not her native land. Like the other residents of Kakasd and thirty-seven other surrounding villages in Tolna and Baranya counties, she was a new settler in the region. Like the others, she came from the multiethnic Bucovina province, annexed by Romania in 1918, after the collapse of the Hapsburg Empire. As a member of the Bucovina Székely subculture she was relocated to this region in southwest Hungary in the migration of 1946-1947.

Because of their isolation from the motherland, Bucovina Székelys preserved a unique, archaic Hungarian cultural tradition; therefore, soon after their arrival, the newcomers attracted the keen interest of folklorists and ethnologists. The opportunity arose to study the Székely settlers in the process of economic, social, and cultural adaptation to their new homeland, different in every respect from their native land. In the company of other folklorists, I myself first conducted fieldwork in Kakasd in 1948, beginning an almost lifelong association with its people. I began as a novice folklorist, an apprentice, who learned the trade through continued visits with the villagers of Kakasd. Each visit—those made during the first eleven years and those made later from 1981 to 1987, after a pause of seventeen years—brought new insights. As time passed, old generations succumbed and new generations emerged, posing new cultural enigmas and puzzles, showing the inexhaustible vitality of tradition and the futility of the scholarly illusion that one can gain full knowledge of a people even in a lifetime.

The settlers of Kakasd (pop. ca. 5,000), Roman Catholic natives of Andrásfalva (one of the five Bucovina Székely villages), came to inhabit fertile farmland. Herds of grazing cattle, rich pastures, well-equipped farmhouses, full pantries, barns, and sheds awaited the new arrivals, but no resident was there to welcome them. The former occupants—descendants of migrant laborers from Germany who populated an area devastated during the 150 years of Turkish occupation—had settled here, in the eighteenth century, in what was later known as *Schwäbische Türkei* (Swabian Turkey), but were accused of collaborating with the Nazis during the Second World War and deported back to Germany. When the Székelys arrived, authorities distributed wealth among them according to family size, not according to their former economic standing in the Bucovina. They came almost emptyhanded, running through war zones between the German and the Russian fronts. Countless personal experience stories recount their adventures; these tales are characterized by the famous Székely deadpan humor. Anna Sebestyén recalls a brief example: When the frightened, hungry, aimless wanderers were passing through West Hungary, villagers treated them to hot soup and potatoes, asking: "Where are you going, brother?" "Towards ruin!" "Where is that?" "Where we are going."

As a Hungarian subculture, the Székelys sustain a proud, historically shaped sense of ethnic identity. Their habitat—the valleys, plateaus and ranges of the southern Carpathian Mountains in Transylvania—was ceded to Romania in 1918. Yet the Székelys' Hungarian roots are extensive and well remembered. Originating in a nomadic tribe of cattle breeders, the Székelys became an important military contingent for the kings of Hungary during the Middle Ages. Earning privileges and land, their sib organization later developed a specific social order based on units called *széks* (sites), composed of six extended families divided into two branches. To defend their own land, they formed a military unit with its own rules, leaders, strategies, and uniforms. Under feudalism Székely society developed a land-holding aristocracy, while those with small or no holdings lost their ranks and freedom from taxation. Poor have-nots regressed to serfdom.

In the eighteenth century the Székelys supported uprisings against the Hapsburgs. In retaliation, Vienna dissolved their military organization and took away their privileges. But since the defense of the southern borders was crucial, the government ordered the formation of a 15,000-man Székely border guard, under the jurisdiction of the Austrian army. The Székelys resisted the recruiters. On the morning of January 6, 1764, military units stationed at the village Mádéfalva opened fire on the protesters, killing 200. Despite other economic factors, this incident remains in folk memory the sole cause of mass emigration from Székelyland (*Székelyföld*).

Many refugees fled to Moldavia, then under Turkish sovereignty, and established scattered villages on fertile riverbanks, near lush grazing grounds. Others eventually returned to Székelyland. Finally, in 1774, the Austrian government offered amnesty to the deserters, liberation from serfdom and free land to those who would settle the uninhabited Bucovina (North Moldavia), newly annexed from Turkey. About 800 Székely families settled in the five villages, named Fogadjisten ("God-Receive-Us"); Istensegits ("God Help Us"); Józseffalva ("Village of Joseph," after Emperor Joseph the Second); Hadikfalva (after András Hadik, the Governor of Transylvania responsible for settling the deserters); and Andrásfalva ("Andrew Village," after Hadik's given name). Soon the settlers found themselves surrounded by other exiles: Germans, Romanians, Gypsies, Jews, Poles, Ukrainians. They all built their own communities and interacted with the other groups, exchanging goods, skills, and ideas, broadening their cultural knowledge and world views. Isolated from their homelands, expatriates of diverse countries preserved their archaic folk traditions while borrowing from each other and creating new forms of folkloric expression resulting from new experiences in the multilingual, multiethnic Bucovina. The Bucovina Székelys' exposure to cultural diversity for more than two centuries is largely responsible for the richness and the peculiarities of their exquisite oral art.

By the time the Székelys left the Bucovina, life had grown very difficult for most. The distribution of property determined the social structure. Due to economic decline and population growth, living conditions slowly deteriorated. My informants recalled that four well-to-do Andrásfalva farmers owned 60 to 80 acres, twenty families owned twelve, and thirty possessed eight. The majority, victims of crop failure and other calamities, lost their holdings and had to earn their living from sharecropping on the estates of the landed Moldavian aristocracy during the seven-month agricultural season. During the winter, they found other ways to complement their meager incomes. Men and women peddled goods, bartered produce with other ethnic groups, hauled timber, and sold dried fruits, cucumbers, and onions. Women made rugs to sell. Marketing, hauling, and working in lumber mills often took people back to the Transylvanian homeland, keeping a nostalgic attachment alive. Andrásfalva's poor district became increasingly crowded as more and more people found themselves unable to buy arable land.

Drought, famine, and cholera epidemics took their toll on the population and contributed to the success of the Hungarian government's resettlement action in 1883, which brought the exiles back to the motherland, to a site on the lower Danube gained by draining the river's floodplain. Four thousand people arrived and turned the wilderness into a human habitat. They built their villages and farms, but within four years they had lost everything to the flooding Danube. Penniless, they had to return to Andrásfalva and accept the charity of neighbors and relatives. Repeated attempts were made to return to the homelands, mainly to Transylvania, before the outbreak of World War I in 1914. Some of the resettlement sites remained viable in the early decades of the century; nevertheless, as early as 1906 many Székely left to seek their fortunes on the Canadian prairies.

After the war, conditions in Andrásfalva deteriorated further. In addition to suffering a general depression and shortages of basic necessities, Hungarians in the new Romanian state were relegated to minority status. No wonder that when Bucovina Germans were relocated to Germany during World War II, the Székelys accepted the Hungarian government's resettlement proposal. In 1941 inhabitants of the five Székely villages vacated their homes and moved with all their belongings to a beautiful fertile area in the Bácska, a multiethnic region incorporated into the newly created nation of Yugoslavia after World War I, but returned to Hungary by Hitler in 1939.

During World War II, the Hungarian government settled the Székelys on the land of hostile Serbs; in the words of György Andrásfalvi, nephew of Zsuzsanna Palkó, "they settled us on the bear's back—the bear shook himself and shook us all loose." On October 8, 1944, the Bácska became a battlefield, and the Székelys had two hours to flee their villages with hastily packed belongings loaded on their wagons. The Székelys badly needed new homes, but they felt guilty about occupying the abandoned houses of German farmers in Kakasd. Furthermore, the Székelys feared that they would soon have to run again.

The migrants from Andrásfalva adjusted to the new land in Kakasd under extremely difficult conditions. They had to learn new agricultural techniques, adjust to new Communist-style cooperative farming methods, and develop a family entrepreneural system that incorporated cooperative farming, contract herding, raising pigs, and working in the nearby coalmines, the state farm, and an enamel factory. After initial mismanagement leading to crop failure and clashes with authorities over the harsh Communist ideological system, the Székelys learned to cope. Particularly after the mid-1960s, when liberalization of the agricultural system opened a free market economy, the Székelys became affluent. Moving from the old German houses, families built comfortable modern homes and developed technologically efficient farms. At the same time, they maintained their clannish, extended family ties and continued to distinguish themselves from non-Székelys. The features they see as markers of traditional Székely identity are taught as primary education to children at home and in early schooling; these same traits are also foregrounded in educating the general public about Székelys through staged cultural displays. Among the most cherished features are the archaic Bucovina Székely dialect, the elaborate Christmas mumming drama, the farewell lament for the dead, certain pieces of the traditional costume, woven rugs, embroidered towels, pillowcases displayed in the front rooms of Székely homes, and, above all, storytelling.

Storytellers were always held in high esteem as artists, public entertainers, and performers of the magic tale, the most elaborate form of oral prose narration. I have collected many tales in Kakasd, from many people: men and women, young and old. Some were specialists in diverse tale genres; some original talents possessed large repertoires while others told only a few tales; some narrated only occasionally; others told stories at public ceremonies of various kinds. I was lucky to arrive at the right time to capture the exceptional art of Zsuzsanna Palkó as it evolved and received center stage during the last fifteen years of her life.

I was able to trace storytelling as far back as eighty years prior to the Kakasd settlement; throughout this period narrative art was a practice highly esteemed among the Bucovina Székelys. Almost everyone was able to recite a tale or list a few favorites and cite cherished narrators; yet villagers unanimously pointed to the district of Andrásfalva, where the poor resided, as the hotbed of the magic tale. The poor families, who traveled in boxcars to the Moldavian estates and spent seven months together as a work team, lived together in barracks. After long working hours, they cooked their evening meal and then shared leisure until they fell asleep. There could not have been a better diversion from back-breaking agricultural labor than telling folktales: stories leading them away from harsh reality to a world that miraculously fulfilled otherwise impossible wishes. Traditional peasantry developed the folktale into a unique oral prose genre fulfilling the need for aesthetic delight. What literary fiction offers to reading, movie- and theater-going, TV-watching urbanites, the orally performed folktale offers to small groups of illiterate and semiliterate people isolated from the technology of mass communication. For the Andrásfalva poor, as for other agricultural laborers elsewhere in preindustrial Europe, the sharecropper's work schedule offered the opportunity to learn and develop storytelling skills, trade stories, compete, and entertain fellow workers at night, after the evening meal. While telling a story, an expert narrator would call out "soup" from time to time to see if everyone was still alert and listening. If the answer "bone" came from many voices, the story continued, but if the answers became fewer and the audience seemed to be lulled to sleep, the teller stopped, only to continue next night, after finding out at what point in the story the audience fell asleep. The storytellers were all men, addressing an audience of both men and women, but women were not accepted as public entertainers: their specialized narrative art was confined to the nursery. Sometimes children managed to sneak in unnoticed, but they were not welcome at this serious adult entertainment, partly because it was not "for their ears," partly because children, unable to sit still for long, disturbed the fun of the adults.

I have traced the careers of many good storytellers of the past. Their memory was very much alive during the first period of my fieldwork in Kakasd. I could even trace repertoires because stories were handed down in families and considerably altered by the individual taste of the recipients. I was able to identify the community corpus of the Székelys of Andrásfalva and Kakasd, living in active use, in latency, or recently revived. In addition to my texts published in 1955 and 1960 and my unpublished recordings made from 1981 to 1987, there is a third source that fills the gaps and completes the body of community heritage: the collection of Ádám Sebestyén. These three complementary sources document fully the intricacies of the storytelling network, as well as the creativity and variability of storytellers over time; there is much to be studied by future generations of scholars. Sebestyén, a Székely farmer, was born in Andrásfalva in 1921. Although he had only two years' grade-school education, he followed his father as lay church singer and master of rituals at weddings and funerals. In his dedication to Székely distinctiveness, he became the chronicler of his people's history and recorder of oral poetic tradition. His systematic and extraordinarily valuable collection was published in four volumes (1979, 1981, 1983, and 1987) containing 466 texts from fifty narrators.

This representative material reveals the lasting impact of a storytelling dynasty: the Zaicz family. József Zaicz, Mrs. Palkó's father, was a farm laborer who worked on the land of wealthy Andrásfalva farmers and told stories to his employers. He often boasted that he knew 365 stories, one for every day of the year. His son János was equally well-liked; even when crippled by old age, he was welcomed to a good meal in exchange for his delicious stories. He was more than just a storyteller. Through the years, his magic-shamanistic powers and knowledge were often mentioned in conversations. His powers are cited even today, when modern technological inventions are mentioned. János was a wise man, a prophet: a visionary who could see into the future. He believed in the Revelations of St. John and continually drew parallels between biblical prophecies and recent events. People believed that many of János's predictions came true, such as that people would engage in wars causing mass destruction; that "iron birds" (airplanes) would ply the skies and "iron horses" (cars) would race on the streets; and that see-through glass (nylon) dresses would be invented. People still believe that other of János's predictions are bound to be fulfilled, and that in the end the earth will perish by fire. János was an avid reader and an eloquent speaker, respected by educated villagers. At wakes, he led the rosary and the singing of hymns. József Zaicz's grandson, György Zaicz—a small, hunchbacked man whose pride in his ancestral village led him to change his family name to Andrásfalvi (from Andrásfalva)—inherited his grandfather's talent for telling stories. György was the only male member of the Zaicz family of Andrásfalva raconteurs whom I knew.

Mrs. Palkó, daughter of József, knew all the tales. She heard them throughout her life but did not tell them publicly until she was nearly 70 years old. She was a plain, modest woman, dressed always in black, wearing a black headsquare; yet her blue eyes sparkled from her wrinkled face. She never learned to read and write, she never went to school, but she helped raise her younger sisters and brothers. As a woman, she could listen to the tales, but she had no opportunity to capture an audience. Her rise to recognition could happen only under extraordinary conditions. When the Székelys settled in Kakasd the social hierarchy of old Andrásfalva collapsed. Prestigious rich families lost their status with the new distribution of the land. The poor people were singing: "Thank God, the world has turned; from poor people, big farmers have grown." Public storytelling, previously confined to the poor district of Andrásfalva, now traveled to the most prominent social occasion: the wake.

It was an essential element of respect for the dead that family members, neighbors, and friends gather in the house of the deceased and spend the night with the body before burial. Storytelling was a major event; the narrator's task was to keep all the mourners respectfully awake from dusk till next morning's dawn. Wakes of important people were highlighted by the performances of the most noted storytellers; for children and young people, however, anyone could be asked to tell tales. At the time of the settlement, none of the Bucovina greats were functional. Márton László, author of *The Book of the Dead,* settled in another community and died in 1949; János Zaicz was ill, unable to speak; he died the same year. It was time for Zsuzsanna Zaicz, the daughter of József Zaicz, to assume her father's role.

She was born in 1880, the third of ten children. When she was one year old, the family moved to the settlement on the lower Danube; six years later they lost everything to the flooding Danube and returned to continue seasonal work in Moldavia. When she was eight, she started to work in the sugar beet fields. After turning thirteen she worked in the households of well-to-do families in the country and in the nearby city, taking care of children, cleaning house, and helping in the kitchen. She also worked harvesting wheat and rye at the threshing machine and serving clients at the general store. She could not expect a dowry from her parents; she had to provide her own. At eighteen she married István Dobondi, who died of tuberculosis after three years of marriage; their two children also died within one year. Five years later she married József Palkó, the foreman of a sharecropping band whom she met during seasonal work. After a good life with her, raising eleven children, József died in 1927.

Life became a struggle for the widow, and she was determined to win. She worked wherever she could. Like a man, she got into the horse-drawn wagon, hauled wood and a variety of goods which she sold or traded. She accepted day labor, went hacking, wove runners, hired out for spinning. As her children came of age, she took her older sons to help her on errands. When the family moved from Andrásfalva to the Bácska in 1941, the children went ahead with their possessions while she stayed on to sell the house at a good price. In Kakasd, she moved in with a daughter's family. That daughter died a year later, so she took up residency with her oldest son's wife, but moved out again when he did not return from the war, "so that the young widow could get a chance to remarry."

Linda Dégh dressed in the traditional native costume in 1986.

At the time I met Mrs. Palkó, only four of her children were still alive. Erzsi Fábián, her sickly youngest daughter, needed her most. The Fábián family worked nine acres; with five young children—aged 12, 8, 6, 3 and nine months—there was much to do and Mrs. Palkó's was the greater share. She did all the cooking, cleaning, and laundry; she took care of the cow, the pigs, and the poultry; she cut wood and hay; she took on herself all the responsibilities she listed as woman's work in her tale "Peti and Boris" (no. 28, below). I never saw her idle or resting, even while she was telling a story. Sitting on the low stool in front of the iron stove, she fixed her eyes on the pans so as not to burn the food that was cooking; she wiped the children's noses and washed their hands. Telling her tale, she would hold one child on her lap while rocking the baby in the cradle. She was always smiling, cheerful; she had a way with children.

In the tiny, crowded, steamy kitchen the children were quiet, well behaved, polite, governed by their grandmother's calm words and many tales. These children knew all her tales; it was their privilege to remind Grandmother of what she had not told me yet. I usually came in the evening, after dinner, when I did not disturb the family's work schedule because it was now time to relax. Erzsi sat on one of the two beds, mending socks or embroidering shirts; her husband Antal sat on the other bed with male visitors. Visiting women brought their low stools and distaffs; while listening they would spin or knit. There was no electricity yet available in the section of the village where the Fábiáns lived. I sat at a small table with the only tiny gaslight on it, barely sufficient for taking notes and operating the battery-run tape recorder that was an extra sensation, drawing a curious audience—everyone wanted to hear his or her own voice emerge from the machine. A number of ambitious village children begged for the privilege of carrying the tape recorder for me.

Mrs. Palkó left her home only if her three daughters-in-law needed help with the laundry, pig-slaughtering, or major housecleaning. Her hands were too full with running the Fábián household; she could do no more for her own pleasure than attend church services, funerals, and wakes, as is expected of old women, close to eternity. She was deeply religious, at peace with the world.

As a storyteller, she was modest, unlike the men who would usually boast and exaggerate their knowledge of tales and claim to have invented them. She never claimed authorship but always made reference to her source. Mrs. Palkó did not see herself as a great artist. When she was awarded the distinguished title, Master of Folk Arts, by the Hungarian Minister of Culture in 1954, she was surprised." I did not deserve this," she said at the ceremony, "my father and my brother told stories all their lives and they did not get any recognition."

Aunt Zsuzsi's repertoire numbered 74 stories: 45 magic tales, 19 jokes and anecdotes and ten stories belonging to diverse genres. Among known storytellers there are many, men and women alike, whose repertoires greatly exceed this number; many told more than a hundred tales and some knew as many as 300 and even 500 (Faragó 1971). Nevertheless, her artistic embellishment of content and style, her thematic originality, her way of blending experienced reality and poetic fantasy mark her as one of the greatest known traditional storytellers. What makes her narration particularly attractive is its variability. She specializes in magic tales, elaborates the plots meticulously in diverse ways, characterizing her actors and detailing situations without stagnating or making repetitions dull. She has many voices: she takes the women's side, pouring out her own feelings, but she is no less convincing as she pursues the dangerous journey of the male hero. She accompanies her stories with commentaries that reveal personal beliefs, opinions, personal positions concerning the order of the world and how it should be. Her sense of humor emerges in her anecdotes, particularly those that criticize the objectionable behavior of girls, young women, and men. When talking about bodily functions, she sometimes uses what urbanites would view as four-letter words. Yet her audience did not consider such terminology coarse in any way. Her speech reflects the typical usage of Hungarian peasant dialects, which lack refined alternatives. Actually, she disliked vulgarities and the obscene jokes popular at older women's work parties and men's gathering at the "father's store" (the pub). I saw her once send a young man away after he came to the door directly from the pub, visibly drunk, and began telling a spicy anecdote.

Aunt Zsuzsi died in 1964, at the age of 84, but her tales, now in print, are continually nurtured by posterity. For the Kakasd Székelys folktales are identity markers, sources of great pride; narrators take great pains to preserve the indigenous archaic dialects of the ancestors. Mrs. Palkó's language is consciously preserved by today's star narrator, Mrs. Mária Fábián, a nurse in the Kakasd kindergarten, who teaches her preschool wards how to tell tales in the time-honored fashion by preserving Székely terms and gleaning "foreign" (Hungarian) words from the tale (Kovács 1980) .

It has been difficult to choose only 35 tales from Mrs. Palkó's extensive repertoire. Because her tales are of consistently high quality, the major principle of selection is variety. The stories that follow present a representative breadth of genre: women's tales, hero tales, jokes, legends, pious tales, and realistic tales. A second principle is distinctiveness: I have favored characteristically Hungarian tales and left out those which vary little in plot or subject from tales well known internationally. For example, Mrs. Palkó's "Rupcsen-Hencsen" is very similar to—and probably derived from—the Grimm Brothers' *Rumpelstilzchen* (AT 500); and "Pihári" is derived from a standard book-tale treatment of "The Youth Who Wanted To Learn What Fear Is" (AT 326); in spite of their excellence, these two tales were omitted in order to make way for such uniquely powerful masterpieces as "The Twelve Robbers" (tale no. 19, below) and "Margit" (no. 35).

So much should suffice to introduce readers of English to the cultural background of Kakasd and to make the following selection of Aunt Zsuzsi's stories enjoyable reading. A headnote prefaces each tale, describing its place in Hungarian and Western traditions, providing specific cultural information, and commenting on Mrs. Palkó's unique narrative touches. A glossary at the back of the book explains unfamiliar concepts, terms, names, and sayings and presents a catalog of formulaic phrases.

If oral tales are by nature international—traveling easily and naturally across linguistic borders—literary translation is always a problematic venture. Vera Kalm's translation, however, is remarkably smooth, preserving the spirit of the original as far as possible.

# Bibliography

Aarne, Antti, and Stith Thompson. 1961. *The Types of the Folktale: A Classification and Bibliography.* Folklore Fellows Communications, no. 184. Helsinki: Suomalainen Tiedeakatemia. [Abbreviated AT in the headnotes to the tales, below.]

Benedek, Elek. 1894. *Magyar mese és mondavilág.* ["Hungarian Tale- and Legend Treasury."] Budapest: Athenaeum. 5 vols.

Dégh, Linda. 1955, 1960. *Kakasdi népmesék.* ["Folktales of Kakasd."] 2 vols. Budapest: Akadémiai Kiadó.

———— 1978. "The Tree That Reached Up to the Sky." In *Studies in East European Folk Narrative.* Ed. L. Dégh. Publications of the American Folklore Society, Bibliographical and Special Series, no. 30, pp. 263-316.

———— 1979. "Conduit-Theorie." *Enzyklopädie des Märchens.* Berlin: Walter de Gruyter. 3:124-26.

———— 1989. *Folktales and Society: Story-Telling in a Hungarian Peasant Community.* 2nd ed. Bloomington: Indiana University Press.

———— 1995. "How Do Storytellers Interpret the Snakeprince Tale?" In *Narratives in Society: A Performer-Centered Study of Narration.* Folklore Fellows Communication no. 255. Bloomington and Helsinki: Indiana University Press and Suomalainen Tiedeakatemia, pp. 137–151.

Denecke, Ludwig. 1975. "Amicus und Amelius." *Enzyklopädie des Märchens.* Berlin: Walter de Gruyter. 1: 454-63.

Faragó, József. 1971. "Storytellers with Rich Repertoires." *Acta Ethnographica* 20:439-43.

Kovács, Ágnes. 1980. "A Bucovina Szekler Storyteller Today." In *Folklore on Two Continents: Essays in Honor of Linda Dégh.* Ed. Nikolai Burlakoff and Carl Lindahl. Bloomington: Trickster Press, pp. 372- 81.

————. 1981- 1992. *Magyar Népmesekatalógus.* ["Hungarian Folktale Catalogue."] Budapest: MTA Néprajzi Kutatócsoport . 9 vols. [Abbreviated MNK in the headnotes below.]

Sebestyén, Ádám. 1972. *A bukovinai andrásfalvi székelyek élete és története Madéfalvától napjainking.* ["History and Life of the Bukovina Székelys of Andrásfalva from Madéfalva until Our Days."] Szekszárd: Megyei Tanács.

————. 1979-1987. *Bukovinai székely népmesék.* ["Székely Folktales from the Bucovina."] Notes and comments by Agnes Kovács. Szekszárd: Megyei Tanács.

Thompson, Stith. 1955-1958. *Motif-Index of Folk-Literature: A Classification of Narrative Elements in Folktales, Ballads, Myths, Fables, Medieval Romances, Exempla, Fabliaux, Jest-Books and Legends.* 6 vols. Bloomington: Indiana University Press.

# A Note on the Texts

Each of the tales is preceded by a headnote provided by Linda Dégh to place the story in its Hungarian and international contexts, as well as to explain terms and situations unfamiliar to non-Hungarian readers. The notes contain some abbreviated scholarly references; the full citations are found on p. xxii of the foreword.

Within the tales themselves, certain words and phrases are italicized: for example, *dog-headed Tatars, shako, their eyes popped out.* Italics refer readers to the glossary provided by Linda Dégh on pages 371–79, below, where the special significance of each term is explained.

"The Twelve Robbers" (tale no. 19) ends with a complex tale-within-a-tale told by the son of the heroine. In order to avoid overly complex punctuation and to set the embedded tale apart from the rest of the narrative, the boy's retelling is rendered in italics.

In six of the tales—nos. 2, 6, 12, 15, 18, and 20—Linda Dégh recorded not only the words of Zsuzsanna Palkó, but also comments from the listeners. Mrs. Palkó clearly responded to some of these comments as she proceeded with her storytelling. In this translation, listener comments are rendered in bold type. For example,

**[Listeners:] I'd have snuffed out that girl's life!**
**They were really heathens.**

Mrs. Palkó's responses to her listeners, as well as her asides to the audience, are placed in parentheses; for example, after this audience comment—

**[Listener:] He didn't know about his wife's illicit dealings?**

—Mrs. Palkó's response is rendered

(No, he didn't know about it.)

## From the translator

As there is no cross-cultural equivalent of the Bucovina Székely dialect in which Mrs. Palkó's tales were narrated and transcribed, I had no choice but to offer them in the English vernacular. While I attempted to retain the "spoken" quality of the tales, avoiding embellishments, I found that compromises, especially in grammar, were inevitable to make the texts readable. Moreover, as the glossary also attests, some expressions defied transference into another context, another language. For instance, in tale no. 25, "The Wager of the Two Comrades," the terms "friend," "pal," "comrade," "neighbor."

variously used to render *koma* (masculine) and *komaasszony* (feminine)—do not capture the quality of the "elective kinship" these words represent in a traditional Hungarian village community. Above all I have tried throughout to preserve the distinctive rhythms and patterns of the narrator's speech. Mrs. Palkó often used long, complex sentences, stringing together many phrases. These proved difficult to punctuate. The series editor agreed, however, to use dashes—instead of the commas of the original transcriptions—to set apart asides, false starts, and sentence fragments, to allow the voice of this master storyteller to shine through.

—Vera Kalm

# The Tales

# 1. I Don't Know

AT 532 (*I Don't Know*); a complex combination of elements of 314, 510A, 530, and 532, particularly widespread in Central and East Europe. The Hungarian subtype, MNK 532 (*Nemtudomka*), lists 34 variants, some identified as "Male Cinderella" because of the close parallel with episode III of 510A (*Cinderella*).

Tape-recorded in 1949 at the home of the narrator. It was one of those cold winter evenings when a few neighbors came over to listen to her tales. It was usually one of her grandchildren who asked for a particular story, and if she was in the right mood for that one, she began to talk, sitting next to the cradle and occasionally rocking the baby with her foot. She learned the story from her godfather, the farmer Mátyás Mátyás, for whom she worked when she was young. " We don't want to be bored," he would tell her while she was hacking beets, "I shall tell a story if you listen." In the course of time, this tale became one of the most popular pieces that she told at wakes, entertaining mourners at the vigil, during which attendance was obligatory from 6 p.m. until the morning bell-ringing. The need for a long story made this extraordinary narrator expand her godfather's original version and display her unique creativity. Six years after Mrs. Ambrus Jordáki's wake, villagers still recalled Aunt Zsuzsa's poignant performance on that occasion.

The original was a retelling of the five-page storybook version of folklorist and writer Elek Benedek (1859-1929). Only the title of the booktale—"Timberland Castle"—as I Don't Know's ambiguous reference to his residence, remained unchanged.

This was the longest and most elaborate tale I recorded from Mrs. Palkó. Even this lengthy telling cannot be called "complete," as episodes and motifs were borrowed from other tale types and the threefold repetition of events is not consistent; nevertheless, it is representative of her superb storytelling art. Her performance is characterized by colorful, artful use of language and style; masterful character descriptions; carefully depicted sentences and mental dispositions; elaborate fast-breaking dramatic dialogues and elaborate details constructed through meticulous description of landscapes, environments, and physical conditions. She often stops or slows down the tempo of events to explain and interpret, and prepare her audience for what is forthcoming. For her the tale is not a cool, objective outsider's account. Deeply committed, she lives in the tale, identifies with her heroes, suffers with them through their ordeals—as if she herself would try to find words of consolation for the steward, as if she would teach I Don't Know the chores of the kitchen help. Her narration is realistic, mirroring experiences of her personal life, yet she keeps the magic world of the tale intact. Like other expert storytellers, Mrs. Palkó knows that the mingled presence of reality and fantasy is essential to magic tales. In her stories, the actors act according to the tale logic; the flow of events is governed by the märchen's world view, and style and form utilize the folktale's vocabulary and inventory of formulas. Mrs.

Palkó frequently uses the same words, sayings, and formulas describing identical situations in diverse tales as, for example: "We are not born all at the same time and shall not die at the same time"(also in "The Sky-High Tree" and "The Princess" in this collection, as well as in her untranslated tale, "The Flea Princess"); "when the others eat oats, then he gets hay" (also in "The Sky-High Tree," below, and "Ej Haj," untranslated). But her resort to formulaic vocabulary does not make her prose repetitious, or dull; on the contrary, it gives her style a specific rhythm and flavor as documented in her special treatment of the following episodes: 1) the consolation of the widowed king; declaration of war and the king's departure; the steward's gradual change of heart; 2) I Don't Know and the soldiers in the stable; 3) the magic horse instructing I Don't Know; 4) descriptions of the city, people on the street, the royal family, and the princesses; 5) the portrayal of the cook; 6) the mockery of the brothers-in-law; and 7) description of the splendor and parade as the young couple enter the royal palace.

———

Once upon a time, beyond seven times seven lands, there lived a king and a queen and they had a beautiful little son. The boy wasn't more than four. He was four years old. They loved him so dearly that they found all their joy in the child. He was very lovely, with a head of golden locks. They delighted in him but their happiness didn't last long for the queen fell ill and died. The child became an *orphan*. Oh, how grief-stricken the king was! He wept bitterly night and day. He couldn't eat, couldn't sleep, all he ever did was weep. He just couldn't control himself. There was a beautiful statue of the queen in the palace. Every single day the king went to kneel before it to pray for her soul but he couldn't pray for all the weeping and sobbing. He was overcome with tears all the time.

The king had a steward whom he had always considered to be very, very fair-minded. The steward visited him every day for he knew that he would always find the king weeping. He went to console him:

"Your Royal Highness, why are you crying so much? Surely you know that *we were not all born at the same time and that we cannot die at the same time.* So accept the will of God, who let her live this long and has now let her die. Such is the order of things. Your Majesty will wed again, take another wife, and go on living. So why keep crying so much?"

And so he tried to comfort him day after day, but the king just continued grieving for his wife. He would never find a woman as beautiful and as good as his first wife was, he said. Well, one day, when he was once again in tears, crying until his heart nearly broke, the steward came to see him and said:

"Great king, can't you compose yourself—do you want to destroy yourself too? And who will look after the little boy if he doesn't even have a father? You may want to die, so deep is your sorrow, but have pity on your small son!"

"Well, if it has to be, it has to be," he said, "I have to accept my fate for I see that I can't get her to come back no matter how much I cry, or even if I kill myself."

"I believe," said the steward, "that one can't forget, for he who truly loves his wife has trouble forgetting. Just accept that *we don't come into this world together and we don't leave it together!*"

Well now, the king asked that the steward should come to see him more often to reassure him, for when he was alone he kept remembering his wife and was always weeping. So the steward visited the king more frequently and consoled him so he wouldn't go on crying forever.

Now then, the boy could have been about six years old. He had grown well and become unusually tall. People might have thought the child was ten, he had grown and developed so beautifully.

One day a courier arrived, bringing a letter, a letter with a seal affixed to it—and handed it to the king. The king accepted it, looked it over and, God Almighty, he found that he was summoned to war. They were warning that the country was about to be invaded by the *Tatars*. The courier said that the king should muster his troops and if he wanted to save his country, he should confront the enemy. If he didn't, they would invade and take away his country.

Well, the king wasn't as sorry for his country or for anything else, as he was for having to take leave of his young son. Most of all he was worried that the boy would have neither a mother nor a father. What would become of the child if he were to lose his life? In those days kings too had to do battle, not like nowadays when only soldiers, officers and noblemen do—the country's "greats" don't go to war. Then, to be sure, kings had to take up arms.

For a while the king was in deep thought.

Then he said: "My heart is breaking for my little boy."

And the steward said: "No, it isn't, no, it isn't breaking, why should it? No harm will come to him."

"To whom can I entrust him? Who would be as good to him as I was," said the king. "Look, steward, I know you as being the most faithful to me, you were the one who consoled me, so I believe you will not treat the boy badly if I place him in your care."

"I'll treat him as if he were my own," said the steward.

It happened that the steward's son was as old as the king's. They were the same age.

"Well, mine is going to school, they can go together. Or, better still," he said, "I'll get a tutor to come to the palace to teach him. I'll not let him go to school. He'll get a good education while Your Majesty is away. Don't worry about the boy," he said, "he'll not have a bad life here, with me. I'll treat him like my own, even better."

"Then," said the king," if you keep my son, take good care of him, have a priest and a teacher give him an education so that he will learn and develop and not suffer any want while I am away—then, God willing, upon my return I shall elevate you to a high position. You will be second only to me."

The king would make him prime minister, if he cared for his child.

"That's agreed, your Majesty," said the steward, "the smallest of your worries should be larger than this, for no harm will come to your boy."

Now then, one day the drums started rolling, the time had come to go to war. They were beating the drums and *calling up the soldiers,* assembling them. When they were ready to leave, all the horsemen gathered in front of the palace, waiting for the king to lead them. But the king was weeping inconsolably, he just couldn't, couldn't part with the boy. He started for the gate, perhaps even ten times, always returning to embrace and hold the child, lamenting that he was unable to leave him. And the steward continued to comfort the king, reassuring him that the boy would have a good life in his household. Finally, after urging the steward once again to be kind to the boy, he was ready to leave. They set forth to the sound of the band playing loudly. And the boy stayed behind. He, too, shed bitter tears for he could now understand that his father had left for the war and God only knew if he would ever return. The steward called the boy pet names, talked to him endearingly, took him to his own mansion which was nearby and brought him over to his son to play, so the child would be cheered. He even let the boy attend school a few times so he could enjoy the company of other children and forget. He was so good to the boy that he couldn't have been any better to him had he been his own.

About a month had passed when suddenly something evil took hold of the steward's heart. He said to his wife:

"Wife, wouldn't it be better if we took less good care of this boy and gave him only the bare essentials? Just enough so he wouldn't die of hunger. Why should we be so good to him? Maybe, somehow, he will perish and then my son would become king. If the king's son were to die, my son could succeed to the throne. We needn't tend to this boy's comforts so much," he said, "and, who knows, he may just die."

Then the wife said: "I don't mind."

So they cut down on his meals and food. They gave him less and less every day. They didn't even let him share what they ate but always gave him something worse. Then they no longer allowed the boy to eat in the room with them—they chased him out into the stables. It is there he had to eat the small slice of dry bread he received. The boy realized the bad turn his life had taken. The servants, too, noticed that the child was always sent out to the stables with only a piece of black bread to eat. They noticed that the steward wanted to put the boy's life in danger. The soldiers felt sorry for him— there were soldiers working in the stables—and he grew to like them so much that he could hardly do enough to please them. He tried to be near them all the time, watching them work and shovel manure, so he took a pitchfork and helped them. They told him in vain that he was the king's son, that such work was not for the likes of him, that he needn't do it.

"Never mind," he said, "I like to work and to help you. You'll get done sooner."

The stable was filled with two rows of horses, horses so fat that they seemed to be bursting. And there was a scrawny colt lying on the floor in a corner. It was so skinny that its legs were dangling criss-crossed and it was too weak to disentangle them. The boy saw it and said to the soldiers:

"Uncle, uncle soldier, what is wrong with this colt, why is it so thin?"

"Well, son," he said, "it is like that."

"Why is this colt not eating like the others?"

"Because they are not giving it the same feed as the others."

"Why aren't they? Poor thing, it could use something better."

"Son," he said, "when the others get oats, this colt gets hay, and when the others get hay, then he gets oats. But we are never allowed to give it the same amount as the others or as much as it would want. Yet it knows how to ask for more. But it is forbidden, once and for all, to feed it the same as the others."

The boy was saddened. He could see that the colt couldn't stand up on its legs, it was just lying there. Every time he went to the stable he spent a long time standing by the colt's side, then by its head, looking at it and feeling sorry for it.

"Oh, poor animal, how scrawny it is," he said. "I am sorry for it."

Well, the soldiers got used to having the boy around. They saw how kind he was, how he helped with giving the animals water and with everything else. No sooner did a speck of manure fall on the floor than he rushed over to pick it up. He wanted to make sure that the royal stables were as clean as the inside of a house. So the stablehands grew very fond of him. Then one day they said to him:

"Son, little prince, it is Sunday and we can't even remember the last time we went to church. We ought to go."

Every Sunday the steward and his wife put on their best clothes, took their son and set out for church. They locked up and let the soldiers keep watch over everything.

"We always have to stay home and keep watch," they said, "we can never get to church. Would you be so kind as to stay here, in the stable, while we go to church so we can attend mass for once? But," they said, "we'll leave ahead of the others and hasten back. In the meantime you'll stay here and look after the horses. Should one of them break loose, all you need to do is get over to the telephone, push the button and somebody—a soldier—will come and tether the horse in its stall. You just take good care!"

"Sure, I will," said the boy, "you may go, I'll keep an eye on everything, I'll even tether the horses if need be—I can do it."

"Don't you try that, son—the horse could kick you, or bite you. Just go and push that button and help will come at once."

So they got dressed and left for church. The boy stayed at home. As soon as the servants were gone, he locked the gate behind them. A big iron gate it was—he locked it, locked it securely so that no one could enter, and went back to the stable. He walked straight over to the colt, stood close to its hindquarters and gazed at it:

"Oh, poor animal, I feel so sorry for you," said the boy, "I am sorry that this poor animal is so scrawny."

All of a sudden the colt began to speak.

It said: "I see, little prince, that you have a big heart, a very good heart. You feel sorry for me, but I feel sorry for you too, as sorry as you are for me. The steward is as wicked to me as he is wicked to you. He is threatening your life and mine, he wants us to perish. But if you listen to me and do as I say, you'll be set free and I'll be set free too. If not, we'll both be destroyed."

"Go on, please, what's on your mind?" said the boy. "I'll listen to you and obey."

"Look, son, today it's already too late," said the colt, "but I'll tell you what you must do. Come next Sunday they will leave for church again and you should let the stablehands go too. Be very careful until then. If they don't find anything wrong, they'll want to go to church again and you'll stay behind. Then I'll tell you to light a fire, burn a cord of wood and bring me the embers, maybe two shovels full, and the rest I'll tell you later. Everything will be fine—but don't talk to anyone about this. No one must know, for if they betray you it means the end of you and of me, at once."

The boy could hardly wait for Sunday—and when it came, the steward and his wife took off again in festive splendor. They went to church. All along the little prince had been staying close to the stablehands, eating with them, sitting around with them, day after day.

Then they said to him: "Well, little prince, you took very good care of the horses, you watched over everything and there was no trouble. Would you agree to do it again?"

"Sure I would, you may go to church every Sunday. I won't go anyway, they wouldn't take me. I'll just stay here quietly and see to it that nothing goes wrong," he said.

So they got dressed up in a hurry and left for church. As soon as they were gone, the boy rushed over to the colt, and the colt said to him:

"Well, little prince, light the fire at once and let it burn."

The wood was dry and on this warm day it burst into flame and burnt to embers in no time. When the embers started glowing the boy took a good shovelful and placed it in front of the colt. The colt gulped down the lot and three more shovelfuls besides, in a matter of seconds. Then it rose up on its legs. Until then it couldn't stand, it just lay there.

"And now," it said, "let me out of the stable."

The boy let the colt leave the stable. It headed straight for the large pile of smoldering embers remaining after all the wood had burned down. The colt swallowed the whole big heap and by the time it finished, it had turned into a golden-haired steed, so shiny that it made the *eyes of whoever was looking at it, pop out*. Its hair was glittering gold and it had five legs.

"Little prince," it said, "you saved my life, now I'll save yours. Go at once and find the cellar key hanging on a nail, take it and unlock the door. As you enter you'll see on your right a sword, a pair of spurs, a saddle and a bridle. Take them and bring them out in a hurry. Then put the bridle on my neck and the saddle on my back, get dressed and climb into the saddle. We'd better start out right away, or else they'll find us here!"

The boy ran down to the cellar, unlocked it, opened the door and found everything, as the colt had said. The saddle was hanging there, as were the sword and a pair of spurs.

"When you are ready to leave," said the colt, "look into my ears."

He reached into the horse's ear and drew out a set of silver garments.

"Now," said the colt, "put on these clothes, the whole suit, and when you are done, climb on my back and let's go. But before we do, I'll tell you also that there is plenty of gold and silver in the cellar, in barrels here and there. Take as much of it as you can stuff in your pockets. Take only the pure gold—it is worth more—not the silver. Fill your inner and outer pockets with all they can hold! Then come, get up on my back!"

So the boy dug into the gold, stuffed his pockets full, went out and leaped up on the colt's back.

"And now we are off—shut your eyes!"

The horse flew, its hooves not even touching the ground. It galloped at such speed that it rose into the air. They traveled until they came to the end of their kingdom. They reached the neighboring land. But just before they entered, when they were at the border, where one realm ended and the other began, the colt stopped and said:

"Now dismount and take a rest."

Well, he was tired—although he had been sitting, he had grown tired.

"Have a rest, my little boy!"

The boy was so beautiful that, as the saying goes, *you could sooner look straight at the sun than at him,* so dazzling was his beauty. His curly locks fell gracefully over his shoulders, his complexion was fair, his eyes a deep blue and his round cheeks had a rosy glow. Although he had been treated badly, he had developed better than the steward's son and grown taller.

"Well son," said the colt, "now I'll tell you what you must do. Here is the gate to the palace. Go there and you'll be admitted by the guards who are standing there. Enter the palace grounds and continue walking. I should also tell you that this is as far as I can bring you and no farther. I must now return, but I'll leave you a small whistle. If you get into trouble, or if you need anything, I'll come at once. You must hide this whistle so carefully that no one will ever find it. But if you are in trouble, or want help, use it and I'll be there. And now I tell you, son, you must go into this city. It is the *capital city.* No matter whom you encounter, do not greet them! If you do, just salute, like the soldiers do, but do not open your mouth and do not talk to anyone, no matter who asks you : 'what is your name, son?' or 'whose son are you?' or 'where are you from?' All you must ever say is 'I don't know.' Nothing more, no matter what they ask. Just say 'I don't know'—not a word more, and keep on walking!"

The colt gave the boy an affectionate kiss and licked his face. Then the boy kissed the colt, over and over again.

Said the colt: "May God be with you, son! I won't say more. If you get hungry, you have sufficient money. There are merchants around here, selling everywhere. This is a capital city. Whatever is good for you, whatever you desire, you'll find it here. They sell everything in the market place, go there and buy what you need and the quantities you want —be it fruit, or baked goods, or other food, sausages, or whatever else. Buy what you believe will be sufficient for you and pay with a piece of gold. The merchant will keep the cost of your purchase and give you back the rest. But you must not talk, not even ask about the price of anything, for then you would have to speak. Just hand over the gold without words and you'll get back your change. This is how you must act everywhere," said the colt. "I trust that you will do your best—I can teach you no more."

Then they took leave of one another and the little horse disappeared, like a whirlwind—it just vanished and the boy entered the city. He approached the gates of the palace and the soldiers let him in, so he went on. But whomsoever he met stopped to look at him. They didn't know the boy but neither had they seen one in their big city as beautiful as he was. There were some who were brave enough to ask:

"Where do you come from, son?"

Or: "Where are you headed?"—"where are you traveling?"—"what is your destination?"—or "where do you come from?"

"I don't know."

"Well, what's your name?"

"I don't know."

This is all he ever answered. And people were wondering what it was with this beautiful child, so clever, yet unable to say more. He could say this much clearly, but nothing else. This astonished them greatly. But he paid no attention to anyone—he went on and did everything the way the colt had taught him. He got into the city, into its very center. It was Sunday: people were going to church with their books and missals. He thought they were headed for church because the bells were ringing. He was on his guard, watching everything since he was a stranger. The men were gazing at him and so were the young women, wondering who this boy was, he was so exquisite looking. He was dressed in fine clothes and was very handsome and no one knew him, no one had seen him before. So several people asked:

"Beg your pardon, young Master, may I enquire where you are from or where you are going?"

"I don't know," he said and uttered not another word.

He wandered over to the market, as he was hungry. There he picked out some rolls and sausages, along with some cold cuts. When the food was assembled, he took a piece of paper and wrapped it all up, as if he were the vendor. He made a nice package. Then he reached for a gold coin and gave it to the merchant, who returned the change, after subtracting the amount of the purchase. He didn't check it, just slipped it into his pocket. Then he turned around and ate his food. He ate as much as he needed. He ought to go back to church—he thought to himself—he should go where the others were going. Why, God wouldn't punish him if he entered His house. So he started on his way to church. Many people were headed that way, forming one long line. It was a great big church, already full of worshippers. He walked up to the front, bravely, as if he were a native of these parts. The priest was just delivering his sermon from the pulpit. He stopped directly in front of him and stared at the priest's mouth, without once averting his eyes. And the same way the people stared at him, not at the priest, not at the church, nor even the altar. All eyes were fixed on the boy, wondering who he was, how smart he was, and why they had not seen him before. Who could he be, what could he be? The king himself was at the church, since this was a royal city, the king, his wife, and three daughters were all there. He, too, just gazed at the boy intently. Who is he, what is he? Soon the mass was over and the people began streaming out of the church. The boy was in no hurry, he let everyone go ahead. In the end he came out, too, and continued on, minding his own business. But one of the people called over to him:

"Where are you from, son? Tell us, young Master, where do you come from?"

"I don't know."

"Well, who is your father?"

"I don't know."

"What do they call you? What is your name?"

He went on his way while the people were watching and wondering whether he could talk or say only those few words. As he was walking, the king caught up with him in his carriage, in the royal coach in which he was riding and ordered it to stop.

Said the king to the boy: "Where are you from, son?"

"I don't know."

"Well, whose son are you?"

"I don't know."

The king didn't take the boy with him then—he drove away. But at home they all started talking about him, who he could be, whether he could be a lost child? He could have gone astray, wandered off, and, who knows, his parents might be searching for him. "The boy should be brought here and kept here until someone comes looking for him. Surely someone from his family will come and then," said the king, "we'll hand him over. But we must get him to come here now, so he won't go on wandering. He must be lost, that seems certain."

So they dispatched two soldiers, sent them out to comb the streets and find a boy of such and such a description and bring him back to the palace. The two soldiers left at once, ran up and down searching the streets until finally they came upon the boy.

They said to him: "Well, young Master, his Royal Highness the king has sent for you. Will you come?"

"I don't know."

"You better know, because you are coming with us. We are taking you to the royal palace. He told us to bring you there, before him."

The boy said: "I don't know."

"Never mind, just come along, you won't have a bad life there."

They took the boy with them, went straight to the palace and announced to the king that they had arrived, that they had found the boy and brought him back. Right away the daughters started clapping their hands:

"Oh my, oh my, what a beautiful boy, what a beautiful boy! Dear Father, don't allow him to leave the palace—we can bring him up here. Who knows where he is from, perhaps someone lost him, let him be ours," they said. "What a lovely boy!"

The princesses were enthralled by him. The king himself was moved. He said: "My son, tell me, where are you from?"

"I don't know."

"Do you have a father?"

"I don't know."

"And your mother, is she alive?"

"I don't know."

He couldn't get anything else out of him.

"Come here, son. I know you are hungry," he said, "come and eat!"

They sat him down at the table in their midst, as they were having their midday meal. The boy ate nicely. He knew how to behave, how to use the serving spoon, how to help himself from the dishes. He ate amply, to his fill.

Then the king said to him: "My boy, you'll stay here with us."

He said: "I don't know."

"Never mind, son," said the king, "you'll find out after being here for a while. You won't be treated badly."

He told his wife that the child must be taught to converse, somehow he had to be taught.

"We don't know what his name is, so let us call him 'Little I Don't Know.' Since all he ever says is 'I don't know', let his name be 'Little I Don't Know.'"

Then the king summoned the chief cook and said to him: "Look, I place this boy in your hands. Take him in the kitchen, let him be with you, let him fetch water, when you need water, or wood, or anything you may want for cooking. Send him to the pantry, or to the larder—let him bring you what you need and little by little he will learn to speak. But first," he said, "take him to the pantry and show him everything, what this chest contains, what that one has, this bag has wheat flour, that one holds rice-meal, the prunes are stored here, the figs there, and God only knows what else there is, almonds, oranges, lemons, and many other things."

She showed him everything: "Well, son, this is here and that is over there."

But each bag had its own little label and just by looking at it, one could tell what was in the bag. Then there was a chest of drawers, as in the stores: one had candied peels, the other orange peels, yet another had sugar, and so on—God knows what else. And on all these drawers too, it was written what each one contained: this one held paprika, that one something else—it was all nicely marked for the cook, when she needed something.

Said the cook to the boy: "Little I Don't Know, go to the pantry and bring me this and that—the things I need."

The boy jumped to it. The cook thought he couldn't even have reached the pantry when he was already back, so fast did he move. The cook grew very fond of him, she wouldn't have parted with him for anything. He was helping her so well. She was astonished that he understood everything, no matter what she said or asked, he understood it and made sure that she always had at hand what she needed. He was so able, yet he couldn't speak. He even knew how to read. He just had to glance at the labels and he knew, he knew what they said.

The king went over to the kitchen every day, sometimes five or six times, to ask the cook how the boy was doing.

"Very well. He is clever beyond words. Whatever I ask for, he goes and does it immediately. I am amazed," she said, "and yet he cannot speak. Maybe he'll learn little by little, from one day to the next."

Weeks and months went by, a whole year had passed since the boy had come to the palace. Everyone grew to like him and the daughters' hearts were filled with love for him. They embraced him, accepted him as their own brother:

"Dear Father, we can never allow you to let him go—even if someone should come looking for him, we will not consent to your letting him leave. He must stay here, with us."

And so the boy continued to develop and to grow nicely. As time went by, he filled out and grew visibly taller. One day the cook talked to him about how he had been with them for years now, about how clever he was and how he understood everything he was told. During this time, the king, his wife, and their daughters drove to church in their carriage every Sunday.

Said the cook: "Little I Don't Know, would you let me go to church? I am never able to go. I can see that you are smart, that you listen to everything I say. You are an obedient child. So," she said, "I'll go to church and I'll give you no other task but to watch the fire. I have put on the soup—it is already boiling and has been skimmed off. I have added to it all that was needed, except salt. So, look, Little I Don't Know, let the meat simmer for another half an hour after I have gone. Then put in the salt, I'll show you, about a tablespoonful or so, and let it simmer some more with the salt, so it can absorb the flavor. But be careful, the flame mustn't be too high and the soup shouldn't bubble, but just simmer on low fire—it'll get richer that way. And don't let it boil over, or it will lose all its fat. So listen my boy, until now you have always been obedient," she said "once again do as I say. Just add a log or two to the fire—it shouldn't be blazing. Do you understand me?"

He said: "I don't know."

"Well, you'll see, it'll be all right if you do as you were told. Look, Little I Don't

Know, I'll leave the church ahead of time—when the priest makes the sign of the cross and gives his benediction to the people, I'll start on my way back."

With these words the cook left. She waved to the boy as she was going. The boy waved too, but didn't say a word. The cook got dressed, delighted that for once she was able to go to church.

As soon as the cook was gone, the boy set to it; he threw the cat into the pot of soup, covered it and let it simmer. Soon the church bells signaled the end of the service and the cook came back.

"Well, Little I Don't Know, has the soup been cooking?"

He said: "I don't know."

The cook ran and quickly stirred the pot with a large spoon and there was the cat, turned upside down, scalded; its hair and skin were all gone and its eyes had popped out, only the sockets were visible.

"Oh dear! Little I Don't Know, what have you done?" she said, "how did the cat fall into the soup? Oh dear, dear! The king will be back shortly and what am I to serve him? What have you done, Little I Don't Know?"

He said: "I don't know."

"I told you to cover the soup and to keep it covered. The cat must have jumped into it." (She thought the cat had jumped into the pot.) "You must have taken the cover off, forgotten about it—and the cat jumped in."

"I don't know."

"What a fine mess you got me into!"

She grabbed the ladle and struck the boy on the back of his neck. She struck him in anger, so upset was she that they would be coming home soon, expecting the soup and there wasn't any. The boy started screaming and wailing—he had never been hit before. Just then the coach pulled into the courtyard. And it had to pass right in front of the door. Sure enough, they heard all the crying. Right away they stopped the carriage; first the daughters jumped off, then the king:

"What is the matter, what is the matter, why is the boy crying?"

"Well," she said, "let me tell Your Majesty what he did. I relied on him to watch over the soup, since until now he has always been obedient. And now, there is a cat in the soup! I don't know how it got there, but there will be no soup for midday."

Said the king: "If there is no soup, there isn't any. Don't we have something else to eat? There are other things to replace the soup. The boy shouldn't be beaten."

The daughters, too, were complaining: "Don't hit the boy! How did you dare hit him?"

Well—said the cook to herself—it is all right if they are angry that I whacked him. That isn't too great a worry, as long as they don't harm me.

Plenty of food was found to serve for the meal, many different things. A king need never be concerned about having enough to eat. And so the incident passed and another week went by. During this time the boy behaved well, he wouldn't have dis-

14

obeyed for the world. He did everything he was asked to do immediately. He was so good that the cook began trusting him again. Then Sunday arrived.

"Well, son," she said to him, "will you let me go to church today? Will you do again like last Sunday?"

He said: "I don't know."

"Son, will you watch the soup today? Look, it has to be kept covered," she said, "and when you add something to it, like salt, you must put the lid back on the pot right away. And don't build too big a fire! So, my dear boy, do as I say and I'll love you and the king will love you, too. You can see how fond the princesses are of you, but if you misbehave, they won't like you."

He said: "I don't know."

"Well, may I go to church?"

"I don't know."

So the cook prepared to leave again, got dressed in her best clothes, left repeated instructions about the meat, to which only salt was to be added in half an hour, and off she went. Little I Don't Know kept the fire going. Then, all at once, when the half hour was up, he poured salt into the soup, a large amount of it, but he used three big ladles full of ashes instead of salt! He poured three big ladles full of ashes into the soup. When the cook came back, she went straight to the soup and stirred it with a spoon. It was as thick as pure lye.

"What is this? Are there ashes in here? Oh dear, Little I Don't Know, this liquid is all murky," she said, "what did you do?"

He said: "I don't know."

"Look at it," she said, "I can't serve this and what will the king say when he finds out?"

He said: "I don't know."

She slapped the boy in the face so hard that the crack resounded.

"This is so you learn to do as you are told. You must not spoil the food! What will the king say to me when he sees that there is no soup?"

"I don't know," he said.

He screamed and yelled that she had slapped him, he screamed so loud that it could be heard in the street. Again, the royal coach was approaching—the king, his wife, and daughters were coming back. Once again they found the boy crying.

"What's the matter, what's the matter, why is the boy crying? Maybe you hit him?"

She said: "I just slapped him once. Look at what he did! He filled the soup with ashes."

"So what if he did, we ate soup all week long, every day, and we'll have it again—don't hit the boy, don't hurt him, I told you before not to hurt the boy!"

"Don't hurt the boy," begged the daughters, they felt so sorry for him.

Well, once again she was out of trouble. They ate their midday meal peacefully, nothing went wrong. And once again the boy started to please the cook by helping her in every way. He swept all over and worked as hard as a slave. He had improved and seeing how diligent he was, the cook began trusting him anew. Then the third Sunday came.

"Little I Don't Know, will you let me go to church?"

He said: "I don't know."

"Look son, this time there is no soup. I wouldn't trust you with it. But," she said, "there is a pig roasting in the . . . 'thing', in the oven, and you, my boy, must watch so the fire doesn't get too big and burn the meat. You see," she said, "it's already done nicely on one side. I'll turn it so the other side will brown slowly and be ready for noon. You don't have to add salt, or anything else, just make sure that the fire is kept low. And I'll go to church."

He said: "I don't know."

The cook left for church but as soon as she was gone, the boy heaped wood in the stove, as much as it could take. The fire grew to be as big as an inferno. He used up all the dry logs so they burst into flame right away. The roasting pig got scorched and started to smoke. Soon the smoke was so thick inside that one couldn't see. Then the cook came back. She was still out in the street when she was struck by the smell. "Oh, this time he burnt the pig," she said. "He burnt it—now what will I put on the table, what kind of roast?" She ran indoors, the kitchen was filled with smoke, she had to wave a kerchief around to disperse it. They were choking, suffocating from it. She opened the oven door, the roasting pig was in flames, burning and smoking so fiercely that it had turned into pure charcoal.

"You, Little I Don't Know, once again you fixed the midday meal! Now what can I put before the king? And what will they say when they discover that I ruined a meal yet another time?"

He said: "I don't know."

Again she slapped the boy in the face so hard that he started to scream, beside himself. Then the king arrived and stood in the doorway.

"What happened this time," he says, "what is going on here?"

The cook burst into tears: "Great King," she said, "I am thankful that until now I was able to serve you well and I was hoping to continue but ever since this boy was placed here, I cannot put a decent midday meal before you on Sundays when he is asked to watch over it. He built such a big fire that the roasting pig became completely charred. I ask you to take him away from here, or I'll have to leave your service," she said. "If you don't remove him, I'll have to go."

"I'll remove him. He'll go, you just stay, but don't hit the boy," he said. "You shouldn't beat him, you should come to me when something is wrong so I can help. You must not beat him!"

And the daughters were crying and complaining that the boy had been beaten. So the king said to him:

"Little I Don't Know, you don't like it here in the kitchen. I wanted you to have a good life, indoors, but you are not pleased and you are disobedient, so I am sending you out as a helper to the barnyard hand. Listen to the man and help him feed and give water to the poultry. Or," he said, "perhaps you shouldn't even do that, just help herd the chickens into the pen at night and count them in the morning when they are let out, and again in the evening when they go back in. This will be your task and you needn't worry about anything else. Better still, I'll place you with the barnyard hand to gather the eggs and help bring them in. Collect the eggs," he said, "and bring them into the house. This will be your job. If you mind the barnyard man, your lot will not be a bad one. Now then, you'll leave the cook, since you can't get along."

The boy was happy that he was sent outside. He behaved well for a week or two—he was very good, always carrying around the basket, busy gathering the eggs. There were so many hens that a huge crate was filled with the eggs they had laid. The barnyard hand was pleased. But the boy did more than collect the eggs. He went to fetch water when he noticed that there wasn't any, and made sure that the chickens always had enough to drink. He helped with everything and did what was needed. This cheered the barnyard man so much that when the king came to ask about the boy, he said:

"He is good, I can't fault him for anything. He does more than expected. He was told that here he need only take care of the eggs, but he is also feeding the poultry, bringing them water, although I tell him that this is my concern. He is even helping me clean the pen every day."

Said the king: "Don't let the boy do those things—he should mind the eggs, that's all."

"Well, I put it to him," he said, "but he likes having his hand in everything."

So the boy continued on his best behavior for perhaps a whole month. Then all of a sudden he was at it again, he started to juggle with the eggs. He threw them up high: as one came down he tossed the next one up so that he held eggs in both hands all the time. But for every one he caught, at least ten dropped to the ground and broke. He carried on this way day after day, until more than a hundred eggs were missing. The barnyard man noticed that the eggs were not accumulating as before and reported it to the king:

"Your Royal Highness, I don't know what is going on," he said, "but the eggs are not increasing in number as in the past. We had large amounts for so many had been coming in, and now we have fewer and fewer every day."

"What could be the cause? Are the hens not laying?"

"I don't know. All I know is the eggs keep diminishing."

"We ought to observe the boy," said the king, "to find out if he is hiding the eggs and giving them to someone. We ought to see."

So, one day the barnyard hand concealed himself and watched what the boy was doing. He saw him gather a big basketful of eggs, set them down in the center of the courtyard and toss them up in the air one after another. The eggs were dropping, and for every one he caught at least ten fell and shattered so that the ground around him was all yellow and littered with shells. Witnessing this, the barnyard man went straight to the king:

"Your Royal Highness, now I get the picture of what is happening. It is the boy's fault that we have fewer eggs. He is playing ball and juggling with them so fast that although he is able to catch some, many more fall down and break."

"Well then, I'll give him something else to do so he doesn't touch the eggs, but I won't send him elsewhere."

Said the king to the boy: "Son, since you don't obey and you are not careful with the eggs, you mustn't touch them again! Leave this to the barnyard hand. Your job will be to bring the poultry back into the pen and lock them up. Then in the morning, when they are let out, you will count them to see if all are there. That's it, nothing else, and don't go near the eggs again!"

The boy did as he was told. He let the chickens into the pen and locked them up. In the morning, when he let them out, he counted them and made note of how many there were. This way the barnyard man knew that they had been counted and how many there were. And so the days went by, even months. The boy was so obedient that the barnyard man grew very fond of him. He wouldn't have let him go for anything. Then, one day, fewer and fewer chickens started showing up on the count. Once twenty were missing, the next time thirty. The barnyard hand became concerned. What could be the reason that the numbers were diminishing? What happened to the chickens? Why were there fewer every day? The king said that the boy should be watched to see if he did them any harm, whether he gave them away, or maybe sold them to someone. The barnyard man concealed himself again to observe the boy with the chickens in the morning. And what did he see? Little I Don't Know stood there with a stick in his hand, counting the chickens up to nine. Then he whacked the tenth so hard on its head that it keeled over and died on the spot. He went on counting out the following nine and hitting the tenth so hard that it expired immediately. He continued this way until he destroyed at least fifty chickens that day. Once again the barnyard hand went to report to the king:

"Your Royal Highness, move this boy away from here, or else you won't have a single chicken left."

"Why is that?"

"He is killing them and that's why we have fewer chickens every day. He counts nine and strikes every tenth dead."

"Well," said the king, "never mind, if this is how it is, I'll place the boy with the gardener to tend the flowerbeds."

He assigned the boy to work in the flower garden with the gardener and said to him: "This boy will be here to help you, and even if he isn't working, he should follow you around—it will make the time go faster for you, too. But you must watch him so he doesn't get into any trouble."

So the gardener took the boy, showed him the whole garden and the flowerbeds, which were very, very beautiful.

He said to him: "Here are flowers of this variety and there are those of another. Do you know them?"

He said: "I don't know."

"These lovely flowers need to be watered and watched over so the birds don't peck at them. You'll like it here, son, you'll see! You'll stay with me."

He said: "I don't know."

Well, the boy behaved beautifully, he was very good. He pulled out every small weed from under the flowers and swept the paths winding between the beds, just to make sure everything appeared neat. The gardener grew so fond of him that he wouldn't have let him go for the world. He could see the boy was smart and considerate.

Then Sunday came—the royal household was preparing to go to church, but the youngest daughter was developing a toothache.

Said the king: "Now, my daughters, get ready, we are going to church!"

The younger one said: "Dear Father, I can't go to church, my tooth hurts so much that I can't stand it."

"All right, if you can't come, you'll stay at home. You don't have to come, but we are going."

So she went up to the first floor and sat in front of the window, looking out. She watched the boy. She saw how briskly he moved, how diligent he was and how well he got along with the gardener. She loved the boy—that is why she didn't go to church, not because of a toothache, she wanted to stay at home to watch him. She loved the boy so much, she didn't know what to do. But the boy was a boy no longer—he had grown and turned into a young lad. He was beautiful, so very beautiful that it was impossible to describe.

One day the gardener said to him: "Little I Don't Know, will you look after the garden, so I can go to church? You see, other young people are going every Sunday and I am always here. Will you watch over the garden?"

He said: "I don't know."

"Look, son, I'll leave you this bell. Just stroll about on these walks and paths between the flowers and ring it continuously. This will scare the birds and keep them away. Take care so that nothing gets in here to pick off the flowers."

The gardener pulled himself together, got dressed up and left for church. Little I Don't Know stayed behind. No sooner was the gardener gone, than he remembered the small whistle that the colt had given him. He took it out and blew into it. All at once a little horse, a little silver-haired horse materialized out of nowhere. Its coat was shiny silver. It came closer and said:

"What is your command, little Prince?"

"I command that this garden, these flowers, be destroyed—not even their roots should remain in the ground! They must be stamped out."

"Reach into my ear, now!"

The boy did so and drew out a saddle.

Said the colt: "Put it on my back! Now look into my other ear!"

He did as he was told and took out a suit of clothes, a pair of boots, a *shako* and other accessories belonging to royal garments, the kind princes would wear, all in glittering silver.

"Now mount me!"

Little I Don't Know mounted the horse but didn't notice that the princess was looking on from the window. He mounted the little horse and rode, circling the garden about three times, until not a single flower was left standing under the horse's hooves—all were trampled down. The flower garden was leveled, the beds had disappeared, as if a herd of swine had stampeded through them and dug them all up. Then he dismounted.

Said the horse: "Now put the clothes, the saddle and everything else back into my ear."

He did as he was told and the little horse vanished again. It was a magic horse—it just disappeared.

Soon they started coming back from church. The gardener was the first to return. Dear Almighty God, when he saw what had become of his garden, he nearly collapsed.

"What on earth happened to this garden, Little I Don't Know? Who was here? Who did such a foul, shameful thing? What will the king say when he finds his beautiful flower garden destroyed, laid waste?"

He said: "I don't know."

"So you don't know who was here?"

"I don't know."

The gardener slapped the boy in the face so hard that he started screaming. Just then the king appeared in the garden. All along his young daughter had witnessed Little I Don't Know's actions. But seeing what a dapper young lad he had turned into, dressed in those splendid garments, *she nearly wet herself* out of sheer excitement and became even more enamored of him.

"Well," said the king, "what happened to this garden? What went on here?"

The gardener said: "Sir, my life is in your hands! I went to church and left him precise instructions. Up until now he has been obedient, he did everything he was told, even more than he was asked to do, and now that I left him this happened and he won't say who came here, who did all this. All the flowers are destroyed."

"Never mind, we'll get gardeners to come and plant them anew. Don't harm the boy"—these were the king's words.

And so, without a moment's delay, the king sent for some six hundred gardeners. They raked and shaped new beds, replanted the flowers and watered them so they all took root and revived again. By the next day the garden looked as beautiful as before.

For a few weeks the gardener didn't dare to go to church. He waited. He could see that the boy was on his best behavior, he was forever running, tending the flowers, watering them, weeding and cleaning around them, so they would bloom and become more and more beautiful. He could see the boy's efforts, so he said to himself: I'll go to church again—he is able and very careful with the flowers, so I'll go.

"Little I Don't Know," he said to the boy, "I am leaving for church. Watch over everything and don't let the birds pick off the flowers or some wild beast trample them down. Be alert and keep ringing the bell to scare them off!"

He said: "I don't know."

"Well, just do as I say."

So, once again, the gardener got dressed and left for church. Little I Don't Know stayed behind, walking around in the garden. Then, all of a sudden—who knows what went through his head—he drew out his small whistle and blew into it. This time a golden steed appeared. Its hair was pure gold. It came closer and said:

"What is your command, little Prince?"

"I command," he said, "that you trample down these flowers so that not even their roots remain in the ground!"

The colt didn't have to be told twice.

"Look into my ear!"

The boy withdrew a saddle, a set of clothes, and everything—down to the spurs—was sparkling gold. When the king's daughter saw from her window what a handsome lad he was, decked out in such finery, she was beside herself. He mounted the horse and began racing it like the devil, criss-crossing and circling the garden over and over again, until not a single flower, or even a single flower bed, remained intact. The garden had completely lost its shape.

Soon the gardener arrived. By then the colt had vanished and the boy was strolling among the flowers. The gardener came and said to him:

"Little I Don't Know, what happened to this garden? Look at it! There are up-rooted, trampled flowers strewn about on the beds and everywhere, even in the street! Who came here, Little I Don't Know—tell me, who did all this again?"

He said: "I don't know."

"How can you not know when you were told to keep watch?"

"I don't know."

And whack! He slapped the boy. But just then the king appeared.

"What's the matter now," he said, "what happened to the garden this time?"

"I don't know, Your Majesty. I went to church and I warned him to keep watch, yet he can't say who came here. All he says is: 'I don't know.' So what am I to do?"

Said the king: "Why did you hit him?"

"How can I not hit him, when he caused such damage!"

"Don't hit the boy, the gardeners are still around," he said, "they'll restore the garden. Don't beat him!"

And when the king's daughter saw the gardener slap the boy, she started screaming from her upstairs window. She screamed for him to stop, forgetting her toothache. That time, too, she had complained of a toothache and didn't go to church. But she didn't reveal to her father that the boy had done all the damage. She wouldn't betray him, for she loved him and thought to herself that she wouldn't ever marry unless she could marry him. That is what she said to herself.

So, once again they repaired and replanted the garden. They watered it and worked on it until the flowers took root. And once again the flowers bloomed and were beautiful. So the gardener turned to the boy yet another time:

"Look, Little I Don't Know, the flowers are lovely again, they have all recovered. I'll go to church and you be on the lookout. You must watch and tell me if something gets into the garden and does damage to it! How is it that when I am here nothing goes wrong and as soon as I leave there is trouble?"

He said: "I don't know."

The gardener left and the boy stayed behind. As soon as he saw the gardener enter the church, the boy blew into his whistle and a diamond-haired steed appeared. Its coat had turned into diamonds.

"Look into my ear, little Prince," it said, "and take out your garments and the saddle. What do you command me to do?"

He said: "I command that all these flowers be destroyed and that not a single tree be left standing in the garden."

A circle of trees surrounded the garden, laden with different kinds of fruit— even they had to be cut down.

Once again he took out the saddle, the garments, the *shako* and the boots, all in sparkling silver. And how splendid were the spurs! When the boy was dressed in full attire, the horse said to him:

"Now you must mount me!"

He did so at once and they circled the garden again, three times, until all the trees were down, lying in a heap, uprooted. Then they stopped. Little I Don't Know dismounted, put back the saddle and everything else and the horse disappeared. Soon the king arrived.

He said: "There are flowers, uprooted flowers, even at the church door."

The church stood apart, quite a distance away from the flower garden.

"Even there," he said, "and the road leading from the church is covered, like on *Corpus Christi* day, when flowers are strewn in front of the priest in the procession. The gardener came and said to the king:

"I don't know what happened to the garden, what went on here, I have no way of knowing and Little I Don't Know can't tell me. I'll never go to church again but I have to say that if you don't remove the boy, I'll leave. I can't continue in your service!"

Said the king: "You are not going anywhere, you are staying and I am taking the boy away from here."

He summoned the boy and said to him: "Little I Don't Know, if you don't like it here, in this lovely garden, where you can smell the fragrant flowers, where everything is neat and clean and you are well treated, I am placing you with the pigs as a herdsman."

He said: "I don't know."

"Whether you know it or not, that's where you are going, son. You didn't like it in the kitchen, or in the barnyard, and you didn't do well here either, so from now on you'll be a swineherd."

He said: "I don't know."

Right away the king removed the boy from the garden and sent him to the swineherd.

"I am placing the boy here," he said. "He is to go with you and watch over the pigs, he is good for nothing else. He caused nothing but trouble everywhere. I don't expect much, but don't hurt him, no matter what he does! Come and tell me if he makes a mistake, but don't hurt the boy, be good to him!"

The boy was well treated, he ate and drank the same as the king—and he had all he needed. By then he had turned into a handsome young lad, so fine, so beautiful that it was a pleasure to look at him.

Well, the king had three daughters and the time had come to give them away in marriage. He let it be known in the land that all eligible young men—sons of kings, barons and princes who wanted to take a wife—should come to the palace, as he wished to marry his daughters. From among them, the daughters were to choose their mates. He made the announcement, posted it in writing and gave each of his three daughters a golden apple.

He said to them: "Well, my daughters, soon the young men will start arriving, sons of kings, princes and barons, all the greats of the land, so you can select a husband! When you find the one you fancy, you'll toss him the apple."

So, once the proclamation was issued and the three daughters had their golden apples, the king said to them:

"Now come and be seated with me on the throne."

He took his place in the middle with his daughters next to him. Soon the young men were forming a line on either side and the daughters were watching them carefully. Then the oldest threw her apple to one of them. Next it was the turn of the second daughter. She looked and looked and finally she, too, threw her apple to a young man. Two daughters had made their choice but the youngest didn't find any one of the young men suitable. She didn't throw her apple to anyone.

Then Little I Don't Know appeared, herding the pigs home. He had trained the pigs to fall in line, like soldiers. And when he started playing his flute, the pigs began to dance. Well! When all the noble young men saw how the herdsman brought his pigs through the gate, how beautifully he played the flute and made the pigs dance, they broke out in laughter and even the king joined in. How could Little I Don't Know teach the pigs to march in formation, like soldiers? As soon as they had all come through, he shoved them into a large pen and went over to see what the brilliant gathering of young men was all about. He went over and took his place in the line. He looked around, observing this one and the next. Then, all of a sudden, as he stood there among the others, the young princess threw her apple at him with such force that he almost keeled over. Little I Don't Know caught the apple. But when the king saw to whom his youngest daughter had tossed the apple, he grew so angry, so livid, that he nearly jumped off his throne. How could his own daughter bring such shame on him? Here were all these brilliant young noblemen, one more handsome than the other, and instead of choosing among them, she picked a swineherd! What got into her? The king, her father, felt deeply shamed and so did her two sisters.

"Now," said the king, "it is all over"—and he descended from the throne. "You, my daughter, have brought shame on me and on my palace. You may pack up and leave! I am disowning you, you are no longer my child! You couldn't choose among all these handsome young men, one more beautiful than the other, but you didn't like any of them and had to choose this swineherd! I am disowning you, you are not my child!"

He threw out his daughter; he expelled her:

"Take him for your husband, you selected him, you live with him, but get out of my palace!"

He drove her out of the palace, beyond the palace gates and there he had a wooden shack built for them.

"This will be your palace, this wooden shack. This is where you'll stay and it won't matter to me whether you live or die."

For his two other daughters the king arranged such a wedding feast that it lasted twenty-four days. In the meantime the couple in the wooden shack were crying miserably—they had nothing, not even food to eat. But the king's daughter wouldn't have been so unhappy if only Little I Don't Know had started to speak, if his tongue had become untied. The real hardship was that she couldn't converse with him. Well, once the big wedding feast was over, both daughters remained with the king. They were pleased and happy and just made fun of the couple in the wooden shack. One day the sons-in-law grew tired of sitting around and said:

"Your Royal Highness, our Father, we wonder if we could go hunting for a little while, and enjoy being out in the forest?"

"Well, sons, sure, if that's what you would like to do, you may go."

So they chose two steeds, mounted them and set out for the hunt. Little I Don't Know planted himself in the doorway of his shack and watched them. He stood there with his hands on his hips, staring at his brothers-in-law. When they got close to him, they said:

"Little brother-in-law, come on hunting with us."

He said: "I don't know."

"You don't know anything, but you knew how to wed the king's daughter. Still, you aren't man enough to come hunting."

With those words the two brothers-in-law set spurs to their horses and galloped away. Little I Don't Know stayed behind. They chuckled and roared with laughter and, feeling mighty proud of themselves, they made fun of him. No sooner were they out of sight, an idea crossed Little I Don't Know's mind and he reached for his whistle. His wife wasn't even aware of it; he took out the whistle, blew into it—and there was the silver-haired steed.

"What is your command, Prince?"

"I command," he said, "that we go hunting too!"

"Then," said the horse, "take the garments out of my ear, the saddle too, fasten it to my back and get on!"

Quickly he withdrew the clothes from the horse's ear and got dressed in the shining silver attire. The steed, the saddle, everything was shining silver. He mounted the horse, but took a different path from the two brothers-in-law, who by then were far away. He chose a shortcut so he would reach the forest ahead of them. As he penetrated into the woods, Little I Don't Know caught sight of a silver duck, a wild duck, and shot it down at once. He took the duck, suspended it on the pommel of his saddle, turned around and headed home. He had to ride a long time before he met his brothers-in-law. They hadn't even reached the forest when he was already on his way back. The two princes saw that someone was approaching, some great nobleman on a silver-haired steed, and they marveled at it for they had never seen a horse with a silver coat. Who could this knight be? When they came closer they noticed that the knight, too, was dressed in silver, shining like a mirror. They were still at a distance when they started saluting and bowing to the stranger. He must be very wealthy, they thought, so they halted and saluted him with their swords. Then, once they met, they said good morning, greeted each other as respectfully as they knew how, and paid homage to one another.

"Well," they said, "you must have spent the night in the forest since you are already on your way back."

"Oh no," he said, "I started out today."

They didn't recognize who he was.

"What a fine duck you shot there—would you sell it to us?"

"Why not," he said, "I'd sell it."

"And what are you asking for it?"

"No bargaining—the price is one hundred pieces of gold."

One of them took the gold out of his pocket, handed it over and said:

"Where are you from?"

"I am king of the timberland castle."

"Oh, that land must be far away—I never heard of a place by that name!"

He had said "king of the timberland castle" because he lived in a shack made of timber boards. Well, they took the duck and started on their way home. But Little I

Don't Know galloped ahead and vanished, like a butterfly. By the time they arrived, he had dismounted, changed his clothes and stood there again in the doorway with his hands on his hips, watching them advance, proudly. They were approaching with the silver-feathered duck dangling from the pommel of the saddle. On the way they had talked about their father-in-law, the old king, about how happy he would be to have such valiant sons-in-law, who shot down a silver duck. They would have earned his respect and felt very proud of it. When they came up to Little I Don't Know, they said to him:

"You see, you wouldn't come hunting with us. Now look at what we brought down!"

He said: "I don't know."

"You never know anything. That's all you'll ever be, Little I Don't Know."

And with those words they left, laughing heartily. As soon as they entered the palace gates the merrymaking began. Their father-in-law was happy that they brought back such a splendid duck. He announced that there would be a ball Sunday evening, a ball to celebrate the valor of his sons-in-law. So the ball took place, a band was playing, while the pair in the wooden shack just listened to the others carousing. When the ball was over, the sons-in-law again prepared to go hunting. They asked the king whether they could have his permission to go out once more.

"Sure, you have my permission!" he said.

So they left. Somehow Little I Don't Know got wind of it and again planted himself in the doorway of his wooden shack, hands on his hips and watched them coming proudly through the gates. They greeted him:

"Good morning, little brother-in-law, come on, come hunting with us! Don't you want to come?"

He said: "I don't know."

"You don't ever know anything. It's good you knew how to wed the king's daughter."

They were peeved and wanted to show their displeasure at the king's daughter being married to such a—such a Little I Don't Know. Having said it, they galloped away. Little I Don't Know waited a while, allowing them time to get ahead. Then he blew into his whistle and the the golden-haired steed appeared:

"What do you command, Prince?"

"I command," he said, " that we follow them and go hunting too."

"Take out your clothes and take out the saddle!"

He withdrew a saddle, the garments, a shotgun, all in glittering gold. He mounted the horse, chose a different path again, and reached the forest before the others. As soon as he entered the woods, he shot down a golden partridge. Who knows what kind of a partridge it was, but it had feathers and they were pure gold. He shot it, suspended it on the pommel of his saddle and headed back. He had put a good stretch of road behind him when he met his brothers-in-law. They were coming toward him. One of them said to the other:

"Look, there is the knight again. It must be the same knight we saw yesterday. But look, this time he is riding on a golden-haired steed. He must be a very wealthy king to have such horses. I never even heard of such horses existing anywhere."

They were still a distance away when they began saluting and paying their respects. When they were side by side, they said to him:

"Oh, you are returning so soon. Had you spent the night here?"

"Not at all," he said, "I just left today."

"Would you sell us that fine golden partridge?"

"Why not?"

"What are you asking for it?"

"A hundred pieces of gold."

They gave him the gold on the spot.

"If you please, if you don't mind us asking, where are you from?"

"I am king of the timberland castle."

"Hurrah! Hurrah for the king of the timberland castle!"—they applauded. "You certainly know how to handle a gun, if you can shoot such fine birds in so little time."

They took leave of one another. Little I Don't Know spurred his magic horse, and as soon as he said *"hip-hop, take me where I want to be,"* he found himself at the wooden shack. He dismounted, put the garments back in their place and the horse vanished. He went inside and gave the gold to his wife.

"Little I Don't Know, where did you get this gold?"

"I don't know." He didn't talk, not even to his wife. "I don't know" is all he said.

She was happy, she kissed her husband and laughed, but her heart was still heavy for he wouldn't talk.

Soon the brothers-in-law arrived: "Look, little brother-in-law," they said, "look at what we shot, can you see? You couldn't shoot anything like this, could you? Well, we told you to come along."

He said: "I don't know."

"You never know anything and that's all you'll ever be, Little I Don't Know!" And so they left in great merriment and rode back to the palace. Once again the king was very happy to have such famous sons-in-law, such excellent hunters, who brought back a beautiful partridge, a partridge with golden feathers.

So once again he announced that there would be a ball on Sunday night. Again there was dancing and merrymaking and no one cared about the other two. When the ball was over, the sons-in-law went out hunting for a third time. As they passed the shack, Little I Don't Know was in the doorway, watching.

They said to him: "Instead of staring at us, come along. But you don't know how to shoot anyway, ha, ha, you don't know anything!"—they taunted him.

He said: "I don't know."

"You can see the fine game we bring back every time and how happy the king is. You," they said, "never do anything to please him."

With these words, they left. Little I Don't Know waited for them to be a little farther along, blew into his whistle and the diamond-haired steed appeared.

"And what do you command this time, Prince?" it said.

"I command that we follow them and go hunting!"

In no time he put on the clothes, saddled up the horse and stood ready to go. He was so beautiful all dressed up, so dazzling that *one could sooner gaze at the sun than look at him.*

And—one, two, three—they were back in the forest. This time he saw a deer with diamond hair and shot it. Its horns, its coat, everything was glittering. He placed it on the pommel of the saddle, cocked his *shako* rakishly to the side and proudly started back to meet his brothers-in-law. When they saw him, they said: "Look, now he is riding on a diamond-haired horse! And good Lord, look at the clothes he is wearing! He must come from an empire! He must be the son of a wealthy emperor at that!"

They were still at a distance when they started greeting and saluting him respectfully.

When they drew near, they said: "Oh, what a beautiful diamond deer you shot! Where did you find it?"

"There, in the woods."

"When could you have left that you are returning so soon?"

"Maybe when you did. Perhaps we left at the same time," he said, "I started out today too."

"Won't you sell us your diamond-haired deer?"

"Sure I would!" he said.

"Well, what do you want for it?"

"For this one, three hundred pieces of gold."

"We better pay it," they said, "our father, the king, will respect us even more for our valor, for what we bring back from the hunt." So, again they handed him the amount he asked for.

Little I Don't Know turned his horse around and galloped away. When he got home, he took the three hundred pieces of gold and placed them in his wife's hands. She was so happy she didn't know what to do. Where did he find all this gold?

Well, this too, came to pass. Once again the king announced a great ball, but the ball wasn't even over when he received a letter affixed with a seal, telling him that the *dog-headed Tatars* were about to invade his country and take it over. Oh, this worried the old king, and even more the young men, that they had to go to war. But worried or not, they had to go. When the day came, they prepared to leave to the blaring sound of the band. They got dressed, packed up, mounted their horses and set out for the war.

As they reached the gates, they saw Little I Don't Know standing there.

They said to him: "All you do is stand there? Why don't you come with us to save the country? The *dog-headed Tatars* are invading our land and unless we save it, it will be no more."

He said: "I don't know."

"You'll know when you're chased out even of your wooden shack—you'll find out! Come with us, grab a weapon and let's go, let's shoot them up!"

He said: "I don't know."

So they went on their way, grumbling and muttering angrily that he knew how to wed the king's daughter but was good for nothing else. They left for the war and Little I Don't Know stayed at home. He waited for them to get ahead and to be out of sight. Then the news came that the *dog-headed Tatars* had conquered at least ten cities. They had overrun them and the people barely had time to get away. Countless numbers had perished for the Tatars had won the battle with an army much larger than theirs. So they returned in sorrow and said to Little I Don't Know:

"You see, you wouldn't come to war with us, yet we are about to lose our land, but you aren't willing to defend it."

It was no use, all he said was: "I don't know."

A time was set for the cease-fire and then the fighting was to begin again. The king *mustered his troops* once more, called up more soldiers since he had lost so many, and prepared for battle. They left with a heavy heart. They knew that they couldn't defeat the *dog-headed Tatars* and their hordes, who far outnumbered them.

They were grim as they started out while Little I Don't Know waited for them to be a distance away. Then he blew into his whistle and the silver-haired steed appeared:

"What is your command, Prince?"

"I command that we go to war and defend our fatherland."

"Now then," said the horse," take out your clothes, your sword and a shotgun!"

Everything he withdrew from the horse's ear was shining silver. He put on the garments, jumped into the saddle and took off at a gallop. The battle had already begun, it was raging and the dog-headed Tatars took one city after another in their path.

When Little I Don't Know got there, he sprinted full speed into the middle of the fray. As the enemy soldiers closed in, he rode up to the front and faced them alone. He drew out his sword and swinging it left and right, he mowed them down, as a reaper harvests crops. They fell in rows like sheaves. By the time he was ready to leave he had destroyed the army, only a handful of soldiers remained to tell the tale. He chased them, God knows how far, back to their own land. So there was no one left to fight, most of the men were dead and the rest had fled. The king was overjoyed that the great knight had helped him out, defeated so many soldiers and got him out of his plight. In the battle he had gained back the cities, all the cities that the dog-headed Tatars had taken.

"Now," said the king, "we must take the knight back with us, we must catch him. Don't let him get away, we must bring him to the palace so I can show him my gratitude for his good deed, for having saved the country."

All well and good, but there was no one to catch—the knight had disappeared like a magician, he just vanished, flew away on his horse. The men returned home, amidst great merriment, happy that by the grace of God they had driven the enemy away and even took a chunk of his land, thanks to the knight, about whom they knew nothing. Who was he? Where was he from? No one could tell.

Then once again the time was set for another battle. The king let it be known that he was ready to fight and designated the day on which the encounter was to take place. He armed his men anew and they started out. Little I Don't Know stood in the doorway.

They said to him: "Little brother-in-law, aren't you coming? We have already been to war twice and you haven't been at all. What do you want? Are you waiting for the Tatars to seize the whole country? You are some son-in-law, you really do your share in defending our land!"

He said: "I don't know."

They galloped away, fuming with anger. Little I Don't Know stayed behind and when he thought that they had reached their destination, he blew into his whistle and the golden-haired steed appeared:

"What do you command, Prince?"

"I command that we go to battle again, defend our country, and stop the dog-headed Tatars from taking over our homeland!"

"Well then, reach into my ear and get dressed at once! Hurry!"

He put on the garments, swung into the saddle, and off they rode. The battle had not yet started when he arrived but when they were about to begin fighting, he moved straight up to the front, ahead of the king. Leaving everyone behind in full gallop, he swept into the midst of the enemy's ranks. Once again he mowed them down in rows, and they fell, just like pelting rain, their dead bodies hitting the ground like hail. He decimated them so badly that no more than ten could escape and run back to carry the news. He even conquered the enemy's *capital city*.

They returned home again and the king begged his men once more to find the knight and not let him go so he could show him his gratitude for saving the fatherland. But the knight was nowhere around because Little I Don't Know was like a magician, he just vanished.

Well, there was to be a third and last battle. No matter who won, this would be the last. So they started out again, armed and with additional men, whom they had recruited.

They shouted over to Little I Don't Know: "Come on, don't just stay home to watch over your wife and sit by her side! Come to the war!"

"I don't know," he said.

They left. He waited for a while, then blew into his whistle once again, and the golden-haired steed appeared:

"Well, what is your command, Prince?"

"That we go to war for a third time," he said. "This will be the last battle, we must help our country as much as we can!"

Little I Don't Know swung into the saddle, drew out his sword and off he rode. By the time he got there, they were ready for the battle. But he didn't wait, he charged into the enemy's ranks and gave them such a thrashing that they soon held up the peace flag . They surrendered, giving up their country, and vowing not to go to war again. "We belong to you and so does our land," they said. That was it. The dog-headed Tatars were defeated and their land taken away.

Little I Don't Know pretended that he was wounded. He had stabbed his leg with his sword and blood was running down his boot. The old king, his father-in-law, saw this.

"Oh dear," he said, "what a shame, the brave knight was wounded."

This time Little I Don't Know didn't run away, didn't escape, but went along with them. They asked him who he was, why he had disappeared twice before when he had accomplished such a great feat in saving their country. Without him the enemy would have surely conquered the land.

Said the king: "You have saved my kingdom, now you must come with us!"

"Well, I won't come right away. I am not saying I won't come—I will, but not now. I want my wound to heal," he said, "and I want to bring my wife with me when I come."

Then the king said: "We understand that you are wounded and that you want to come with your wife; our pleasure will be all the greater. So I am inviting you for Sunday night. I'll organize a ball and expect you and your wife to come to my palace."

"I'll be there, I'll come, for sure."

He took leave of them for a moment and returned home. They headed back too and hoisted a peace-banner, a victory pennant, happy that they had won the war. They had saved the fatherland and what a big country they had gained in addition! There was great joy and merrymaking. The sons-in-law were singing their hearts out, they couldn't contain themselves.

Then Little I Don't Know said to his wife: "Well, wife, until now we haven't been conversing, but from now on we are. I recaptured our land—the dog-headed Tatar would have taken it all if I hadn't been at the second battle. I went to war twice and I saved our country both times. I even conquered the dog-headed Tatar's own land. So," he said, "now the war is over, but your father hasn't yet been able to talk to me, instead he invited me to go back home with them now, to thank me for my good deeds and find out who I am and where I come from. I told him I can't go just yet because I am wounded. But I am not wounded really, I had stabbed myself so they could see that there was blood. I don't feel any pain though. There will be a big ball Sunday night and we are going, both of us. Now they'll learn the truth about who the swineherd son-in-law is, and who the other two, the two proud sons-in-law, are. Now," he said, "the king will find out everything."

Oh, how happy the wife was—she threw her arms around him and hugged and kissed him:

"Why didn't you say anything until now?"

He said: "Now the time has come, now I had to speak out. I wasn't allowed to before."

"How could you stand it all these years and, dear God, how could you, a royal prince, live in this wooden shack, endure everything and not say a word!"

"Well, now I spoke up and from now on I'll be myself. Let's get ready for the ball on Sunday night."

The big ball had been announced and all the country's greats were invited. Already the band was playing hard and the guests began to assemble but they were not yet ready to go over. Then Little I Don't Know blew into his whistle and the silver-haired steed appeared:

"What do you command, Prince?"

"I command that a carriage be brought here—it should be sheer glass and the edges and trimmings all in diamonds, the wheels in gold and the axles, God knows what." He decided everything and described what it should be like. "There should be four horses, all black, as black as sloe, but their coats should be shiny and the four horses should be harnessed one in front of the other, and even the rings on their halters should be pure gold. There should be a liveried coachman because," he said, " we are going to my father-in-law. And now I want my wedding celebrated. Everything must be as fine as I say it should be."

As soon as he uttered the words, there was the glass carriage. And what a carriage it was, even its windows were inlaid with God only knows what! No human being has ever seen anything like it, anything as beautiful! And four pitch-black horses were harnessed to it. They were festooned with flowers and the fine straps of their halters were embellished with diamond trim and rings. This made them look even more splendid. No one had ever seen horses more beautiful.

"Now then, wife, let's get dressed. And." he said, "I want a whole set of new wedding garments brought here for me and for my wife. We'll get ourselves ready and go!"

No sooner had he expressed the wish than everything was there. Royal garments, the kind kings would wear, with red and gold tassels. Good Lord, what all there was! The *shako* was pure, shining gold and so were the spurs—eyes could not be laid on them, they were glittering so. And the bride, what a robe she had, the likes of which no one would have ever seen! One couldn't tell whether it was made of velvet or silk or what else, it was so beautiful. . . . The bridal wreath was sweet, lovely, and she held the wedding rose in her hand, the rose she would carry for the ceremony. Everything was nicely taken care of and when they looked at each other, standing in front of the big mirror, they couldn't stop marveling at how beautiful they were.

Then they took their places in the carriage, the liveried coachman seated in front, and departed. When they got there, the soldiers, the palace guards, were standing in a row on both sides, waiting for the guests and saluting them when they arrived.

Then, all of a sudden, they saw a carriage approaching. But a carriage of a kind they had never seen before. How beautiful was the carriage and how beautiful the horses, fit more for an emperor than for a king! Many people had come here and many balls and weddings had been held, but a carriage like the one arriving now had never yet entered the king's courtyard. They telephoned the palace at once that a guest was on his way but that they couldn't tell whether it was an emperor or who else, for *ever since their eyes had popped open,* they hadn't seen anything as beautiful as the beauty that was now approaching. And what horses and what a carriage! They could only belong to an emperor. All the guests leaped to their feet and streamed out into the hall to see who was coming. The band was blaring so loud that the earth trembled. It was playing a welcoming march. Well, they entered through the gates quietly. With wide eyes and mouths agape the gathering was staring at them. Who could this be that even the king was trembling at the arrival of such an unexpected guest, someone, someone—not a king, perhaps an emperor of a foreign land, who knows from where? They came and stopped in front of the palace doors. Right away the country's greats rushed forward to gaze at them. They wanted to uncover the mystery.

When the king saw his son, or whoever he was, and his daughter, so beautiful, all dressed up next to her husband, he didn't know it was Little I Don't Know. He didn't recognize him. He recognized his daughter but not her husband. They mentioned their name, who they were. The noble guests should know who they were, when they mingled among them. The young woman gave her father's name, the name of the king whose daughter she was.

"Dear Father," she said, "I came to put an end to a deception. This is my husband, my mate, whom I have chosen, my fiancé. It is with him that I'll exchange vows, whom I'll wed in your presence. No matter that you expelled me, excluded me from your palace, you are still my father and I am your child."

When the king heard this, he fell to his knees and asked his daughter and his son-in-law for forgiveness. He didn't know what he had done, for he didn't know with whom he was dealing. He was deeply distressed and in his shame and anguish didn't know what he should do.

He said: "Don't hold a grievance against me and please forgive me!"

His son-in-law, Little I Don't Know, said: "Please rise, Your Majesty, my Father—don't prostrate yourself, I am not worthy of your prostrating yourself before me. I am not worthy of it."

And at his daughter's feet, the king said: "My dear daughter, forgive me for acting so shamefully with you, for disowning you as my child. I regret it with all my heart and I'll make good for everything, only let there be no ill feelings!"

Right away the father took his daughter into his arms and then gently ushered them inside. The two sons-in-law were sitting at the table alongside their wives and the couple was seated next to them. The youngest daughter was in her full wedding attire, so beautiful that the others, including the sons-in-law, would have done better to disappear. Moreover, Little I Don't Know was very beautiful himself, as he was when he was a child, but now, fully grown and dressed up, he was so splendid looking, that they couldn't stop admiring him.

Then, once they were inside, they recounted everything. Little I Don't Know revealed whose son he was, that he was a royal prince, for his father too, was a king. He told them why he had to leave the royal palace and his country, how the steward had treated him, that his father might have perished in the war, but that he didn't know whether he was dead or alive, for he himself had to get away. He had been ordered not to speak until the right moment came and that is why he never said anything. It was he who had destroyed the flowers, not some bird or wild animal, it was he with his steed who had trampled them down.

And he said: "My dear bride saw it, she was looking out the window, she knew it was me."

Said the king: "And still she didn't betray you. She watched while I was torturing you, moving you from one place to another and she didn't let on that you were at fault."

"Well, she didn't want to give herself away, or me. But now," he said, "that we belong to one another, we want to make it clear that we love each other and don't wish to leave matters as they were. God bless our old father the king, and God bless us with him!"

"Now then," said the king, "if this is how things are, I shall hand you my crown in the presence of all the reigning princes and the country's greats who are here, for you are worthy of it. You may be the youngest and your two brothers-in-law are older than you are, but it is you who deserves the crown."

He handed over his crown and the whole realm to Little I Don't Know, who became the ruler of the land. As to the other sons-in-law, one became a king over in the dog-headed Tatar's country, and the other—who knows what became of him? Maybe a prime minister. They are all alive to this day, if they haven't died.

# 2. Zsuzska and the Devil

AT 328 (*The Boy Steals the Giant's Treasure*); MNK *328 (*Incula*) is its female counterpart, not listed in other national or regional European classifications. It easily combines with 327A (*Hansel and Gretel*) and 327B (*The Dwarf and the Giant*). In Hungary, both male and female versions are popular.

Mrs. Palkó's version is closest to an early (1873) text from Transylvania with the same title, that reached the general public through school primers. It was probably this version that she had heard, for "it was read from a book and then I learned it." Aunt Zsuzsa enriches the story by featuring the hardships of poor people, working girls who have to earn their living by serving in households far from their family homes. Before the Second World War peasant girls like herself worked in urban or manorial households solely to obtain enough money for the dowry (bedding, towels, clothing) that was necessary for getting married and starting a new household.

Tape recorded in 1948 at the family home at the request of Mrs. Palkó's oldest grandson, aged twelve.

———

There was once a poor man who had three daughters. They were very poor and had to work hard to earn their daily bread.

One day the oldest daughter said: "Dear Father, thank you for caring for us until now. The time has come for us to go and enter into service."

The girls thought that even the youngest was of age to get married— and she had nothing, not even linens for the dowry.

They bid farewell to their father and all three left. They went past the village and turned into the open fields. They walked until twilight without reaching a town. Then they came to a forest and on its edge stood a house. Said the sisters: "We'd better stop in here and ask for shelter."

All three entered, said good evening and were beckoned in. The master of the house, his wife, and three daughters were inside.

Said the oldest of the girls: "We came to ask whether you would be kind enough to take us in and let us spend the night here."

The master of the house said: "You may stay. Where are you traveling? What is your destination?"

"We left home, looking to enter service somewhere," said the girl.

"Well, you might as well stay here—I could use some workers."

Right away they gave them supper and made up their bed. There was only one room and they lay down, together with the man's daughters, six of them in a row.

When they woke up in the morning the master of the house said: "The two older girls will go out to work in the field and the youngest will stay in the kitchen."

The youngest girl was called Zsuzska. She was well off in the kitchen while the older two had it much worse outside.

When one week had passed since their arrival and they came back from work, the girls went to lie down on the porch, all five of them, side by side. The youngest was always kept late in the kitchen. When she was done, she too went out, ready to go to bed. She knelt down, said her prayers—and when she finished, she prepared to undress. But, she thought, first she would look through the keyhole to see what they were up to inside. Well, when she looked in, what didn't she see! God Almighty, the man was not a man but a real devil, and he was not wearing the clothes he usually wears—he was naked. His whole body was covered with hair, he had long nails and, to boot, he had two horns and a tail. His entire body was hairy like a dog's and he had two big, red eyes. Now she knew with whom they were dealing. The girl was very frightened. She undressed, went to bed but couldn't fall asleep. She rose again and went over to the door to look in and to listen to what they were saying.

Suddenly she heard the devil say to his wife: "Do you know what I thought, wife? I'll kill these three girls and pickle their bodies in salt in a barrel. We'll have enough to eat while they last."

When she heard this the girl continued listening:

"And when do you intend to kill them?"

"Tomorrow night. There are no people on the road then, so no one will know."

"Well," she said, "How will this be? How will you know which one is ours and which is the other, when they are lying side by side?"

"Don't you worry about it. Tomorrow morning when you make up the bed, I'll bring in three stones and place them at the heads of the strangers, and I'll put pillows at the heads of our girls. I'll wait for them to go to sleep and then I'll cut their throats with a big knife so they won't have time to scream. Then," he said, "I'll leave them there till morning and in the morning I'll cure their meat with salt."

The girl heard all this. She lay down beside her sister and waited for the devil and his wife to fall asleep. She waited to hear him snore. When she could tell that he was sleeping, she rose and woke her sister. The sister was angry at Zsuzska for disturbing her sleep, but she insisted:

"Wake up my dear sister, *I need to go out,* but I am afraid to."

"Other times you were not afraid to go out and now you are? You don't let me sleep, you are disturbing me," said the sister.

Zsuzska burst into tears. Her sister felt sorry and went out with her after all.

"Come farther back with me, to the side," Zsuzska said, "they mustn't hear what I want to tell you. I didn't call you because I am afraid to go out. I am not afraid. But do you know in whose house we are in service?"

"Whose?"

"In the house of a real devil from hell. I saw with my two eyes that he is the devil. And what were he and his wife saying? That they want to cut us up and pickle the meat of our bodies. Tell me, dear sister, what should we do to escape from here? He also said that he'll kill us tomorrow night, and, so as to be sure to recognize us in the dark, he'll put a stone at our heads instead of a pillow. They'll wait for us to be asleep and then he'll come with a big knife and cut our throats, all three of us. I say to you that now, tonight, we can't go anywhere any more but let's not be here when he comes to murder us tomorrow. When I wake you, we should leave."

Well, they lay down again and slept until morning. Then the two girls went to work in the field and Zsuzska stayed indoors.

And that is how it came to pass. The devil brought in three stones and put them at their heads. In the evening they all went to bed. The girl waited for the devil to lie down and when she thought that he was asleep, she got up, took the stones and placed them at the heads of the devil's daughters. The youngest girl, Zsuzska, switched them around and put the pillows under their own heads. Then she lay down and went back to sleep.

Suddenly she heard the devil get out of bed and come in. A knife was gleaming in his hand. He felt the stones and immediately cut the throats of the three girls, one by one, in a row. Then he left, went back to bed and when he was snoring, Zsuzska began shaking her sisters:

"Shh, shh, don't say a word."

They grabbed their bundle and in no time they were out the door. Yes, but the youngest one lagged behind and as they passed by the window she shouted:

"Devil, you killed your three daughters, not us—we are leaving!"

When the devil heard this, he leaped up to follow them, but it was pitch dark. He went out on the porch, looked and found that it was all true.

"Just you wait, you lousy, filthy whore, you'll not get the better of me! I'll catch you!"

He bounded out the gate and ran after them, but they had seen a freshly plowed field and hid in one of the furrows. The devil ran and ran, and after a while, when he didn't catch up with them, he stopped to listen for the sounds of their footsteps. But he heard nothing, so he turned around and went home.

"I'll get you sooner or later! I'll have my revenge for the death of my three daughters!"

They kept quiet in the field. When they could tell that the devil had gone home, they jumped up and ran. They ran, across the forest until they reached the shore of an ocean, where a ship was ready to depart. The older girl went up to the captain and asked him politely where it was sailing.

"It is crossing the ocean."

"Would you allow us to come? I must tell you that we have no money for we are the children of poor people, but if you do, God will reward you, for misfortune has befallen us."

And they told him how they fared, that they had been in service with the devil. The captain felt sorry for them and let them board the ship. They crossed over to the other side of the ocean. When they disembarked, they thanked him kindly and went on their way.

They walked until they reached the *capital city* and there all three went to see the king. He was just coming out of the door then, so they greeted him as best as they knew how. They didn't really know how to greet a king—being the children of poor people, they hadn't been taught.

"Well," said the king, "what is your trouble? What brought you here?"

"We would like to enter service somewhere."

"You might as well stay with me."

The king was a bachelor, he had no wife. There too, the two older girls were given work in the field, and the youngest was assigned to the kitchen. They were sweating out there, for it was very hot, while she was well placed in the kitchen. But Zsuzska was very clever, very hard working—the king grew really fond of her and so did the cook. They gave her gifts on several occasions; in addition to her wages she received gifts. And every time she boasted about it, about how fortunate she was, so that her sisters began to feel jealous.

One said to the other: "You see how lucky Zsuzska is, how well she is treated, she doesn't have to stand the hot sun, as we do. Still she is given presents, she receives gifts." They were very jealous of her. Then they began thinking of how they could lose the girl, that is how far they went in their jealousy.

One day the king was out walking in the courtyard. The older girl approached him:

"Your Majesty, I'd like to say something, if it's no offense."

"Just say it, since you have started!"

"Have you heard, Your Majesty, what Zsuzska has been saying? She is saying that when we were in service with the devil, she saw a pair of shoes in his kitchen. With these shoes one can stride across the ocean. She said she could steal them."

This wasn't true, of course, they said it out of envy. Well, the king didn't need to be told twice—he summoned Zsuzska immediately:

"What were you saying, my girl, that you saw shoes at the devil's that would let you stride across oceans, and that you could steal them?"

"Oh no, great King, I didn't say that, nothing of the sort."

"Not another word," said the king, "whether you said it or not, it is all the same to me. Bring them, or else I'll have your head impaled on a stake!"

Her sisters thought that they'd have the devil catch Zsuzska and they'd be rid of her. And Zsuzska burst into tears, protesting that she had never said anything like it, but no one listened; she had to pull herself together and go to fetch the shoes.

So, weeping she left at dawn. But by the time she arrived the lamp was lit, it was evening. She saw the devil chatting with his wife, they were already after dinner. She waited for them to go to bed and to be asleep. Then she quietly entered through the gate; the dog didn't bark, he knew her. She went to the door, it was unlocked for the devil never locked his door. There was some sort of pantry in the house, and the shoes were in it. She went in, slowly, grabbed the shoes and out she was again. No one had noticed her but she didn't have sense enough to leave—she called in through the window:

"Devil, I am taking your ocean-striding shoes!"

When the devil heard this, he jumped out after her, but Zsuzska ran so fast, faster than he, so that she reached the ocean in no time, slipped into the shoes and was transported to the other side. Well, she crossed the ocean! The devil *somersaulted in anger,* he had no choice but to return.

"Don't you worry, I'll get you!"

So the girl went to see the king: "Here are the shoes, I brought them."

"All right, my girl," said the king, and gave her a gold coin as a present.

In the morning Zsuzska went to her sisters to show them what she had received.

They said: "So you brought the shoes?"

"Sure I brought them! Why wouldn't I have?"

The sisters grew even angrier when they heard that she had brought back the shoes and received a gift from the king.

The next day the king was in the courtyard again and the girls stopped him.

**[Listeners:] I'd have snuffed out that girl's life!**

**They were really heathens.**

**It was long ago and it wasn't true.**

"Have you heard, great King, what Zsuzska has been saying?"

"What?"

"That she saw a golden head of cabbage in the devil's garden and that she could fetch it."

"If she said that, she'd better bring it to me."

Right away he went and said to Zsuzska: "You said that you could steal the golden head of cabbage from the devil. Go at once and get it, or else I'll impale your head on a stake."

Well, the girl felt a little sad, but she thought she would try, maybe she could bring it.

The next morning she got dressed and started on her way. Once again she arrived when the lamps were being lit. She hid and waited for the light to be out. Then she proceeded alongside the garden, up to where she knew the cabbage was growing. The dog didn't bark. There was a very tall fence; she climbed over it and went and cut off the cabbage. Then she leaped across the garden and began to run. When she was near the window, she shouted once again:

"Devil, I am taking your golden cabbage!"

"Just you wait! Wasn't it enough that you murdered my three lovely daughters, then you got my ocean-striding shoes, and now you are taking the golden cabbage? Just you wait, I'll catch you!"

By the time the devil came running after her, she had reached the ocean, stepped into the shoes and crossed over. When the devil turned up at the ocean shore she was already on the other side. He was so furious that he was tearing his hair out, but there was nothing he could do. He returned home and the girl went to see the king. She told him that she had brought the cabbage with her, and once again the king gave her a beautiful gift.

Zsuzska went to find her sisters and told them with pride about another present she received from the king. And they grew even angrier that they were not able to lose her. So they waited for the king to be outside and spoke to him once more:

"Have you heard, great King, what Zsuzska is saying?"

"What?"

"She is saying that the devil has a one year-old son who is sleeping in a gold cradle and she could steal it."

"Well, if that is what she is saying, she'll have to bring it to me."

Right away the king summoned Zsuzska: "I hear that you said that the devil has a one-year-old son who sleeps in a gold cradle next to their bed and that you could steal it. I want you to go and fetch it," he said, "and if you don't, I'll have your head impaled on a stake."

Oh, the girl burst into tears for she thought that this was a task she couldn't accomplish.

She said: "Your Majesty, I didn't say that."

"Look, my girl, if you said it, you'll bring it."

Yet she hadn't, but envy is very powerful. The girl wept for she knew how difficult this would be. She had to enter the devil's room for the cradle was there, at their bedside, where they were sleeping. Still she set out and came there about the time they were lighting the lamp. She waited for the devil to be asleep, and then she went in very slowly, leaving the door open. She grabbed the cradle and rushed out the door! As she passed near the window, she put the cradle on her shoulder and shouted:

"Devil, I am taking your little boy!"

When the devil heard this, he didn't just leave by the door, he leaped through the window! He ran after her but couldn't catch up with her. He nearly, nearly did, but God was merciful to Zsuzska—the devil couldn't get her. When she reached the shore, she slipped into the ocean-striding shoes, took one step and found herself on the other side. The girl had crossed the ocean and the devil was throwing himself to the ground and *turning cartwheels,* so furious was he.

"Oh darn! Wasn't it enough that she murdered my three lovely daughters, she took my ocean-striding shoes, took the head of golden cabbage? And now she has taken my beloved, beautiful son? Well, just wait, you whore! You'll pay for this!"

The girl went straight to the king and announced to him that she had brought back the devil's son, along with the cradle. The king praised her, patted her on the back and gave her two gold coins as a present.

**[Listener:] He could give me one too.**

Zsuzska ran and showed them to her sisters. They nearly burst with anger.

"Well, never mind," they thought, "we'll send her again!"

They waited until the king was outside and approached him yet another time:

"Have you heard, Your Majesty, what Zsuzska has said?"

"Just tell me. What?"

"She said that the devil has a bagful of gold walnuts. The bag is in their chamber, where they are sleeping, on the beam over their heads. She said that she could steal it."

"All right, if she said that, then she'll have to bring it."

The king went in and summoned Zsuzska:

"Zsuzska, is it true that you said that?"

"Oh, Your Majesty, it isn't true; I didn't say it and I won't be able to bring it for the walnuts are just above their heads. They'll rattle when I touch them. This will wake them up and I will fall into their hands."

"Look, my girl, it is no good protesting. If you don't bring the bag I'll have your head impaled on a stake, but if you do, I'll take you for my wife."

The girl wept and wept that she couldn't do it. She wept bitterly: "To heck with it, I don't care! It is all the same to me now! I'll risk my life. I see that I have to die one way or the other, at least I'll try."

So she left again and got there about the same time as before. She waited for them to be asleep and then she went in. She walked by their bed and stopped. She was so quiet that she hardly took a breath for fear of waking them. She reached up for the bag and wondered how best to take it down. She grabbed a corner of the bag and began tugging at it. Slowly, slowly she tugged and pulled but in the midst of her tugging and pulling, the bag opened and the walnuts poured down onto the devil and his wife. The whole bag emptied onto the devil and his wife. They both sat up in bed.

"Well now," said the devil, "I told you, didn't I, that I'd get you! I told you that sooner or later you'd come to grief! What did you want this time? Wasn't it enough that you murdered my three lovely daughters, that you stole my ocean-striding shoes, took the golden cabbage and then my beautiful beloved son? Did you also need the golden walnuts? Just you wait, now I've got you in my clutches!"

He grabbed the girl and took her into a small room; it was as dark in there as in a jail. He locked her in. Then he and his wife collected all the walnuts, tied up the bag and went back to bed.

When morning came the devil said: "So, wife, now that I have caught the thief, I'll go down to hell and invite the devils, for I am giving a ball tonight. And you, go and light the oven and when it is red hot, take the girl, strip her naked, put her into a pan and roast her! I want us to have a fine roast at the ball. Do you understand?"

"Sure I understand. I'll do it."

"Make sure that the roast is ready when my pals arrive!"

The girl heard all this. The devil left and the woman stayed behind, and, right away she started heating up the oven. She heated it until it was red hot. Then she went to fetch the girl, grabbed her and pulled off her clothes:

"Now lie down in this pan!" She placed the pan onto an oven-peel: "Now lie down and this will be the end of you!"

Said the girl: "Whatever you order me to do, I'll do. But show me first how to lie down in this pan, then I'll do it myself."

"You don't even know how to do that?"

"No, I don't. I have never seen it done, so I don't know."

"All right. Wait, that much I'll do. I'll show you."

So the devil's wife lay down in the pan. Zsuzska grabbed the peel and shoved it in the oven! She shriveled up inside in a second, like bacon-skin. Zsuzska ran back into the house, pulled the walnuts down from above the beam, but she did not take the time to put on her clothes, she was too frightened. She gathered them under her arm, flung the bag of walnuts on her shoulder and ran.

**[Listener:] She did the right thing!**

She got dressed only when she reached the other side of the ocean—she was naked until then. She went to the king straight away and told him that she had the walnuts but it had taken her three days to get them.

"Well, Zsuzska," said the king, "I thought you had perished."

"Oh no," she said, "I kept my wits about me, more so than the devil's wife." Then she told the king about how she was held prisoner and how they had planned to roast her in the morning. The devil had gone to invite his friends for the evening and had instructed his wife to prepare a fine roast for the feast.

"But I was smart enough to say that I didn't know how to lie down in the pan, that she should show me first, and then I'd do it. When she was lying in the pan I pushed her into the oven and she was roasted."

**[Listener:] Oh, that was cruel!**

Said the king: "Is this how it happened, Zsuzska?"

"It is. God helped me—I brought back the walnuts."

"Well, you brought them, so from now on you'll be queen."

And he took Zsuzska for his wife. She then told him that nothing of what the sisters had said was true, that they spoke out of jealousy and wanted to be rid of her.

"If your sisters are such enemies, tell me, what sort of a death sentence should they be given?"

"I don't have the heart to condemn them to death, they are my sisters. But," she said, "pay them what they are owed and send them back home so I won't have to see them again. They were my bitter enemies. Let them go home!"

So the king paid them, he and Zsuzska were wed, and they lived happily ever after to this day, if they haven't died. And this is how Zsuzska fared with the devil.

**[Listener:] So the devil became a widower.**

# 3. Death with the Yellow Legs

AT 332 *(Godfather Death)*; MNK 332 lists 23 regular and 3 unusual versions. This popular tale type is pretty consistent throughout Europe and Hungary; Mrs. Palkó generally follows the pattern, but makes her version unique by expressing her personal feelings and compassion. She learned it from her brother János, the famous storyteller, and I recorded it in 1948 at the home of the Zsók family during a visit.

Poverty and undeserved wealth constitute the underlying theme of this moral story. Why is God unjust, cursing poor people with so many children that they cannot even find a godparent to baptize the last-born? The desperate father rejects Jesus and St. Peter and accepts Death, whom he finds more equitable. But when the poor father succeeds and assumes the luxurious life of the wealthy (even his smallest child wears gloves!), he cannot stop wanting more. Here, as in "Peasant Gagyi" (tale no.15) "Józsi the Fisherman" (no. 9), "The Fawn" (no. 8), and "Gábor Német" (no. 34), Mrs. Palkó displays her image of the lives of the rich: rolling in loads of money, jewelry, silver, and gold, and surrounded by splendid gardens and castles. Being insatiable and breaking a promise are wrong, according to Aunt Zsuzsa: the hero must die.

———

Once upon a time, beyond seven times seven lands, there lived a poor man. He was *as poor as a church-mouse, and he had as many children as there are holes in a sieve,* and one more. His wife was heavy with child and soon her time came to give birth. She said to her husband:

"Go look for a godfather so we can have the child baptized."

"Where shall I go? Whom should I call?"

"The village is large enough, there are plenty of people. Call one of them!"

"True, but each one has already served as a godfather for us."

"Never mind, one of them may come again to baptize this one too."

The poor man went to the end of the village and to the end of the next village and asked everyone he met. But they all said:

"Well, pal, I have been at your baptisms twice already; find yourself another godfather."

He received the same answer in every house. He went through the village but couldn't find a godfather. He went home and complained to his wife:

"You see, wife, we are poor, we can't arrange a big baptismal feast, so we can't find a godfather. If we could have a big feast, they would all offer to come, but don't worry," he said, "someone will turn up."

The poor woman and the man wept. He said:

"You know what, wife, I'll get a big stick, attach a piece of iron to one end, and go out to the highway. I'll hide in a ditch there, and when I see someone coming, I'll ask him to stand godfather to our son. If he doesn't accept, I'll strike him on the head so he'll die instantly."

Well, the poor man took off at night, in the dark. He went out to the highway, crawled into a ditch, and listened whether anyone was coming. Soon he heard two people approaching. When they reached him, he leaped up and faced them.

"Who are you?" he said, "Stop!"

Both men stopped: "What do you want from us?"

"What I want is that my child, who was born today, be baptized. But I can't find anyone who would accept to be a godfather and hold him at the baptismal font. What about you? Who are you?"

One of them said:

"I am Saint Peter and the other is Christ our Lord."

When he heard who they were, he said:

"You are not wanted as godfathers, even if you agreed to come, you are not wanted."

Said Christ the Lord:

"And why not, poor man?"

"Because," he said, "you are not fair. Christ our Lord, you are not fair!"

"Why not?"

"Because you gave me so many children, I don't even know their names, while there are gentlemen who live in clover and they have no children. They could even buy them with money, but you don't let them have any. And I have so many of them that in every corner there are five or six, crying from hunger; my two arms aren't sufficient to support them. Go on your way, you are not wanted!"

So Saint Peter and Christ our Lord left and the poor man crawled back into the ditch. Then he heard someone else coming. He jumped up and stood in front of the person:

"Halt! Stop!"

The person stopped.

Said the poor man: "Who are you?"

"I am the Death with the Yellow Legs. What do you want from me, poor man?"

"What I want from you is what I want from everyone I meet: to be a godfather to my son. I ask, for I have no one who would take my child to baptism. I have to do it this way."

"Look, poor man, I can see you are desperate," he said, "don't worry, I'll be there in the morning for your child's baptism."

"But be there, for sure!"

"Quite sure, I'll be there."

So the poor man went home and said to his wife:

"Hurry, get ready and swaddle the boy, I found a godfather for him."

Death arrived in the morning and knocked on the door:

"Good morning, pal, here I am!"

He took the boy in his arms and baptized it, there, in the house:

"Well, pal, I baptized your son, but that is all. I have no gift to give you, for all I own is this scythe on my shoulder. This is my weapon, my wealth."

But when Death saw how many tiny children there were about, he was shocked. More of them were naked than clothed.

"I am sorry, pal, that I can't give you anything," he said. "But listen to what I have to say. I'll put up a sign over your door now, with golden chalk, in golden letters, saying that here lives the world's most learned doctor. And you, if you have a few pennies, go to the pharmacy, buy a couple of small boxes and some drops for the digestion and be ready to start doctoring, because they'll soon be here. As soon as they see the sign from the road, they'll come asking for you and you must be prepared with the medicine. But I am also telling you, when they take you to a sick person, just look for me, for where I'll be standing. If you see me at the head of the sickbed, don't begin any treatment. Say that it is too late, nothing can be done, the person must die. But if you see me at the foot of the bed, you may go ahead with confidence, the person will recover. No one will be able to see me, only you."

With those words he took leave of his friend and left. The poor man said to his wife:

"Wife, do you have a penny or an egg, so I can go to the pharmacy?"

They had to borrow from the neighbors. He went and bought some drops for the digestion and some ointment. When he came home, there was a carriage standing at the gate, waiting for the doctor. As the poor man approached, they said to him:

"Does the doctor live here?"

"He does."

"Where is he then?"

"Right here!"

They said:

"If you are the doctor, how is it that such a famous doctor goes around in tatters? But if you really are the doctor, please come—a count has a very sick son. He is so sick that they are watching him in his bed, afraid that he will die."

The poor man climbed into the carriage right away and they left. It didn't take them long to get there. He went in and found a young lad so sick that he couldn't open his eyes. His father and mother were there, heartbroken, weeping at his side. The doctor went over to the patient, took his hand, felt the veins for the pulse, but first he looked around for his friend. He saw him standing at the young lad's feet. Then he said:

"Sure, with God's help I can save him."

He took out the drops, asked for a teaspoon and poured the medicine into the young lad's mouth, drop by drop. He palpated his stomach, then the veins in his hands, rubbed some ointment behind his ear and sat down beside him. Within a few minutes the young lad opened his eyes. The doctor said to him:

"How do you feel, son?"

"I feel better," he said.

Then he gave him more drops and put on more ointment. Suddenly the young lad spoke up:

"Mother dear, I am hungry."

He hadn't eaten anything for weeks. On the third day he got up and walked around in the house. A week later he went to church, he was so well. The count ordered two carriages to be filled with money, with silver and gold and with banknotes; he had a pair of oxen hitched up to each and had one of his servants take the doctor home, along with the money.

Soon the news spread that the doctor had brought the young lad back from the dead. It spread everywhere, and he amassed so much money that they were bringing it to him by the carriageful. Even his youngest was now wearing fancy clothes and they all looked like sons of gentlemen.

Some time later another count came and asked him to go see his daughter who was on her deathbed. If he cured her, he would get six carriagefuls of money; silver, gold and banknotes. There again, Death was at the girl's feet, the doctor treated her, and on the third day she was up and about. He received everything, as promised, delivered all the way to his home. He became so rich that he bought himself a three-story dwelling and lived in it. Even his youngest son was wearing a gold ring, money was piled up in the cellar in barrels and the tills were full.

Then a royal carriage drove up and the coachman said: "Doctor, Sir, please come with me, the king is very sick. They say there isn't another doctor like you in the whole world, for you have brought many people back from the dead. The queen said that if you can help, she will give you so much money that you couldn't ever spend all of it."

Well, he had plenty of money but he was maneuvering for more. He went along and entered the sick king's room. First he looked around to see where his friend was standing. Death was there, at the king's head. He examined the king's head, his hands and his feet and said:

"I can't treat him, he is about to die."

Oh, but the queen and her daughter were lamenting:

"Do treat him, you helped so many patients recover, if you treat him he'll get well too."

Said the doctor:

"Why didn't you call me before? Now it's too late."

The queen said:

"Just treat him, even if he dies, do what is necessary, I'll pay for it if you treat him, the same as if he stayed alive; just begin treatment."

"The money would be welcome," he thought to himself, since he had all those children, and he said:

"Only two people can stay in the room, everyone else must leave!"

He thought that somehow he would be able to help. He said to the two people: "Take the bed and turn it around."

They turned the bed around but Death was still at the head. Then he asked them to turn the bed around the other way, but Death followed and stayed at the head. When they turned the bed around a third time, Death became very angry. He gave his friend an irate look, but no one else could see him. The poor man noticed, however, that his friend was aggravated. Then Death left the room and he started with the treatment. He began his doctoring and brought the king back to health. It took three carriages to haul his money home and by then he wasn't concerned about Death. He had a beautiful manor house, a lovely flower garden, never lacked anything, and his money was piling up in barrels in the cellar.

One day the doctor, his wife and the children sat down for their midday meal. They began talking about how poor they used to be and what had happened to them. How rich they had become. Even their youngest son was wearing gloves.

Suddenly there was a knock on the door. It was his pal. Said the doctor: "Oh, dear friend, we have been expecting you for a long time. How good that you came."

"Well," he said, "it's not very good."

"Why not, my friend?"

"Because I came for you, to take you away."

"Where? Where do you want to take me?"

"I came because now you have to die. You remember that I told you when I wrote the sign in golden letters that you must only treat the sick when you see me at the foot of their bed. You see, you defied my command, you didn't do as you were told. The king's time had come, I was sent to take him away. You would have had twenty more years to live, but since you cured the king, now he will live for another twenty years and you must die. You exchanged your life for his."

The doctor started to cry: "My dear friend, allow me to go on, none of my children are married yet; let me help them leave the nest, please let me."

"I won't allow anything, friend, you must die."

"Well then, at least come down to the cellar with me so I can show you what I have acquired."

"That I'll do, I'll come down with you."

He took him into the cellar. It was lined with two rows of barrels, filled to the brim.

Said the poor man: "Look friend, I have enough to live on and you are removing me from among the living. Aren't you sorry for all these children? Should they remain without a father?"

"No, my friend, I am not sorry for them, they have plenty to live on. You disobeyed; now you must die."

"At least allow me to take you out into the flower garden, allow me to show it to you."

They went out into the flower garden. There was a fish pond, its bottom was pure glass, and it had a fountain in the middle, with a pump. On top of it sat an elephant. Out of this fountain the water flowed into a golden trough.

"You see, my friend, all this is mine."

The doctor was thirsty, he wanted water badly but there was no glass or cup to drink from, and he was embarrassed in front of his friend to bend down into the trough. But Death knew it, he could see into his heart, he knew how thirsty he was. He could see, too, that the doctor was ashamed. So he looked away and went ahead, while the doctor bent down and quickly took a drink from the trough. But then Death spun around and with the scythe cut off his head. There he remained, dead. Death plucked his soul from behind and went back to the house:

"Go and lay my friend out on a bier."

"Is he dead?"

When they brought him up, they were all weeping and lamenting, but to no avail—once a person is dead, he is dead. Then the friend took off and they stayed there with all the money and the mansion. The boys took wives and the girls got married and they are all alive to this day, if they haven't died.

# 4. The Glass Coffin

AT 407B (*The Devil's [Dead Man's] Mistress*); MNK 407B. Elements of this tale are traced to seventeenth-century devotional literature featuring the devil as seducer, and to folk beliefs about the sexual attacks of the incubus. This tale type is remarkably consistent in Hungary: only 8 of the 49 listed variants are combined with the affinial AT 365 (*The Dead Bridegroom Carries off his Wife [Lenore]*), which in these cases serves as introductory to 407B. Regarding its constituent episodes and motifs, the tale is deeply rooted in local belief in evil spirits, the return of the malevolent dead, and avoidance-magic. Throughout East Europe it exists as both magic tale and belief legend. Mrs. Palkó learned it from a Romanian girl in the Bucovina while they worked on a sharecropping team.

The tale begins as a simple village event. Girls gather for the spinning bee, as was customary for the Székely during winter months prior to World War II. They prepared the yarn for the loom to weave the cloth for underwear and linen goods for their families while their sweethearts joined them for courting games to ease the work. A man who grabbed an "accidentally" dropped spindle was rewarded by a kiss.

The heroine of "The Glass Coffin" pays dearly for her sinful longing for a boyfriend: the devil appears—that is, the incubus (*lüdérc*), an evil spirit in Bucovina Székely folk belief—and "uses her." She escapes by following the advice of a village wise woman—so far, the story is completely legend-like. It becomes a magic tale only when the girl is reborn as a flower that the prince takes home. Not all versions end tragically, but Mrs. Palkó believes invoking the devil cannot go unpunished.

Recorded at Mrs. Palkó's home in 1950.

―――――

Once upon a time, in a land far away, a woman had a daughter, who was very unhappy because no one loved her. She was getting on in years and no one had yet courted her. She would go to the spinning house with the others in the evening, and all the girls would have sweathearts there except her. Well, she was very sad about this and ashamed; yet she was a pretty girl, but she had no luck. She couldn't cast the thought out of her mind, and it kept her awake at night, brooding over why nobody loved her. She was hard working and she was pretty, still no one turned up for her. This worried her greatly. One evening the girls gathered again. They all had their lovers with them and there they were sitting together, chatting and whispering to each other, while she looked on in sorrow.

51

Then there was a knock at the door and in came a fine, handsome lad, the likes of whom they had never seen. His boots were as shiny as a mirror—they could see their reflections in them. The coat he was wearing didn't have its equal in their whole village, or in the entire world. The girls had never seen a lad more beautiful. He greeted them and they welcomed him. He looked around and saw right away that there was a girl alone, no man was sitting next to her. He stepped inside, shook hands with everyone and sat down beside her.

Suddenly the girl dropped her spool while spinning. He grabbed it and said:

"What is it worth to you to get it back?"

Said the girl: "Its only worth to me is that you give it back so I can go on spinning."

"That is not how it is. I won't give it to you until I get a kiss—then I'll return it."

The girl was very embarrassed—she was prudish, never having had a lover before. But the lad didn't hand over the spool until he gave her a kiss. The girl jumped up and moved away, she went to fetch a glass of water. Right away the other girls began to whisper to each other that the lad was courting her and, well, they were jealous.

Time passed, it turned nine o'clock, and they were preparing to go home. As was customary, the lads left the house first and the girls stayed behind. They said to her:

"This young man is interested in you, surely he will want to marry you. Oh, how lucky you are! Where could he be from, this handsome lad?"

No one could guess where he came from, where he belonged, who he was, what he was. They went out and started on their way home. Well, the lad was there, waiting for the girl, and walked her to her house. She didn't go in right away, as girls normally do—she stayed with him outside, chatting.

She kept asking him: "Tell me, where are you from?"

"Why does it matter to you where I come from? I love you and I want to marry you."

He visited her for three weeks and during this time the girl became so thin that everyone was wondering what had happened to her. There was an old woman living in the neighborhood. She asked the girl to come see her. Said the girl:

"I came. Now what do you want, grandma?"

"Look," she said, "I called you to ask you about something. I heard that a young man is seeing you. Who is he?"

"I asked him but he wouldn't say."

"He wouldn't even say where he is from?"

Said the girl:

"No. But you know, he is so handsome that he could be a prince. His clothes are so fine that a king's son would have no better."

"And you, why are you so thin?"

"I don't know. I just feel that I am getting weaker every day, losing weight."

"Look, my dear girl," said the old woman, "I don't like this love relationship of yours. You must prepare a spool of thread, of very thin yarn, and make sure there is plenty of it. Then you must thread a needle through the yarn and stick it in the spool. When the young man comes to see you, follow him and show him out. He'll stop to chat with you and while you talk, put your arms around him, as if you were embracing him lovingly, so that the needle sticks to his coat with the thread fastened to it! When he takes leave of you and starts on his way, hold the spool in your hand and let the thread unravel until it unravels no more and stops somewhere. Then, quickly, begin winding up the spool and follow the thread until you reach the end. This way you'll see in which village and which house it'll stop, because he himself won't tell you. You'll know, my girl, where this lad comes from, the thread will lead you there. The next morning come to see me and tell me what you saw and where you saw the lad!"

And that is how it came to pass. The following day the lad appeared early, they chatted for a while, then he rose:

"I'll go home now."

The girl accompanied him, followed him out of the house. While they were talking and whispering tender words to each other, the girl put her arms around the lad and made sure that the needle and the thread stuck to his coat. He didn't notice it. They took leave of one another and he left. As he walked on, the girl let the spool unravel. He quickened his pace and the thread unraveled faster, until suddenly it came to a stop. "Now" said the girl, "he must have reached his house." Quickly she began rewinding the spool and set out to follow the thread. She went far, over hill and dale until she came to a bare field, in the midst of which stood an old, abandoned church in ruins. From it, from this church issued the thread. She wanted to open the door to see who was inside. But the door was locked. Now what should she do? She hoisted herself up on the side of the wall, up high to the window, and looked in. She saw her lover standing in the place where the altar used to be, chewing on some dead bones. He was crunching them with his teeth. And the lad looked like the Devil. He was all black, with two large, red eyes and black horns; the girl could see that he was the Devil in person. She jumped down from the window and started to run. It was morning by the time she got home. She went straight to the old woman, weeping and lamenting. She told her where she found the handsome lad who had been courting her, where he was living, what he was doing and eating. "Oh," said the old woman, "my dear girl, what misfortune befell you! You were very unhappy that no one, no young man was courting you, you took it so much to heart that the Devil came to tempt you. And now you won't be able to escape him, unless you heed my words and do as I tell you."

"Dear grandma, teach me what I must do to be free of him!"

The old woman said: "Lock the doors, and if the lad comes calling, don't let him in the spinning room!"

And that is what happened. She locked the doors and sat down to work. Then the young man came and when he couldn't enter through the door, he went to the window.

He said: "Let me in, my dear!"

"I will not! I don't want you, neither my body, nor my soul wants you!"

"Let me in, for if you don't, your father will die!"

"I don't mind—even if he dies, I won't let you in! I'll have nothing to do with you!"

That night her father died. The next day in the evening the lad appeared as before, and again the girl locked herself in. He couldn't get in through the door, so he went to the window and said:

"Let me in!"

"Certainly not! Neither my body, nor my soul wants to have anything to do with you!"

"If you don't let me in, your mother will die."

"I don't mind—even if she dies, I won't let you in."

By midnight her mother was dead.

Once again the girl visited the old woman and asked her to help:

"Dear grandma, teach me how I can free myself of him."

The old woman said:

"My girl, have them prepare a glass coffin for you, lie down in it and tell your relatives that when they take you to the cemetery they shouldn't carry you out through the door, but through the window—otherwise you can't escape him—and they should bury you alive."

And that is what came to pass. They placed her in a glass coffin the very same day and buried her. Then her father's relatives went home and stayed at the house so it shouldn't stand empty. They spent the night there.

Soon after they returned from the cemetery in the evening, the young man appeared. But the door was locked again. He tried to open it and when he couldn't, he went to the window and called out:

"Let me in, my dear!"

Her aunt said to him: "She'll not let you in on this earth any more. She is dead."

"When did she die?"

"Well," she said, "we just came back from the cemetery. We just buried her."

"If she is dead, let her be dead. I am now going to roam the world for seven years and I'll find her wherever she's hiding," he said. "And if during this time I see her anywhere beyond the eaves of the house, she'd better beware and her relatives too!"

"We are not afraid," said the aunt, "she is dead and buried."

Then the lad left with much clatter and in a big gust of wind. On the third day after the girl was buried a rosemary sprouted on her grave. It was in full bloom, with twin blossoms intertwining, waving to and fro together. The passers-by marveled at the beautiful flower that had grown on the grave.

One day a prince drove by in his carriage. He saw the flower from afar and noticed how beautiful it was. When they reached the cemetery gates he ordered the coachman to stop. He alighted from the carriage, went over to the grave, picked the flower, and took it home. He placed it between two windows in the room where he slept, and watered it every day for he grew very fond of it.

One day the prince went hunting and his servants, his bodyguards, went along.

One of his servants said to him: "Your Royal Majesty, I'd like to tell you something—I would and I wouldn't, for I am afraid that you'll punish me."

He said: "You broached it, so go ahead. If you don't, you'll die."

"I didn't know why" he said, "I was no longer getting the food that you left on the table, or the glass of water—it stood empty. I didn't tell Your Majesty before, but I spied and I saw who eats the leftover food and who drinks the glass of water. I watched and I saw with my two eyes that the rosemary steps out of her vase, shakes herself and becomes such a beautiful maiden that *one doesn't have to light a candle, her beauty illuminates the room*. She sits down at the table, eats the food that is left, drinks the glass of water, and goes back to the window. She tumbles, head over heels, becomes a rosemary again, and returns to the window."

"Is this true?"

"This is the truth, Your Majesty, I saw it with my two eyes."

Said the king: "Maybe you dreamed it."

"Oh no!" he said, "I really saw who finishes the leftover food."

"Well, if this is so, here is what we'll do: When I am in my bath and you bring me the drink that will help me sleep, you'll have to suffer a slap in the face for me. As you carry the drink, pretend to trip on the sill, so it will spill into the bathtub. I know," he said, "that the old cook will slap you in the face, but I ask you to put up with it for me. I'll fill the glass with bathwater, drink it and tell the cook not to bother you— 'nothing spilled, I drank it all.' Then I'll pretend to fall asleep in the tub. You'll carry me to my bed and I'll be awake to witness for myself what you have said."

And that is how it happened. The following day when they returned from the hunt, supper was ready, waiting for the king. He sat down, ate his fill, leaving the rest, and went to take his bath. While he was in the bath, his valet brought the drink, tripped on the sill, and poured it all into the tub. The cook jumped up and slapped the valet in the face, hard.

She said: "You, clumsy mama's boy! What kind of a soldier are you, if you trip even on the smooth floor?"

Said the prince: "Don't! Don't hurt him—look, I drank it all!"

He had filled the glass with bathwater. Then he stretched out, as if he had fallen asleep. His two valets went over, lifted him out of the tub, laid him down in his beautiful, white silken bed, and covered him. He slept as soundly as I did just now. Around midnight he woke and saw the window open and the rosemary step down on the floor. She shook herself and turned into such a beautiful maiden that *one could sooner gaze at the sun than look at her*. Her radiance filled the room with light, as if a lamp had been burning. She went to the table, sat down and ate. The king was waiting to see this. She drank the glass of water and then rose. And as she was about to return to the window, she had to pass by the king's bed, it was the shortest way. The king took her by the waist and put his arms around her. The maiden let out a scream:

"Let me go! What do you want?"

"I won't let you go! I want to take you for my wife."

"This doesn't please me," she said. "There is a curse on me, I cannot be in this world. It is forbidden."

Said the king: "Don't be concerned. You don't have to be out in the world. You can stay inside, in the castle. Here you'll have all you need, to eat, and to drink. I'll give you two maids who will dress and undress you, cook for you, and look after you—you'll never have to take even a single step outside the door."

"Well," she said, "Prince, it'll be for a long time and you'll not allow it, or tolerate it, that I should spend my days sitting indoors. But I cannot go out beyond the eaves, for that would be the end of me, until the seven years are over."

"Oh," said the Prince, "I'd allow it, even if it took twice seven years, as long as you are mine! Just remain quietly with me, no harm will come to you!"

The prince protested so much that the poor girl stayed. They got along well together. They had a priest come to the house and were married by him. They lived happily for a while. A little girl and a little boy, twins, were born to them and they blossomed and developed in the castle, like flowers.

Then, one day, the king said to his wife: "Wife, I am tired of this way of life."

"Why, my dear husband, why?"

"Because, you don't know, but I am so ashamed that I cannot go out into the park for a walk. Everyone goes with their wife and I am always by myself. People confront me saying that they heard I had a wife yet I never take her out for a walk, like the others do. I answer with all kinds of lies, once that you are unwell, the next time that the children are sick and now I don't know what to say any more. I am embarrassed. They are even hinting that maybe I married an ugly woman, that I am ashamed to take her out, to let others see how ugly she is. So, dear wife, I ask you to come for a walk with me tomorrow evening—let me show the world that I am not ashamed of you."

"You see, my dear husband, I told you in advance what would happen. Why didn't you let me be? You plucked me off my grave, but now why don't you leave me alone now that you have brought me here? Why do you press me when you know that I cannot go out before my time is up?"

Well, her husband felt sorry for her and said nothing further. He continued going on his walks alone.

A few weeks passed and he spoke up again: "Wife, will you come to church with me today? Who knows in which part of the world the Devil is roaming, where he is—he won't find you here, in church. We'll go in a carriage and come back the same way."

She said: "I am telling you, until my time is up, he'll be looking for me everywhere."

The king went on complaining that now he was embarrassed before the other gentlemen about never taking his wife anywhere.

"Well, let it be. I'll go, if you wish, but I believe I won't come back any more."

Said the king: "Sure, you'll come back. You'll be next to me in the carriage and I won't let him take you. He will not attempt to pull you away from me, off the carriage. Besides, it's not customary for the Devil to go to church."

"All right," she said, "I see that you are determined to take me, so take me!"

The woman bathed her two children, hugged and kissed them, weeping, then got dressed, stepped into the carriage and they drove off. They entered the church, the woman said her prayers but her eyes were constantly searching whether the Devil was anywhere to be seen. When mass was over and they were leaving, she suddenly spotted him standing there, waiting for her. She pressed her husband's hand:

"You see, I told you he'd be here. Well, he is."

"Oh no!" he said, "It is just your fear, you are imagining."

"I am not imagining," she said, "I can see him clearly—he is baring his teeth at me."

Said her husband: "Come closer to me, I'll hold you, he won't take you away, I won't let him!"

But the woman began to shiver and tremble, so frightened was she. As soon as they were outside, beyond the eaves of the church, the Devil grabbed her. She let out a scream.

Her husband said: "Have no fear, wife—there is no one here, I don't see anyone."

"You don't, but I see him! Listen to what he is saying, that he is taking me now, that I must go with him, that he won't let me return home!"

No one could see him, only the woman. She knew that nothing would save her, so she said to him:

"Let me go home and take leave of my children."

Said the Devil: "You may go, but hurry, I'll not wait for you long!"

So, the poor queen went and the Devil stayed outside her door. She pressed her children against her, hugged and kissed them over and over again and said to them: "You can thank your father that you'll not have a mother any more."

Her husband said: "Don't cry, you are inside now and won't go out again."

"Can't you hear him howling, demanding to know how long I'll be, why I am not rushing?"

"I can't hear anything," he said.

"He is screaming in a horrible voice that I shouldn't wait for him to come in after me!"

Then the poor woman embraced her children once again, took leave of her husband and stepped out.

The Devil grabbed her instantly and said: "So, you couldn't hold out, you couldn't wait for a little while longer. You only had one week, one day, one hour and one minute left for the seven years to be over. You would have been as free as a bird, you could have come and gone wherever you pleased, I wouldn't have had the strength to pursue you. But now you are mine! Tell me, what form of death should I inflict on you, what would be the most painful?"

Well, the woman couldn't utter a single word. The Devil let out such a shattering scream that she collapsed in shock and he snatched her soul.

Her husband arranged a splendid funeral for her.

He was sorry enough that he didn't wait for the time to be over, but it was too late. So the king remained alone with his two children, unless he took another wife. And that is all there is to the story. Take it, or, if you don't believe it, leave it!

# 5. The Count and János, the Coachman

This popular legend—comprising *Motif-Index* numbers E371 (return from dead to reveal hidden treasure) + E415 (the dead cannot rest until certain job is completed) + 463 (living man in dead man's shroud)—is listed in the MNK as AT 326*, indicating its type-affinity with 326 (*The Youth Who Wanted To Learn What Fear Is*). Mrs. Palkó explained the dead count's behavior by telling another legend: her father-in-law's account of an attempt to dig up buried treasure that failed because of greed. Furthermore, to clarify her point, she added another related personal legend that came to her mind:

"The dog sees the dead man and is afraid of him. My mother told us that she was in service at a certain place where there was a bad woman. No hired man could stand it longer than one day with her. When Mother got there, the woman died. She was buried, and she went home. She says, that she saw her—as she came out of the furrow, the dog saw her. But he was so afraid of her, he barked fearfully, not in the way that he would bark at a living person. But how long it lasted, I don't know. From the furrow she passed into the garden. There was something hidden there. She was waiting for somebody to force her to say why she was waiting. It's like this: whoever hides something quickly—hides money—has no rest; one only has to remove it from where it is hidden. If only somebody had forced her to speak!" [Shorthand notes, 1948]

———

There was once a count and he had a coachman. The coachman was called János. The count was greatly beloved by his servants for he was very fair-minded. One day he fell ill. With two or three doctors in attendance he received every possible care, but to no avail. He died, leaving a great fortune. His wife gave him a splendid funeral; still he kept returning and rattling around in the attic, or in the room, so loud, that she was at her wit's end. She even went to complain to János:

"Look, János, why is it that my husband continues haunting this house? It scares me to death. He keeps throwing dishes on the floor, yet not one breaks."

János said: "I'll stay in the house for one night."

And that is what happened. He lay down but wasn't asleep yet when the count came and started making noise in the attic. He was pounding so hard that the ceiling nearly caved in. Then he came into the room and began throwing things this way and that. He continued until about eleven o'clock, when he quieted down and left.

"Well, Madam," said János the next day, "I'll find out why your husband comes home to haunt you."

Said the woman: "You see, János, I gave him a fine funeral, and still he comes back to haunt the house. Why, I don't know."

"Please go into town and buy me a glass coffin and a set of brand new clothes to wear, for I am going to die. But first," said János, " let me have a pot of gold."

She gave him the pot of gold. János carried it out into the stable and buried it in a corner. Then they bought a glass coffin and János got dressed.

He said: "I'll lie down in this coffin now, and you take me to the cemetery and place me next to the count, in the vault."

And that is how it came to be. They took him there, but he wasn't dead; he was alive. Candles were burning in the crypt. When it turned nine o'clock, János saw the count rising from his coffin and bending over to see who was alongside him.

"Well, János, you came here too? You are dead too?"

"I didn't come here—they brought me. I am dead; they buried me today."

"Then come along," said the count, "let's go home together!"

They went back, and the count started banging about in the house and throwing everything on the floor. Nothing broke, but when János threw something down, it shattered.

Said the count: "János, you are not dead."

"Oh yes, I am!"

"Then why are the things breaking that you throw down?"

Soon the time came for them to leave.

János said to the count: "Sir, tell me, why do you go back to haunt the house so much?"

"And you, why do you go back?"

"Count, Sir, you answer first, then I'll tell you."

The count said: "I'll tell you why. Look, János, there are three barrels full of gold buried in the pantry. No one knows about it, and I cannot rest until someone removes them from there."

"Well, now it is my turn to say why I go back home."

János took the count to the stable and showed him the pot of gold.

"No one knows about this either; that is why I go back."

"Let's go, János. It is nearly time, we'd better return to the crypt. Let's go."

The count left in a hurry, but János didn't follow him. Since he was alive, he could stay behind. He went to the gold the count had talked about, removed it and put one barrel away for himself. He gave another barrel to the woman.

She said to him: "János, wait! I want you to have half!"

"I don't need it, keep it all to yourself."

János told the woman about the count and the treasure. The count stopped haunting the house, the countess got married again, János became a wealthy farmer and took a wife. They are alive to this day, if they haven't died.

The dead return to haunt a house where they hid something during their lifetime, but only if no one finds it and removes it. Especially any kind of iron, or money. Beelzebub keeps watch over the money; he puts his hand on it.

My father-in-law told the story that once, in the old days, thieves had stolen some money and buried it in the ground. There was a shed, where they used to do the cooking in the summer. A peartree stood in front of it which always bore a lot of fruit. One day my father-in-law came back from the road, unharnessed the horses and led them back into the stable.

Every seven years buried money starts smouldering, burning off the rust. When this happens, one has to throw a rag over it. My father-in-law didn't do it, yet he wouldn't have had to dig down deep. He told his buddies what he had seen, and they agreed to join him in digging up the money at night. It is only good to dig at night. And the men really have to be close friends and united in their purpose. So, four of them went in the dark and began digging for the money. Soon their spades hit a barrel.

They said: "Well, we got it!"

Then a priest looked in from the garden and asked: "Will you let me have some?"

"You are not helping us dig, so we won't give you any!"

That very moment the money disappeared, amidst great clatter. The priest must have been the one to keep watch over it. They should have shared it with him.

# 6. The Princess

AT 403A *(The Black and the White Bride)*, with elements from 533 *(The Speaking Horsehead)*; MNK lists 31 full and 14 deviant versions corresponding to the widespread European prototype. Mrs. Palkó learned this tale from her brother János. I recorded it from her at her home in December 1950 while the whole family awaited the arrival of the Christmas mummers.

This is the smoothest, most poetic among the forsaken heroine tales in her repertoire. She features warm family relationships, loving care between parents and children, sister and brother. Her descriptions are particularly poignant when presenting situations and people—the radiant beauty of the princess contrasted with the coarse, sunburnt "peasant" looks of the substitute queen; the king, mourning the loss of his wife; his concern for the future of his country and admonition to his son to be a just ruler so that the people will love, not hate him; the pain of separation of sister and brother; and the brother taking responsibility for his sister's welfare. Mrs. Palkó is on the side of the poor: only poor people do good without expecting a reward—although they are finally fabulously rewarded, like the fisherman and his wife. Otherwise in this tale only the clothing differentiates the rich from the poor; the prince liberated from prison is recognized as king as soon as he puts on his regal attire.

———

Once upon a time, beyond hill and dale and beyond the seven seas, there lived a king and a queen. The queen was as beautiful as a shining star. They had a very lovely daughter and a son, a prince and a princess. The daughter was so exquisite that there was no one like her in the entire world. Stars were glowing on her two cheeks and a moon on her forehead. When she wept her tears were like golden beads and when she walked rosemaries bloomed in her footsteps. It was impossible to find anyone more beautiful.

The king and the queen delighted in their children The son was handsome too, but the daughter had no equal. Their joy didn't last long, however, for the queen fell ill and died. The children became *orphans*. Their father, the king, wept for seven days and seven nights—his tears never stopped flowing, so deeply did he mourn his wife.

"Well, my dear daughter, I'll never marry again for I couldn't find another woman like your mother. I'll stay by myself until I die."

In his sorrow the king became deathly ill. He summoned his son and his daughter:

"My dear son and daughter, I know that I'll die soon and you will be orphans. You must cherish one another as your greatest treasure, look after each other and love each other as brother and sister! You'll have no one else to comfort you and guide you. I am asking you on my deathbed to always love and protect each other!"

Then the king spoke to his son: "You'll be king after me, you are entitled to the crown. You must take good care of the country and always comport yourself as I have, so that the people will love you. They shouldn't harbor anger against you, but hold you in their affection."

Having uttered these words, the king died. His children wept and wept; they were heartbroken at losing their father and becoming orphans.

Well, brother and sister went on living from one day to the next. They were loving and couldn't do enough for one another. In time the young lad became tougher and the girl was ready to think about marriage. They had both grown stronger.

Said the lad: "My dear sister, I'd like to take a wife, but whom to ask? I don't know. So I decided to go searching and leave you here. I shall not return until I find someone just like you. If I can't, I will not marry."

The girl said: "My dear brother, what will I do until then?"

"God will not abandon you and you must look after yourself! Your bodyguards are here and so is the steward—they'll watch over you. I believe that if I find someone, I'll be back very soon, and if not, I'll go looking all over the world. But before I leave, let's go into town and have our pictures taken."

They went to a photographer. The prince said to him: "Take a picture of my sister. It should show her as you see her here, now. I'll pay you anything you want, but the picture must show her as you see her."

The photographer took the picture. He succeeded in portraying her exactly as she was in real life—she could almost speak. She almost could. Then the prince had a picture taken of himself. He gave it to his sister and kept hers for himself. He fastened a gold chain to it and put it around his neck. He wore it so he could always look at her. They went home. He gathered his belongings and prepared to leave the next morning.

In the morning he said: "Well, my dear sister, we now have to take leave of one another. Don't cry, for I'll be back, as sure as I am alive. Don't cry—God will protect you."

They parted, the lad mounted his horse, a fine steed, and rode away. The girl followed him to the gate and gazed after him for as long as she could see him. And when she could no longer see him, she went inside, weeping.

She was forever weeping. Meanwhile the lad traveled farther and farther, until he reached the neighboring land. He entered, went straight to the royal city and stopped on the side of the road, in front of the king's castle. He tethered his horse to a post and stood there, reflecting on which way to go. Just then the king's son came out on the balcony. He looked and wondered about the lad and about the pendant around his neck. He couldn't see it well from afar, so he summoned a soldier and sent him to the lad, inviting him to come over. The soldier went and said:

"Who are you? Please, be so kind and come to see the prince!"

Well, he walked over, leaving the soldier with his horse, lest it break away. The prince descended from the balcony to greet him. They shook hands.

He said: "Who are you?"

He told him that he was the son of a king, and so on and so on.

"Me too," he said, "I am heir to the crown. Is the photograph you have for sale? Why are you wearing it around your neck?"

"Oh no! It's not for sale," he answered, "no amount of money could buy it from me."

"Well, who is this girl?"

"She is my young sister."

"And where are you going?"

"I am on a journey," he said, "because I have decided that I'll keep on going until I find a girl like my sister and take her for my wife."

"Tell me," he said, "is she as she appears on this photograph?"

"More beautiful, in real life she is even more beautiful," said the prince.

"Look, I ask you, let me go see her and if I like her, I'll marry her."

So he thought about going back. If his sister took a liking to the prince, he could become her husband and she would be less lonely, she'd miss him less.

He said: "Look, prince, I'll return with you, but only if you'll marry my sister. I don't have time to waste and I have a long way ahead of me. It will take a while, so I'll go with you only if you take her for your wife."

"If she proves to be as I see her on this picture, I'll marry her for sure!"

He didn't tell his old mother what he wanted to do. The prince had an old mother and the old queen was a witch. A real witch of a woman. She had an attendant, a maid, who knew that the queen was a witch.

"Don't ever tell my son where I go at night," she told her. She would mount on a broomstick and take off. That is how the maid knew that she was a witch.

"Don't betray me, my girl! If you keep secret who I am, I'll not rest until my son asks you in marriage. I'll make sure that he asks you and you'll become queen."

Well she promised not to betray her. The two of them got along well together.

The old queen had overheard her son talk about wanting to marry the princess. She became concerned that if the maid learned of it, she'd betray her.

Meanwhile the two princes came to an agreement. They ate, drank, and sat at the table together until dawn, when they were ready to leave.

Said the old queen: "Son, take me along. I want to see the girl you'll bring home."

"You may come, Mother, for you are my mother. If you wish to come, come. You'll sit in the carriage, with your attendant, your maid, who dresses and undresses you. There will be room enough for you and for my bride," he said.

So she was preparing to go, too. The next morning they rose and after breakfast the two princes got on their horses, and the queen and her maid climbed into the coach. They ordered twenty-four young lads to accompany them. Twenty-four soldiers escorted them. So—the two princes on horseback, the queen mother seated facing her maid, and the coachman in the driver's box—they took off. Well, eventually they arrived in the other country.

Said the prince: "Here we are. This is my country."

"I am glad," said the prince, "I could hardly wait to be here and to see her."

Right away they proceeded home.

"This is the royal fort. Here is the king's palace."

They reached the gates and were let in. When the princess saw her brother, she was so overjoyed, she didn't know what to do. She ran outside and began plying him with questions. But then she noticed that there was another regal looking lad, she could tell from his attire that he was regal. She thought to herself: what is this young man doing here?

They came face to face, introduced themselves and entered into the room. They sat down at the table. The princely lad couldn't take his eyes off the girl. He had liked her on the photograph but when he saw her, he liked her even more. Well, he didn't know how to tell her why he had come. He didn't know how to present it to her. While they were sitting at the table, food and drink were served. They drank, but the princely lad just couldn't stop gazing at the girl. He nearly devoured her with his eyes. He fell deeply in love with her.

"Princess," he said, "I'll tell you my most secret thoughts. No one knows, except your brother, why I came here from so far away. Ever since I saw your photograph, the one your brother carries, I have not been able to sleep. I'll die if you cannot be mine. So I came to find out your answer. I came to take you for my wife, if you'll have me."

The girl became alarmed; she didn't know what to say.

"I want to know your answer. Will you be my wife or not?"

The girl asked her brother what she should do. Should she marry him? Should she take him for her husband?

"Look," he said, "I saw his good appearance, but what he's like, what his heart is like, I really can't say. I don't know him from the inside out but I can tell you, if you fancy him, you may marry him."

The girl liked him, he was a handsome lad, not a weakling—a nice, regal looking lad, with a stately bearing.

"All right," she said. "I will."

Right away they exchanged rings, became engaged and the following morning started on their way, back to the lad's country.

"Well now," said her brother, "take what you want, what you need for the journey, but nothing else. Take only what you need."

The princess put on a beautiful gown. They climbed in the carriage; the lad helped the princess into her seat. She sat in the back with the queen mother, facing the attendant. The carriage went ahead and the two young men on horseback followed behind. So, they took off and were on their way.

Soon the prince called out: "Mother, watch over my fiancée, my bride, don't let the breeze get to her. Take good care of her!"

"I am here, beside her. If it gets to her, it gets to me. I am as concerned about her as I am about myself."

So they continued on the road, flanked by soldiers on either side and followed by the riders. When they were farther along, the prince called out again: "My angel, look after yourself! Don't let the breezes or anything harmful touch you!"

She didn't hear him well.

She asked: "What did the prince say?"

"He said that your golden hair, reaching down to your heels, should be cut off."

The princess said: "Dear God Almighty, is this true? What harm is there in my long hair? Why does my hair bother him? Why does he want to cut it off?"

"Well, he didn't say why. He said it, so we have to do it, we have to cut it."

The old queen cut the girl's golden hair as she sat there—she sheared it all off. The girl cried bitterly, she was heartbroken for her hair. She became very sad, her spirits were completely dampened. Why did he want to do this? Put her to shame, even before they reached home?

They continued on their journey. Soon the prince called out again:

"Look after yourself, my angel! Don't let anything happen to you! Mother, you too, make sure no harm will come to her."

"What did he say?"

"He said that I should poke out your eyes."

"Well, if that's what he said, you'd better cut off my head, but don't take my eyes. Did he take me from my home to become my murderer, rather than my savior? If they take my eyes, what will my life be worth? What will I do without my eyesight?"

"What the prince commands, has to be!" The queen took a penknife out of her pocket and gouged out her two eyes. She wept and wept bitterly, she didn't know what to do, she was so distressed.

They came to a big stream. A bridge led across it. When they reached the bridge, the prince called out:

"Don't worry, my angel, we'll soon be home!"

And the princess again asked: "What did he say now?"

"He said that I should undress you, leave you naked; that I should take away your clothes and, at the other end of the bridge, I should throw you into the muddy pond."

(But she didn't even say that she was repeating the words of the wicked prince; she said:) "I should strip you of your clothes and push you into the muddy pond at the end of the bridge."

And she said: "Well, push me. My life isn't worth much any more. I might as well drown!"

Right away the queen stripped her of her beautiful gown, took off her lovely golden necklace, the golden ring and the golden earrings. She stripped her of everything and pushed her stark naked into the murky water. Then she made her attendant wear the princess's clothes and jewelry, and she pinned up the princess's hair on her head, to make it look as if it were her own. The attendant was a coarse peasant girl, really ugly. She dressed her up and made a princess out of her.

[Well, let's leave the poor princess there, in the pond!]

They arrived at the royal palace. The lad immediately dismounted and came to help his bride get off the carriage. But when he saw her, he almost had a stroke.

"What a beautiful girl she was when I took her from her castle," he said, " and now she looks so different. What happened? This is not the same girl I brought here! This is not a princess."

Said the old queen, the witch: "What's the matter, my son? Have you lost your senses? Of course it's the same girl!"

"*Why does she look like such a peasant?* She wasn't like this. She has bushy, black eyebrows and big, black eyes, when her eyes were a beautiful cornflower blue and she herself was exquisite. And how lovely were the sun on her forehead, the stars on her breasts and the moon on the nape of her neck. She isn't the same! Don't make me out to be blind," he said, "I am not blind."

The old queen said: "Come here, prince. Come here and tell me, is this your sister?"

The prince got off his horse, came over and said: "I don't recognize her as my sister. My sister didn't look like this. This is not her."

The old queen, the old witch grew angry: "Do you call me a liar? Do you dare to tell me, old queen that I am, that this is not your young sister? Take him and throw him into jail at once!"

She had the prince locked up. She had him thrown into jail, into a dark cell, and she continued lecturing her son:

"What happened to your eyesight? Can't you see that she is the girl you brought? Do you expect her to be as beautiful as when you took her from her palace? You should know that a princess is not used to being outdoors—she must have become coarser from being in the air. She'll be beautiful again in a few weeks, once she is inside the castle, her beauty will return. Don't be so dumb," she said, "you can see that it's her, you can tell from the clothes and the jewelry she is wearing!"

She befuddled her son's mind so completely that he finally agreed that this was the princess.

"Well, all right, Mother, there is nothing I can do. I made her leave her home, brought her here, so I won't go back on my word. I'll marry her, but there will be no wedding until she gains back her beauty, for now *she looks like a peasant*. A coarse peasant," he said, "she isn't the same as when I got her."

So they took her into the palace. Days went by, then months, still there was no wedding.

Meanwhile the poor girl was left in the pond. She swam and splashed around until she managed to struggle over to the shore. There she grabbed some branches and saved herself from drowning. She sat in the murky, muddy water. Not far from there lived a fisherman, who went fishing every day and every day he caught two fish. There were only two of them, he and his wife—they had no children. That morning the man went fishing again. He cast his net in the water, but all he caught was a frog. He cast it a second time and a third time, and then the net became so heavy that he couldn't lift it. He just couldn't.

"God Almighty! What is in this net? Is it entangled in a bush that makes it so hard to move? He kept on tugging and pulling at it until finally he hauled it out. A big mass was in it, entirely covered in mud, so he couldn't tell whether it was a human being or an animal. The fisherman became alarmed.

He said: "Speak up if you are a human being, or else I'll kill you on the spot!"

She said: "I am a human. Take me out of here, for God's sake! If you believe in God, take me out of here!"

Well, the man hauled the net out, took the girl and led her to a clean stream, for she was covered with mud. He took her to the stream and bathed her. Her body was so white and delicate that he had never beheld such beauty since he first saw the light of day, but she was completely blind.

"Oh dear," he said, "how on earth did you land in this pond?"

"How did I land here, dear uncle? How did it happen? I came," she said, "and I met with thieves, who attacked me and demanded my money. When they found that I had none, they stripped me of my jewelry and my clothes. Then they gouged out my eyes and pushed me into the pond, since I couldn't give them any money."

The man felt deeply sorry for her.

"Look, my girl, I'll take you to my humble cottage, only my wife and I live there, and in the name of God, I'll provide for you. You don't have your eyesight so, in the name of God, I'll provide for you."

"Well, God will reward you if you offer me shelter," she said.

He was about to take her with him but the girl said: "I am ashamed, I am all naked."

He removed his coat and wrapped it around her.

"Look," he said, "don't be ashamed!"

As they entered the gate, the fisherman's wife came to meet them:

"Who is this girl, this female, whom you bring here?"

"Look, don't be upset, I fished her out of the water. She is a poor blind girl."

"Oh dear, why did you bring her into this poverty? We don't have enough to eat ourselves and now there is someone else we have to feed."

"Don't say anything, wife. We must do something for God, we have to care for her, for the sake of the Lord." [The girl felt very bad when she heard this.]

"Look, she is all naked."

"What can I give her to wear?" said the woman, "all I have is what I have on!"

"Take it off and put on something less good! Quickly, make her lie down—who knows how long she spent in that muddy pond. Thieves attacked her and put her eyes out."—

**[Listener:] Why didn't she say she was a princess?**

(She didn't say who she was.)

Well, she ushered her into the house, gave her food, her own clothes and put her to bed. The girl wept and wept, distressed about her fate. She wept bitterly and the man comforted her:

"Don't cry, my girl, God will help you!"

He went fishing and this time he caught three fish.

"Look, dear wife, God ordained this. Never yet have I caught three fish, always only two. And now," he said, "I got three."

And so a week went by; they cared for her for a week.

Then the girl said: "Dear Mother" (she called them mother and father), "please lay a rug on the floor and give me a comb, so I can comb my hair."

"Let me do it, my girl, I'll comb your hair," she said. "Without eyesight, how can you do it?"

She began combing her hair and combed out a bug. A bug of pure gold.

"Oh," she said, "I have never seen such a beautiful, golden bug."

"Put it into a small box," said the girl.

She did so. When the father came back from fishing, the girl said to him:

"Take this golden bug to the royal city. Go up to the royal palace and try to sell it. Maybe they'll buy it there. If they ask you what you want for it, just say: an eye."

So the man went into the city and up to the palace. Only the old queen was there.

"What are you selling?" she asked.

"A gold bug."

"What kind of a gold bug?"

"Here it is."

"What do you want for it? What does it cost?"

"All I want for it is an eye."

"An eye, what for?"

"One of my little lambs scratched out the eye of another. I want to replace it."

"Don't be such a fool," said the queen. "Do you expect me to give you one of my own eyes? Where else can I find an eye for you? You'd better leave the way you came."

So the man left, full of sorrow. As he reached the steps going down —for he had been upstairs—he met the young queen.

He said to her: "Look at this gold bug."

She thought about it. Maybe if she showed it to her husband, the king, he would be happy that she acquired it:

"Well, what do you want for it?"

"I would give it in exchange for an eye, if one could be found."

"I'll look," she said. "There was one around, but I am not sure where."

She searched the entire upstairs. There was a pantry and in it was a table, and in the drawer of this table she found the eye. It was there, covered with dust and shriveled.

"Look here," she said, "you may have this, if you like, but I don't have any other."

He handed her the gold bug and set out for home, overjoyed.

"I am back, my girl," he said, "it turned out well, I received an eye."

"Oh, my dear Father," she said, "please bring me a glass of water!"

He placed the eye in her hand, brought her a glass of water and she lowered the eye into it. After five minutes the eye revived, it looked as fresh as when it was taken out. The girl inserted it back into its socket and daubed some saliva around it. It healed and became once again as good as when she was born, she could see so well with it.

"Dear Lord Jesus, I regained one of my eyes!"

The following day she asked once more: "Please, comb my hair."

This time she combed two gold bugs out of her hair and along with the gold bugs, she combed out a gold platter. By now her hair had grown so long that it reached down to her waist. It was pure, shining gold.

"Dear Father, please take these two gold bugs over there and again only ask one eye for them. No matter how much money they offer you, say that all you want is one eye. And if they ask you why, say that you need it for your lamb. One of them had its eye scratched out by another and needs it."

So the old man went once more.

Said the queen: "I have never seen such a merchant, he is always looking for an eye. I don't want to part with my own, so where should I find one?"

She had forgotten that she had one saved. But the young queen knew it. The old man met her again in the palace.

She said to him: "Well, what do you want?"

"I am here to sell two gold bugs."

"What do they cost? What do you want for them?"

"Nothing more than one eye. It could be any kind, as long as it's an eye."

"Wait, there must be another one around. I'll go look for it, maybe I'll find it."

Suddenly she came running: "Look, I found another eye, but once you take it I have no more to give you."

"This one will do fine," he said and handed her the two gold bugs.

Once again the girl placed the eye in a glass of water and when she removed it— it was as fresh as when it was taken from her. She replaced it in its socket, daubed some saliva around it and it healed so well that her eyesight became as good as when she was born. Even better. She went over to her father and kissed his hands and feet, in gratitude for giving her back her sight.

"Well," said the father, "you see, dear wife, with the many plattersful of gold she combed out of her hair, we are now rich."

They bought a small cow, slaughtered a pig, bought themselves new clothes, stored up some flour, and acquired land. They had become wealthy, the girl had combed so much gold out of her hair.

She said to them: "Dear Father, I thank you very much for saving me from death, for bringing me to your house, and for being so kind in taking care of me. Now I must leave."

"Where will you go?"

"I'll go and keep on going until I find my brother. He may be dead, or he may be somewhere and I'll go until I find him."

They cried and begged her to stay, but to no avail. She dressed up nicely—she had asked her father to buy her new clothes—and when she was ready, dear Almighty God, she was as beautiful as before. She went into the city. She stopped a stone's throw away from the royal palace and looked for someone she could ask about her brother, someone who could tell her what had become of him.

"Dear God, I don't know anyone here. Whom could I ask?"

And as she stood there thinking, the prince came out on the balcony. He looked down and saw the girl.

"Jesus Christ," he thought to himself, "she moves just like my bride used to. Her movements are the same.

**[Listener:] Did he recognize her?**

(He recognized her.) Right away he sent a soldier to ask the girl to come over.

The soldier went and said: "Please, Miss, the king is calling you."

She refused to go. She wouldn't go to the king for anything, she'd rather turn around and go elsewhere, but she wouldn't face the king. The soldier went back. He had called her, he said, but she refused, she wouldn't come, she had important business to attend to somewhere.

The prince didn't give up. He came down from the balcony. The girl saw him approaching and quickened her pace.

He followed her and said: "Miss, please stop. Stop, so I can have a few words with you. Why are you running from me?"

But she walked even faster. Then the king started running. Shame or no shame, he decided to run and catch her. When the girl saw the king running after her, she nearly collapsed, she was so frightened. She didn't know what the king would do if he recognized her.

She said to him: "Why are you so impolite?"

"And you, why are you running away? I am not the devil, nor am I a murderer," he said.

Then the girl stopped.

"Where are you from and who are you that you are such a stranger to this city? Where do you come from? Who are you?"

"You can see who I am," she said. "Don't you know me?"

"If I did, I wouldn't ask."

But he already knew. He saw that as the girl was walking, rosemaries bloomed in her footsteps.

"So don't ask!"

And the girl pressed on; golden beads streamed down from her eyes in such profusion that the path turned a brilliant gold in her wake. Then the king was convinced that everything about her, even the sun on her forehead, proved that she was the same girl.

He said: "Miss, it appears that you are the princess. Don't be afraid of me and admit who you are!"

"It is true, I have important business here. But don't ask me who I am and don't pretend that you don't recognize me. You know me well. You know me and perhaps this time again you want to kill me," she said. "Haven't I suffered enough?"

The king became alarmed.

"I am not a murderer," he said, "I am the son of a king! How can you say that I want to kill you? I am no murderer! I am a royal prince! I am the ruler of this country."

He wasn't sure. The girl knew him but he didn't know her for sure, but observing her movements, her shape, he thought she must be his bride.

"Look," said the king, "just tell me briefly, what are you doing here?"

Said the girl: "I am looking for my brother, my own brother."

"And who is your brother?"

"My brother is the prince with whom you brought me here. You brought me here into all this misfortune. It was you who came after me into my father's house, to my country, to our palace, to take me for your wife, and on the way here you had me murdered."

"How did I have you murdered, princess? Murdered by whom? I want to understand what happened. What kind of talk is this? I know nothing about it."

"Well, now you'll know, because I'll tell you. When you brought me with the old queen, your mother, and we were on the bridge, why did you call out to her to cut off my hair?"

"I called that out to her?"

"And the second time, why did you call to her to poke out my eyes?"

The king began to shiver, waiting to hear more, and not knowing what to expect.

"And the third time, when you and my brother riding on horseback reached the bridge, didn't you call back that I should be stripped of my clothes and of my jewelry and thrown into the muddy pond? You did, and now you pretend that you know nothing about it and you keep asking me who am I, what am I?" she said.

The prince fell to his knees and said to the girl: "Please forgive me, for I know nothing about all this! I know nothing, so I ask you to tell me, but without such reproaches, what happened to you during the journey? I did call out to my mother repeatedly, but it was to urge her to watch over you, and I asked you to look after yourself so that no harm would come to you."

"But she said that first you wanted my hair cut off, so she cut it; next you wanted my eyes gouged out, so she gouged them out; and finally she pushed me into the pond and said that this is what you had asked her to do. Well thank you very much, if this is what you had in mind for me when you took me away from my country and from my father's palace! But, you see, God is kinder than a wicked man—he knew I was innocent and gave me back my eyesight. And I can thank a poor fisherman for it."

"Now," said the king, "follow me to the palace. Now the two evil women will suffer for what they did! Now I'll have my revenge! Come with me."

"I won't take a single step with you until you bring my brother here, before me!"

"All right."

"Where is my brother?"

"Well," he said, "We'll get him right away."

He just remembered then that his mother had him locked up in prison. He summoned a guard and ordered him to free the prince and bring him over.

"First," said the princess, "you must tell me whether he is still alive, or whether he is dead!"

The guard rushed to the prison and found the prince alive. He came back and gave the king the news.

Said the king: "Get him out and take him to the bath and to the barber. Clean him up, give him back his royal garments and let him come here all dressed up. If his sister sees him now, her heart will break!"

The prince had grown a beard in the year he spent in prison. His face was hairy, filthy, dirty. God knows what he looked like, emaciated, only skin and bones. Well, they took him out of there, dressed him nicely and brought him over to his sister. When the two met, they hugged and kissed and wept and the prince, the prince from that place, wept along with them. Then he remembered how his mother had insisted that he must have lost his senses; how she had pressed him: "don't you recognize your own bride? How can this be? She just became a little coarser, peasant-like, not being used to the warm weather. She'll be all right once inside the castle, she'll recover." A year had gone by and she was uglier than ever. "Now I understand my dear mother's actions," he said.

He took them inside the palace and right away ordered the soldiers to fetch two stallions, the wildest ones. He had them tie the two women by their hair to the stallions' tails, and ordered the two lads to whip the horses and circle the fort with them twelve times. Twelve times they circled around until the women's bodies were torn to shreds. Then he nailed the shreds to the wall of the fort and had them riddled with bullets so that nothing but dust was left of their remains. And then, without further delay, the prince invited priests and bishops to come to the palace for a *wedding feast*. He threw such a big party that the merrymaking lasted for twenty-four hours. They were married and are alive to this day, if they haven't died.

# 7. The Serpent Prince

AT 425A (*The Monster [Animal] as Bridegroom [Cupid and Psyche]*) is one of the more coherent and relatively autonomous folktales within the large group of female adventure stories centered on a Search for the Lost Husband (AT 425-449). Strong affinities among these tales lead to liberal and whimsical borrowing of motifs and episodes. Separate narratives—variously identified as AT 425A-425P, 430, 432, 441—emerged, spread and merged in time and space—which made the task of classifiers of regional and ethnic subtypes difficult, as is apparent from the confusing configurations of the MNK. My survey of forty variants told by noted community narrators led to the identification of an established Hungarian ethnic redaction of AT 425A (Dégh 1994).

Among known variants, Zsuzsanna Palkó's was particularly revealing. She heard it from Anna Petres, an older woman, when she was fourteen. It was among her standard repertoire pieces, well rehearsed, and refined by the inspiration of wake-audience commentators. I recorded the tale in 1950 at her house when she entertained the usual audience of neighbors after all the children were asleep. She identified with the heroine with particular fondness and compassion; after all, in the symbolic language of the magic tale, this is the story of marriage in traditional patriarchal society; it could be anyone's story.

The events of the tale are built on the following institutional principles and cultural facts: the expectation that the first-born be a boy; a fear of unnatural birth that puts blame on the mother; entrapment of the girl to force her into an arranged marriage; and the conflict in which the male drive toward polygamy and freedom from family ties is pitted against the Christian concept of monogamous marriage. This tale clearly follows a biographical pattern, representing a segment of the critical transitional phase of woman's life: marriage, subordination, acceptance of domestic service, and fulfillment in motherhood.

But the story of the woman is incomplete without the story of the man, the Serpent Prince—always a snake in the Hungarian ethnic redaction, and robustly sexual. Born as a misfit in consequence of a parental misdeed, he regains normalcy through marriage. But he cannot stay in the domestic haven projected by feminine values; he is driven by search of adventure but makes his wife responsible for his action. The two biographies make one interdependent story about the asymmetric marital relationship of woman, the domestic; and man, the public.

Mrs. Palkó's recital is almost faultless, neatly framed by formulaic introduction and conclusion. Her professional competence is shown at the point that she notices that she has left something out. Without embarrassment she assures us that she will make the correction later, and she does so. At the end, however, she does make a mistake by including a dissonant episode that unnecessarily turns the second wife, an innocent bystander, into a villain. The addition of the episode of the ambitious substitute wife and her plotting witch mother from related tales (403, 408, 450) seems accidental, because in this tale there is no scheming. The Serpent Prince abandons his first wife and marries an unsuspecting other who has to put up with the humiliation of discovering that the filthy beggar woman is her husband's real wife; then the second wife has to witness a family idyll in her own bedroom. But Mrs. Palkó's powerful dramatization of the sufferings of the central heroine still does not put the blame on the real culprit, the leisure-loving prince. It is the other woman who must suffer for calling the princess a whore as she buys herself nights in the prince's bedroom. In culture-specific terms, there is only one marriage between man and woman because marriage vows can be pledged only once. The real wife is the *hites* (or "the true one," with whom the pledge was made), as opposed to the *hitetlen* ("false one"). Mrs. Palkó's wake audience was moved by the marvelous restoration of the family—the reward that ends the tale—and gratified by the traditional formulaic punishment of the *deus-ex-machina* villains.

———

It happened long ago, beyond the beyond, even beyond the seven seas and beyond the glass mountain. There was a castle hill and below it an enormous willow tree. The willow tree had ninety-nine branches and on the ninety-nine branches sat ninety-nine crows, and if you don't listen to this story, they will peck your eyes out!

There was once a king and a queen. They were very sad for they had no offspring.

"Wife, it is your fault. You are at fault for you don't want us to have even one child."

"Don't say that, my heart is aching as much as yours that we have no children. But if God doesn't want to give us any, what can I do?"

Well, one day the king went to attend to his own affairs in parliament. The queen felt deeply distressed. It was bad enough that she was without child; to make matters worse, her husband spoke ill of her. She threw her arms up towards the sky:

"Dear God, why I am not worthy of having a child? If you don't want me to have a child, give me a snake son, so I can at least have one offspring."

As soon as she uttered the words, there was a snake son.

"My God, I must have offended you! Why did you bless me with this ugly beast? What will my husband say when he sees it? And the strangers, what will they say when they'll learn that a snake child was born to the king?"

Soon she telephoned her husband to call him home. He came running to find out what was wrong.

"Look," she said, "this is the boy we have. God gave him to us because I asked."

"Why did you ask for such a boy?" he said.

"In my bitterness I said to God that if I am not worthy of a child, at least he should let me have a snake son. He was born right away. Now what should we do?"

Said the king: "We will not have him baptized for I am ashamed, and I don't want even the priest to know the kind of offspring God gave us. We'll name him later.

But you must not nurse him, just give him something and make sure that he eats it. Don't let him take your nipple in his mouth, lest some harm come to you."

Well, they made up a nice soft bed in a basket for the snake child and placed him into it. And they put the basket into the fanciest room, where usually no one entered. They put him in there. The queen brought him food and drink. He learned to eat and swallowed everything he was given. He developed and grew every day before their very eyes—still, as parents, how could they not have been grieving? They were grieving because they were ashamed. They could never take him out into the world, they thought, for fear that someone might see him. They would always have to keep him a secret.

When the snake grew to be as big as the axle of a carriage, he curled up in thick rings in the basket and held up his head, watching. His mother was loath to enter his room. She found him frightening, he was so large and repulsive. One day when she took the snake his midday meal and he had eaten his fill, he started to whistle, but he whistled so loud that the walls began to shake. He hadn't done anything like that before.

Said the queen to her husband: "Can you hear our son whistling so loud? I wonder what is wrong with him?"

"Go ask him. Something must be troubling him because until now he never whistled!"

So his mother went into his room: "Tell me, son, what is wrong with you? What do you want? What does this whistling mean?"

"It means, my dear mother, that I'd like to have a mate."

"Oh, my dear child, who would take you?"

"Well," he said, "I'll tell you whom to bring here. The king of the neighboring land has a very, very beautiful daughter. I want to take her for my wife. I am sending you as my emissary to ask for her hand in marriage. Say that a king's son has sent you and that he is waiting for a reply! And say no more, only that she should come with you for a trial visit and if she and the prince like each other, she should stay."

Who knows what kind of a world it was then, for the father let his daughter go with the queen to see the prince and if she liked him, she could stay. So the queen brought her home but instead of taking her straight to the snake, she led her into another chamber, which she and the king used as their sitting room.

"I went and brought the princess," she said to the king.

"All right, you brought the princess back but don't let her into our son's room; first give her something to eat and drink and then take her to our son. Don't show him to her until then!"

They set the table right away, but the princess said: "Where is the prince?"

"He'll come soon. You must rest now because you are tired, and have some food and drink. He'll be here by the time you have finished."

They sat down to eat and drink and talk. All the while the princess was trembling with excitement, wondering whether she would like the prince when she saw him. But the prince didn't appear.

Said the queen: "Come, let us surprise him, he may be in his room! Come, let's see!"

They entered the room and found it empty. The old queen went into the back, where there was a shelf installed in the corner, and there was the basket. As she approached, the serpent prince lifted his head and looked around.

Then the girl caught sight of him: "Oh dear! What is this snake doing here?"

"This is our son," said the queen.

The girl let out such a scream that she collapsed on the ground and fainted.

"God Almighty, don't abandon me!" she said. "Is this the kind of lad that I, a princess, deserve? Let me out of here!"

They helped her up, splashed some water on her, and she came to.

"My dear daughter," said the queen, "come, he won't hurt you. He is gentle, he'll do you no harm—he just loves you and wants you to be his wife."

"I'd rather have my head cut off," she said, "and be buried anywhere, than become his wife! Have you lost your senses? Do you want me to marry a snake? How could you take me away from my father's palace? Why did you take me and bring me here? And why didn't you tell me what your son was like?"

"Well, I didn't tell you, for I thought that if I told you, you wouldn't come. Now stay here," she said, " and be patient, you'll see, you won't regret it, he'll be very good to you."

"I don't care if he is a thousand times better, I don't want him! I detest looking at him, he is a wretched animal, a revolting, wretched animal!" she said. And I should lie down in bed beside him? I'd rather kill myself!"

The queen begged her to have patience and not to be so upset and frightened. She locked the door behind her and left the girl in the room. The girl didn't know what to do. She ran from one window to another. They had bars on them, iron bars. There was no way out. The king and the queen left the house. She ran around in circles, she was about to *lose her mind in despair*. She ran around in circles weeping, kneading her hands in desperation, how to escape, what to do? Somehow the day would pass but what would happen at night? She screamed and cried bitterly, but no one had pity on her, no one let her out.

Well, when evening came the queen brought in the meal. The girl was watching the door, ready to slip out. But the queen immediately locked the door with a key so she couldn't get out. She was forced to stay. The queen had just put the food down, but found it again untouched in the morning. She couldn't eat one bite of it, she just couldn't take anything. All night long she was pacing up and down, screaming and lamenting, they could hear from the next room how she was crying. So, to avoid listening to her they went out, but they didn't release her. This went on for a week. The girl didn't eat, not even a single bite, didn't lie down to sleep, all she did was walk around in circles, while the snake kept trying to comfort her:

"Don't be afraid, my angel. I'll do you no harm. If you knew how much I love you, you wouldn't be afraid."

"You just keep your love from me! It would have been better if God had taken you the minute you saw the light of day! And now you dare to expect me to become your wife!"

The girl went on protesting and the snake kept trying to appease her with soothing words, tapping his tail.

After a week went by, the princess thought to herself: now she didn't care any more. She hadn't slept a wink all this time, nor had she anything to eat or drink. She was utterly exhausted, ready to die. So she decided to lie down and rest.

All the while the snake was lying on his stomach, blinking at her. Then he moved forward. The bed was ready, the queen had made it up for them when she got there. The girl fell asleep right away, she was so worn-out. Suddenly she woke up feeling the snake creep up on her bare leg, slithering into bed. She let out such a scream that the king and the queen leaped out of bed:

"Our son is killing the girl in there!"

They ran in to see and found nothing wrong except for the snake crawling into bed. The girl screamed and *screamed so hard that her eyes were popping out.*

"Get away from me you ugly beast! Go away you wretched animal, don't you come near me!"

And the snake spoke gently: "Please let me lie down beside you. I won't hurt you!"

The king and the queen having looked around, walked off and locked the door behind them. They left them there.

All night the crying and fighting continued. They woke up in the morning: "This night passed—I got away from him, but what will happen the next night? I wish I had a knife, or something," the girl said, "so that I could stab myself and die! I cannot stand to have him come near me in bed! I am so frightened of him that *I could die of despair.*"

Well, it was no use, the tools she could have used to kill herself had all been put away. The following night went the same way. The snake crawled up into her bed. By then the girl had started eating. The queen brought in the meal, the girl sat down at the table while they let the snake eat separately. "It is all the same now," she thought, "I am miserable but at least I shouldn't be miserable and hungry!" And so she began eating regularly.

One night, as she lay down, the snake slid into bed beside her. She grabbed a pillow and put it between them. She placed a pillow there to separate them, so the snake wouldn't touch her.

"It is no use for me to weep and cry; he sneaks into bed anyway, but at least he won't come near me," she thought. She put a pillow between them and went to sleep.

When she woke up, there was such a beautiful prince lying next to her, such a dazzling, regal-looking lad, that *one could sooner look at the sun than at him*. He was such a handsome, beautiful lad. She stared and stared at him. Was he a vision in her dreams or what? Such a handsome, beautiful lad, the likes of whom she had never seen *since her eyes had popped open*. She had never met a lad like this. She thought to herself:

Where has this prince come from?

She looked and the snake was nowhere to be seen. She put her arms around the lad and he woke up. She said to him:

"How did you come here, prince?"

"I didn't come, I am at home here. This is my home."

"How can this be?" she said. "Are you the snake?"

"I was, but now I am no longer," he said, "I have slipped out of the snakeskin."

"Well, don't slip back into it, for God's sake, I beg you! You are such a handsome lad, why did you put on that horrible animal skin? I was so repelled by it that I nearly *died of despair*. If you are a prince, why did you get into a snakeskin?"

"I had to do it."

He didn't say why or what had happened. All he said was that it had to be this way for a while. The girl was delighted. She gazed and gazed at him, so enchanted was she with her lover and one day she became pregnant.

Then the princess started grieving that her beloved was a prince by night and during the day he crawled back into the skin and became a snake again. He didn't show himself, not even his parents saw that he could transform himself. But the princess continued begging for him not to put on the snakeskin.

"Well, I have to," he said, "for it belongs to me, it is my cloak."

She went on thinking about it. Now she was able to lie down beside the snake and fall asleep because he could change and become a prince. And what a beautiful, handsome lad he was! But even if one day he came to shed the snakeskin for good, and even if this were soon, it would be too late.

The girl had heard that nearby lived a woman, a sorceress, who could perform all kinds of magic. So she went to see her one day when the old queen was not at home. She went over to the woman in the neighborhood.

The sorceress said to her: "What is wrong with you? Why are you so thin? Just skin and bones, you look like a skeleton. What is going on in your life? Don't you have enough to eat, or are you sick, or are you grieving? What is the matter?"

She said: "Don't even ask, my sorrow is so profound. Don't think that I am thin because I lack food. I am well off."

"Then why? How can a princess have such great troubles?"

She said: "Oh yes but I do! They have to do with my betrothed."

She told her, she related everything: how she came to the palace and why, and how she wasn't told that the royal son was a snake. The sorceress only heard about it then that the king had a snake son. Until then she hadn't heard it from anyone. No one had talked about it.

Said the princess: "At night he becomes such a beautiful prince that *one can sooner look at the sun than at him,* he is so dazzling, but at dawn he crawls back into his snakeskin. I am unhappy because he won't stop doing it, turning into a snake. And when he is a snake I am so frightened of him because he is so large, so huge that I could die, *fall into despair.*"

"You know what, princess? I'll teach you what you must do, if you want him to be rid of his snakeskin," she said. "When you both go to bed and he falls asleep, you must get up, light a fire in the stove and once it is blazing, throw in the snakeskin and burn it. When he wakes and asks you where is the snakeskin, his cloak, you must answer that you haven't seen it. Then he will say : 'what is this bad odor that I smell?' And you must reply that you had combed your hair and tossed some into the stove. That is what caused the smell."

Well, the princess accepted the woman's advice. "If it is true that he will be freed of his snake kin, I'll give you so much gold and silver that you'll never know poverty, or lack anything ever again," she promised.

"Just do what I told you and it will be all right, you'll see," she said.

The princess went home. Evening came and they went to bed. Once again the princess woke up at night with her husband next to her. He was beautiful, like a flower. If ever he had to leave her she would be heartbroken, she thought, he was so beautiful. The snakeskin was there, on his back. She slipped out of bed and lit a fire in the stove. When it was blazing, she gently removed the snakeskin, threw it into the flames and burned it.

Soon the prince woke up. He said: "Where is my cloak? And what is this bad smell in here?"

"Well," she said, "I was just combing my hair. I cast some into the stove and that causes the smell."

"Don't lie to me for I can see into your heart and I know that you burned it. But you'll be sorry, not I! All you needed to do was wait one more month," he said. "In one month, one week, one hour, one minute and one second, my time would have been up. There is a curse on me and I was to have worn the snakeskin until then. But now that you dared to burn it, that you did this without telling me, you'll have to suffer for it, and you'll be sorry! And now listen!"

The prince rose from his bed:

"You get up too," he said. "Let us see each other while I am still here."

He went out and brought back a dry hazel rod and a grain of wheat:

"Wife, I am telling you now I am leaving. I am leaving and you'll never hear from me and you'll never know where I am. I am giving you this dry hazel-rod so that you can plant it. You must plant it, nurture it and water it every day. You must watch over it so that nothing digs it up. Water it with your tears and with well-water and when the hazel-rod begins to sprout leaves and bear fruit, then you may set out to look for me. When you are ready to bring me some hazelnuts and bread made from the grain of wheat, then you may come after me!"

Next he put a band around her waist and a gold ring on her finger and said: "You will give birth to your child only when I put my arms around your waist, and you will remove this ring when I touch your finger with mine. And you must not come looking for me until you crack a nut from this dry hazel-rod. You must sow this grain of wheat, care for it and let it multiply until you reap enough for baking a loaf of bread. Only then must you set forth to find me. Any sooner would be to no avail."

The woman wept bitterly, asking him to forgive her. What she did was not her own idea, she had followed someone's advice.

"Well, if someone advised you then ask that person to help you and comfort you now!"

"Don't leave me! Please forgive me! Aren't you sorry to leave me in my present condition, the way I am?"

"You are the way you are, but you will not be free of the child until I hold you, nor will the ring snap off your finger until my finger touches yours."

With these words the prince shook hands with her, kissed her and left. And the princess wept and wept so bitterly that her heart nearly broke.

The king and the queen asked her: "Why are you crying so?"

"The prince went into exile."

"Where has he gone?"

"He went into exile. He said to me that I would look for him in vain until this dry hazel rod took root and bore fruit, and until this single grain of wheat multiplied over the years so I could bake bread with it. Then, I should take the bread and the hazelnuts and go find him. And only when I find him and he puts his arms around my waist, may I give birth to my child. How can I stop crying," she said, "when will all this come to pass?"

"Look," said the king, "maybe you were up to some mischief and he got angry. Otherwise he wouldn't have left you here."

Well, she didn't have the courage to tell the king, her father-in-law, or her mother-in-law, what had happened. She didn't dare to say why the prince was so upset.

So she planted the hazel rod and watered it, watered it every day, with her tears or with well-water. She never stopped weeping. She planted the grain of wheat and built a small fence around it so that no chicken or other animal could scratch it out. By the following year the grain sprouted some stalks. She harvested the wheat and sowed it again at the right time and continued to water and care for it. With God's help the dry hazel rod took root and sprouted leaves. But by the time it was fully grown and in bloom, seven years had passed. And she, a mother to be, got so heavy that she could hardly move. She wept inconsolably.

"How can I bake a loaf of bread?" she said. "The wheat is plentiful and there are hazelnuts, but which way should I go looking for him? Well, I'll start out in God's name and keep going until somewhere I hear something about him."

So she packed some provisions for the road, took a little money with her along with the loaf of bread and set forth. She went on and on, crossing from one land into the next and into the one after that on her journey. And when she was barely able to walk, she reached an enormous open field.

"Dear God," she said, "it is getting dark and I see a big forest in the distance. Somehow I have to get through it. What will happen to me at night when I have to cross the woods ? Please God, make a little cottage appear. Even if the devils live in it, I'd ask them for shelter, so as not to spend the night in the open under the skies."

As she reached the edge of the forest, she saw a light shining through the trees.

"I don't mind who lives there, I'll ask, maybe they'll take me in for the night."

She went and knocked at the door.

Someone cried out: "Come in."

An old woman was sitting by the fire. The hearth was large, the kind they used to have in the old days. She was stoking the cinders with an iron. Her nose was so long that its tip came down to her breasts.

"Good evening, grandma!"

"Good evening to you! What are you doing in this *god-forsaken place where not even a bird can fly?*"

"Misfortune brought me here. Would you kindly take me in, so I don't have to spend the night in the open? Wild beasts might attack me."

"I'd take you in, my girl, but I don't know if my son would get angry when he comes home. He is not here now. Perhaps he won't mind."

"If he's likely to get angry, I'd rather leave."

"What are you doing here? Why are you wandering about in these strange parts?"

"Where should I be wandering, dear grandma? I ask you because you are old, you have seen and heard a lot and been here and there. Have you ever heard of the serpent prince?"

"Well, my dear girl, I have grown old, most of my life is behind me—but I have never heard of him. I say to you, sleep here tonight, and start on your journey again tomorrow. By nightfall you will see another house like mine. My aunt lives in it. She might be able to tell you something about him, for she is older than I."

"Thank you kindly for your advice," she said.

She had dinner, made up her bed and lay down. In a little while the son came home. He burst in the door:

"Mother dear, what is this strange smell? Who is sleeping here?"

"Don't be angry, my dear son, a poor woman wandering about asked for shelter and I let her in. She is searching for the serpent prince. Have you heard of him any-where, son?"

"Well, my dear mother," he said, "I have been all over the world and peeped into every nook and cranny, even into the bottom of wells." (The old woman was the mother of the Moon.) "I have crossed forests and fields and streams, looked everywhere, but I have never heard of him."

The poor woman was very sad. She couldn't sleep, not even a wink. She wept so much during the night that the pillow under her head was soaking wet. She rose in the morning, washed and prepared to leave.

"I'll go now, dear grandma," she said, "I found no consolation for my great sorrow."

"Just do as I said, my girl. If you come upon my aunt, she may know something, she is older."

"All right, grandma, thank you very much."

"Look, my dear," she said, " I'll give you a gold bobbin—put it away for you may need it."

She thanked the old woman, put away the gold bobbin and started on her way. It happened that by evening she reached the other house and knocked at the door.

A faint voice answered: "Please, come in."

She entered the room. Once again she found an old woman, even older than the one before. She too, had a long nose, so long that it reached down to her navel, even farther. She looked up, but could barely see, her nose was in the way.

Said the girl: "Good evening, dear grandma!"

"Welcome, my girl. What are you doing here, in this *god-forsaken place where not even a bird can fly?*"

"Well, misfortune brought me here, my sad fate. I ask you, would you take me in? Would you be so kind and take me in for the night?"

"Sure," she said, "*this is God's shelter and man's resting place.* It is possible that my son will get angry but I'll placate him. I am the Sun's mother."

"May I ask you," she said, " you have been around a long time, you know much and have seen a lot—have you heard of the serpent prince anywhere?"

"No, I haven't, my child. Most of my life is behind me but I have never heard anything about him. Maybe my son knows. Come and eat while I make up your bed. I can see that you are tired." The poor girl was in tears and couldn't stop lamenting.

The old woman felt very sorry for her. As soon as she went to bed but was not yet asleep, in came the Sun:

"Oh dear," he said, " what is this bad smell here, mother?"

"Don't be angry, my son, a poor wandering woman had asked for shelter. I took her in," she said, "she is desperate."

"Why is she desperate?"

"Well," she said, "she wants to find the serpent prince. Did you hear of him anywhere, son?"

"My dear mother, I go around the whole world, I cross rivers and forests everywhere. I shine into every place, light up every corner, and look into every window," he said, "but I have never heard of him."

Said the old woman: "Poor woman. If she learns that you don't know anything either, she will be heartbroken. Maybe, if she looks up my old aunt on her way," she said, "she might have something to say about him."

When they rose in the morning, the old woman said to her: "My dear girl, my son couldn't say anything. He never heard of the serpent prince. But if you went to see my aunt, about the same hour you came here, she may be able to help. She is even older than we are. And if she cannot tell you, then I don't know what to say, how you'll find him."

Then she gave the young woman a reel:

"Well, my girl," she said, "my niece gave you a bobbin, so I'll give you a gold reel. Take good care of it, for you may need it!"

With those words she served the young woman breakfast and sent her on her way. She started on her journey and she walked and walked, although she did more weeping than walking. Eventually she reached the other house. By then it was evening and dark. She gathered up her courage and knocked at the door:

"Please," came the answer, "you may come in."

She entered and saw an old woman with a nose so long that it touched her knees. She looked up at her:

"What are you doing here, my dear girl?"

"I bid you a good evening, grandma!"

"A good evening to you too, my girl. What are you doing here, in this *god-forsaken place where not even a bird can fly?*"

She said: "My misfortune brought me here, grandma. Would you give me shelter for the night?"

"*This is God's shelter and man's resting place, so do come in!*"

The old woman made her sit down and asked her why she came.

"Well, dear grandma," she said, " I see that you are old, you have seen a lot, heard a lot and learned a lot—tell me, have you heard of the serpent prince anywhere?"

"I haven't, my girl. Maybe my son can say something about him when he comes home, but I can't."

Right away she gave her something to eat, made up her bed and bid her to lie down to rest. So she lay down but couldn't fall asleep. She waited for the son, waited to find out whether he had any news for her.

Soon she heard a rustling sound. In came a light breeze, the kind that combs the wheatfields. It floated in through the door.

"Dear mother, what is this strange smell here?"

"My son," she said, "don't be upset. I took in this poor, wandering woman. Have you heard of the serpent prince anywhere? She is looking for him."

"Well, no, mother dear, I haven't," he said. "Yet I slip through the fields, the forests and the grassy meadows, I drift over everything, but I have never heard of him.

Maybe my brother can say something, when he gets home."

The Breeze had a meal and went to bed. In a short while a loud noise started up outside, and there was such banging and cracking that they thought the roof of the little house was breaking asunder. There was such a strong windstorm!

Then the storm entered: "Good evening, dear mother!"

"Welcome, my son."

"What is this strange smell in here?"

"Don't be angry son, a poor, wandering woman came and asked for shelter, so I took her in," she said. "But before I give you your supper, let me ask you, have you ever heard of the serpent prince? She is looking for him."

"Maybe," he said, "I took off a corner of his castle yesterday."

The woman heard this from her bed and she became so overjoyed that her heart nearly burst from happiness. At last there was news about him!

"Son, then you know where he lives?"

"Sure I know," he said, "didn't I just say that I took a corner off his castle?" He was the Hurricane Wind.

"Well, son," said the old woman, "be so kind and take this poor woman there in the morning. She is in such a state that she can barely go on living."

"We'll see when the day breaks."

She served him a good meal and they all went to bed and fell asleep. When they rose in the morning, the old woman said: "Listen to me, my girl, I can bring you some comfort now."

But she already knew, she had heard it, for she had waited up for the Hurricane Wind.

"You see," the old woman continued, "he came home and said that he had taken a corner off the serpent prince's castle. So I asked him to take you there, for you would never find it on your own. He promised to do it."

They gave her some food, but in her excitement she couldn't eat or drink. She didn't want anything. She just waited, anxious to leave and to get there as quickly as possible.

The old woman handed her a gold spool and a ball of thread in pure gold:

"Look, my girl, I give these to you. Put them away carefully, you may need them."

She thanked her kindly and put the gold spool and thread away.

Said the Hurricane Wind: "Mount on my back and close your eyes!"

She climbed on the Hurricane's back, shut her eyes, and—*"one, two, three, take me where I want to be"*—they landed near the castle.

He set the woman down and said to her: "Ask the guards who are standing at the gate to let you in. Ask, and if they let you enter, walk in and the rest is your concern!" (I forgot something, but I won't add it now.)

So the woman entered the grounds and headed straight for the king's castle.

She began strolling up and down in front of it, holding the gold bobbin in her hand. The queen, sitting at her window, saw her and thought she was a merchant selling a gold bobbin. Right away she sent down her maid to ask whether the gold bobbin was for sale. The maid came running and said:

"Is this bobbin for sale?"

"It is. I would sell it."

"Then follow me to the palace," she said.

She went, gladly, and the queen said to her: "What do you want for this bobbin?"

She said what the old woman had told her to say: "I don't want anything else, just let me spend one night in your husband's bedchamber, and you may have the bobbin."

The queen thought about it and decided that this was not a matter of great consequence. She said: "I don't mind. Meanwhile go to town for a walk, until he returns. He went hunting and won't be home until evening—then you may come back."

Well, the poor woman didn't feel like strolling about—she sat down in a corner and stayed there, weeping all day. What would happen next? Evening came and the king returned. They had their supper, ate and drank and he went to have his bath. They filled a big tub with water and helped him into it. And as the snake prince was having his bath, his valet brought in his drink that would lull him to sleep, and handed it to him. He gulped it down and fell asleep there in the tub. He dropped off right away and became limp, unconscious. His two bodyguards lifted him out and took him over to his bed all made-up in silk, and covered him. Then the old queen, the false queen, opened the door and pushed the young woman inside:

"Go," she said, "see if you can make him horny, go."

She shoved her inside and locked the door. The woman waited for the king's servants, his bodyguards, to fall asleep. They were in the adjoining room and there was not even a door separating them. Only a carpet was suspended in the opening, so that should something happen to the king they would be there to attend to him. But they were not yet asleep when she began:

"I came, my dear husband. Wake up, put your arms around my waist so I can give birth to my child and put your finger on the gold ring, so I can take it off, for I am dying! I brought the bread made from the grain of wheat and the nuts borne by the hazel rod. Wake up, wake up, my dear husband!"

She carried on this way until dawn, but he didn't wake. He lay there as if he were dead. The woman wept bitterly.

She walked around the bed, who knows how many times, repeating:

"Wake up, my dear husband! I have been looking for you. I came and brought with me all you have asked. Free me from my burden, or else I'll perish!"

Morning came. Suddenly the queen flung the door open:

"Get out, you beastly whore!"

She chased her out. The young woman left in great sadness. What should she do? She went down to the ground floor to think. One night had passed already and nothing had happened. What would become of her if the second night passed the same way? She took out the golden spool and started to unravel it. The queen caught sight of her from the window:

"Run down, my girl, and ask the merchant whether she will sell the golden spool."

The girl went and asked: "Is it for sale?"

"It is," she said.

"Then please come with me to the palace, to see the queen."

She didn't have to be asked twice, she went.

Said the queen: "What do you want for the spool?"

"The same price as before," she said. "To be your husband's sweetheart for one night."

Oh, well, thought the queen, that doesn't amount to much. I'll give him a drink that will lull him to sleep and there will be nothing to worry about.

She said: "All right. Meanwhile, go out."

She asked the woman whether she was hungry, or whether she could offer her something. Nothing, she wanted nothing. Yet it had been a week since the poor woman had last eaten. She went out to a corner of the castle and there she stayed and lamented:

"Dear God, I can only get in once more and if all I can achieve is what I have achieved so far, I'll die. My heart will break there, on the spot, for I cannot stand it any more." Even her hand began to swell. She couldn't grasp anything with it, it was so puffed up. When evening closed in again and the king returned from hunting, she went back to the castle.

"Wait," said the queen, "the king hasn't gone to bed yet." She pushed the woman into a small room and there she remained, weeping. All of a sudden the queen opened the door and let her out:

"Go," she said, "see if you can make him horny, go."

Once again they had given the king a drink to lull him to sleep, so they let her try her luck. She went in and this time didn't wait for the bodyguards to fall asleep. She didn't care either that the queen, whose chamber was next door, might also be awake.

She began again: "Oh dear, dear! Wake up, my husband! I came to you once more. Wake up my dear husband for I brought you the bread from the grain of wheat and the nuts from the hazel rod. Put your arms around my waist, so I can give birth to my child and touch my finger with yours, so I can take off this ring, or else my heart will break here and now!"

Then the third day arrived. The poor woman took out the ball of gold thread and strolled about with it in front of the castle. The queen saw her from her window and right away sent her maid to ask her to come up. She went.

"Is this ball of gold thread for sale?" she asked.

"It is for sale."

"And what do you want for it?"

"No bargaining—what I want for it is that you let me spend one night with your husband."

"I'll let you," she said and bought the thread.

"And now you may go out into town and walk around until the evening. My husband will be back then, not before."

So the poor woman went out. She sank into a corner and wept bitterly.

"Dear God, what will become of me if once more my efforts are of no avail tonight?"

Meanwhile the king was out hunting yet again.

On the road his valet said to him: "Your Majesty, I'd say something, but I don't dare."

"Go on," he said, "you started it, so go on!"

"My life is in your hands, Sir. Here is what happened," he said. "For two nights running, when we take you out of the bath and you lie down on your bed to rest, the queen lets a woman into your chamber. 'Go, see if you can make him horny, go,' she says and pushes her into the room. Then the woman waits for a while. I think she wants us and the queen to be asleep so we wouldn't hear anything. Then she begins: 'Wake up, my dear husband, wake up and touch my finger, let the gold ring fall off, for I am so swollen that I'll burst! I brought the bread from the grain of wheat and the nuts from the hazel rod. Wake up, wake up, my dear husband! Have pity on me!'"

That night the king stayed awake. He didn't fall asleep, for his valet had poured the sleep-inducing drink into the bath. He just pretended to be asleep. He went limp in the bathtub, his two servants lifted him out and placed him on the bed. Then the queen shoved the woman into his chamber:

"Go, see if you can make him horny, go" she said.

The king waited for her to say it three times, then he sat up. He was lying down until then. He recognized his wife at once. He put his arms around her waist and right away she gave birth to such a beautiful golden-haired child that *one could sooner look at the sun than at him*. There was no need for cloths, or for candles—the room was bright and shiny, bathed in light. They rejoiced, for not one child but twins were born to them. Two boys and both had golden hair. The king was happy. He touched the woman's finger with his, and the ring snapped off. He helped her lie down in his place, in the bed. He was overjoyed with his sons. He sent his bodyguard to bring a woman over to help. He went and brought back the emperor's midwife, who immediately set about to attend to them. She bathed them and swaddled them and placed them on either side of the table. The king was so happy that he walked around on tiptoe, so his steps wouldn't be heard and his wife could rest. That is how he got dressed. He offered her all kinds of fine things to eat and drink, but she felt ill—she couldn't take anything. Well, the king didn't close an eye all night—he just paced up and down by his wife's bedside. At daybreak, when it became light, the queen came at last. She flung the door open:

"Get out of here, you beast, you whore!" she said.

The king leapt in front of her:

"Whom are you calling a whore? Who is the whore here?"

The queen, the former queen, became so alarmed at this turn of events that she nearly collapsed. And right away the king called out: "Catch that woman, the former queen, and throw her into a cellar!"

They took the queen and thrust her into a cellar. Then the king summoned his advisers to counsel him on which woman was better, the wedded or the unwed. Which was better? Which one should he honor? Which one should he keep?

They said: "The wedded one, the one you had wed."

"How could you elevate the illegitimate one and discard the one you had wed?"

"It is right that you should respect your wedded wife."

"Well then," said the king, "I am ordering you now to bring two of the most unruly colts out of the stables and tie the wicked woman and even her old witch of a mother to their tails! She had covered up for her daughter all along, lest something be discovered, so she deserves no better."

They tied both women to the stallions' tails. Two lads, each with a whip in his hands, flogged the horses while they circled the fort twelve times, until the women's bodies, even their bones, were shattered to pieces. And those the king wanted destroyed, so he had them nailed to the walls of the fort and burnt so that not even dust would be left of them. Then they arranged a big baptism, a big feast. They invited the kings, princes, and barons from all over, and asked the godparents to come for the christening. They also brought in the bishop, renewed their marriage vows, and *lived as happily as two turtle doves*. They are alive to this day, if they haven't died.

# 8. The Fawn

AT 450 (*Little Brother and Little Sister*; closely, perhaps generically related to AT 403), a relatively stable narrative that begins with the second marriage of the father to a woman who wants to kill her stepchildren. The cannibal-motif (G36) appears also in the West-Slavic region. The MNK lists 48 variants: 26 follow the outline and the rest incorporate elements from AT 313, 327A, 510, 403A and 707. MNK identifies the introductory part as a combination of MNK 450A** + 450B** + 450, as in Zsuzsanna Palkó's story.

"The Fawn" is among the tales Mrs. Palkó learned from her father, János Zaicz, the renowned public entertainer of old Andrásfalva. It was "his tale" and she started telling it to her Kakasd neighbors only after his death. I recorded it at her home in 1950.

The dramatic power with which Aunt Zsuzsi creates realistic characters is remarkable. She intertwines elements of everyday village life with elements of magic so subtly that the listener does not even notice that he has been taken from our world into another. She elaborates every detail with great patience; nothing is passed over or left unexplained. Unusual or absurd acts are given convincingly credible interpretations. For example, the first part of the tale presents miserable family conditions: constantly crying hungry children (here, as in "Death With the Yellow Legs" [tale no. 3, above] and "Margit" [no. 35], the problem of fertility in poor families is exposed) and the woman's desperate effort to feed the father, the breadwinner, and quell the children's insatiable appetites. Unlike the international versions, in which a stepmother wants to get rid of the children, Mrs. Palkó's tale makes the real birthmother the would-be killer who elaborates a secret strategy to murder her children for food.

The initial situation of hunger and poverty provides the foundation for a story that is built like a cathedral, with engineered precision and strict logic, brick by brick, episode by episode: the gluttony of the children, the desperation of a mother who cooks her own flesh, and the idea of consuming her children follow naturally, as does the elaborate murder plan. To augment tension and keep the audience terrified, Mrs. Palkó repeats the parents' plot three times, each time argued from a different vantage point. First the parents discuss it; second, the girl who heard it informs her brother; and third, when Mrs. Palkó reports the plot as it is enacted. These are simple but effective artistic tricks that help convince listeners that this is not a tale but a real event that they have accidentally come to witness. Up to the point where the children are rescued, the tale is completely realistic. The alien magic world of the tale opens with animal transformation and continues with the wonders of the royal palace and the world of folktale justice.

Mrs. Palkó reinvigorates traditional tale elements by giving them a psychological frame; she never tires of elaborate interpretations. She explains the smallest detail: for example, the mother's use of vinegar to stop the bleeding after she has cut a large chunk of meat from her thigh. Mrs. Palkó calls attention to an unusual but unremarkable act that becomes later an important element in the course of events: the girl asks her brother to accompany her to the outhouse where she earlier had no fear to go alone (an element also found in "Zsuzska and the Devil" [no. 2]). She is tireless in exploiting the available stock of tale formulas, and commonplaces such as proclamations of war (also in "I Don't Know" [no. 1] and "The Twelve Robbers" [no. 19]) and the substitute wife's pretense of sickness.

In this tale, as in "The Serpent Prince" [no. 7], Mrs. Palkó admits to a slip. She almost neglects to say that the king follows the fawn on his third visit with his sister—an element that brings the tale to its happy conclusion.

———

Once upon a time, beyond the beyond, beyond the seven seas and beyond the glass mountains, there was a poor man and a woman. They had as many children as there are holes in a sieve, and one more. They were as poor as church mice. The poor man worked as a day-laborer. He earned his daily bread with his two hands.

One day he said to his wife: "Wife, I don't even remember when I ate meat the last time. Tonight I'll bring some home from work, and you'll cook it for me. Let me at least once eat my fill of meat, for I cannot bear the work of threshing with such measly food. I cannot get a decent meal since we have so many children. All we ever have is cheap dishes."

"Bring some," she said, "I'll cook it for you, gladly. I wouldn't mind having some myself."

So the poor man went to work. The woman waited for him in the evening and, sure enough, he brought back eight pounds of meat.

"Well, there should be enough," he said, "make it in a stew—that will stretch it."

"All right," she said.

They woke the next morning and right away the woman began cooking the meat. During the day they ate whatever they found. Toward evening there was work to do outside; they had a few hens laying eggs. She went out to give them feed and water and look after them. She did what was needed in the yard. She said to her daughter, the oldest one—who was thirteen (then came a boy who was nine years old):

"Well, my girl, I am going to take care of the work outside; meanwhile you watch over the meat, add some salt to it and let it simmer. It should be ready by the time your father comes home."

"All right, dear mother."

The woman went outside to attend to her work, and there were all the hungry children. The girl stirred the pot to make sure the meat wouldn't burn, then cut off a piece and tasted it to see if it was done. When the other children saw this, they all rushed over to the pot and each took a slice or two of the meat. They didn't leave a single piece. Not one piece of meat was left in the pot when they were finished.

Then the poor woman came back in. She ran to stir the pot and found that there was not even a morsel of meat in it.

"God in Heaven, where did the meat go? What did you do?" she said.

"I only took one slice, dear Mother, to taste whether it had to go on cooking."

"And where is the rest?"

"Well, each one of my brothers and sisters took a piece," she said. "I told them not to touch it, but it was no use, and now it is all gone."

Oh dear, the woman became very upset. She was alarmed. What would she serve her husband when he comes home? The poor man was expecting to eat some meat. And now there wasn't any, what to do? What could she do when there was none? Well, she went into the pantry and cut off the four pounds of meat, two pounds from each leg. Then she went and rinsed it, washed it well, chopped it up and put it on the stove to cook. She had bandaged her legs with something, stopped the bleeding with vinegar, and went on cooking the meat. Evening came and her husband arrived home:

"Well, wife, is dinner ready? I am very hungry."

"I think it's ready by now. I'll serve it to you right away so you can eat."

She went and served the meal. The children were still crying for she had given them a thorough thrashing. One was under the bed, another by the oven, still another under the table, and one was in the crib. There were enough of them to spread around; they were in two or three places.

"Why are the children crying?"

"I beat them because they were bad."

But she didn't dare say what they had done. She served the meal and they sat down to eat. She gave the children their food separately. When the man ate his fill, all the children went to bed. The two older ones slept on the porch. There was also *an oven and some slept on top of it.* Not having room for everyone in the house, she let the older ones sleep outside. The woman and the man were chatting inside.

Said the woman to her husband: "How did you like the dinner?"

"The meat had such a fine, sweet flavor. I haven't eaten such good, sweet-tasting meat for a long time."

"Do you know what kind of meat you ate?"

"Well I know what meat I bought," he said.

"It wasn't the meat you bought."

"What happened to it?"

"The children ate it. That's why I beat them so hard that they are still crying. I went out to attend to my work and by the time I came back in, they had finished it all."

"Then where did you get this meat?" he said.

"Look here. My leg is bandaged. I took the soft meat from my leg, from both of them," she said, "and I cooked it."

"Oh, my! Is human flesh this good? I didn't know, I have never eaten any. And look what I discovered now!" he said.

They thought the children were all asleep, in bed.

"Look," he said, "I have been thinking. Tomorrow we could slaughter the girl and the day after tomorrow the boy, the older one. They are a little fatter than the others. We could slaughter them, cure their meat in salt, and while it lasts we needn't worry about having enough food to eat."

Well, the woman agreed, she thought it was a good idea. But the boy heard it, he was not quite asleep on top of the oven; he had listened to what his father and mother were saying. The others had dozed off.

"It'll be all right," said the man, "as long as no one gets to know about it. We live next to the highway and if they scream, it can be heard outside."

"Oh," said the woman, "I can make sure that there will not even be an 'ouch'! They should both be going to school, but tomorrow I won't let them. I'll say that I have to give a bath to the girl, wash and comb her hair, and the boy must sweep the court-yard and tidy up outside, so they cannot go to school. And then I'll wash the girl's hair—but I'll sharpen the knife ahead of time and hide it away. And when she sits down on the chair and I'll start combing her hair, I'll cut her throat so fast she won't have time to scream," she said. "All will be well. We'll salt the meat in a basin and there will be enough for us to eat tomorrow and even the day after."

The boy listened to all this. And when they had finished planning how it would all come about, they went to bed and fell asleep. As soon as the boy heard them snore, he shook his sister, the older girl:

"Dear sister, wake up and *come out with me.*"

"Why do you want to go out?"

"Let's go out to pee!"

"How many times have you been out on your own—why do you disturb me now? Go by yourself!"

"I won't go, I am afraid," he said, "come with me."

"And other times you were not afraid? What is wrong with you?"

"Come, don't let me beg you so much. Come out with me, I have to go."

Well, the girl wasn't pleased but she got up and they went out:

"So go and pee!"

"No," he said, "let's go back to the corner of the house."

The girl followed him, very annoyed that he didn't let her be, that she'd be wide-awake and not able to fall asleep again.

He said: "My dear sister, I didn't ask you to come out because I am afraid. I am not afraid—I have been out before and would have gone again. But listen to what I have heard from our father and mother. You were asleep but I wasn't. Listen to what they have planned to do."

"What?"

"They said that we didn't know what kind of meat mother had cooked the second time, that she had cut a soft piece out of her leg and served it to us for dinner. And when they thought that we were asleep, she began asking my father whether it was good, whether he liked the meat, and he answered: 'It was very good, I haven't had such sweet-tasting meat before.' And she said: 'Do you know what that meat was?' 'Sure I know, I bought it. It was beef.' She said: 'No, it wasn't. I took a piece of tender meat from my leg and cooked it. What you had bought was eaten up by your children. It wasn't even done yet and they ate it. And I was expecting you, my husband, to come home. There was nothing else I could do, so I cut the meat off my leg.' 'Does human flesh taste this good?' he asked. 'We'll do something different. There are enough of them anyway, tomorrow we'll slaughter the girl, she is bigger and fatter, and the day after the boy. This way we'll have enough to eat while the meat lasts. But how should we do it so no one hears about it? We live near the highway, if they scream, someone may come in.' 'No,' she said, 'I won't let them go to school tomorrow and I'll say that I have to wash and groom the girl's hair, and the boy must sweep the yard, chop wood, and attend to his work. So I'll keep them at home. I'll send the boy out to sweep, I'll wash the girl's hair, and when I start combing it, the sharpened knife will be ready and all I have to do is draw it across her throat and it will be done.' 'All right,' he said. He agreed.

"Now tell me, dear sister, what should we do so we don't die? Do we need to die this young? My heart breaks at the thought of it. What could we do? Let's you and I agree—no one can hear us now."

The girl said: "Do you know what? I'll wait until tomorrow. I won't go anywhere at night for I am afraid. But tomorrow, after mother washes my hair and I am winding the ribbon around my finger, you rush in the door, grab it from my hand and shout: 'I need this for a whip.' Then I'll burst into tears and cry that you mustn't take my ribbon, you shouldn't take it; you'll jump up and start running, and I'll run after you, shouting and screaming that you can't take it, that you can't take my ribbon away! This way she won't notice anything and you keep running as fast as your legs will carry you. We'll reach the fields—where we don't have to worry that someone will see us—and make our way through the tall wheat. We'll run wherever our eyes will lead us. We won't let them kill us!"

And so it happened. Morning came and both were trembling for they knew what was awaiting them. The woman started grumbling—her husband had gone to work, and she began shouting at them:

"You two," she said, "you don't have time to go to school today. I must wash and groom your hair, Juliska, and you'd better go out to chop some wood for tomorrow, Sunday, and tidy up the yard. Both of you will have work to do at home."

"All right, dear mother," he said, "I'll chop wood and do what needs to be done."

The boy went out and set to work. Inside the woman untied the girl's hair, washed it and handed her the ribbon:

"Smooth it out with your fingers, so it won't be so wrinkled."

The girl began smoothing and folding the ribbon. Suddenly the boy bounced in and grabbed it from her hand:

"This is just what I need for my whip!" he shouted and ran out the door. He heard her scream:

"Mother, he took my ribbon! What will you use to braid my hair? I'll run and get it back from him at once!"—and she slipped out.

The woman said: "Don't run anywhere, my dear, we'll find another one."

"I won't let him use it for a whip. It is my ribbon!"

She rushed out to follow the boy, but God knows where he was by then, he ran so fast.

She ran after him: "Stop," she shouted, "let me have my ribbon!"

She ran in pursuit of him, and they shouted back and forth to each other all the way to the end of the village. They ran beyond it, bounded into the fields, and skipped between the standing corn and wheat as best they could. They ran on, past the fields, into the next community and then past that until they left their country behind and entered into the neighboring land. They came upon a forest, so dense and large that it was completely dark.

The girl said: "Look brother, how big this forest is. Once we are in it, we need to fear no longer. They wouldn't find us in the midst of these woods. And here, I believe, no one will recognize us anyway for we are far from home."

They entered the forest but kept on running there, too, going deeper and deeper.

Suddenly the boy said: "Oh, my dear Juliska, I am thirsty, so thirsty that I could die."

"Dear brother, be patient, there is no water here. Maybe we'll find some further on."

Then they reached some soggy ground full of puddles, where water was standing in the footprints left by animals. Nowhere else was there water, it only seeped up through the animal tracks, or it was rainwater or something. Anyway, it was water.

Said the boy: "Look, dear sister, these are the prints of a wolf and they are filled with water. I'll drink from them."

She said: "Don't, dear brother, for if you do, you'll be turned into a wolf and eat me up."

The boy became alarmed and didn't drink. Then they came upon some bear tracks.

"Look, dear sister, these are bear tracks. I'll drink from them."

"Don't drink, dear brother, for you'll be turned into a bear."

Well, he didn't drink then. They went on and came upon the prints of a fawn. The girl didn't see—for her brother was behind her—that he bent down and took a drink of the water; he said nothing to her about it. Suddenly she looked back and saw that a fawn was following her. Then she knew that he had drunk from the deer tracks and had turned into a deer.

"Oh! Oh! My dear brother, until now I had someone to speak to, but now I won't even have that, I'll have no one to speak to, to converse with! I told you not to drink from the tracks of wild animals for you'd be turned into the one from whose tracks you drank."

So the fawn followed her, sauntered behind her, not lagging back too far, while she walked ahead. The fawn had a lovely head, it was beautiful. They reached a clearing, with only one tree standing in it. It was a meadow. The hay had been cut and piled into a stack.

The girl said: "My dear brother, let's hide under this stack and rest—I can't bear all this running and walking any longer. Let's get some rest and then we'll go on."

Said the fawn: "I don't mind, little sister, let's climb in under there."

They crawled under the haystack. The girl's clothes were in tatters, they'd been torn as she ran in between the bushes. The thorns had caught and ripped her dress so that she was almost naked. She crawled in under the haystack and the fawn settled down beside her. Then she took a handful of hay, stuffed it into the opening and they bedded down. They were not yet asleep when they heard voices. They became alarmed— God knows who could be out there. They feared that it was their parents pursuing them. The girl, who no longer looked like a child, stuck her head out to see who was talking.

She saw that it was the king, who had come out for a hunt with a number of his soldiers. They tethered their horses to the tree, loaded their guns and sat down to eat in the clearing, a little to the side of the haystack. They sat there, chatting. The girl quickly pulled back her head, lest they notice her and discover that they had been listening.

Said the king: "Now we'd better start our meal. Let's eat and then we'll begin the hunt."

So they all pulled out their bundles, took out their food and prepared to eat. The king sat down too, drew forth his bag, ready to start eating. His bag was filled with rolls. He took the first one and threw it to his dog. He had a hunting dog, a greyhound, and he gave him the first roll. Then he took another one, some lard and who knows what else, and began to eat, but the dog snatched the roll away from him. The dog had the habit of running and eating his food not where it was given, but out of everybody's sight. So he snatched the roll and took it to the side of the haystack to eat it there. He put his two front paws on the roll and was about to bite into it. But the girl noticed it, grabbed the roll from the dog, broke it in two, and gave one half to the fawn and ate the other. The dog ran back to his master and sat down in front of him. Wagging his tail, he looked straight at the king, licking his chops. The king just stared at him:

"Poor dog," he said, "he is starved! He hardly took two bites and devoured the roll."

He gave him another one: "Here, have your fill!"

Once again the dog snatched the roll, ran with it and dropped it down near the haystack. And once again the girl reached out and grabbed it. They were as ravenous as wolves. She shared the roll with the fawn. The dog ran back to the king.

"Well," said the king, "something isn't right. This dog couldn't have eaten up the roll so quickly. I've given him rolls before, but he never finished so fast, and two rolls were enough for him. He must be burying them somewhere."

He said to one of the soldiers: "Go see where he takes the roll. I'll give him another one and you look where he takes it. Maybe he buries it; he is a dog who buries things."

So the soldier went and followed the dog, making sure that he wasn't noticed. He saw the dog run to the haystack, deposit the roll, and a beautiful white hand reach out to grab it. But the soldier didn't dare to look at who or what was under the haystack. He rushed back to the king and said:

"Your Majesty, I saw that the dog doesn't eat the roll—he takes it over to the haystack and then a beautiful white hand reaches out from under the haystack and draws it in. Surely the same thing happened with the other two rolls, since the dog went there a third time."

The king said: "We must see who is there!"

The king jumped to his feet, took his gun and, with a soldier, went over to the haystack. He had the soldier pull away the hay, and he called out:

"Who is in there? Who is under the hay? If it's a human being, let him speak up, but if it's a ghost, I'll shoot right away. If you are a human being, speak now! Who are you?"

The girl was very frightened.

"I am no wild beast, I am a human being, don't harm me! I never hurt anyone, don't harm me!"

"Then come out, come stand before me! Who are you? What are you?"

"I'd come out," she said, "but I am ashamed, for I am almost naked. I am ashamed because my dress was torn off."

"Well," said the king, "I'll give you my cloak; put it on and come out!":

He gave her his cloak; she wrapped herself in it and came out. The king, who was a handsome young lad, looked her over. Well, she was a lovely, beautiful girl—he took a liking to her instantly.

"Tell me, girl," he said, "how did you get here?"

"How did I get here?" She told him how. She told the truth:

"I was driven out of home and country."

She told him that their father and mother wanted to kill them, so she ran away with her brother.

"Come," said the king, "I'll take you with me to my palace."

"Oh, no! I don't know who you are!"

"I am a prince, the king's son."

"Oh prince, how can I go with you when I have my brother here, with me?"

"Where is he?"

"He is in there," she said.

"Let him come too."

"But how can he? He was turned into a deer. He is a fawn. I told him," she said, "not to drink from the tracks of wild animals. He didn't drink from the tracks of wolves, I had talked him out of it, he didn't drink from the tracks of bears, but then he found the tracks of deer, and without telling me he drank from them and was turned into a fawn. He followed me and I wouldn't ever leave him for he is my beloved brother. He may be a fawn, but he is my brother."

Said the prince: "You may bring him with you!"

The girl called the fawn. He was so beautiful that the king said:

"Even if you don't want to bring him, I will, he is so beautiful. He is a beautiful animal. Come with me, the fawn will want for nothing. I'll look after him. I'll take you for my wife and the fawn will stay with us, no harm will come to him in my care."

The girl was very happy. The king took her in his coach, left the hunters behind and drove home with her. He took her home and immediately gave orders for her to be given a bath and be dressed in royal garments, as becomes a princess. And so it happened. They bathed her and dressed her and she turned into such a beautiful maiden that *one could sooner look at the sun than at her.*

"Well," he said, "*you are mine and I am yours only the shovel and the spade should separate us.*"

Then he called in the cook: "Do you know what I want to tell you, cook? Take this fawn with you in the kitchen. He should eat what I eat, drink what I drink, and *not a single hair should be missing from his coat.* And if he loses a hair, you must pick it up, place it in a golden box and report to me that one hair fell from his coat and where it is. The fawn must not be missing a single hair."

He said to his wife: "Look, wife, anything the fawn wishes, I'll try to give him. I won't turn my back on him, I'll do everything to please him. And don't be concerned about him—he'll have a very, very good life. I'll watch him every day and make sure that he'll want for nothing."

The girl was very happy. And that's how it was. The king made it the cook's duty to give the fawn the best of care. She took him into the kitchen and he ate what the king ate and drank what the king drank. He developed nicely. He was so beautiful that the king could see himself reflected in his coat; it had turned so shiny from the good life. And the king rejoiced in his wife, for she had become pregnant. He rejoiced that God would bless them with offspring.

But their happiness was short-lived, for one day a knight appeared and handed the king a letter affixed with a seal. He took it and read it. Well, the message in it was that the *dog-headed Tatars* were about to invade his country. If he wished to save it, he must gather his troops and confront the enemy.

Oh, the king became so upset that he didn't know what to do. The cook, who was a sorceress, had a daughter and for this daughter she stole food from the palace and whatever else she could. It was her greatest wish that somehow she should meet the king and that he should ask her to be his wife. Well, the king read the letter out loud and grew very sad.

"Dear wife," he said, "we have to part. The message came that war is imminent, I must confront the *dog-headed Tatars*. It is very sad for me to leave you. I don't know what will become of you. If only my dear mother were alive to take care of you, but she is dead, so to whom can I entrust you? I can only leave you with the cook and hope that she'll look after you. But my greatest worry is that I may not return in time for the birth, and the little baby will need much attention. Who will care for it and attend to it?"

"My dear husband," said the queen, "you must not grieve. Don't worry, God will be with us, He won't abandon us. As long as He protects you from those ill-fated bullets, you need not grieve for me, for I am in my home and I'll manage."

Then the cook came and the king said to her: "Look, you have been here for quite a long time. For ten years I have known you as a fair-minded woman. I'll entrust my wife, the queen, to you, so that you care for her as for your own child, even better. And when, God willing, it'll be time to give birth, see to it that no harm comes to her!"

"Well," she said, "Great King, you mustn't be afraid of me, you can trust me. I'll look after her as if she were my own, even better. Don't grieve, don't worry, don't torment yourself!"

Soon the day arrived when it was time for them to go. The soldiers, trumpets blaring, halted in front of the palace. They stood and waited for the king. But the king couldn't bring himself to leave the house. He started out at least ten times, kissed his wife over and over again, made for the door and returned every time:

"My dear wife, take care of yourself! Take care, so no harm will come to you! If you fall ill, or feel unwell, send for the doctor, let him stay with you and attend to you!"

"Don't worry about me," she said, "may God protect you and bring you back safely!"

They took leave of one another and the king departed.

Well, the cook took good care of the queen. She prepared fine meals and served them to her. One day her daughter came along to help. She dressed and undressed the queen and brought her food. No one else needed to wait on her, she took it all upon herself.

Then, by the grace of God, the hour arrived for the queen to give birth. A lovely, golden-haired boy was born to her—he was like an angel. She rejoiced in the child but she also wept—if only his father could see him, how happy he would be!

Time passed. One day the evil spirit of jealousy took hold of the cook. She began plotting with her daughter to do away with the queen and strip her of her royal garments.

"I'll put them on you, I'll dress you in her clothes, then you'll lie in, with the baby beside you, and you'll be the queen," she said.

"Oh, that'll be fine!"

One day the cook said to the queen:

"Your Majesty, I'll not give you a bath today, but I'll groom your hair. I'll comb it and wash it, as one can get lice from lying in bed a long time. If even a single louse is found in your hair, the king will kill me."

"Yes, sure," she said, "I never had lice in my life."

"No, of course not," she said, "you kept yourself clean, but now with the baby just born and your fever, lice can appear in no time."

"All right, I don't mind."

She bathed her that day, took off her clothes so she was naked, soaped her down and washed her. Not for the world would the queen have thought, or suspected, that this would be her last bath. When they were done, the cook said:

"I won't dress you until I have combed your hair. But, please, Majesty, sit up on the window ."

It so happened that the ocean came up all the way to the foot of the palace. The cook made the queen sit in the window and, all of a sudden, pushed her out. She fell into the ocean, but she didn't drown; she turned into a golden duck instantly, and swam away.

The poor little child remained there with the cook's daughter. The cook set it down beside her stepmother and she held it as if it were her own.

A short time later the king returned. All along the fawn had wept so much, his eyes never dried, for he knew that they had pushed his sister into the ocean. The king came home and went straight to his wife's bedside:

"How are you, my dear wife?"

But he nearly had a stroke when he saw how ugly his wife had become.

"What happened to you, my dear wife? You were different when I left."

"Well," she said, "don't ask! All the weeping ruined me. The sorrow over your leaving destroyed me. I was forever grieving, and then the childbearing; I don't know when I'll recover from it, when my beauty will be restored."

But the king was not convinced, he had doubts. He wondered—why had her complexion turned so ugly? Why had his wife become so unsightly, without any shape or form?

"Look, son, look, childbearing took its toll, and all the grieving and weeping," said her mother. "You must understand that she wept so much, worrying that you might perish, not knowing what would become of you. But you'll see, her beauty will return, her looks will be restored."

So the king let up. Maybe she'll be set right again.

But that didn't happen. She turned uglier by the day instead of more beautiful. She put the little one to her breast, pretending to nurse him, but there was no more in her nipple than in my own. So the little one cried and cried from night to morning and morning to night, he just cried, and all the time the fawn cried with him.

One day the sorceress mother said to her daughter: "My girl, I don't like the air around here. Look, the fawn is forever crying and the king is suspecting something. I say to you that you should pretend to be deathly ill and ask the king to come back from parliament, for you are about to die. And when he comes, you must tell him that you feel you are about to die, but if he does as you say, you'll stay alive. You must tell him that in your dream an old man came to you and said that the king should kill the fawn and let you eat its heart and liver. If you do, you'll recover your health. If you don't do it," she said, "the king will find out our secret, for the fawn keeps crying."

So the daughter sent for the king in parliament. She was lying in bed, languishing.

"What is the matter with you, wife?"

"What is the matter?" she said, "I feel that I am about to die."

"Why? What happened to you?"

"My body is aching all over, I know I'll die from it."

"What should I do? I'll call a doctor."

"Don't get me a doctor, he can't help me. But listen to what I saw in my dream: I dozed off, and there was an old man, a white-haired old man before me, and he said to me: 'My girl, you are very ill and if the king doesn't kill the fawn and let you eat from its heart and liver, within three days you'll be laid out on a bier. Tell the king to have the fawn killed and its heart and liver cooked for you, and as soon as you eat them you'll be well again.' If you do it, maybe you'll keep your wife; if you don't, I'll die."

"Just think about it—how can I have the fawn killed when I love him so? Remember, when I asked you to be my wife you said you won't come with me unless I take the fawn too. You said that 'if I become queen, I don't want a kingdom or anything else, but I'll never part with my brother.' And now you are asking me to kill him?"

"Look, if you pity the fawn more than you pity me, then let me die."

"Well, if it is your wish that he should be killed," he said, "he is your brother; I won't pity him more than you do. Wait for two days—if you don't improve, I'll have him killed."

The queen agreed to wait two days. The next day the fawn spoke to the king, for he went to see him and said:

"What is the matter with you, my dear fawn? Why are you so sad?"

"Oh, my dear brother-in-law, I 'd ask you to grant me a wish."

"What is your wish?"

"That you should tie my little nephew to the back of my neck so I can take him to the flower garden, stroll around with him, for he was crying all night and I feel so sorry for him. I keep hearing him cry. All he does is cry, day and night."

But the fawn didn't say what they had done to his sister.

"Look fawn," said the king, "since I had promised that I'll never deny a request you make, I'll grant your wish. I give you my permission." And he himself secured the child to the fawn's neck. But the queen started protesting:

"Don't put him on his back! He'll drop my child, don't put him there!"

"What do you want? Let it be," said the king, "let the fawn take him around!"

He fastened the child to the fawn's neck and led him down into the flower garden. The fawn ran, looking around him; there were paths in between the flowers and delicious fragrances. He carried the child, rocked it to and fro—and the child quieted down, he didn't utter a sound. The fawn made straight for the far end of the garden, where the ocean swelled up against it. The ocean washed the side of the palace but it circled the flower garden.

When he reached the shore, the fawn called out: "Dear sister of mine, dear little sister, rise from the bottom of the ocean! I brought your offspring so you can nurse it and swaddle it. Change your baby's clothes and suckle it for they are sharpening the knife for my tender little neck and washing the basin for my red blood." He said it three times: "Little sister, little sister, rise from the bottom of the ocean, I brought your offspring! Suckle it, swaddle it, change it and nurse it, for I cannot bear all the crying. And they are sharpening the knife for my tender little neck and washing the basin for my red blood!"

All of a sudden a gold duck appeared, cutting through the water as it swam. When it reached the shore, it thrust itself out of the ocean, tumbled head over heels and became a beautiful queen. She was a thousand times more beautiful than before. She came, put her arms around the child, covered it with kisses, unwrapped it and didn't begin to nurse it until after she had washed its clothes and spread them out on the flowers to dry. Then she sat down and put the child to her breast. But her tears kept streaming down on the child's face. A beautiful child it was. She nursed it and wept. And the fawn wept with her.

"My little sister, little sister, I am condemned to die. They'll cut my tender throat and they are already washing the basin for my red blood."

There they were, the two of them, weeping. As soon as she finished suckling her son, he fell asleep. She dressed and swaddled him in clean clothes and placed him onto the back of the fawn's neck. Then she flipped head over heels, thrust herself into the ocean and swam away.

The fawn took the child home. He was altogether quiet, there was no more crying. The king unfastened the child, covered him with kisses and laid him down onto the bed, next to his mother. The child slept through to the next day, without a sound.

Said the king: "You see how helpful it was for the fawn to take the child into the garden. I don't know whether he got tired, or enjoyed the outing, or what, but he quieted down. Before he was always crying."

"Well," she said, "he is sleeping because I nursed him, and not only once."

The next morning the fawn went to the king again.

"What is the matter, little fawn?" said the king. "Have you another wish?"

"Yes, I have, my dear brother-in-law. Fasten my little nephew to the back of my neck again and let me take him around in the flower garden. I won't be able to do it for long."

Said the king: "You may do it." He brought out the child, secured him to the fawn's neck, and let the fawn into the flower garden. Right away he ran to the back, to the edge of the ocean and began calling again:

"Rise, rise, little sister, come up from the bottom of the ocean! Bathe your child for no one bathes him the way you did before you perished; no one bathes him and he just cries, day and night. Come out, my dear little sister, for they are washing the basin for my red blood and sharpening the knife for my tender little neck!"

All of a sudden the duck appeared, parting the water as she swam. Once again she thrust herself out of the ocean and turned into such a beautiful queen that *one could sooner look at the sun than at her.* And once again she lifted her son and pressed him to her heart. She unwrapped him, bathed him, washed his clothes and diapers and spread them on the flowers to dry while she suckled him. The sun was bright in the sky, it was summer and the diapers dried while she nursed the child. Then she swaddled him again and said:

"My dear brother!" She kissed the fawn and he kissed her. Then she kissed the child, placed him back onto the fawn's neck and sent them on their way. The fawn took the child home—he was fast asleep and only woke the next morning.

"After all, it is good that he takes the child around, dear wife. I am loath to slaughter this little fawn. Don't you see what a fine nurse he is? This alone makes it worth saving his life."

"Well, if you pity the fawn more than you pity me, if you love him more, then let me die."

"If it's what you want," he said, "I'll have him killed tomorrow."

They woke the next morning and the king went to see the fawn. He was grieving for him. His tears were flowing and the fawn was weeping too.

The king said: "Have you another wish, my dear fawn?"

He said: "My wish is that you fasten my little nephew on the back of my neck once more, and let me carry him around."

The king did so and said: "Come back soon!"

Well, the fawn ran into the garden—he galloped until he came to the edge of the ocean.

Then he stopped and called out: "Rise, rise to the shore, my little sister! I brought your offspring again—suckle it, for henceforth no one will bring him to you. They are washing the basin to hold my red blood and are sharpening the knife to cut my tender little neck. We can still meet today, but never again."

Then the golden duck appeared and thrust itself out of the water. (I am ahead of my story, I left things out!)

The king had come out after them. He watched them and said: "I'd better see how the fawn carries and rocks the child, so that if I have him killed I'll know what to do. I'll take the child around myself so he'll sleep."

The king came on a secret path among the flowers and saw how the fawn crossed the garden running, then came to a halt at the edge of the ocean and began calling:

"Little sister, little sister, rise from the bottom of the ocean, for I brought your offspring for the last time. Suckle it and bathe it for you'll never see me again. Bid me farewell for they are washing the basin for my red blood and are sharpening the knife for my tender little neck."

The king listened. No one appeared. The fawn called out a second and third time:

"Little sister, little sister, rise from the bottom of the ocean and come here. I brought your offspring—suckle it, swaddle it in clean clothes and nurse it, for they are sharpening the knife for my tender little neck and are washing the basin for my red blood."

Then, all of a sudden, the duck emerged from the water, flipped head over heels and turned into a lovely queen. She was a thousand times more beautiful than before the ocean had swallowed her. She took her son into her arms and pressed him to her heart:

"My dear, beautiful child, I may never see you again! Where and how could I have sinned so much that they separated me from you? Tell me, my dear brother, what do they have against you, why do they want to kill you, when you never hurt anyone or anything? And still they find that you deserve to be killed?" The queen clasped her arms around the fawn and, bending down, she held him close against her.

The king came up behind her and said: "What's going on here? What's going on?"

The queen was startled, she straightened herself and the king recognized her as his wife.

"Oh, my dear wife, where have you been all this time? You are my wife, aren't you?"

"I am," she said.

They fell into each other's arms, held and kissed one another and wept.

And the queen recounted everything they had done to her.

Said the king: "I am not at fault, for I had no knowledge of anything. When I came home they misled me, told me that my wife had turned ugly from all the grieving in bed. When I asked why she looked so *coarse, peasant-like*, they said her beauty will be restored, that nursing the child took much out of her and made her lose weight. This is how they lied to me," he said, "and made me believe that she was my true wife. Don't worry, dear wife, they'll pay for this! I'll cure the sick woman!"

He couldn't part with his wife. He kept kissing her and the child. And the fawn, with a flip, tumbled head over heels and turned into a handsome youth. He shed the skin of a fawn that he'd had to wear until now. Then the four of them made their way back. The king, his wife and the little child—and the fawn transformed into a young man. As they approached, the queen caught sight of them from the window.

"Oh, mother, with whom is the king coming? He is bringing guests, a very fine woman and a fine young man. I don't know, but he might be a prince," she said, "they are so handsome, so beautiful."

"Never mind, my girl, when they get here we'll offer them hospitality!"

But then the old woman recognized them, for she was a sorceress— she knew that it was the true queen.

Said the king: "Now let the mother-in-law and her daughter come before me! Let them receive the reward they have been seeking. They'll get the reward they wanted!"

"How did you dare tell such a big lie to a king! That she had turned ugly from all the grief and withered from nursing the child! And this poor, innocent offspring of mine kept crying because all he was offered was a coarse, dry nipple to suck, while she was telling me that the child was crying because he was sick. They dared tell me such a lie! They dared lie to me and have me believe that she was the queen, having thrown my dear wife into the ocean to the fishes! But God doesn't tolerate deception, and innocence had to come to light. They'll get what they deserve!"

Right away he ordered two stallions to be brought up and had the two evil creatures tied by their hair to the horses' tails . They were to be driven alongside the ocean, its full length, back and forth, back and forth! "That will take too long," said the king. "I want to see with my own eyes how they perish. Drive the stallions here, on the ocean shore, until their bodies are torn to bits." The skin had been ripped off their muscles, all had turned into jelly, their flesh and everything.

"Burn them," said the king, "and let the ashes of the evil ones be blown away by the wind!"

Then the king gave a big ball and invited everyone, kings, princes, and barons. They brought over the bishop and held such a splendid wedding feast that the band never stopped playing for four days. Even the ducks came up from the bottom of the ocean and danced, and all the fishes came from the sea. So they were wed again and are alive to this day, if they haven't died.

# 9. Józsi the Fisherman

AT 465C (*A Journey to the Other World*) + 750A (*The Wishes*); MNK lists 18 variants of 465C (*The Fish Maiden*).

Mrs. Palkó learned the story from Márton László, a noted storyteller who entertained Andrásfalva sharecropping bands during seasonal labor. As a master of ceremonies at wakes, he compiled a handwritten *Book of the Dead*, also including tales to be useful for the diversion of mourners. In terms of content, Aunt Zsuzsa's text follows the early Székely version of János Kriza (1863), adapted by Benedek's storybook, but stylistically she has completely recreated the tale to fit the social and economic conditions and peasant ideology of her time.

There is a momentary hesitation at the beginning, as the hero's characterization accords with both the lazy simpleton (AT 510) and the strong boy (AT 650) as they are typically presented in folktales, but soon it becomes clear that for Mrs. Palkó the tale is about the life-and-death struggle between the poor and the rich, the weak and the powerful. To the outsider, Józsi is a lazy dog, a passive good-for-nothing who cannot even fend for himself until a fairy marries him. He does not move a finger, he only complains and feels distressed; the fairy does everything for him. She is the driving force behind the action. Why should Józsi deserve so much, why does he become the embodiment of superior morality and why did the Lord use him to set an example and teach mankind a lesson? In the philosophy of this tale, deprivation in and of itself is sufficient to make Józsi a candidate for a folktale career. Left without a family, without means and hope for survival, Józsi is an ideal tale hero. As a serf, he owes free services to the local nobleman, he is taxed for his bare existence: a dwelling, a plot to grow crops and a permit to fish on the land of the squire. Serfdom was abolished in Hungary in 1848, but the feudal-patriarchal relationship between master and servant persisted because of the economic distance between the village poor and the landed nobility. This social and labor relationship supplies the ideological base for the tale. In the duel of squire and serf Mrs. Palkó employs a masterful reversal to restore justice and secure a satisfying resolution for the tale. The fairy's helpers perform the impossible tasks ordered by the squire while Józsi is asleep. But fulfilling the final, outrageous, sacrilegious command—inviting the Lord for lunch—backfires. Not Józsi, but the squire must fulfill the final impossible task, the condition set by Christ: to accept the invitation. But the squire has no fairy wife, and cannot deliver. His greed, envy, desire for his neighbor's wife, cowardice, and, above all, disrespect of the Lord bring about his downfall. On the other hand, Józsi's humility, the fairy's preparation of the food the squire failed to offer, earns divine approval, answering the common prayer Hungarians recite before meal: "Come, Jesus, be our guest, Bless what you have given us."

Tape recorded in 1950 at Mrs. Palkó's home.

———

Once upon a time, beyond seven times seven lands, there lived a poor man. His name was Józsi the Fisherman. He was so poor that all he had to his name was a small cottage and a few nets with which he went fishing every day. They called him Józsi the Fisherman for fishing provided his livelihood. He had a young son who was so lazy that he never wanted to do anything. He just passed the time, went out into the street, and there he stayed playing in the dust. Yet he was getting to be quite big. His father always said to him:

"Oh, my dear son, what will become of you when I die? You never want to do any work. You see, I am getting old and fishing is becoming too much for me."

And the boy answered: "Don't worry, dear father, there will be time for me to work once you are dead."

Well, the boy didn't want to work, but the poor man went fishing every day; every third day he caught a fish or two, and they lived on that all day. It went on like this for a long time.

Then one day Józsi the Fisherman said: "Wife, I feel I am going to die; I am very ill. What will happen to you when I go?"

"Well, I don't know what will happen, but it won't be good."

The poor man died that day and they buried him. They were so poor that they had nothing to eat. Then the woman became ill, and she, too, died. Józsi was left alone. But even then he didn't shape up, he just returned to sit by the side of the road and puttered around in the dust. Well, the women were kind-hearted—many times they felt sorry for him and brought him a piece of bread or two. But when they realized that not for anything would he go to work, and all he ever did was laze about, they became angry and decided not to bring him any more bread. Once he really got very hungry, he would find work and earn something, they thought. And that is what happened. Józsi had nothing to eat. So, all of a sudden, one day he looked for the creel and the net left by his father, put them on his shoulder and he went off to the water. He stepped into it, cast his net, drew it out, but all he caught was a frog. He cast it again, pulled it out—still nothing.

"It would have been better if I had gone with my father at least once; I would have learned how to fish."

He cast the net for a third time: "Maybe I'll strike it lucky." He cast the net and drew it out. This time he caught a fine goldfish, it was beautiful. He gazed at it, the little fish was bouncing around in the bottom of his net. Then Józsi grabbed it, put it in his hat and carried it home. He carried it home, placed it into a bowl and said: "Well, little fish, I'll take you to the squire and offer you to him as a present. He'll be happy and perhaps he'll exempt me from three days of labor or so, from what I owe him."

But as he put it in a bowl and was about to go out the door, the little fish spoke up: "Józsi, don't take me anywhere! One good turn deserves another!"

So Józsi put the bowl down, and the little fish flipped around and turned into such a beautiful fairy maiden that *one could sooner look at the sun than at her.*

She said: "Well, Józsi, I'll be your wife. *You are mine and I am yours, and nothing but death can part us.*"

This made Józsi very happy. He was so overjoyed at having such a beautiful wife that he didn't know what to do. But the thought that they had to eat, too, didn't occur to him, yet they had nothing, for they were very poor.

Then the fairy said to him: "Józsi, I am hungry. We should eat something."

"We should, sure, we should, I could eat too, but today I didn't go fishing so there is no food."

"Józsi, are you that poor? Hasn't your father left anything? Didn't you inherit from him?"

"All I have is the creel and the net."

"And what did you live on?" she asked.

"Well," he said, "my father went fishing every day, and every day he caught three fish, and three fish daily were sufficient for us."

"Why Józsi, didn't you have any land, or cattle, or anything?"

"We did have a *hectare* or so of land," he said, "but, do you see that big mountain? *It is as steep as the Calvary.* The land was never ploughed and only bird droppings were spread on it. It's not accessible by carriage, so it couldn't be cultivated, or fertilized, it's completely barren. It's very hard to climb up on that mountain, on that ladder."

"Still, let's go, the two of us, let's look at it."

"Let's go, I don't mind."

So they set out for the mountain together. They left in the morning and by nightfall they were at the top. But the mountain was so steep that Józsi had to scramble up on all fours. The fairy flew but Józsi got so tired that when they reached the peak, he threw himself on the ground. He said he needed to rest for he could hardly speak.

"Just lie down, Józsi, and rest!"

Józsi lay down and fell asleep immediately. The fairy got up and drew forth a lash, a big whip. She cracked it so hard that the mountain moved. And, God Almighty, there came the dragons, so many that they made the clouds turn black.

A fairy came forward and said: "What do you command, fairy princess?"

"I command that a castle appear on top of this mountain, and that it be *fastened to the sky with three gold chains.* It should have three hundred windows and one hundred and fifty doors. But the hinges must all be made of gold and the handles all of diamonds. And everything that belongs in a castle, all kinds of furniture, should be there, and the castle should be decorated as befits a king."

"Now then," she said, "lie down, fairy princess, and go to sleep!"

Józsi hadn't awakened yet. The fairy princess lay down to rest, too.

When she woke, she was in such a splendid castle that *her eyes nearly popped out* and her mouth fell open. She couldn't stop marveling and staring at all the beauty. She quickly walked through one room, then inspected all the others. Each was filled with furniture, bedding, pictures, and was beautifully decorated. She would have gladly sat there for a week without eating, just looking around.

Then Józsi woke up. He opened his eyes, rubbed them and rubbed them, and kept looking and staring.

He said: "Are you here, my angel?"

"Can't you see me? I am here, beside you."

"I don't know whether I am dreaming or awake, I don't know where I am," he said, "in a castle—or where am I? When did this castle come to be here?"

"Never mind when it came to be. You know that when you lay down, you lay on barren ground," she said, "and where did you wake up? This is ours, God gave this to us."

"Praise the Lord," said Józsi, "then I must be king. It seems that now that I am next to the queen, I am king."

Well, they were happy in the castle. All the fairy had to do was think, and by magic they immediately had cakes and roasts and whatever else was best in the world; one thing was fancier than the other. *The table was so laden that its legs were bent from the weight of the food.* There was wine and a great variety of drinks.

"Come, Józsi, sit down and let's eat!"

They sat down, ate, drank, rejoiced together, and chatted. Then Józsi said: "Oh, my beloved, I would very much like to invite the squire. I'd like to invite him for the midday meal on Sunday."

"Józsi, I see that this would please you, but I am telling you that if the squire sets foot in here, I will no longer be yours."

"Well, how?"

"You'll see how."

"Do you think that he can take you from me, that I'd lend you to him? Never! *You are mine until death do us part.*"

"I know that I am yours until death do us part, but if you have the squire come here I won't be yours any longer. Still," she said, "if that's your pleasure, invite him. But I will not sit down in the room with you when the squire is here. I'll set everything out on the table as it should be, and then I'll hide. I'll get out of his way, so he doesn't get to see me."

"All right, wife, and you'll come out from hiding once he is gone."

So Józsi went and invited the squire.

"Józsi, where do you want me to come for the midday meal? To that little shack of yours, to that pen?"

Because he was such a poor lad, all he had was a small cottage.

Józsi said: "Never mind where, sir. Come to where my father left me the *hectare* of land. That's where I live. Look around and see where I live, where the castle stands."

The squire thought that he was getting confused.

"Well, all right, I'll come, Józsi. If that's what you have, I'll come."

"Please do."

Then he went home and told his wife that the squire had accepted. So they watched and waited for him to arrive.

All of a sudden, Józsi came running and said: "He is coming in a carriage. How he'll make it up this mountain, I don't know, but he is coming."

"So then let him come."

The fairy set out everything on the table as it was fitting, all kinds of food and drink in profusion.

"And now," she said, "I'll go into the adjoining room and won't come out as long as the squire is here."

All right. Józsi watched the squire come in through the gate. The fairy retired into the other room and drew the curtains shut so he wouldn't see her.

Well, when the squire entered, he shook his head:

"My God, when was this beautiful castle built here?"

"It wasn't built long ago, you wouldn't have seen it before."

"And who built it?"

"Well, I did."

"How?"

"The way God willed it. God gave it to me, never mind how. I invited you for a meal and your business is to eat and drink as much as you can. But when I built it and who built it, shouldn't be your concern."

"Oh my! Aren't you a proud one, Józsi!"

"I am not proud at all."

They ate and drank and the squire became so inebriated that he was barely conscious. He staggered about.

Then he said: "Józsi, where is the wife?"

"My wife left home."

"Well now, you invited a guest, so why didn't she stay?"

"She doesn't want to be here when we have a guest," he said. "She prefers for us to be only the two of us, so when a guest comes, she leaves home."

"All right, Józsi, we ate and drank and have partaken of everything, it is time for me to go home."

"Stay a while longer, squire."

"I won't stay," he said, "night is closing in and I am drunk. I might tip over, fall down somewhere."

"So if you fall down," he said, "you'll get up."

"Better not," he said, "do you know what? I am going home now."

They went out; Józsi helped to harness the horses and sat him into the carriage. But he was so drunk that he swayed back and forth. The fairy queen glanced out the window for she thought she would go down in the front, once the squire had left. She looked out and the squire caught sight of the fairy. He became desperately enamored of her, deathly sick with love, as soon as he saw her. But he went home. He was so ill that he had to be lifted off the carriage. They took him inside, placed him on the bed and asked him repeatedly what was ailing him.

"I am so ill that I'll die."

He had some masons working for him outside in the yard, some men. They were very surprised that the squire hadn't been out for two days to inspect their work. It was his habit to go and see several times a day how they were progressing. But now he hadn't been to check whether they were working or sitting around; he hadn't gone to see. They were very astonished.

"I'll go find out what's going on with the squire, why he doesn't come out to us."

"Go!"

He went in and saw that the squire was so ill that he had turned blue all over.

"What is wrong with you, squire? We were wondering why you don't come out to us, as you always do. Are you that ill?"

"I am," he said, "I feel my end is near."

"Then let us go and get a doctor so he may revive you."

"To bring a doctor would be of no use," he said, "don't bring him, he wouldn't help me."

"Well, what's the matter?"

"I won't tell you, for you can't ease my troubles."

"Just the same, tell us what is the matter—maybe we can help!"

"That scoundrel, Józsi the Fisherman, invited me for a midday meal. He has such a beautiful wife that I fell desperately in love with her, though I only caught a glimpse of her through the window. I am so sick at heart that I'll die if she cannot be mine."

Said the mason: "Sir, is there no way that she could be yours?"

"How could she be when she is his wife? To take someone else's wife is not lawful."

"That's not what I am suggesting, squire. Give him a task he wouldn't be able to fulfill, and tell him that if he can't, you'll take his wife and his castle. If he can't accomplish it, it would be your right to take them."

"So what can I ask that he wouldn't be able to do?"

"Summon him and tell him: 'Józsi, my son, I am telling you to build a golden bridge by tomorrow morning, spanning from my castle to your castle. The bridge must be pure shining gold and its railings made of diamonds. Alongside the golden bridge there should be a—what do they say, what do they call it—a *paved road*, lined with trees on either side, and on the trees there should be birds of many varieties, so that when a man goes down that road he should weep and spring to dance at once. It must all be finished by eight o'clock, and if it's not, I'll take your wife and all your possessions.'"

Józsi felt very sad. He started on his way home, his head sunk down to his knees. But his wife was looking for him and she saw how grief-stricken Józsi was. When he reached home, she said to him:

"What's the matter with you, Józsi? Why are you so sad?"

"How could I not be?" he said. "Here is what the squire ordered me to do. That by tomorrow morning I should build a bridge, spanning from my castle to his castle. It should be pure gold, down to the last beam, and the two sides should be made of diamonds. There should be a paved road alongside the bridge, starting from the gate, it should be lined with two rows of trees, and all kinds of birds should be singing on them. Well, how can I accomplish all this?"

"Don't be sad, Józsi; just lie down and go to sleep!"

Józsi lay down, his wife had comforted him. When he woke in the morning, he was nearly struck dead when he saw that from his castle to the squire's castle such a bridge had been built that one could barely look at it, for *one's eyes would pop out*. A beautiful *paved road* was there, with a row of trees on either side, and the birds sang so enchantingly that—he swung into a dance, and the travelers began to dance, too.

"Well, it's ready."

When the squire rose and saw it, he became even more ill. He was so ill that at dawn they had to run for the doctor, but he didn't help at all.

Said the squire: "Now I am sure to die. That dogcatcher accomplished this, too. So," he said, "I cannot have his wife and I'll die of it."

"Not so, squire," said one of the masons. "You must give him another task, one that he won't be able to complete."

"What more can I tell him to do? If he was able to accomplish this, he will fulfill the other tasks, too."

"Well," he said, "summon Józsi and tell him: 'there, next to the castle is an enormous rocky mountain.' Tell him to remove that mountain overnight so that the ground in its place is level. He should plough, plant the land with vines; the grapes on them should grow and ripen so that by eight o'clock in the morning they can be pressed into wine. And the wine should be ready so that when you wake up at eight o'clock, it should be there in a glass, on the table. This he surely cannot do, and then," he said, " his wife will be yours."

Oh, the squire was happy, he liked the idea so much that his condition improved. He summoned Józsi and told him. Józsi became very alarmed. How could he accomplish this?

"Look, Józsi, it is your concern what you do and how you do it. It must be done and if it isn't, I'll take your wife away and even your castle will be mine."

He went home, his heart filled with sorrow. His wife saw him.

"What's the matter with you, Józsi?"

"Look," he said, "what he told me. Something that is surely impossible to do. He told me to level this big, rocky mountain in one night, and that its place should be as smooth as the top of a table. I should plough it, plant it with vines—and the grapes should grow and ripen so that by eight o'clock in the morning there should be wine on his table. How can this be done?"

"Never mind, Józsi, don't grieve; just go to sleep!"

She made him lie down. In the morning they rose. The squire rose too, and the wine was there beside him, on the table. He looked out the window, there were real grapes in such abundance that they were sinking to the ground. Like suckling pigs, the grapes dangled on the teats, on the things, in clusters.

"Oh, my God," he said, "this, too, was of no use."

He wasn't glad to have the vineyard. He grieved that he would now die, for Józsi's wife couldn't be his.

"Well," he said, "now I'll die, that is certain. Even this he was able to accomplish. There is nothing else I can think of, so I must die."

Said the mason: "You must give him one more task. Thrice is better than twice. If he fulfills that too, then I'll also say that it is to no avail. But I don't believe he can make good on this one."

"What?"

"Let him come here."

He summoned Józsi.

"What is your wish, squire?" he said.

"My wish is that you should go up to Heaven and invite Saint Peter and Christ the Lord to come to me tomorrow for a midday meal. If you don't do it, and if you don't bring Them, I'll take your wife and all your possessions."

Well, Józsi was very upset. This was really impossible to accomplish.

"It is your worry. All I say is that if you don't do it, I'll take your wife and everything you own."

He wept and wept so hard that his handkerchief was soaking wet from his tears by the time he arrived home.

His wife said: "What's the matter, Józsi?"

"Oh, my God, if only I had listened to you and hadn't invited him for a meal. You told me that if I invited him you won't be mine. All the crafty squire wants is to separate me from you. Now he said that if I don't bring Saint Peter and Christ our Lord over on Sunday for the midday meal, he'll take you and everything I have to my name. Now, how can this be done? How can anyone get into Heaven if he hasn't died? How can one get in there before?"

"Never mind, don't worry Józsi, just lie down and go to sleep!"

Józsi lay down and fell asleep. The fairy queen drew forth the whip and cracked it three times, so loud that the noise made even the earth tremble. All of a sudden the dragons appeared, swooshing through the air. She stepped in front of them.

"What is your command, fairy princess?" said the head-dragon.

"I command that you take Józsi up to Heaven so he can invite Saint Peter and Christ our Lord for the midday meal on Sunday."

Right away the largest dragon came forward:

"Climb up on my back, but shut your eyes!"

Józsi mounted on the dragon's back, closed his eyes and the dragon carried him, zooming through the air at great speed. In one second they reached the gates of Heaven. He jumped off, went up to the gate and knocked.

Saint Peter called out: "Who is there?"

"It's me, Józsi the Fisherman."

"What do you want?"

"Open the gates and let me in!"

"Oh, my dear Józsi the Fisherman, it is difficult to get in here. A sinner cannot get into Heaven; he is not allowed in. It's not as easy to get into Heaven as you think."

"Then send Christ our Lord out here so I can speak to Him!"

"That I can do. I'll send Him out."

Christ our Lord knew well that Józsi was coming, so He went to the gate:

"What do you want, Józsi?"

"The squire sent me," he said, "to invite You and Saint Peter for the midday meal, tomorrow, Sunday."

He said: "Yes, Yes, Józsi, my son, go back and tell the squire that we'll come. We'll come but he must plough a *hectare* of land, sow it with barley and draw a harrow over it. The barley must sprout, grow and ripen. He should harvest it, take it to the mill, have it ground into flour and there should be barley bread on the table for the midday meal when we get there. We'll come, for sure, but everything must be the way I said."

"All right then," said Józsi, "all right, I'll tell him."

He mounted on the dragon's back, and, *"hip-hop, take me where I want to be, to my home,"* and he was there. He went to report to the squire that he spoke to Them and They said They'd come. They'll come for sure, but some things the squire must do. He must plough a *hectare* of land, sow it with barley, the barley must grow, be mowed down, taken to the mill and ground, and there should be warm barley bread on the table when They arrive.

Oh, was the squire alarmed!

"I cannot accomplish this," he said. "Tell me, how can this be done? So quickly, in such a short time, how can barley bread be produced for the table? No human being is capable of this."

"Well, this is your worry. I gave you Their message. I'll go home now."

The squire didn't know what to do. He was tearing his hair out and scratching the skin off his face. Why did he send him to Heaven—now God had set a task for him to accomplish. Right away he called in the masons:

"See what you taught me, what you encouraged me to do? That I should invite Saint Peter and Christ our Lord, for a midday meal. And now, look what he said. Can this be done? It is impossible to produce bread in one night, when the field hasn't even been ploughed yet. This cannot be done."

Józsi went home. When he left there was nothing alongside his castle. When he returned, there was a plot of land, a field of barley, so beautifully ripe that it had turned rosy. They mowed it, took it to the mill and by morning they had baked a loaf of barley bread. From that barley, at Józsi's. But this the squire didn't know. Had he known, he would have taken it from him. But he didn't know.

Meanwhile they were discussing what should be done, how it should be done. If They come and he is not ready, what should he do?

Said the squire: "Do you know what? One of you should go up into the tower and watch when They are approaching. The other should lock up the poultry, the dogs and whatever else there is, and lock the stables. Clean up everything, lock up the pigeons too, they mustn't fly around, and bolt the iron gates, so They can't enter. Or else we are in trouble, if They come and what He had ordered hasn't been done. Even the flies should be hiding and no one should be visible, as if the castle were abandoned. This way, maybe They'll turn away—otherwise They won't.

They locked away everything: the chickens, the ducks, bolted everything and concealed themselves. One of them went up into the tower so he could see when They were coming. The squire hid somewhere else.

Then, all of a sudden, he called down from the tower that They are coming, They are coming.

"So, let Them come, They cannot get in, the big gate is locked."

They reached the gate, Peter pressed down on the handle and said:

"This is locked. Almighty God, it is locked!"

"Never mind, let it be locked. We'll return home, let it be locked."

They turned around and started on Their way back. They walked, and when They were half way, near Józsi's, Peter looked behind him and said:

"Oh, my God, the entire castle, the squire's, is engulfed in flames! Oh dear, it will burn down and everyone in it will be incinerated!"

"Let it be, let them burn. They don't deserve anything else. Such an envious man deserves no better."

For he was an envious man—the devil of envy had taken hold of his heart. "All he wanted was to rob this man of his wife and of all his possessions. An envious person," He said, "deserves nothing else."

They continued on their way. As They went, Józsi the Fisherman came running to meet Them and fell to his knees.

"Dear God Almighty," he said, "I wonder if You'd visit our castle? Come in for a meal!"

They went in. The table was beautifully set. The barley bread, all brown, was there, along with many different things, white bread too, for the fairy made anything they desired appear by magic. They sat down nicely and ate.

Said Christ our Lord: "Well, Józsi, he was always envious, he envied your possessions and your life. But, I've put an end to that, he won't envy you any more."

"How did that happen?"

"It happened because they burned. Anything and everything he had, burned. They concealed themselves from Me, so let them remain concealed. But you," He said, "you have always conducted yourself well, and that you must continue to do! And don't forget God; He will bestow His grace and His blessings on you in abundance."

With these words Christ our Lord and Saint Peter went on Their way. And Józsi the Fisherman and his wife are ruling in their castle to this day, if they haven't died. This is the end of the story; there is no more to it.

# 10. The Sky-High Tree

AT 468 (*The Princess of the Sky-Tree*) + 302 (*The Ogre's Heart in the Egg*); the MNK classifies this type as AT 317 (*The Stretching Tree*), and identifies 40 variants that show great diversity in combining type and episode clusters of related hero tales. The most consistent element of this tale is its frame-story, in which the hero climbs up the tree to rescue the stolen princess. According to regional and ethnic preferences, this type may include, precede or follow other tales. In the Hungarian language territory the tree-climbing episode emerges as an ethnic core element originating in proto-Hungarian shamanistic belief and practice. It appears sporadically also among Hungary's immediate neighbors, in Ukrainian, Slovakian, Romanian, Gypsy, Serbian, Bosnian, Croatian, Slovenian, Austrian, and ethnic German variants, but it did not enter the broader bloodstream of European magic tale tradition (Dégh 1978).

Aunt Zsuzsa learned this tale from her father, János Zaicz. Her version, a combination of AT 468 and 302, occurs only five times in recorded Hungarian tradition. Her performance, at her home in 1948, was smooth and well proportioned but without new formulations. Her application of formulas and repetition of episodes is notable but the liveliest and best is the princess' strategic maneuvering to persuade the dragon to tell her where his strength is located.

––––––

Once upon a time, beyond the seven seas, there was a king who had a beautiful wife. She was so beautiful that . . . that no one in the whole wide world had a wife as beautiful as his. They had a very lovely daughter, who was just like her mother. They rejoiced in her and loved her dearly.

When the little girl was of school age, her mother became ill and died. The king was so grief-stricken that he didn't eat, didn't sleep, just mourned his wife day and night. But his daughter kept comforting him:

"You know well that *we don't come into this world together and we don't leave it together.* We must accept the will of God!"

The king reflected for a while: "My God, how young this little girl is, I mustn't weep so much, for my tears cannot resurrect my wife."

He said, "My dear daughter, I can tell you that I'll never take another wife, for I wouldn't find anyone like your mother. There is no one like her, so I'd rather stay as I am."

Said the girl: "My dear father, don't remain as you are. I won't be here forever, and then what will you do, all alone?"

The king said: "I don't mind, my daughter, but I will not take a wife again, I'd rather stay like this, a widower."

The girl said: "Well, dear father, then I won't marry either. I won't leave you in your great sorrow."

The king had a flower garden. There wasn't another as beautiful as his, perhaps in the entire world. All the varieties of flowers that existed were in that garden. Fragrant flowers, one more beautiful than the other, and in the center of the garden there was such a tall tree that its crown reached to the sky. One day the princess went for a walk in the garden.

As she strolled about, she thought: My God, why would I want to get married? I'll never find a flower garden anywhere as beautiful as the one I have.

No sooner had she spoken these words than such a big wind started up that she thought the tree would be uprooted and topple over. The gust of wind snatched up the princess and lifted her up to the top of the tree. But no one saw that the girl had disappeared. Her father waited for her—it was time, so he expected her to come home. She didn't come. He sent the cook after her—still she didn't come. The cook searched every nook and cranny in the flower garden but couldn't find her anywhere. He sent the soldiers into town to comb the streets and they didn't find her. The king didn't know what more he could do, so he posted an announcement that his daughter was lost—if anyone knew of her whereabouts, they should let him know. But it was all to no avail. Now the king wept for his daughter all the time and his heart nearly broke. He summoned his advisers so they could tell him what he should do. How could he find out where his daughter was? But no one was able to guess where she could be.

One night when the king lay down and dozed off, he saw in his dream that during the windstorm on Saturday, the whirlwind caught the girl and carried her up to the top of the tall tree. She was now in the castle of the dragon with twenty-four heads. This is what he saw in his dream and when he woke he said, "My God, this dream is a sign."

The king issued a proclamation that if a knight came forward who would bring his daughter down from the top of the tree, he would give her to him in marriage, and he would bestow on him half of his kingdom, and— after his death—his entire realm.

To be sure, when the announcement was made, they all came, sons of kings, princes, barons, and handsome knights with stately bearing, as straight as a burning candle. They all came, one after the other, and said they would bring the princess down. But there was not one lad among them able to scale that tree. They climbed up to a certain height but they all fell down—one broke his arm, another his leg, yet another his neck. Oh, was the king unhappy! He wept all the time, grieving that no one was able to climb up the tree and he would never see his daughter again.

The king had a swineherd, a young boy, tending the pigs. He could have been fifteen or sixteen years old. His name was Jánoska. He took the pigs out into the woods.

One day, when he was out with them, feeling very sad—for he, too, was sorry for the princess—Jánoska stopped at a tree and leaned on his herdsman's crook. He stood there musing, then he said:

"Oh well, the dear, kind-hearted princess is lost. We won't see her any more."

Suddenly a little pig came up to him and said:

"Jánoska, don't be sad, you'll bring the princess down."

Jánoska looked at the little pig; until now he hadn't heard it speak.

"What are you saying, little pig? This is idle talk."

It said: "It isn't idle talk, Jánoska, just listen to me. Go to the king and tell him that you'll bring her down, and then he'll give you his daughter in marriage. But before you start climbing up after the girl, you must tell the king: 'Great King, I'll bring her down, but first I ask you to have the buffalo cow slaughtered and from its hide seven pairs of loafers and seven sets of clothes made for me, and when they are worn out, I'll be back.'"

Said the little pig: "János, I am also telling you that when you climb up on the trunk of the tree, you'll reach a thin branch, a branch so long that it stretches one and a half times around the world, but so thin that you have to crawl along on it. If you can get to the end of that branch, you'll surely be able to make it to the top of the tree. But be careful not to fall off, for if you do, even your bones will be shattered to smithereens. Then you'll come to where the leaves begin—before that point there are no leaves on the tree. The leaves are so large that each one holds an entire country. Once you are there, you can be confident that you'll get the princess, that you'll find her."

He thanked the little pig for its good advice and the same evening went to see the king. He sank to his knees and greeted him respectfully.

"Now then," said the king, "what's on your mind, my son?"

"Great King, if it doesn't offend you, I have a request to make."

"What is it, Jánoska, just say it!"

"Your Majesty, if you permit me, I'll go after the princess to the top of the tree and bring her down."

The king, who never even smiled since his wife died, burst out laughing.

"Oh, Jánoska, Jánoska, what excuse for an idea have you brought before me?"

"The idea that I'll climb up and bring her down—just give me your permission."

"My God," said the king, "all those valiant knights couldn't make it, and a boy like you wants to bring her down?"

"That is my concern; just say that I have your permission."

"Well, my son, you came this far, I'll permit you to go, but if you fall off, you'd better die on the spot, for if you fall, I'll kill you then and there for having been so insistent."

"Then, Your Majesty, if I have your permission, have the buffalo cow slaughtered and have them make seven pairs of loafers and seven sets of clothes from its hide.

God willing, I'll still be wearing them when I return and bring the princess home."

So the king had the buffalo cow slaughtered and ordered seven suits of clothes and seven pairs of loafers made for him.

When they were ready, Jánoska put on the clothes and bundled together whatever else he needed to take with him. The king packed some provisions for his journey, so he wouldn't want for food or drink.

Said the king: "Well, Jánoska, may God be with you. May you return with my daughter, for then you'll be fortunate, too."

Many people had gathered to witness the miracle of him climbing the tree. Huge crowds came to see how he would do it. Jánoska always carried an ax with him, so he took it and when he came to the foot of the tree, he planted it in the trunk and climbed like a cat, but first he said farewell to the world, down below him. Then he pulled out the ax and planted it higher up. The trunk of the tree was very tall—it took him a long time to reach the branches. That's why it was so hard to climb. So he kept pulling out the ax and planting it higher and higher until he reached the branches of the tree. Then in a minute or two Jánoska was lost in them—he could no longer be seen from the ground. He climbed up and up and up until he came to the long branch, the one the little pig had mentioned.

"Oh well," he said, "the little pig was right—it's difficult to crawl out here!"

The branch was very thin. He couldn't walk on it, so he lay on his belly and crept like a worm. When he came to the end of the bare part of the branch, he stood up, closed his eyes and said: "Good-bye, world"—and, like a frog, he leaped across onto a leaf. He got very tired. He rested a little, and when he felt restored, he looked around and said:

"My God, there is the same world here as down on earth. They plough and sow, there are cities, even twenty-story buildings." He walked and ambled along but didn't meet anyone, not a single soul, yet the city was very beautiful. Then, as he passed in front of big, multi-story buildings, observing this and that and looking right and left, he heard a voice:

"What are you doing here, Jánoska?"

The voice came from an upper story—it was the princess, asking him where he was going.

"I am looking for you, princess."

The princess said: "Ssh, quiet! My husband must not hear, or he'll kill you. Come upstairs."

She came out to meet him and ushered him in.

"Come in—my husband isn't at home, I can talk with you a little until he returns. Oh, Jánoska, do you know that my husband is the twenty-four-headed dragon? If he learns that you came to take me back, it'll be the end of you. What is my dear father doing?"

"God knows what he is doing," he said, "he is forever weeping. His eyes never dry for all the tears he is shedding."

He told her quickly how many princes had tried to come up after her, but none had succeeded. The king had promised that he who brings her down will receive her in marriage.

He said: "So I tried, too, and God helped me to get here. But I am not going down without you. I'll take you with me."

"Please, Jánoska, be quiet, don't let the dragon hear you say this."

Right away she set food and drink before him and bid him to partake of both.

"Now, Jánoska, I say to you that I'll hide you, so my husband won't find you here when he comes home." And she hid him under a washtub. "First I'll tell him who is here, for he is very nervous, then I'll have you come out from hiding."

Soon the dragon came. But he came with such force that when he was still seven miles away, he hurled his club forward and the gate sprang wide open.

"János, he is near, he's already hurled his club forward."

He entered, roaring: "What is this strange smell in here? Who was here? I could smell it from the road that there was a stranger here."

"Oh," she said, "don't be angry, my dear husband. Our herdsman came up from the earth down below. He came looking for me for he was sorry not to see me, and he wants to continue in my service here."

"Well, where is he? Let him come forward!"

"I'll let him, but don't hurt the poor man, he came to continue in my service."

She raised the washtub and bade János to come out. The dragon stepped in front of him, looked him over, snapped him up with his mouth and swallowed him. He gobbled him up and spat him out, snapped him up again, swallowed him, then spat him out. He did this three times.

"Well, you came here to serve your queen, *but I'll see whether you are worth your keep or only half.* And now sit down and eat with me!"

Jánoska ate and drank. When the dragon had finished eating and drinking they went out to the stables. He showed him his horses and his cattle and what had to be done.

Among the horses, in the back, in a corner, lay a colt. It was so scrawny that it couldn't stand up, so weak that it couldn't disentangle its legs. And the other horses were so fat that they nearly burst.

Said the dragon to Jánoska: "You know, Jánoska, you must feed, water and curry these horses. But the colt lying over there doesn't need to be curried and it shouldn't get the same feed as the others. *When it wants hay, you give it oats, when it wants oats you give it water*, but never give it what it asks for."

And so he showed him everything. Jánoska stayed in the stable and the dragon went back in.

Well, the days passed, one after the other. The young man had already been there for a month, always on his best behavior and doing what the dragon ordered. He trusted him so much that he stopped telling him what to do. Jánoska took care of everything as if he had been born there. The dragon was very pleased—the lad did all that needed to be done.

One day the dragon went hunting and Jánoska was in the stable, feeding the animals. He stopped and stood behind the scrawny colt:

"Poor colt, why are you so scrawny? You can't even stand up, you poor thing!"

Suddenly the colt spoke: "Jánoska, I see that you have a kind heart. Now there is no time to talk, but I'll tell you more later."

There was no time, for the dragon soon came home. He looked at everything and found that all was in order. He liked Jánoska; he ate with them at the table. The following day the dragon left again and Jánoska went to the stable to attend to the cattle.

Then the colt spoke once more: "Jánoska, I see that you are a kind-hearted lad. I know why you came. It's difficult to take the princess back from here, you know. But if you listen to me," he said, "you'll be lucky. Look, Jánoska, tomorrow is Sunday. Now go inside and tell the princess that she should use guile and sweet talk and find out from her husband where he keeps his strength. She should keep asking him, though he will not want to tell her—but she should cajole him, somehow draw it out of him, and then you must come and tell me!"

And that is how it happened. Jánoska went in and said to the queen: "Your Majesty, Princess, I say to you that you should find out from your husband where he keeps his strength. Your Majesty, I say to you that if you want to see your father again, you must find out from your husband where he keeps his strength."

"Oh, Jánoska, this will be difficult to do, he will not tell me," she said—but she promised to use flattery and honeyed words to get it out of him.

Then the dragon came—he hurled the club ahead of him with such force that the gate ripped open. Seven yard-long flames billowed out of his throat as he was approaching. She gave him supper and they ate and drank. The following day he left again.

The dragon's wife said to him: "My beloved, don't go hunting today, rest up at home. I am always alone, it is weighing on me. I wish you'd stay home with me for a day."

She bent over and began caressing him, showing him sympathy. The dragon became overjoyed—he thought she loved him. Yet she loved him as much as she loved manure, but there was nothing else she could do.

"My dear husband," she said, "if you are fair with me, you won't deny me if I ask you something."

"What, my dear wife? What do you want from me?"

"There is nothing else I want," she said, "merely to know where you keep your strength!"

"Oh, my dear wife, why would you want to know that? This never came up before and no one but me knows where my strength is."

"You won't even tell me? I am your wife."

"No, I won't. I'll tell you everything, but I won't tell you that."

Said the woman: "Then you don't really love me, that's why you don't tell me, for if you loved me more, you wouldn't deny me."

And the woman began to weep so her husband felt sorry for her: "Don't weep, my beloved," he said.

"How could I not weep, my dearest, when you just admitted that you don't truly love me."

"But of course I love you."

"If you loved me, you would tell it to me."

"Listen, my dear wife, this is a big secret, no one may know about it."

"I have always heard that when a woman weds a man, they become one, body and soul, so why do you conceal this from me?"

"Look, my dear wife—but no one must ever know!"

"Of course not! What kind of talk is this?"

"Well, I'll tell you where my strength is. There, in the forest, is a silver bear, and there is a stream, and every noon the bear goes to that stream to drink. If someone shot the bear and split its head in two, a boar would jump out. If someone shot that boar and split its head in two, a hare would jump out. And if someone shot the hare and split its head in two, a box would jump out. If someone smashed that box with two stones, they would find nine wasps. They are my strength. If the wasps were destroyed, I would have no more strength than a sick fly. That's why this is such a big secret and no one must know where I keep my strength."

"Well, well," said his wife and kissed him. "Oh, my beloved, you didn't want to tell me, yet there is no one in the whole world to whom I would betray you. And now, my dear husband, let's have a drink!"

She brought up a carafe of their strongest wine and they sat down.

"And now let's drink to your health!"

They filled their glasses and clinked them. The man emptied his in one gulp. The woman pretended to drink but poured her wine on the floor.

"So," said the man, "this time let's drink a glassful to your health."

They filled their glasses again. Her husband drank his, but the woman only pretended to drink—she emptied her glass in her bodice.

Then she said: "Let's drink to Jánoska's health too!"

When they finished drinking they chatted for a while, but the woman saw that her husband was a little drunk, for the wine they had was really strong. She said to him:

"My dear husband, let's have one more, to our long life!"

They drank that too and then the man keeled over, like a log, just fell down. He was fast asleep and snored loudly, lost to the world. Then the woman went out and called Jánoska:

"So, Jánoska, I found out where his strength is, I got it out of him."

Right away she told him. Whereupon Jánoska went to see the colt in the stable and said:

"I know where he keeps his strength. In the forest there is a silver bear who at midday goes to drink from the golden stream. If it could be shot there and its head split in two, a boar would jump out. If someone shot the boar and split its head in two, a hare would jump out, and if that hare were shot too, a box would drop out of its head. In that box are nine wasps, they are his strength. If someone smashed the box and destroyed the wasps, he would have no more strength left than a fly."

"Now then," said the colt, "Jánoska, go and light a cord of wood and when it burns down, bring me three shovelfuls of embers."

Jánoska ran and built a good fire. Once the cord of wood had burned down and became glowing embers, he took three shovelfuls to the colt. The colt swallowed them and when it was done it rose to its knees:

"And now let me out of the stable!"

He let the colt out and right away it gulped down all the remaining embers from the cord of wood, and when it finished, it turned into a golden-haired steed. Its hair was pure gold and it had five legs.

"Now, Jánoska, run to the cellar at once, you know where to find the key!"

"Yes, I know," he said.

"Run down into the cellar, you'll see hanging there a golden saddle and a set of golden clothes for you. Put them on quickly, bring up the saddle, fasten it onto my back, and take the sword, too, that is there, hanging from a nail!"

Jánoska did everything as he was told; he brought the saddle, the sword and got dressed in the suit of clothes.

"Now mount on my back and let's go!"

They took off and penetrated deep into the forest. The colt knew well where it wanted to go, it was familiar with the place. When they arrived, the bear was just drinking from the stream, then, having caught sight of them, it began to roar and charge in their direction.

Said the colt: "Have no fear, János, be brave!"

As the bear came close, the colt kicked it so hard with its fifth leg, that it fell to the ground. Jánoska leaped over and with his sword split the bear's head in two. He split the bear's head open and a boar jumped out. The boar attacked Jánoska, ready to kill him, but the colt with its fifth leg kicked it too, and it keeled over. Then Jánoska ran with his sword and split its head in two. A hare jumped out of it and started running, but the colt ran faster and kicked it so hard that it tumbled over. Jánoska cut its head open and the box sprang out. It bounded and skipped around but János took two large stones and smashed it to smithereens—nothing was left of it.

"Now," said the colt, "we can go home safely; there is nothing to fear."

They went home and found the dragon lying in the same spot where he had keeled over.

He said: "Jánoska, you took my strength away, didn't you? Never mind that you took it, but at least let me keep my life!"

"Sure, I'll let you keep it!"

Jánoska grabbed his sword and cut off all the dragon's twenty-four heads. That was the end of the dragon, he was dead.

"And now," said the colt, "tell me, János, what do you want? Do you want to be king in this country? You could be, if you so choose—it is all yours, but if you want to take the king's daughter home, you can do that too."

János said: "I thank you for offering me this land, but I have no desire to stay here. I am going home. I feel very sorry for the old king—I want to bring his daughter back."

"Well," said the colt, "if you want to bring her home, you may. Take from this treasure, this gold, as much as you can, there is plenty of it here. Then mount on my back, both of you, I'll take you."

Once they had mounted on its back, the colt said:

"Now close your eyes." They did, and before they had time to say *"hip-hop, take me where I want to be,"* they were already there, in the king's courtyard.

They went in. The old king was near death; he was about to die from all the sorrow. János went up to him and announced that he had returned:

"Great King, I brought back your beloved daughter for whom you were grieving so much."

He said: "Where is she?"

The king opened his eyes and the girl spoke up:

"Here I am, dear father."

She fell into her father's arms and the two of them, the three of them, wept in their happiness.

"Now, my son, János," he said, "you brought me my daughter, so henceforth you are the king of this land. I'll give you my daughter and my realm, I'll hand everything over to you."

No sooner had the king uttered these words and given his blessings than he died. János took the king's daughter for his wife and they are alive to this day, if they haven't died.

# 11. The Blackmantle

AT 505 (*Dead Man as Helper*); building on the affiliated European tale types AT 505-508, which focus on the rescue of an enchanted princess with the aid of a grateful dead man, Mrs. Palkó's version elaborates on the partnership of the living and the dead and its consequences. One may say that, compared to the well known European märchen—also popularized by the literary version of Hans Christian Anderson's "The Traveling Companions"—this is a fragment. The princess is not possessed by the devil; there is no diabolical riddle contest, with life-threatening consequence for the suitors who fail the test. Instead, in Mrs. Palkó's tale, the prince takes to the road to find a bride whose beauty is comparable to his mother's—a plot element signifying an incestuous relationship. The mother's ability to change colors like the rainbow—a mark of great beauty—is a feature that first appears in an early nineteenth-century Hungarian version of this tale.

The prince's travel is interrupted as he passes by a cemetery where he rescues a corpse from beatings and pays off its debts. This incident distracts the story from its normal course as a magic tale and leads it into the realm of legend. From this point forward, elements of the magic tale are perfunctorily summarized while, in contrast, the full-fledged legend develops from a matrix of local belief: the indigenous Bucovina Székely fear of the malevolent dead.

In the magic tale version (MNK 507), the dead man is benevolent: to share the princess (by cutting her in two) is to purify her, to cleanse her from the seeds of the devil. But Mrs. Palkó's narrative offers a religious lesson about dealing with evil spirits. One should not help those whom God has condemned; only a priest can perform the holy mass of exorcism to lay souls to rest.

Mrs. Palkó heard this tale long before it became part of her repertoire. In fact, she remembered it only in 1956, after I kept pressing her for more tales. Yet she could not recall her source, not even if it had been a part of the Andrásfalva tale stock; it seems never to have belonged among her favorites. She may have heard an incomplete version or, more likely, she reconstructed this legend from the rudiments of the tale. But, whatever the magic tale has lost, the legend has gained. Not only did she highlight the prince's struggle against the dead man with colorful dialogue and dramatic turns, she also transformed the story significantly, adapting it to the Kakasd belief system.

———

There was once a widowed queen who had a son. One day he said to her: "Mother, I'd like to take a wife."

"Well, my son, I don't mind," she said, "but only if you find a girl who is like me; otherwise I won't give you my permission." (For the queen had the power to change into seventy-seven different colors.) "She must be exactly like me: her height, her beauty, and everything about her must be the same—then you'll have my blessing."

"If this is your wish, dear mother, I'll set out tomorrow."

The next day he took leave of his mother, saddled a horse, mounted it, and took off on his journey. He rode day and night; he rode all the time and only stopped to feed his horse. Once, when night had set in and the road led alongside a cemetery, he heard the sound of pounding and beating, as if four people were threshing wheat. He halted and listened. It was night time—whom could they be beating in a cemetery? He waited for a while and walked into the cemetery. He saw that a grave was uncovered, a corpse was lying on the ground, and four men holding big stakes were hitting it with all their might.

The prince said to them: "What are you doing here, men?"

One of them answered: "We are beating the corpse."

"Why?" he asked. "Why don't you leave him in peace? He is dead."

"We are beating him," he said, "because he deserves it—that's why we're beating him."

"Why does he deserve it?" he said. "What do the dead know?"

"We'll tell you, Your Majesty," he said. "In his lifetime this man owed money to the entire village. He made debts but never paid them. He had borrowed from the whole village but didn't pay anyone. He owed us, too," he said, "and now we'll beat him until we beat the money out of him."

He said: "Look, leave this man alone—let him rest in peace. He can't pay you back any more. Tell me what he owed you."

The man told him: "He owed me this much."

The next one said: "To me, this much"—and the next: "This much is what he owed me."

Said the prince: "I'll pay you the money, the debt he owed you, but put the coffin back in the grave and let the man have his peace!"

So they replaced the coffin, covered the grave, threw the stakes on top and left. The prince gave them the money—even more than the man owed them—mounted his horse and continued on his way. He rode for some time in such darkness that when he raised his finger he couldn't see it. Suddenly he heard a voice. He looked here and there, left and right—he couldn't see anyone. Yet someone was talking. He rode on—the voice was still there.

Then he said: "Who are you? Who is there? I can't see you but I hear you talking."

Came the answer: "Don't you know me? It's me," he said, "the one you saved from the beating, for whom you paid."

"How can that be?" he said. "You are dead. How did you get out of the grave?"

"I wanted to," he answeered. "I wanted to come with you to pay you back for what you did for me."

Said the man: "I didn't give you a loan; I paid them off so that they would leave you alone and let you rest."

"Still, I want to come with you. I know where you are going and I know why. I'll go with you—I'll be your companion."

This didn't please the prince. He was afraid—he knew the man was dead.

"Look, don't bother to accompany me," he said, "go back to where you came from; I don't fear being alone!"

"Listen," he said, "I know the purpose of your journey, and I also know where you can find the girl you are looking for. I'll help you."

The prince saw that it was no use insisting, that the man wouldn't go back, so he relented. But he said: "How is it that I can't see you? I hear you talk, but I don't see you."

He said: "I have a blackmantle—when I put it on, no one can see me."

They continued their journey until they came to a large *capital city*.

He said: "Here we are in this *capital city*. Here you'll find the girl you are looking for."

They stopped in front of a palace, and he said:

"This is where she is. She is the king's daughter. Go inside—I'll wait for you here. Go and discuss the matter, explain why you came. Then come and tell me what the king said."

And that's how it was. The prince went in, greeted the king politely and paid homage to him. He told him of his intentions, that he would like to ask for his daughter's hand in marriage.

Said the king: "Look, son, several young men wanted my daughter, but not one succeeded in winning her. You, too, you'll succeed only if you descend into the chamber of the Red Sea and there you find a pair of shoes; if you bring them back, you may have my daughter. But so far not a single lad has been able to bring them."

The prince left and told the ghost what the king had said to him.

Said the ghost: "Don't worry, prince, I'll get them for you—you just stay here! Don't come with me," he said, "I'll go on my own."

So the ghost left and in less than a quarter of an hour he was back. He brought the shoes and handed them to the prince.

"Go, take them to the king and give them to him!"

The prince went in and announced that he had the shoes.

"All right, son, but I won't give you my daughter until you descend into the chamber of the White Sea and bring the wedding gown from there," he said.

The lad returned to the ghost and told him.

"Don't worry, I'll get it for you," he said.

In less than a quarter of an hour he brought it. The prince went and announced to the king that the gown, too, was here.

"Well, son, you are valiant," he said, "but I won't give you my daughter yet. You must still go to the chamber of the Red Sea and there you'll find a gold ring; bring it back, it will be your wedding band."

Again, the prince went and told the ghost what the king had said.

"I'll obtain that for you, too," he said.

He left and soon he returned with the ring. The prince went to see the king and announced that now the ring, too, was here.

"All right, son." Right away he called the princess—the engagement was announced and they all sat down at the table for a big feast. The ghost came in as well and sat down, but no one there could see him. The lad, the prince, with whom he had come, saw him, but no one else. The very next day they called for the priest, invited guests, and began the wedding feast. Then it was time to go to the wedding ceremony. They climbed into a carriage; the lad took his seat next to the bride and the ghost—who got on, too—sat down at her other side. The prince became very angry—he looked daggers at the ghost:

"Why are you here? Where do you think you are going?"

"I am going to church, too."

"Don't you sit beside my bride! If you want to go, go—but not in this carriage! I am the one who's going to be married!"

"Well, I want to be there too," said the ghost. He didn't leave. They arrived at the church, alighted from the carriage and went inside. The ghost followed them. They knelt down at the altar and the ghost knelt down, too—the prince on one side of the girl, the ghost on the other.

Oh, dear—thought the prince—what does he want? Why did he come up to the altar?

He didn't dare speak to him for they were in church. Then the priest began conducting the marriage ceremony, and as the couple answered, so did the ghost. Every time the bridegroom made a vow, he made one too.

Well, they were wed, and as they were leaving the church, the bridegroom said to the ghost:

"What do you want? You are dead—why do you haunt me? My bride and I were just married—why didn't you stay where you belong?"

"Because," he said, "I wanted to be married, too."

They climbed into the carriage and the ghost got in with them. The prince didn't know what to do, he was so angry.

He said: "Get out of my carriage, go away! My bride and I were wed, and this has nothing to do with you. Leave me!"

"I wouldn't think of it! I was united with her in marriage, too," he said, "half of her is mine. Half of the bride is mine."

Said the young man: "Listen! Don't let me hear such talk again that half of her is yours! You'd better go back where you belong, where you came from. I didn't save you from the beating to have you follow me and haunt me!"

"No matter what you say," he answered, "the two of us acquired her—half of the bride is mine."

When the wedding feast was over they climbed into the carriage again, for the prince was taking his bride home. The ghost climbed in with them. By the time they reached the cemetery from where he had come, it was evening—it had turned dark.

He said to the prince: "Have the carriage turn into the cemetery."

"Why should we go into the cemetery?"

"You'll stay for the night, and you may leave in the morning."

The prince thought that maybe the ghost would remain in the cemetery. So he drove in and unharnessed the horses. They went into the mortuary, and there they stayed until daybreak. Meanwhile he had sent a telegram to his home asking that twenty armed soldiers be sent to him. The soldiers arrived as expected.

"What is your command, Your Royal Highness?"

"Over there you'll find a grave," he said, "and on it are four stakes. I command that you take those stakes and beat this corpse—I'll show you where—as hard as you can."

One of them asked: "Where should we strike? We can't see anything."

"Strike where I point. And when you get tired, four others should take over, but you must continue the beating!"

They struck again and again and the dead man kept groaning. Finally he said they shouldn't beat him any more—he'd stop following the prince, he'd stay where he was. When all twenty soldiers had their turn at beating him, the king said:

"Now, place him back in the coffin, push him down into the grave and cover it up!"

They covered up the grave and started on their way home. The prince thought that finally he was free of the ghost. But when they arrived and drove into the court-yard, the ghost was already there. The prince took his bride, introduced her to his mother—then he turned around and went to see the priest. He told the priest how he had fared with the dead man, that he had saved him from the beating, had paid his debts and now he couldn't escape from him. He recounted everything the way it was; his marriage in church made no difference—the ghost wouldn't leave him. The priest told the prince not to worry—he would marry them in the royal palace, for it was their wish to be wed again at home.

He said: "Just come for the ceremony and let him come, too. If he wants to be there, let him come!"

When the young couple knelt down for their marriage vows, the ghost knelt down with them. The priest took a sash, placed it on the lad's head, and said a prayer. Only he knew what prayer it was. Then he made the sign of the cross over the lad, blessed him, and waved incense in front of him. But when the priest began using holy water in benediction, the ghost moved away from the altar. He stood behind the couple. Then the priest took the censer, swung it to and fro, and the ghost retreated another three steps. And when the priest sprinkled holy water again and said more prayers, he left the church. He left and never came near the lad again. The incense frightened him. Then the priest went to the house, took the censer and the holy water with him and blessed the entire palace. The ghost never appeared again.

Said the priest to the king: "Royal Prince, you shouldn't have rescued him from the beating—his soul was doomed forever. He was damned. With all the drinking, the debts, he never gave a thought to God; all he thought about was drinking and doing evil. He was damned."

So, the couple were married a second time and held a wedding feast. The old queen liked the bride—she had her qualities, she could change into as many colors. They are still alive today, if they haven't died. This is the end of the story. And this is how the prince fared for having been so kindhearted. The dead man had even said in the cemetery: "Let's cut the bride in half—half is mine and half is yours." That is why he had called for the soldiers.

# 12. Prince Sándor and Prince Lajos

AT 517 *(The Boy who Learned Many Things)* + 516C *(St. James of Galicia)*; MNK 516/D* *(Amicus and Amelius)*.

The first tale, AT 517 or 725 *(The Dream)*, provides a frame for the main story and serves two purposes: it introduces the superior quality of the hero of humble origin (the motif of the learned son acquiring knowledge through understanding the language of animals occurs in several tale types) and it exposes the father's envy of his career-oriented son. In folktales, the acquisition of superior knowledge is surrounded by secrecy, a theme also present in "András Kerekes" and "The Twelve Robbers" (tales 13 and 19 in this collection). The hero is told that he will die if he reveals his knowledge; yet he makes his revelation and remains unharmed. The hero's promise may refer back ultimately to a secret pledge, a mystical tradition of medieval wandering scholars, but it may also represent fear of the revenge the father will take if he learns the bird's prophecy (as in "András Kerekes").

The tale of Amicus and Amelius (or Alexander and Ludovicus) originates in a widespread European epic about an ideal sacrificial friendship. Entering hagiographic literature in the eleventh century, the legend later spread through chapbook literature and into vernacular folktale tradition, retaining personal names and placenames, a tone of moralizing piety and chivalrous, courtly scenery (Denecke 454-63) that also distinguish the Hungarian oral variants, which were inspired by eighteenth- and nineteenth-century chapbook texts. Thus, Mrs. Palkó's version shows a certain literary influence. She learned the tale from Regina, wife of her son Pius, during the initial Székely settlement of Kakasd (1946), two years before I recorded it in 1948. But the tale must have circulated in the community long before, probably at wakes. Márton László recorded it in the 1934 copy of his *Book of the Dead*, a collection of hymns and prose texts pertaining to the rites of the wake.

Mrs. Palkó's oral performance, unpretentious and straightforward, creates a polished artistic form free of the artificiality of the heavy-handed written versions. Aunt Zsuzsa's account strips away the chapbook language and reclothes the tale in the splendor of traditional folktale diction; this is a prime example of the process through which oral artists transform received materials into folklore. The two texts are almost identical; she modifies only at points where things hard to explain are mentioned, or where she interprets situations or conflicts in ways more suitable to her community. For example, her hero is the son of a simple peasant, while Márton's hero is a nobleman: Sándor, a peasant's son, relinquishes his claim to a princess, allowing his noble friend to marry her. The father sends his son to a priest to study (rather than to a scholar, as in Márton's version; in the Bucovina sense, the ideal learned man is the priest). Mrs.

Palkó omits the preaching and extensive moralizing found in her source and maintains only one of its many religious rituals: the fasting and praying that bring about the miraculous healing of Prince Sándor. Evidently, her descriptions of magic healing are based on the canon of the Roman Catholic church. It is noteworthy that God's justice here embraces not only the healing of Sándor (from the affliction caused by his unfaithful wife), but also the wife's punishment as the disease is passed on to her.

———

Well, long, long ago, beyond seven times seven lands, there was once a well-to-do farmer. He had a small son called Sándor, who was such a beautiful child that there wasn't another like him. Not only was he beautiful, he was kind-hearted and smart. His father sent him to school and there, too, everyone liked him. His schoolmates liked him and his teachers were very pleased with him, because he was such an upright, decent boy.

One day the teacher said to the boy: "Tell your father that he should send you to secondary school so you may yet amount to something!"

The boy went home and told his father what the teacher had said.

"Oh, my son, let the teacher talk—he has it easy, but you are the only one I have, and what shall I do in my old age? There is all that land and a lot of work—and I should be left alone in my old age? No, you'll finish primary school and I won't send you any place else!"

Once the man was on his way to church when he met the teacher. He said to him:

"Uncle, why don't you send your son to secondary school? It is a great pity that you don't."

And so the man changed his mind. He agreed.

"Tomorrow, my son, I am taking you to the city."

He took the boy to a priest and said: "Reverend Father, I'll leave you this boy so that you make something of him. I'll pay for it."

So the child remained and the priest placed him in a monastery.

After four years had passed, the boy returned home. He had passed his exams—he could become anything he wanted to be—he was free. His parents were so happy to see him that they didn't know what to do.

His mother said: "What should I make for your midday meal? What do you like best?"

"Dear mother, make whatever you please. What is good for you will be good for me, too."

So his mother prepared a fine meal and they sat down to eat. He was a very beautiful boy, his mother just gazed at him, she loved him so much. Suddenly a little bird came chirping to the window and the boy burst out laughing.

Said his father: "What are you laughing at, my son?"

"I am laughing at the little bird."

"You didn't laugh at the bird, my son—tell me what you were laughing at."

"Well, what shall I say, dear father? Don't ask me and don't expect me to tell you, for if I do, I'll die."

"Son," he said, "don't tell such a big lie that you'll die. No one has yet died for something like this."

"But I will."

"Well, my son, if you die, I'll bury you, but speak up."

He said: "Dear father, if this is your wish, I'll tell you—I have to die one way or another. The little bird said, it chirped, that one day I'll be such an important gentleman that my father will hold the washbasin for me, so I can wash myself, and my mother will hold the towel for me so I can dry myself."

His father became very angry, as if someone had set him on fire.

"What is this? How do you want to become such an important gentleman? Is this why I sent you to school and labored for you that you should rise above me?"

His father didn't say anything more. That's all he said. The next morning they rose and he said:

"Well, son, today we are going away."

He harnessed two horses and went inside.

"Get dressed, son!"

"Where are we going?"

"Don't ask, son, we are just going."

The boy got dressed—they went out and climbed into the carriage. The ocean wasn't too far from them. He took the boy and threw him into the ocean, stark naked. Then he turned the carriage around and returned home.

His wife asked him: "Where did you leave the boy?"

"He is in a good place."

"Why? Where did you put him?"

"Let it be. He is in a good place where he is."

"You didn't by any chance kill your own child?"

"I didn't kill him, I threw him into the ocean."

"Oh, you heartless man, you drowned your own child in the water?"

"Stop yammering, someone might hear you. How did he dare to say that he wanted to become such an important gentleman that he would rise above me?"

Well, the woman just wept day and night. But the boy didn't drown in the water—he swam across to the other side. God gave him the ability to swim well. And when he reached the shore, he pulled himself out onto dry land, but he didn't know where he was, he was not familiar with the place. It was a sandy area and the sun was shining, so he sat down on the warm sand and started thinking.

"Dear God, what offense did I commit against my father that he could do this to me?"

He began to cry. And as he sat there, crying, a carriage pulled up. It came to a halt, a man jumped off and began filling the carriage with sand. While he was working, he heard the child crying. He went up to him and said:

"What are you doing here, my son?"

He said: "I am sitting."

"How did you get here? Why did you come?"

"I came from far away, uncle—the water brought me here, but where I am, I don't know."

But he didn't say that his father had thrust him into the water. He said he had been shipwrecked and managed to get to the shore.

"I cannot orient myself and find out where I am."

The man said: "You are not in a bad place here, you are in England. Son, would you come with me?"

"Where to?"

"I'll take you to the *capital city,* it's not far. I am a servant of the king, a servant of the king of England—I'll take you there with me. I'll tell the king where I found you and he'll put you to work in some position."

He took the boy into his carriage and wrapped his cloak around him so he wouldn't be cold. As they drove, the man said:

"This king is so wise that kings from all over come to him to learn wisdom."

So he took the boy with him. When they reached the palace, he reported to the king that he found a boy on the ocean shore and brought him along.

Said the king: "Go, call him in. Let me see who he is, what he is!"

He called in the boy.

The king asked him: "Where are you from, my son?"

He told him where he was from, that he had been in a shipwreck and the water had cast him out on the shore. The boy spoke so well that the king took a liking to him.

"Well, son," he said, "you'll stay here with me and you'll serve as a footman at the table."

He was very pleased for he was a clever lad, skillful, and he liked every part of the work.

At that time a prince was there too, who had come to learn wisdom. And the king of England had a daughter, whom the prince, who was studying wisdom, fancied greatly. He was in love with her but the girl didn't like him.

Then Sándor came. The girl was very beautiful but she was choosy, and as Sándor moved about the table, she took a great liking to him. Sándor noticed that the girl fancied him but acted as if he didn't know.

A short while later the girl said to him: "Sándor, how is it that you don't even want to look at me? If only you knew how my heart is longing for you!"

Sándor said: "Princess, I thank you kindly. I see that I am liked, but we cannot fall in love, that's not possible."

"Don't you fancy me?"

"Oh, I do, but this cannot happen."

"Tell me why not?"

"I'll tell you why. Because I am not of royal descent. His Majesty, the king, wouldn't permit it, so it's better not to talk about it. This can't lead anywhere."

The girl said no more, but the way Sándor spoke had hurt her.

Soon a Prince Lajos arrived—he, too, came to learn wisdom. He and Sándor looked so much alike that they could have been born to the same mother. Their speech, their beauty were so similar that it was impossible to tell them apart.

Well, the king made Prince Lajos his cup-bearer, so he and Sándor were always working together. The king was surprised that they weren't brothers, they resembled one another so closely.

One day Sándor noticed that the princess had her eyes fixed on him all the time.

He said to her: "Princess, here is Prince Lajos, he is of royal descent. Your father won't object if he learns that you are in love with each other. He won't keep you apart, for he is a prince."

"It's no use. He may be a prince and there is great resemblance, but I prefer you Sándor," she said.

But Prince Lajos was different in one way. He was shy, not as daring—he didn't like to talk much, while Sándor was very good at flattery.

One day the king held a big ball and invited all the neighboring kings. The prince, who had been there first, noticed that the princess was in love with Sándor—still he asked the king if he could take his daughter for his wife.

Said the king: "I'll not rule on this. If she loves you, I won't deny you, but if she doesn't, I can't force her to marry you. It depends on her."

Fine, but he hadn't talked to the girl, for she didn't like him. So the neighboring kings gathered for the feast and Sándor was busy, bustling about the table. The king of France was there too. Lajos was serving the drinks. The old king of France took a great liking to Sándor. He had chatted with him and was impressed with the way he spoke.

He said to Sándor: "Where are you from, my son?"

Sándor told him where he was from.

"Look, son, I have a daughter and I am getting on in years. I'd like to see her get married and to know who would be left in charge of the country. I thought that you could become my son-in-law."

Sándor said: "Great King, I thank you for the offer but this cannot happen."

"Why not, my son?"

"Because I am not of royal descent. I am only a peasant's son, but I had schooling."

"Son, I am not interested to know whose offspring you are. It is sufficient that you are clever and bright and that I like you, and I think that if my daughter saw you, she wouldn't reject you. There are witnesses here," he said, "let them hear that when I send you a telegram you must set out for France without delay. You should know that I am getting weaker and it is my wish to see, while I am still alive, in whose hands the country will be left."

Well, Sándor thanked the king for his offer and promised to go when he called him. Meanwhile, the three of them were there, and the prince who had arrived long ago was hoping that the king would give him his daughter in marriage. Sándor heard this and said to the princess:

"Look here, Lajos is so deeply in love with you that words cannot describe it, but he is too shy to talk to you. Why don't you love him? He and I are the same—you should love each other!"

Sándor had a gold ring made and gave it to her on Lajos's behalf.

"Look, Princess, Lajos sent you a ring as a gift for your name day."

"And why didn't he bring it himself?"

"He is shy. He said I should give it to you on his behalf and if you accept it, he'll talk to you."

Well, she accepted the ring, thanked him and said: "I'd like to speak to him."

"I'll tell him that he should come and speak with you."

So Lajos went. Sándor labored until he brought them together and got them to love each other. Then the first lad noticed that the girl was in love with Lajos and he confronted her father, the king:

"When we talked, you said that I might have a chance, and now it's King Lajos who wants to take her for his wife?"

Said the king: "Look, my son, I cannot love for my daughter. If she loves him more, what can I do? I'll talk to her and if she prefers you, I don't mind, she can marry you."

Meanwhile Sándor received a telegram asking him to come to France at once. So he announced that he was being called.

"You must go then, for the old king is getting weaker."

Sándor bid farewell to all, said thanks for the friendship he was shown and left.

When he arrived there, the king was indeed on his death bed. Right away he handed over the country to Sándor, but he couldn't be crowned until he had wed the king's daughter.

(And now let's leave them for a while, until their wedding.)

Back at the court the old king had gone so far as to consent that they should fight it out in a duel, King Lajos and the other one, Fendrik. He who defeats the other will win his daughter's hand, and there should be no rancor between them. But Prince Lajos was worried, for Fendrik was a tough lad—he was big and strong and lionhearted. The princess noticed that Lajos was sad. She said: "I see that you are grieving. It seems that you won't be able to get the better of him for you have a tender heart. If he defeats you and I have to be his, I'll die, because I don't love him."

Prince Lajos said: "Well, I don't know what will happen."

Said the princess: "I know, if Sándor were here, he would overpower him. You have a tender heart. But Lajos, I'll teach you. Go to see Sándor. Tell my father that you are being called home to your father's death bed, and if he consents, go to France, to Sándor, but make sure that no one sees you. Tell Sándor that you'll stay there and take his place, if he'll kindly come here for a few days. So you'll stay there and replace him. In this way, we'll get around this business, somehow!"

Lajos ran to the king at once and said to him: "I just received a telegram, my father is dying."

"Go, my son, and when you can, come back!"

Lajos pulled himself together and took off. Who knows where he went, but he asked Sándor to come see him.

"My dear friend," he said, "you have already done a lot for me. I am asking for your help once more, if you are willing!"

"What is it?"

"Look at the trouble I am in. The king said I should fight in a duel with Fendrik and he'll give his daughter to the one who'll defeat the other."

Sándor said: "Dear friend, this presents a small problem."

"Why?"

"You came at a bad time."

"Sándor, what are we to do?"

"This is the very day for which my wedding was set. How can I change places with you? Unless you wed my betrothed—no one knows us anyway!"

Lajos said: "Fine, then I'll stay here."

"Well, I say to you, you may wed her but you must remain loyal to me."

And Prince Lajos replied: "You have nothing to fear, you'll find her as you left her. I'll keep my loyalty to you."

So they came to an agreement. Lajos remained and Sándor went back to the king of England. No one knew that Lajos wasn't Sándor, and there no one realized that it wasn't Lajos, the two lads were so much alike.

The duel was set for the next day and the time came for them to face each other. Prince Sándor put on armor and got himself a fine sword and horse. There were so many people, the entire town had gathered to see who would defeat the other. The king was seated on a throne, with his daughter at his side. They watched to see who would come out the stronger. The two lads charged one another on horses and clashed with their swords, but neither could overpower the other in the first encounter. When they engaged a second time, Sándor struck with such force that he cut off his opponent's hand. It dropped to the ground together with the sword, and Fendrik, wounded, fell off his horse. There was great cheering and jubilation that Prince Lajos had won the girl.

Then they went back home. As soon as they arrived, Prince Sándor approached the king once again and told him that his mother was very ill, he had to go to her.

"All right, my son, if she is that ill, you must go and see what the trouble is. But don't stay too long—let us hold the wedding."

And that's how it happened. Sándor pulled himself together and left for France. There, Prince Lajos and his bride had already been married. Prince Sándor called on Prince Lajos and asked him how the wedding feast had gone.

"It passed, you have nothing to fear. You'll find her as you left her."

Well, all right. So, Sándor went in and Lajos prepared to leave.

"Sándor, what you did for me was to put your life at risk when you fought with that knight. So, if ever you are in trouble, just let me know, I'll be there to help you in any misfortune. And if anyone ever asks me for something in King Sándor's name, I'll do all I can. Now, here, take my ring, I give it to you as a remembrance, and you let me have yours!"

They exchanged rings, Lajos thanked him profusely for his kindness and set out for home. The girl was very happy to see him.

"You see," she said, "I am glad I thought of what we should do, so there would be no trouble."

Well, they went on living for God and were wed.

Fine, but there was Sándor. He went home and right away had a different conversation with his wife. She was astonished that at night Lajos had put a sword between them, with its sharp edge exposed. This cut the bride to the quick. They had slept that way for three nights. And that's when Sándor returned. Well, the young wife was angry and Sándor noticed that she was upset, but he didn't know why. He spoke endearing words to her, cajoled her, flattered her, but his bride just turned away from him. When evening came and they went to bed, she turned her backside to her husband. She didn't want to talk to him.

"Why are you angry with me, my angel?"

"You didn't care for me until today, so now it is my turn not to care for you. Tell me, what was the idea of putting a sword between us until now?"

Sándor burst out laughing. He said: "Look, I just wanted to test you."

"What for?"

"To make sure that you are not afraid, but I won't do it again."

"Whether you do it or not, you are loathsome to me. I hate you!"

Her husband just laughed and tried to cajole her.

"Look, Sándor," said the young bride, "when I was inclined towards you, you put a damper on my feelings. I'll never fancy you again and we won't have a good life together."

Prince Sándor said: "Oh, you'll recover from this. We're young."

"That's what I wanted, but now I'll take my revenge because you placed the sword between us."

Sándor thought that although she was a little angry, she'd get over it. But the woman began to stray, she fell in love with the steward; she became enamored of him. When Sándor was asleep she got up and went over to the steward. Sándor noticed that his wife was straying. He followed her, watched her, and found her making out with the steward. He listened to their conversation. He heard his wife saying to the steward that she'll poison Sándor, put poison in his food so he would die, for she didn't want him. Sándor thought that she'd never do it, that this was just idle talk. But she did it, she mixed some kind of poison into his food. Sándor had an iron constitution—he didn't die but became very ill. He was all swollen, completely disfigured. Sores covered his body, his eyes were bulging, he looked so coarse that no one would have said he was King Sándor.

Still his wife persisted. She went abroad, before a big court where justice is administered for all the kings, and there she denounced her husband. She wanted a separation because he was straying from her. She claimed that her husband had come down with the black plague, and she didn't want to live with him. Even the doctors refused to treat him; they said he had an infectious disease. She had no use for him and, in any case, they had told her that she should chase her husband away—she shouldn't live with him.

She drove him away and King Sándor had to go into exile. What's more, the doctors wouldn't treat him—he had an infectious disease, they said.

So she chased him out of the palace. King Sándor went into a big forest; there he wandered around, but soon he ran out of food and had nothing to eat. He was sick with the plague, yet he wanted to eat, he was ravenous, always hungry. He was in such a state that people would get out of his way on the road. They were afraid to walk in his footsteps, he was so disfigured. Well, he began to ponder his fate. He wasn't able to die, he wasn't alive or dead, he was overwhelmed with suffering. He thought that he might go see Prince Lajos and wouldn't stop until he got to him. So he set forth and went, begging for food on the way. No one knew who he was, he became so *coarse looking*.

It was evening when he arrived—the lamp was lit and Prince Lajos and his wife were having their meal. He knocked at the door—"please, come in," they said. He entered, with a knapsack on his back and a cane in his hand, wished them good evening, and they received him.

He said: "Your Majesty, I came here to ask you kindly, in King Sándor's name, to give me shelter for the night, for I am sick."

When Lajos heard that he asked in King Sándor's name, they took him in, though they were repelled by his *coarse, peasant-like appearance*.

"Please, sit down!," they said, but they didn't recognize who he was. They offered him a seat and Prince Lajos asked his wife to have some food brought in so he could eat. Right away they ordered the cook to prepare a meal for him and set it before him at another table to the side.

All of a sudden he said: "Your Majesty, in King Sándor's name I ask you, permit me to eat at the same table with you."

Once again he consented. They moved his plate over and they ate together.

When the wine was poured, the king said: "You must have some wine too!"

"Your Majesty, allow me to clink glasses with you, but let's exchange them, so I'll drink the wine from your glass and you'll drink from mine."

King Sándor and his wife looked at each other and agreed to this, too. He gave his glass to the beggar but only because he asked in King Sándor's name. They exchanged glasses, and what did he do? He took the ring from his finger and slipped it into the glass, the ring that Lajos had given him. They exchanged glasses, clanked them and drank the wine. The ring touched the king's tooth—he removed it, looked at it and saw that it was his own ring.

He said: "How did you get this ring?"

"I don't know."

He summoned his cup-bearer and asked him from where he had taken the wine.

"Your Majesty, from the same barrel as the other."

"And the glass?"

"From the kitchen, as usual."

"Well, how did this ring get here?"

"I don't know anything about it."

Then he turned to the sick man, who said: "I put it in there."

"But how did this ring get to you?"

He said: "Oh, Lajos, my dear friend, don't you recognize me? Don't you remember that we exchanged rings? Have you forgotten me?"

Prince Lajos felt uneasy. "Who are you then?"

"You don't know me, do you?"

"How should I know you when I've never laid eyes on you until now?"

"Oh, but you have," he said, "I have done you many a good turn, don't you remember? I am King Sándor."

Lajos's wife fainted when she heard him say that he was King Sándor. They freshened her with water and revived her.

"What is wrong with you Sándor? What happened to you?"

Sándor said: "You see, Lajos, my good friend, my own kindness brought this about."

"Why? Tell me!"

So he began his lament: "When you left and I began talking to my wife, she just turned away from me. At night she turned her back to me, didn't care for me, and when I cajoled her she said that since I put the sword between us she came to hate me. She would never love me again, she would take her revenge. And she did, she began to stray and became the steward's sweetheart. She left me at night and went over to him. I followed her and listened to what they were saying. There they were, making out, and she said she would poison me. She gave me enough poison to die, but since I have a tough constitution it didn't kill me—it keeps torturing me instead. I became ill, all swollen, even the doctors wouldn't treat me. They said it was a contagious disease, and since then people stayed clear of me. To make matters worse, my wife brought a complaint against me at the court abroad, saying that I had the black plague. They separated us and she expelled me from the country. You see, it's only my goodness that caused this."

Prince Lajos and his wife began to cry. He said: "Look, Sándor, we'll put you up in a room and call for a doctor."

"It's no use, don't do it," he said, "doctors won't treat me because they believe it is a contagious illness. But I thought of something else."

"I thought, Sándor, that we'll put you in a separate room, in a clean room with a clean bed and all three of us will make a vow to fast. Perhaps God will help you."

Right away his wife went and made up a nice white bed, with the blanket and everything all in white. They even gave him a bath and then put him to the bed.

Lajos said: "We'll do it, Sándor, the three of us will pray, maybe you'll be cured."

Three days passed and on Friday night Sándor had a dream. He saw an old man come up to his bed and say to him:

"King Sándor, you are very sick and there is only one remedy for what ails you. Tell Prince Lajos that he has three sons—he should cut their throats, collect their blood in a bowl and use this blood to wash you with his own hands from head to toe. This will be your medicine."

When he saw this, King Sándor woke up at once and began to think: Dear God, how can I tell him this? How can I expect him to cut the throats of his own sons, three of them, not just one? I'd rather die than say one word.

The next night King Lajos saw the old man in his dream. He told him the same:

"Cut the throats of your three sons and wash him—this will be his medicine." King Lajos said nothing to his wife nor to Sándor.

When Sunday came the queen said to her husband: "We are fasting today—what shall we do, go to church or not?"

Prince Lajos said: "You go, but I'll stay. Let's not leave Sándor all by himself, ill as he is!"

So they harnessed the horses to the carriage and his wife departed for church. Prince Lajos stayed at home. He didn't say a word to anyone, went into the small room and cut the throats of his three sons. He poured their blood in a bowl and went to see King Sándor.

He said: "Now, Sándor, I'll wash you from head to toe. Let's see if you get better."

He washed him and as soon as he was finished Sándor stood up on his own:

"Oh, Prince Lajos, my dear friend, nothing, not even my nails hurt."

He recovered his beauty—his sores vanished as if they had never existed. He was cured.

Then the queen came back from church. She saw that Prince Lajos and Prince Sándor were sitting at a table, chatting, and when she left, Sándor was barely able to move from his bed. Once again he was as beautiful as he used to be, before he experienced all the misfortune. She went in and laughed out loud:

"What happened, Sándor, have you recovered?"

"God gave me back my health."

Oh, she was so happy, she hardly knew what to do.

She said: "I wonder what helped, the fasting or the prayer?"

He answered: "Both, the fasting and the prayer."

King Lajos said: "Wife, what would you have done if someone had told us to cut the throats of our three sons and wash him with their blood, for that would make him well again?"

The queen thought for a while, then said: "Well, maybe, maybe, if someone had said that he will surely recover, I would have allowed even that."

King Lajos said: "Well, it is done."

"What is?"

"What I have just said, come into the room!"

He ushered his wife into the room. Sándor followed them so he could show him, too, that he had cut his sons' throats. And there were the three boys, holding hands in a circle, singing and dancing. They had risen from the dead. Their mother and father embraced them. All that was left was a thin line around their necks.

**[Listener:] You saw this as if it happened today, didn't you?**

(I used to cook for the kings and they would carry in the food.)

Oh, they were so happy, they covered them with kisses. They invited guests and rejoiced together.

One day Sándor said: "It's time for me to go home and see what my wife is up to!"

"Don't go home, Sándor. Stay here, stay with us!"

"My mind is not at peace."

"Then go, but be sure to come back!"

Sándor went home. When he got there his wife was in bed, dying—she was all swollen, her face and her body were blown up like a balloon. Sándor entered.

"What's the matter with you, dear wife?"

"Oh, Sándor, Sándor," she said, "you have recovered but I'll die."

He said: "What's wrong?"

"I am dying, God has punished me. I caused this sickness and now it reverted to me, for I poisoned you so that you'd die, and now God has turned it back onto me. Forgive me, I was at fault."

"I forgive you, I am not angry since God brought me back."

The woman died the same day. He buried her in great splendor, mourned her for a short while and then returned to Lajos. They began discussing whom he could take for a wife.

Lajos said: "Sándor, I have a young sister—marry her. You know I want only the best for you." So Sándor proposed to Lajos's sister and they were wed. *They lived as happily together as two doves.*

One day Sándor said to his wife: "Wife, I have a mother and father. I would so much like to see them, but they are a little far away."

"It doesn't matter, we must look them up."

Right away Sándor summoned two soldiers and wrote a letter to his parents. He didn't tell them that it was from their son. He just wrote their name and asked them to expect the king of France for a midday meal on Sunday, for he was coming to visit them. He wrote down where the soldiers should go, into which country, which community; he put down his father's name, the street and the house number.

**[Listener:] He was a farmer working on the land, a peasant.**

He sent the letter saying that they should expect the king of France for Sunday's midday meal, and that he would be there with his wife.

The soldiers left, they crossed the ocean and reached the country of the parents. They went on and found the house. The soldiers had the rank of officers. They entered, saluted and asked whether such and such a man lived here. "Yes," they said. They had grown old.

"Well, we've been sitting here for a while," they said, "here is the letter, you may read it, but we can also tell you that the king of France is sending you word that you should expect him for the midday meal on Sunday. He is coming with his wife!"

The old man became so alarmed that he started to shake. What could the king of France want from him? He and his wife looked at each other, why would they come here?

"I don't know, but one thing is certain—that they'll be here."

The soldiers rose and left. The old man was deeply distressed.

Said the woman: "Old man, I wonder, could something of our secret have been revealed? Maybe they are coming to pry into that?"

"Oh, I hope not! But why would the king come here?"

Then they began to be concerned about cooking and baking, preparing the dishes to put before the king. They hired a cook and they baked fancy cakes. They had the means, for they were prosperous farmers—they were just consumed with worry over where all this would lead.

Well, Sunday came and they were waiting. Suddenly the king arrived in a coach. He alighted and they entered into the house. The table was ready, nicely set. They didn't know how to receive them, what to do with them, when they came in. So they beckoned them, asked them to be seated at the table, and to take food and drink.

"We thank you kindly, but first we'd like to wash off all this dust."

Quickly, they poured water into a washbasin.

The old man said to his wife: "Go, look for a fine towel!"

The king and his wife washed and the woman stood there, handing them the towel. They dried their hands and sat down at the table. They ate heartily and drank.

Then the king said: "Are you just the two of you, old people?"

"The two of us, only the two of us."

"No children?"

"No."

"Never had any?"

"We had one but he died."

Said the king: "What sort of illness carried him away?"

The old man became so alarmed that he began *chewing vigorously on the stem of his pipe* and the woman poked him in the ribs.

"He contracted a fever and died."

"Well now," said the king, "aren't you lying to me?"

He was so frightened that his hair stood on end.

"It's not my habit to lie."

"Yet it seems that you are lying."

"No, I am not."

"Didn't you throw your son into the ocean?"

Well, had God not protected him, he would have *died of despair* on the spot.

"You see, you said your son died of illness when in reality you threw him into the ocean."

The words got stuck in his throat—even his eyes became petrified.

"What would you say if your son came home, if he were alive?"

He said: "Oh, he won't come home, he is deep in the bowels of the earth, he died a long time ago."

"Yet, see, your son is alive! Can you believe it?"

"Well, I can't say you lie, for as king you stand above us, but as far as I know even his bones have turned into dust."

"Look," said the king, "you cast him into the ocean because the birds had chirped that one day he'd become such an important gentleman that his father would hold the washbasin for him so he could wash, and his mother would hand him the towel. For this you cast him into the ocean. But he didn't die, he is alive today. I came to show you that you held the washbasin for me and my mother held the towel, and for this you needn't have pushed me into the ocean. But I forgive you, I am King Sándor, the ruler of France. This is my wife and you are my father and my mother, and I came for a visit to see if you are still alive. I also want to ask you whether you'd come with me, to be near me until you die."

Well, the man couldn't say a word in reply—he fell to his knees before his son. He begged him for forgiveness, asked that he should forgive him for he hadn't known what he had done.

Then his mother said: "I'll go, my son, I don't want to be separated from you"—

but the man wanted to stay:

"I have lived here all my life; I want to die here in my own home."

His mother said she'd go, she wanted to die near her son.

"Father, I'll forgive you, and if you don't want to come, I won't force you." So, he said farewell to his father and they took his mother with them. She stayed there until she died. He buried her in great splendor and they are alive, perhaps to this day—and tomorrow they'll be Lajos's guests!

# 13. András Kerekes

AT 517 (*The Boy Who Learned Many Things*); MNK 517 (*The Boy Who Understands the Language of Birds*). This tale possesses only one close variant—the probable source of Mrs. Palkó's tale—with the same motif combination, collected in Transylvania (1879) and rewritten for one of the Benedek storybooks. This pious plot is an ideal vehicle for wake entertainment. It found entry into *The Book of the Dead*. Mrs. Palkó had heard it from Márton László and also from her brother János, but she formulated her own version that clarifies and elaborates certain passages by adapting episodes from other tales. My recording is from 1950; Mrs. Palkó told the story upon the request of her nephew, storyteller György Andrásfalvi.

"András Kerekes," the career story of a priest, features Aunt Zsuzsa's great respect for schooling and advancement through diligent study. After all, in Hungarian peasant experience, priesthood was the only possible career a gifted boy could achieve. In several of her tales, this illiterate woman speaks about the education of male heroes, but in this case it is clear that, for her, clerical status is achieved through monastic education. In its opening scenes, the tale resembles "Prince Sándor and Prince Lajos" (tale no. 12, above): an angry father, envious of the son who has risen above him, throws the boy into a dry well. The next episode involves rescue by a nobleman, who adopts the gifted boy and experiences three narrow escapes with the help of his wisdom. In the following part, Mrs. Palkó expands upon Márton László's sketchy episode concerning the envy of the nobleman's son as cause for Jánoska's departure. With a good sense of proportion, she adds a scene which frequently appears in such other tales as "The Three Golden Sons" [AT 707] and "The Twin Brothers" [AT 303]): the hero is embarrassed when his stepbrother reminds him of his lowly origin. In order to heighten the dramatic impact of the scene, Aunt Zsuzsa tells it twice.

From this point, the priestly career is smooth, and the story shifts its focus to the parents: the guilty father and the innocently suffering mother seeking absolution that only the pope can give. The culmination, the dialogue between parents and son, the pope and the sinners, is well structured, leading to recognition and forgiveness.

In general, the telling of this tale is simplicity itself: the narrator does not deviate essentially from the book version. She simply strips the tale of all artificiality and adds dramatic dialogues, translates the laconic and awkward written text into the language of the folktale, giving the unknown tale a homey familiarity.

Once upon a time, beyond seven times seven lands, there lived a man. He had a beautiful young son. The boy attended school; he was very smart, and his parents had high hopes for him to complete his education. Indeed, he took his studies very seriously.

One day when he came home from school, his mother said to him: "Go, my son, ask your father to come in for the midday meal!"

As the boy went out to call his father, a flock of sparrows flew into the courtyard and began to chirp. The boy burst out laughing. He laughed out loud.

His father said to him: "What were you laughing at, my son?"

He said: "Father, I can't tell you what I was laughing at, for if I do, I'll die."

"Why would you die? Of course you won't, my son. Go on, tell me what you were laughing at."

"Father, believe me, if I tell you I'll die."

"Look, my son, many boys told their fathers everything and kept no secrets, yet I haven't heard of a single one dying for it. You won't die either."

"Please, father, believe me, I'd die. I can't tell you, no matter what you do to me."

"Well," he said, "never mind, son, it doesn't matter. Did I send you to school and raise you so that you keep things from me—things of this sort?"

"Father," he said, "I won't tell you. I see that this troubles you, but I won't tell you for I'd suffer for it badly."

His father fell silent. They ate their midday meal and the next morning they rose early. The old man harnessed two horses to the carriage:

"Son," he said, "get dressed and climb into the carriage. You'll see what will happen!"

He didn't even tell his wife where he wanted to take the boy. They climbed into the carriage and took off. They drove out to the *paved road*, I mean the highway, and near that highway was a dried-up well.

He made the boy shed his clothes until he was stark naked and said to him: "Well, my son, you kept a secret from me, you didn't tell me what you were laughing at—here is where you'll die."

"Father, you wouldn't murder me, would you? I committed no offense against you."

"No," he said, "you withheld from me what you were laughing at—you wouldn't obey me."

He stripped the boy of his clothes and threw him stark naked into the dried-up well. The well was caved in. But water had seeped up from the bottom, and it had rained so water was standing knee-high, muddy water in which leeches had bred. There were leeches in abundance and nesting wasps, too. As soon as he cast the boy in the well, the wasps landed on him, and the leeches stuck to his legs. He screamed his heart out, but the man didn't care—he went home. He left the boy clamoring for him to come back and help, but to no avail. A while later a carriage came down the highway. An important gentleman was returning from a big fair. As he drove by he heard the screaming.

"Coachman," he said, "stop the horses; we must see what the crying is all about."

Well, he brought the horses to a halt, jumped off the carriage and went in the direction of the sound. He couldn't see the boy's body; it was entirely covered with wasps; leeches clung to his legs and were biting him, sucking his blood.

The coachman turned around and said: "Milord, Sir, come and see what a beautiful boy is in the well. He can't get out."

The squire walked over and looked.

He said: "We must help him somehow. Surely he fell in and his parents don't know where he is. How can we get him out?"

The boy was submerged in water, unable to climb out.

Said the squire: "Take the reins off the horses, lower them into the well and let him hold on to them."

The boy clasped the reins and they pulled him up.

The squire asked him: "How did you get here, my son?"

"My father threw me in."

"Why? What sin did you commit for your father to do this to his own child?"

"I didn't do anything wrong. I don't know my sin," he said, "but I know he was angry with me. He was irate and this was his revenge."

"Why was he angry?"

"Because I understand the language of the birds," he said, "and I didn't tell him what they were saying. He became furious because I wasn't allowed to tell him."

"Well now, son," he said, "come with me—I'll take you to my house. I have a son who is your age—you'll go to school together."

The boy was overjoyed that he was saved from all the suffering and rescued from the well.

"I just bought a set of clothes for my son at the fair—I believe they'd fit you—I'll give them to you."

They set forth. He sat the boy in the carriage, and they went in search of some water to wash the mud off his body. They came to a fishpond, stopped and washed him thoroughly. He was such a beautiful boy that the squire couldn't stop rejoicing over him.

He said: "How beautiful they are, the two boys! They are the same size, the same age."

He asked the boy how old he was, and he told him.

"My son is exactly the same age."

Well, he took the boy with him. As they were driving, suddenly two crows alighted on the side of the road and began to caw.

The squire said to him: "Tell us, my son, what are these birds saying?"

"I'll tell you," he said. "The crows are saying that soon we'll reach an oak tree on the side of the road, a big oak tree. The squire will want to stop in its shade to feed the horses, but it won't be good if he stops there, for lightning will soon strike the tree and we'll all perish. I am telling you, Milord, Sir, don't stop there, go on farther."

Said the squire: "Look, son, I don't see any darkness in the sky—there are no clouds. When the weather is so clear there usually is no lightning. Often it strikes later."

"Still," he said, "if you heed my words you'll be lucky; if not, we'll all perish. As you wish."

They reached the tree. The squire had thought it over and decided that it was better to go on, so they continued. They were barely beyond gunshot from there when a tiny cloud appeared in the sky and began to spread and spread. Then the rain came; it poured so hard that it was dreadful. Lightning struck—it felled the tree and split it to pieces.

"You see, Sir, if we had been there, we would have been struck."

"God bless you, my son! You saved us from death. You are a good boy."

From then on he was even more fond of the child.

They drove on. Then, once again, a flock of crows alighted on the road and began to chirp.

Said the squire: "Now tell me, son, what did the sparrows say?"

"Well, Sir, they said that here you would have to go straight ahead, for that road would lead you straight home. But you mustn't go that way," he said, "for the road narrows and two carriages cannot stay clear of one another, nor can they turn around, so narrow is the road. There are ditches on either side—it is impossible to get out of each other's way. And there, on that narrow road, a tree has toppled over and is blocking the way. You can't get through there with the carriage. But when you come to a point where another road leads off, a country road, turn into it," he said, "it'll take you back to the highway farther on. Just be sure to avoid the narrow road, you can't travel on it with the carriage."

"Look," said the squire, "I came through there with the carriage a little while ago. Nothing was wrong, there was no tree blocking the way."

So they drove on and soon they came to the tree. It was there, as the boy had said. A big tree had toppled and was lying across the road. They tried to get through, every which way, but to no avail. The horses couldn't get across, nor could the carriage be pulled through. They wanted to turn around but were unable to do that either—the road was too narrow, and there were deep ditches on both sides. They had no choice but to dismantle the carriage. They hauled it on their backs piece by piece and pushed it over to the other side of the tree. Then they led the horses across, reassembled the carriage and continued on their way.

"Well, son, I didn't listen to you and we paid for it. But never mind, from now on I won't oppose you, I'll do whatever you say."

They drove on. All of a sudden two crows settled on the road and began scrabbling about in the horse manure, strewing it all around. They cawed as crows were in the habit of doing.

Said the squire: "Tell me, my son, what are these crows saying?"

"Sir, they are saying that we should hurry. Drive as fast as you can, for your mansion was plundered last night. Burglars got to it, and all they left intact are the four corners of the mansion. If you hurry and get there quickly," he said, "you'll be able to recover the loss, but if you delay, they'll haul everything away. Whatever they took, they didn't take far; they stashed it in the back of the garden, under the heap of cornstalks. Although they hid their loot for now, the crows say that they want to carry it away tonight."

"Well," thought the squire, "I didn't listen to you before and we had a difficult journey. I'll heed your words this time and drive the horses faster."

He tightened his grip on the reins and began driving the horses so hard that they were covered in sweat by the time they got home. The woman was in tears when she came out to meet her husband:

"Come quickly, a great calamity happened in the mansion. Last night burglars broke in and robbed us," she said.

He leaped off the carriage and left everything. The servants unharnessed the horses and led them into the stable. He ran to the back, to the place the boy had mentioned. He searched the stack of cornstalks and found everything; the burglars had hid it all out there.

"Thank God, it is all here!"

They carried his belongings inside.

"Well, son, I was fond of you before, but now you have become like my very own. I'll buy you what I buy for my son, you'll wear clothes like him, you'll eat like him, and I'll have you educated together with him, the same way."

They were happy. The next day they took the boy to school. They dressed him in the clothes he had bought for his son. The boy was so beautiful, even more beautiful than his own. And the two boys liked one another. They went off to school.

Then the woman said to her husband: "Tell me, where did you find this clever little boy?"

"Oh, if you knew where I found him," he said, "and from what fate did I save him!"

"Well, tell me!"

"His father had cast him into a dried-up well. But if the well had been really dry, he could have climbed out. It was caved in, rain had gathered in it and water had seeped up from the bottom. Poor thing, he stood in water. So many leeches stuck to him that his legs appeared all black. His body was covered with them and bloody all over. He was crying bitterly and screaming. We heard him as we came down the road, went over to him and saved him from death. I brought him with me so he'll become our son, too. We'll raise him in the name of God. He is a clever boy—you can tell from the way he speaks."

That day, when they came back from school, their own son said: "They like this boy so much in school, even better than me. He is very smart, very clever, he may yet amount to something."

They raised the boy well, they treated him the same as their own son. But his mother told the boy who belonged to them how they had found the child, that his father had found him and rescued him from a dried-up well. God knows who the boy's father was—he must have been wicked to have thrown his son into a well.

"Your father saved him and now you are brothers. Embrace each other as brothers! I see," she said, "that he is a smart boy and so are you. We have paid for the school and when you are finished, we'll send you to a higher level institution."

So the boys went together every day. They got along well for a while. One day they were let out for a ten o'clock break to play and rest as usual. They played ball. Who knows what happened, how it happened, but the boy who was the stranger, accidentally hit his step-brother and opened a gash in his head.

He began to scream and yell: "What did you do to me? Why did you hit me on the head? I'll tell my parents at home what kind of brother you are!"

"Brother," he said, "don't be angry!"

"You are not my brother! You are the brother of the devil! Is this how you show your gratitude for having been rescued by my father from the well, where the wasps and leeches devoured you? He saved you from death and you thank him by bashing in my head! Don't worry, you'll pay for this, you nobody! You don't even know where you come from, who your father is, and now you are such a big guy," he said, " that you have to fight with me!"

He insulted him and called him all sorts of bad names. The boy was very embarrassed for all the schoolchildren heard it.

"You are not my brother—you were stark naked when my father found you and gave you my clothes! Even today you are wearing my clothes, and this is the thanks I get? You nothing, you nobody! Who knows who you are?"

The boy went home crying: "I thought you were my father and mother."

"Why are you crying, my son?"

"My brother abused me. He shamed me so that I wished the earth would open and swallow me up! No one should hurt me this way!"

"What happened, my son?"

"Look, they let us out for a ten o'clock break and we started to play ball. When I raised the bat to hit the ball, he appeared in front of me, and I struck him by accident, so that tears welled up in his eyes. I didn't want to do it, I swear, I didn't want to do it! Then he called me all sorts of names, and said that this was my way of thanking his father for taking me in, for picking me up naked on the road and dressing me in his clothes. 'You don't know to whom, or where you belong,' he said. 'You don't know who your father is. He wanted to murder you, he wanted you to die, and my father saved you! And now this is how you behave! You believe that you are the big boy around here, but you are not, it is I who am bigger! You are only a stepson, though you don't act like one. You didn't even have clothes to wear,' he said, 'and this is how you show your gratitude?'

"I feel deeply hurt—I cannot stay here any longer. Dear father and mother, I thank you for taking care of me until now, for having saved me from death. Whatever he would have said, however he would have sullied me, it wouldn't have hurt me so much if he had done it at home, and no one would have heard it. But there, in front of all the children, he revealed that you found me as you have, and I am ashamed of this. I am going and I'll keep on going across the world until I die, but I won't stay here."

They tried to prevail upon him: "Don't go, son, you are not wise enough yet! Let it go this time, it will all come right, and we'll be good to you. Don't leave us, son!"

"No, I won't stay here any longer," he said.

When they realized that there was no convincing him, they gave him a bag with provisions for the journey, money and whatever else. They even gave him a set of clothes. Who knows, they thought, where he would stop, whether he would have the means to buy clothes, or find someone who would offer him something to wear. They sent him on his way with kindness. The boy thanked them, kissed them good-bye and left. He took to the road, poor thing.

"Dear God, how unfortunate I am in this world," he said. "My father disowned me, yet I was innocent. And here, I had to experience shame once again. I couldn't stay, although I would have had a good life," he said, "but now I can't stay. I'll keep going until I find a place where I can stop."

So he continued walking, bravely. Then, suddenly, he saw that a priest was following him. He slowed his pace to let the priest catch up with him.

He greeted him: "*Praised the Lord Jesus Christ, blessed be His Name!*"

"*Praised the Lord, for ever, my son!* Where are you going all alone through these fields, where no one else is walking?"

"I am going until I find shelter."

"Where are you from, my son?"

"Where am I from?"

Well, he poured his heart out to the priest. He told him how he fared with his father, and how, in the name of God, a squire had taken him home. He would have been well off there, for they treated him kindly and took good care of him. They accepted him as their own son and he considered them his parents. But they had a son of the same age who abused him in school in front of the other children, and this he couldn't tolerate. He was too ashamed.

"Now then, my son," said the priest, come with me to the rectory, I'll look for some work for you. I'll look for a place where you can learn something."

The priest could tell from the way the boy spoke that he was really smart. He spoke very intelligently and the priest became fond of him. He took him to his residence and right away asked his cook to give the boy something to eat. He made him sit down so he'd rest.

The boy told him how he had fared with his father, that he had never talked back to him, that he had listened to his every word, obeyed him always and was a good son.

"I don't know what took hold of my father that he was capable of doing this to me."

"Don't grieve over it, my son, let it be, and be happy that you are alive! God will not forsake you. One day your parents will come to you, pleading."

Well, he placed the boy in a monastery. He was a parish priest so he couldn't keep the boy with him, but he placed him in a monastery among the clergymen and told him to take his studies seriously. He recommended the boy warmly as *an orphan* and urged them to see to it that he studied well and strove to achieve something.

"What do you want to be?"

"I'd like to be a priest."

"You seem to be clever enough, so you may even become one."

Well, the boy studied hard. In a short time he became a priest. The boy became a full priest, he was ordained.

One day the priest said to him: "What is your intention, my son? Will you stay here or will you go somewhere else?"

"I might as well stay here. Where should I go? Back to my parents? I wouldn't do that, I'd rather stay here."

The boy continued studying and soon became a parish priest. He rose so quickly through the ranks that next he became a bishop. They placed him in charge of a diocese in a city which had a bishop's seat. He comported himself well, very well. Now he had a good life.

(But let's go back to his parents.)

When his father threw him into the well and went home, his wife said to him:

"Where did you leave Jánoska?" (That was his name, Jánoska.) "Where did you leave him?"

"Where did I leave him? In a good place."

"Well," she said, "you didn't by any chance kill your own son?"

He said: "Never mind. Let him sit there, under the gallows."

"How could you do this to him?" Did you sink so low that you became your own son's murderer?"

The woman wept and screamed: "Tell me where you took the boy! He is the one son we have," she said, "and you have done away with him!"

"Look," he said, "I threw him into a dried-up well. Next to the highway there is a caved-in well, I cast him in there. He wouldn't tell me what he was laughing at, so now let him be miserable, let him suffer."

Said the woman: "Look, I cannot rest until you bring the boy back from there. What do you think? You'll go to confession—what will the priest say when you tell him that you killed your own son?"

"I got very angry with him, you see."

"Listen," she said, "maybe the boy isn't dead yet. Let's bring him home."

They harnessed the horses to the carriage and drove out to the well. But the boy wasn't there any longer. The squire had taken him. The woman fainted, there beside the well.

"Surely the boy sank into the muck—it's all soggy here—and he stayed alive until he went under. And when he was submerged, he must have suffocated. Well, my husband, how will you enter the hereafter, now that you have killed your own child?"

She went on harping at her husband. She was forever quarreling with him. But one day she had to accept that their son was no more. They went to confession, both of them. And the man had to confess what he had done to his son.

The priest said to him: "Look, this is a great sin, a mortal sin that cries to high heaven. I'll hear your confession but I cannot let you take Holy Communion. It's not in my power to allow you to partake of Holy Communion. Only the bishop, or the pope, can give you absolution for this sin, for what you have done to your son."

So they went to confession to another priest. But after they confessed they didn't receive Holy Communion there either. They went to several places, to no avail.

One day the man said to his wife: "Let's sell the house, turn our land and everything into money, and let's leave here forever. Let's go and keep on going until we get to the bishop," he said. "He'll hear our confession and maybe he'll give us absolution for our sins, and Holy Communion. It's no use going to confession elsewhere," he said, "we won't receive Holy Communion, and we'll be damned. If a clergyman who is higher up doesn't release us from this sin, we'll be damned forever."

They sold their house, their land, the cattle, the colts, everything. With saddle bags slung on their shoulders and clutching walking sticks in their hands, they set forth on their journey. They walked until they reached the place of the bishop's residence and there, in that city, they went to the bishop and confessed.

Said the bishop: "Good people, your sin is great. It's not in my power to give you absolution. Perhaps I should write to the pope, or you should go to him yourselves and ask him to hear your confession. Maybe he'll absolve you."

Well, they said they'd go to see the pope, by foot, all the way to Rome. But the pope was their son. It was their son who had become pope. The old pope had died so they brought him in because he was so smart. He reached that rank, he was now the pope. So they went there, to that city and they went to the—what do they call it—the seat of the pope. A guard stood watch there. The pope was guarded the same way as an emperor, or a king. They asked the guards to please let them in to see the pope.

One of them said: "Wait, let me telephone first and find out from the pope if you should be admitted or not."

Well, by evening they were let in. And when they reached the next sentry post, having passed six of them already, they were ushered into the papal palace.

The very last sentry said: "We telephoned the pope to let him know that there were some people here who wanted to talk to him, and to see if we should allow them in."

Then they were let in. The sentry at that post let them go in. They entered and fell to their knees at the pope's feet and beseeched him:

"Most holy Father, we are great sinners. No priest or bishop would give us absolution. They said that it wasn't in their power to grant absolution to such a great sinner. They said that maybe the pope can help us. So we came to you, Holy Father, to ask you to hear our confession. We'd like to confess and receive Holy Communion."

"Well," he said, "that may be possible."

The pope sat down in the confessional. The man went first and confessed truthfully what he had done and why.

"Oh," said the pope, "you committed a terrible, grievous sin. You had no pity for a child of your own blood, you did away with him, threw him into the dry well. He must have either gone under or been eaten up by the vermin there."

The man said: "I don't know what happened, whether he died or escaped. I know nothing about it. But what I do know is that I cast him in there."

"Well," he said, "I'll have you do penance, and you must do it faithfully. The penance I'll give you is great, and you must complete it!"

He had him say prayers so the man went to a church and prayed all the time without letup, all day, every blessed day. The pope heard his wife's confession, too, but she wasn't guilty.

"I cried so much," she said, "and begged him to go to the well and take him out so he wouldn't die. But when we got there the boy was gone. Whether he died, or went under, I can't say. We didn't see him."

The pope knew already that they were his parents. He knew it.

He said: "Would you like to see your son again?"

"Oh, would I!" she said. "To hold my child in my arms, to press him to my heart, would allow me to go on living! This way I am consumed by grief!"

He said: "Maybe he isn't dead."

"Well, I don't know what to say. I know that he threw him into that big well—it was a very dangerous place, full of wasps, and perhaps he threw him in naked. There were many leeches. He must have collapsed in shock. And there were plenty of frogs, and the boy was afraid of them. Surrounded by them, he must have *died of despair*," she said.

"Listen," said the pope, "call your husband! Let your husband come here."

Well, the man came and sank to his knees again before the pope.

He said to him: "Rise! Do you want to see your son again?"

"Of course I do, most Holy Father! But it's no use, I won't see him again for he must have perished."

"Still," he said, "if you found him, what would you do?"

"Dear God, that cannot be expressed," he said. "There isn't a human being that could describe the joy I'd feel if I found him alive, and if he'd say that he is my son. There is no way to describe it."

"But if he were alive," said the pope, " have you regretted in your heart of hearts what you have done to him?"

"I regretted it already then. It was revenge and anger," he said. "I acted out of rage, then I was sorry, but I didn't find him in the well when I went back to look for him. I thought I'd die but I couldn't."

"Look," said the pope, "don't you recognize me?"

"I know that you are the Holy Father, the pope," he said. "But how could I recognize you when I've just met you?"

"Your sins are forgiven," he said. "Your wife's and yours, for I see that you have truly repented. You won't leave here. You'll go to confession and receive Holy Communion every day. I'll get a room for you. You mustn't worry about anything, just say your prayers. I am your son—János Kerekes, son of András Kerekes."

Oh, his father fainted—he passed out. He was unconscious, and they had to wash him to revive him. His mother fainted too—both of them had fainted. Then he rushed over to clasp the pope's feet and covered them with kisses.

"Please, forgive me!"

They kissed his hands and feet and begged him for forgiveness for the cruel deed he had done.

"It is forgiven; I bear you no rancor. I accept you as my father, for you are my father—and you, you are my mother. You are my parents," he said, "and I won't let you go on wandering anywhere. You'll remain here, with me, and when you die I'll bury you. Until then I want you to live in comfort!"

They are still alive today, if they haven't died. This is all, and *tomorrow you can have them call!*

# 14. The Psalm-Singing Bird

AT 550 (*Search for the Golden Bird*) + (*The Sons on a Quest for a Wonderful Remedy for Their Father*); MNK 500B* (*The Psalm-Singing Bird*)—MNK registers 40 variants of the type. The content of Mrs. Palkó's text is faithful to Benedek's storybook original by the same title. She heard it from her brother's recital and later from her son Linusz, who read it to her from a book during their temporary stay in the Bácska (1941-1944). Her stylistic modifications are significant because they correct some of the awkward formulations of the printed model and clarify obscure detail.

This was one of her favorite tales for reciting at wakes—many people heard it from her at these long nightly vigils and advised me to ask her to tell it. This was the second tale she told me, in 1948, at the home of the Zsók family, where I was staying and where neighbors and relatives gathered during winter evenings. This explains why she was somewhat nervous in her recital and slipped at the point where her hero was about to enter the castle to fetch the psalm-singing bird. She stopped, looked around, admitted with a smile, "I am not recounting it well"— and then corrected herself. Well into the story, she felt comfortable enough to make a humorous reference depicting herself as an eyewitness of the story's events: she could "see it clearly to this day" how the two brothers pushed their youngest brother into the muddy, leech-infested pond. Her personal style shines through the narrative, particularly in the presentation of the king's wealth, his intent to erect a lasting monument to himself by building a church without equal, the account of the adventurous acquisition of the bird, the hero's betrayal by his older brothers, the adventures of the disguised hero, and his victorious return.

―――――

Long, long ago, seven times seven lands away, there was once a king who had three sons. He was a very wealthy king; he had a lot of money.

One day when they were all seated at the table having their midday meal, he said: "Wife, what can I do with all this money? I'd like to do something so I'll be remembered after my death." All five of them agreed that it might be best for him to have a big church built, one that would remain in the family, and be passed down from kin to kin and from generation to generation. They concurred that this would be the best. Right away they summoned the master builders and craftsmen and measured out the area where the church would stand. They had bricks, boards, lathing, and beams brought in, all that was needed for a church. The construction took ten years; then it was completed. It was so large and so beautiful that there wasn't another church like it in the

165

entire world. The king had ordered everything that belonged in it: images, statues, candle-holders, the finest and the best of everything. Even the bell he had sent for was such that when it pealed it could be heard three villages away.

Well, when the church was finished, furnished with everything according to his wishes, the bishops, popes, and kings came to inspect it and all of them said that it had no equal in the whole wide world. The queen and her sons were overjoyed, but the king was always sad. Whenever his sons entered his room, *they found him with his head bent in sorrow.*

His oldest son once asked him: "Great King, my father, why are you grieving? Every time we come into your room, we see you lost in your thoughts."

"Oh, my son, I cannot tell you, for even if I did, you wouldn't be able to do anything about it."

His oldest son left and the middle son entered. He, too, asked him: "Great King, my father, I am very keen to know, why you are so sad?"

"Oh, my son, don't ask me. I won't tell you for you can do nothing to help."

Then the youngest son went in, the one that was closest to his heart. He loved them all, for they were his sons, but he was especially fond of the youngest.

"Father," he said, "if I don't offend you, I'd like to ask you what is weighing on you? You have said that you'll have a church built and once it is completed you'll have no sorrow, no worry. Now the church is finished, as you wanted it— what is troubling you, then?"

"My dear son," he said, "I won't tell you for you can't help anyway, so it is better for me not to tell you."

But the young king insisted: "Father, I won't leave here until you tell me. Perhaps I can do something."

"Well, in that case call your brothers and I'll tell you."

The young prince went out and called his brothers. They came and stood in front of their father, side by side, in a row.

Said the king: "My sons, you were curious, so I'll tell you what I am grieving about, although I know that it's no use—there isn't anything you can do to help. Look my sons, the church has everything and it is beautiful, everyone likes it. There is but one thing missing from it, and I am racking my brains about how I could acquire it. That, however, is very difficult."

"What is it, father, please tell us!"

"Well, my sons, what is missing is a psalm-singing bird and that is very hard to get."

The young prince said: "Father, we three brothers will go and we'll keep on going until we find it. We won't return without it so we won't see you grieving any more."

The oldest son also spoke: "We'll leave today."

"Wait, first I must go into town."

The old king went into town, to the shop where they made gold rings, and had three of them crafted for his three sons. Each had his name nicely engraved in it, and he brought them home.

"Here you are, my sons, these three rings are for you—put them on your fingers," he said. "When you come to a crossroads stop and bury the gold rings. Then you should separate, one of you should go north, the other south and the third west. And when you return and come to the crossroads again, the first thing you should do is to look for the rings. If you find one rusty, you'll know that the one to whom it belongs is in trouble. But," he said, "wait for each other there and come back home together."

The young men thanked their father for the rings. He gave them his blessings and they left.

They traveled, leaving their country behind and entering the neighboring land. They went on until they came to a crossroads.

The oldest prince said: "Here is where we must stop."

They stopped for a while. They fed their horses and took some food and drink.

"And now let's hide the rings."

There was a well at the crossroads, and they paused alongside it. They lifted up a big stone, set the rings down and placed the stone back over them. Then they mounted their horses and took leave of one another. The youngest prince headed south while the other two continued north and west respectively.

(Now let's leave the two older sons to their journey.)

Meanwhile the little prince crossed forests and fields in his travels and came to a wide, desolate plain. No town or village was visible anywhere. He walked on all alone in the vast, strange land.

Evening was drawing close, the sun was going down, and he set to thinking: Dear God, if only I'd come upon a house where I could ask for shelter! What will I do in the middle of the night in an unfamiliar place?

As he was musing, he caught sight of a small hut. He'd go in and ask for shelter, he said to himself, even if the devils lived in it. He knocked at the door and heard a deep voice answer:

"You may come in."

The young man entered and saw an old woman sitting there, with a nose so long that it knocked at her breasts.

"Good evening, grandma!"

The woman turned around and looked at him: "Good evening, my son. *What are you doing in this forsaken place where not even birds can fly?*"

"*My misfortune cast me here,*" he said. "Would you be so kind and give me and my horse shelter for the night?"

"Well, where are you headed, my son?"

"Oh, grandma," he said, "I set out in search of good fortune, but first I need to ask you, have you heard of the psalm-singing bird?"

"My son," she said, "most of my life is already behind me, but I have never heard of the whereabouts of the psalm-singing bird. But," she said, "I am telling you, I have an older sister, about a day's journey from here—you could go to her and ask her if she knows something. She is older than I, maybe she has heard about it. However, your horse won't make it that far, while I have one that will. Take it and on your way back you'll return it to me."

They rose in the morning and exchanged horses.

"Look, son, when you've gone about half-way, you'll reach a well. Drink from its water but don't give any to your horse! On your return you may let your horse drink too, but not on your way there!"

The lad thanked the old woman for her good advice and after exchanging horses he set forth. As she had said, he came upon a well. He went over and drank of its water, and what did he see in the well? A beautiful maiden, but only her head was visible—her body was completely submerged.

"Here you are, prince," she said, "I give you this silver wand. Watch it carefully for you'll need it. When you come back, return it to me!"

He thanked the maiden and continued on his way.

About the same time as the previous night he reached the other house. He halted, tethered his horse and walked in bravely. He bade good evening, but first he knocked at the door, and there again a deep voice answered:

"You may come in."

He entered and there was another old woman sitting by the stove, but her nose reached down to her navel.

"Well, son," she said, "*what are you doing here in this forsaken place where not even birds can fly?*"

"*My misfortune brought me here*, grandma," he said. "I'd like to ask you if you would give me and my horse shelter for the night."

"Sure I would. *It is God's abode and man's resting place.* You may come in."

Right away he led his horse into the stable and went into the room.

"Dear grandma," he said, "have you heard of the psalm-singing bird anywhere?"

"Oh, my dear son," she said, "I have been around, wandered in many places, yet I have never heard of the psalm-singing bird, although most of my life is behind me. But I have an older sister, about a day's journey from here—she is even older than I," she said. "I am telling you, when you have gone halfway, you'll find a well. Drink from its water, but don't let your horse have any!"

The young man thanked her for her good advice and left. He traveled until he reached the well and walked over to it. Once again he saw a beautiful maiden in the well, up to her neck in water.

She said to him: "Well, prince, I know where you are headed. I am giving you a golden wand, take good care of it for you'll need it." He took the golden wand, thanked her, mounted his horse and rode off.

When evening closed in he found the next house. He alighted from his horse and knocked at the door.

The old woman said: "You may come in."

"Good evening, grandma!"

"Good evening, my son. What are you doing here? Where are you going?"

"Oh, dear grandma," he said, "I started on a long journey, but there is something I'd like to know from you. Have you heard of the psalm-singing bird anywhere?"

"Why, son, why do you want to know?"

"I'd like to get that psalm-singing bird," he said.

"My dear son," she said, "you are attempting a formidable task. Ninety-nine sons of kings, princes, barons, and exceptional, bright young men have all tried it and not one of them has returned. They have all perished. Well, son, you can try, I don't mind," she said, "but you heard, ninety-nine of them have already lost their lives. However, if you listen to me and do as I say, maybe you'll be successful. Look, son," she said, "you'll come to a well—drink from its water, but don't give any to your horse. There you'll receive a diamond wand. Hold the three wands in your hand—the silver the gold and this one—for they are magic wands. And now I'll teach you what do. You'll leave here and you'll reach the ocean. In the ocean there is an island and on the island stands a castle. This is an enchanted castle. *It revolves on the spurs of a rooster and is suspended from the skies by three gold chains*. It has as many windows as there are days in the year, and," she said, "its two hundred and fifty doors are made entirely of gold and diamonds, from the hinges to the frames. It is difficult to get to the castle, there are no boats going there. But when you reach the ocean shore, strike the waters and they'll part, letting you walk up to the castle with your feet dry. When you are halfway there, a twelve-headed dragon will come towards you, and," she said, "this dragon will be spewing fire for seven miles. But you mustn't be frightened! Be brave! So when you have gone halfway into the ocean, go face the dragon with confidence, and don't wait for him to catch you. You must strike him with your wand first. With every strike you'll sever one of his heads, and you must strike twelve times to cut off all the heads. Once they have fallen off you can proceed without fear. The dragon is the lord of the enchanted castle. When you come to the castle, jump up on the stairs, for they are spiraling upwards"—(I am not recounting it well. I should say)—"strike the castle so it'll stop turning, and then, my son, hurry and get in. But there is such beauty inside the castle, such splendor that you must be careful not to be blinded by it," she said. "If you gaze too long, you'll be trapped there. Look straight to your right, for there, suspended in a gold cage, is the psalm-singing bird. Take it quickly, turn around on the spot, and without looking left or right, rush out the door! If you do otherwise," she said, "you'll remain there forever."

The lad thanked her for the good advice and set forth. He came to the third well and in it, too, there was a beautiful maiden. She offered him a diamond wand and said he should give it back on his return. He wove the three wands together and galloped away on his horse. Soon he reached the ocean and came to a halt at the shore, gazing at the beautiful castle. It stood on an island, as the old woman had said. He took his wand, struck the waves, and they immediately parted, making it possible for him to walk through the ocean without getting his feet wet. When he was half way there, he saw a dragon coming toward him with tremendous force, spewing fire. Well, the young man shuddered a little when he caught sight of him, but immediately remembered what the old woman had said. He mustn't get frightened, he mustn't be afraid, he should go up to him bravely and hit him with the wand. So he chopped off one of his heads and struck again until all twelve heads were severed. "Now," he said, "I have nothing to fear but God." He reached the castle, struck it, and it stopped turning. He walked up the stairs to the door. It was locked but when he touched it with the wand—it sprang open. Dear Almighty God, what splendor there was in that castle! *His eyes almost popped out* for all the brilliance. But he remembered the old woman's warning that he mustn't gaze at anything, just look to the right where the cage of the psalm-singing bird was hanging. He spotted it right away, ran over to take it, and turned around to walk out the door. He still had one foot inside and was just about to withdraw it when the door slammed shut and tore off his heel.

"Dear God," he said, "the old woman was right to tell me to be careful, not to linger. One more minute and I would have been trapped forever. That door opens by itself only once every seven years."

Well, he had the bird. He mounted his horse and rode away. He climbed out on the shore from the ocean, and the waters immediately closed in behind him. He rode until he reached the well, but the maiden was no longer in it.

"Prince," she said, "I thank you for having delivered me. I have been in this well for ten years. The dragon had cast a spell on me and I was to remain here until a prince came to rescue me; only then could I get out," she said. "You became my savior. Be sure not to miss my mother's house, for she'll reward you."

The prince gave her back the wand and continued on his way. Soon he reached the old woman's house. She came to the door to thank him for saving her daughter. Inside, the table was set and laden with the finest dishes.

"Come, my son, eat and drink, I know you must be hungry!"

When he ate and drank to his fill, he bade the psalm-singing bird break into song. It sang beautifully. The old woman's nose was so long that it knocked against her knees—still she began to dance, so enchanting was the bird's singing. Then she gave the prince a scoopful of diamonds.

"Son," she said, "this is yours for having freed my daughter. I see you were lucky, you were able to get the bird, but it will sing only in your presence. If you perish somewhere, it will sing no longer."

Then she packed some provisions for his journey, so he wouldn't go hungry. He mounted his horse and rode away. He came to the next well and there, too, the maiden was now outside. He handed her the golden wand and thanked her.

"Well, prince," she said, "you delivered me. Be sure not to miss my mother's house, for she'll show you her gratitude!"

And that's how it was. As he approached, the old woman came running to meet him:

"Come, my son, come, you brought me great joy! Ten years ago that beastly dragon cast a spell on my daughter and I haven't seen her until now."

In the house the table was set and all sorts of fine foods were spread out on it.

"Come, my son, eat and drink!"

Once again he ate and drank and was given a scoopful of gold.

"Take it, son, this is yours."

Once again he received good provisions for his journey—he thanked the old woman and continued on his way. He reached the third well and there, too, the maiden was already outside. He gave her back the wand and she said to him:

"Be sure not to miss my mother's house!"

When he came to the house, he found that the maiden had got there ahead of him. There again he was welcomed graciously, given hospitality and a scoopful of silver. They exchanged horses—he mounted his, and rode off.

He rode for about three days and during this time he didn't eat once, although he had food. He was in such a hurry to see his brothers. He thought they were waiting for him. He galloped at full speed, rushing ahead to get there as quickly as possible. He thought he was bringing great happiness since he had the psalm-singing bird with him.

He came to the crossroads and went over to the well. He lifted up the stone and saw that his ring was as shiny as when he received it from his father and slipped it on his finger, but his two brothers' rings looked rusty.

"Dear God," he said, "my brothers are in trouble. Which way should I go to find them? I won't stop to eat, it doesn't matter, I want to get to them as quickly as possible, or get news from someone about where they are."

He pressed on but didn't see anyone whom he could have asked where to look for them. He would have liked to know what happened to them, whether they were dead or alive, but there was no one around.

As he was riding, preoccupied, he caught sight of a squire's estate, with many workers. He thought it best to go over to them hoping that one of the men could give him some news about his brothers. When he came closer he saw that the men were harnessed to plows, tilling the soil. Indeed that's what they were doing. And behind each plow there was an overseer with a whip in his hand, hitting the men so hard that blood was oozing from their bodies. He came to a halt and stared.

"My God, I haven't ever seen such a thing, that a man should be made to pull a plow! What have they done to be punished in this manner?"

He would have liked to know. And as he was standing there and they passed by him, he recognized his two brothers among them. They were tilling the soil, pulling the plow. They were covered with blood and filth and were completely emaciated. When he recognized his brothers among the men, he felt so sorry for them that his heart nearly broke. He'd go until he found the squire of the estate, he thought to himself, and ask him why they were being punished. He came to a mansion and just then the count appeared in the gallery. He dismounted, went over to the count, greeted him as it was fitting and said:

"Esteemed Sir, what crime have these men committed to be punished so severely?"

He said: "That shouldn't be your concern."

"Sir, I beg you," he said, "how much money would it take to have the men released?"

The count burst out laughing: "What are you saying? Not even your father and grandfather would have enough ransom money to have them freed."

"Why are you whipping them? For what crime?"

"That is not your concern," was his answer.

"I'd like to get at least two of them out. Please tell me how much I need to pay!"

"Do you have three hundred pieces of gold?" asked the count.

"I do," he said.

"Well then, show me the two men you want released."

The count went with him. They went over to where the men were tilling the soil. They had just come to the edge of the field, and when his two brothers turned the plow and were facing them, he pointed:

"These are the two I want freed."

The count called the supervisor and told him to let the two men go. He paid the three hundred pieces of gold and left, taking the young men with him.

On the road he said to them: "My dear brothers, what did you do to this count that he punished you so severely?"

They answered: "Nothing. We did no harm, he just captured us and harnessed us to the plow. He took our horses, stripped us of all our belongings, and tortured us."

"Well," he said, "let's go! Do you know of a place around here where one can bathe?"

"Yes, farther down there is a fish pond," he said.

They went as far as the pond.

"Now go into the water and wash yourselves clean. Meanwhile I'll go into town to buy you two horses and two sets of clothes, complete, from boots to *shakos*. I'll bring back a barber, you'll get dressed and we'll go to eat. I don't know if you are hungry, but I am. I haven't eaten for three days."

They waded into the pond to bathe and the prince went to town. He went into a big store and asked for two sets of clothes, the kind princes would wear. Right away they were brought to him, along with hats and boots, for princes wore boots, not shoes. Then he went and bought two steeds with saddles, outfitted as was proper for princes. Next he found a barber and asked him to take his tools and go with him. He'd pay him whatever he asked for, as long as he'd go, he said. He had the barber mount one of the horses and they rode off. Well, suffice it to say that while he was shopping and spending time in town, in the midst of bathing the two brothers began plotting against him, plotting to take his life.

The older prince said to the younger one: "Do you know what I thought? That it would be a good idea to do away with our brother."

"Why?"

"Because our father always loved him more than us. He was dearer to him. If we now go home our father will despise us when he learns that he got the psalm-singing bird, not us, and that after what happened to us he set us free. Our father will say that we are good for nothing and once again he will become the favorite."

Well, this is how the brothers were plotting, but he had no inkling of their plans. He came with the barber, the horses, and the clothes.

"My dear brothers, come out of the water. The barber is here, he'll clean you up, cut your hair, give you a shave, and make you look right. You'll put on your fine clothes and we'll go to eat."

And so it happened. The barber spruced them up and they got decked out nicely.

"And now," he said, "we'll look for a big tree and settle down in its shade."

They sat down—he unpacked the provisions he had brought with him and spread them out. The young prince was very hungry for he hadn't had any food for three days, yet he was unable to eat, he was so overcome with happiness. The two brothers ate and didn't bother to ask him why he wasn't eating. He couldn't eat, he was so filled with joy at having found his brothers. Well, they ate and drank, mounted their horses, and rode off. But the young prince had taken no food at all. They continued on their journey until they felt hungry again.

Said the prince: "Let's sit down and eat for we are hungry again. I myself am very hungry."

They sat down and brought forth the food. When the young prince reached out and took a piece of cake, the two others slapped his hand so hard that he dropped it. The prince thought that they were teasing him. He reached for the cake again, and again they slapped him, only harder.

"What is it, my dear brothers? Are you joking with me, or what? It seems to me that first I was unable to eat for joy at having found you, and now you are not letting me."

"We won't let you eat!"

"You won't let me have my own food?"

"No," he said. "You may eat only on condition that you let us take out one of your eyes."

Said the prince: "You'd have the heart to cut my eye out?"

"Well, if you want to eat, you'd better let us do it," he said, "for if you don't, you won't eat."

The prince thought that rather than die of hunger, it was better for him to let them take one of his eyes out, if they had the heart to do it.

Then they allowed him to have a few crumbs of bread.

He said: "You took my eye out and this is all you give me?"

"We'll give you more," he said, "if you give us your other eye."

"I'd rather you shot me in the head than let you have my other eye. Do you think that I'd consent not to be able to see our father when I get home? I'd rather you shot me dead!"

They drew forth their pocket knife and cut out his other eye, too. And still they didn't give him sufficient food, just barely enough to keep him from dying of hunger. When they ate their fill, they mounted their horses, and started on their way. They had their brother ride between them, since he couldn't see to guide his horse. Soon they came to a stream. A bridge led across it and on the other side there was a pond, full of mud, reeds, and leeches—(I can see it clearly to this day). When they reached it, they stripped him of his clothes and pushed him into the pond. They took the psalm-singing bird, tied his horse to theirs, and sped off, leaving him behind.

"What we'll do," he said, "is that we'll tell our father that we got the psalm-singing bird. On our way there we took leave of one another at the crossroads, and we haven't seen him since. We searched and searched and asked around but we haven't heard anything about him."

They made it home to the king, but his first question was: where is the young prince?

"Well," they said, "we parted at the crossroads and that was the last we saw of him. We kept looking for him, inquiring about him, but we couldn't find him anywhere."

On hearing this the king never stopped weeping. He had no pleasure in the psalm-singing bird, he was just grieving for his son.

They placed the psalm-singing bird in the church, but it didn't sing for anyone, not even one song. They were very astonished at this and gave it the finest candies and chocolates but to no avail.

(Now let's leave them in their home.) The king was grieving for his son, but the young prince didn't perish in the water when they threw him in. A fisherman pulled him out, and what happened to him? The pond was a magic pond, and he regained his two eyes in it.

Said the fisherman: "Son, why are you in this water? And why are you all naked?"

He answered: "I was traveling when I was set upon by robbers. They stripped me of my clothes, took my money and threw me in this pond. But," he said, "you saved me, dear uncle, and I'll not forget it!"

"Well, my dear son, I pulled you out, but I can't take you with me, for I am so poor that I am barely able to survive from one day to the next."

"You needn't take me. I thank you for having rescued me," he said, "I'll look to enter service somewhere, and be taken care of there."

The young man went on his way. There was a farm close by—he went there and hired himself out as a laborer.

He said to the squire: "First I need a suit of clothes."

He told him the same, that he had been attacked by robbers who had stripped him of his clothes.

Right away the squire brought him some clothes and showed him the work to be done in the stable. The lad conducted himself well, and the squire was pleased with him. They trusted him so that the lad ended up doing everything—they had no misgivings about him. The count, owner of the farm, had a daughter.

One day the count ordered the prince to harness two horses to a carriage—for they were going away—and asked him to watch over everything. They didn't say where they were going, they just left.

The lad finished his chores in the stable and strolled over to the mansion. Just then the count's daughter came out to the porch after the midday meal. He walked up and down in the flower garden facing the porch and watched the girl washing the dishes.

He called over to her: "With your permission, Miss, if I don't offend you, I'd like to ask you a question."

"Please, do!"

He said: "I'd like to know where your parents went."

"I shouldn't tell you, but you belong here so maybe you won't betray the confidence."

"I wouldn't betray my master! There isn't a living soul to whom I would divulge the secret."

"They went to the neighboring land," she said. "The king there had a church built, a beautiful church. It was in the announcement that there wasn't another one like it in the entire world, as beautiful and as large, and there was even a psalm-singing bird in it. People from all over were going to marvel at the church, so my parents went to look at it too. My father knows the king, for when they were children, they were in the same school. They went there to see the church."

"Be so kind, Miss: when your parents return, let me know what they saw."

"Yes, of course," she said, "right away".

The lad was happy. He'll have some news about home—he'll know whether the king is still alive. He felt sorry for his father. Well, they stayed away for two weeks, then they came back. The girl served them a midday meal and in the afternoon the lad strolled over to the porch once again. That's where the girl always washed the dishes.

"Tell me, Miss, now that they are back, what did they say, what did they see there?"

"Oh," she said, "my father said that there isn't a human being who could describe the beauty of that church. The psalm-singing bird is in it too, but the king is sad for it isn't singing. No matter what they offer it, it bows its head, thanks them, but doesn't sing. They are extremely concerned about what could be the matter with it. The king called in his advisers to consult them on why the bird wasn't singing. They couldn't find a reason but the twelfth adviser suggested that the bird wasn't singing because the person who had acquired it wasn't present. The princes had that adviser cast into jail for making them appear to be liars, for saying that the person who got the bird wasn't around, when they were the ones who found it. And so it is that the bird isn't singing."

The prince was glad to have all this news from home. He continued for a few more days, then he resigned.

He said to the count: "Esteemed Sir, I thank you for your kindness to this day, but I am not staying any longer."

"Why not, my son?" he said. "Perhaps your pay is too low—I am willing to raise it."

"That's not the reason," he said. "I wish to go home to see my parents. I haven't seen them in a long time."

"Well, all right, son," he said, "but stay put for three days and let me find someone to take your place."

The count found another servant, and he paid the prince his due. They took leave of one another, and the young man set out for home. He went to the *capital city*, then over to the palace. He walked into the courtyard, looked for the steward and told him he wished to enter service.

Said the steward: "We need a swineherd, the one we had left yesterday. We need to replace him."

The lad stayed there and right away they sent two soldiers to show him the feeding station.

Well, he herded three hundred pigs. He got himself a flute and played beautifully, walking alongside them. And he trained the pigs to fall in line, better than soldiers would have done, when he was herding them home. As soon as they got in, he played a happy tune on his flute, and the pigs began to skip around and dance. The townsfolk were all laughing at how becoming it was for the pigs to be skipping to a tune.

There were very many people. They came flocking to the church in admiration as if there had been a fair. When Sunday arrived, the swineherd paid someone to take the pigs to the range. He said he wanted to go to church to see it. No one knew him for he looked like a simple lad, a servant. He went to church and when he entered through the door the psalm-singing bird began to sing so beautifully that the sound reverberated throughout. Oh, was the king happy! But he wondered why the bird had started to sing all of a sudden. As soon as they left the church, he summoned his advisers. The twelfth adviser was also let out of jail. He asked them why the bird had started to sing. The twelfth man said that the bird sang because the person who had acquired it was there, attending mass. They threw him back into jail. Then they decided that the following Sunday they would post two guards at the church gate and two guards at the door. They would give the people blank slips of paper on which everyone was to write their names. They would hand these to the guards upon entering the church and so it would become clear whose entrance prompted the bird to sing.

Well, that Sunday the lad went to church again. He was given a slip of paper and he wrote his name on it. As he entered and they collected the papers, the bird began to sing so fervently that its song filled the entire church. They took the paper from him and kept watching him. Someone was made to stand beside him. Then two constables grabbed him, took him before the king and reported that it was upon his entrance that the bird began to sing.

The king said to him: "Who are you, my son?"

"I am from the town."

"Whose son are you?"

He said: "Yours, Your Majesty."

"What do you mean," he said, "who is your father?"

"Your Majesty is."

"Son, make yourself clear. Explain your meaning."

"I'll explain it, dear father. Don't you recognize me? Wasn't it enough that my brothers wanted to take my life—now you have disowned me too?"

"What is your name, son?"

He gave his name.

"Father, you still don't recognize me? I am your youngest son who got the psalm-singing bird for you."

Then his father embraced him and covered him with kisses. "Now tell me, my dear son, where have you been until now?"

"Well, father, this will take a long time."

Right away they sent the lad to the bath. They washed him, dressed him up and led him into the room. They convened the advisers, ministers, everybody, and sat down at a table. There were kings from foreign lands, the two older princes were at the table too, and they placed the young prince beside them. Then he began telling the tale of his journey, how he had obtained the psalm-singing bird, how he had gone looking for his brothers and how they had dealt with him. They took his two eyes, gave him nothing to eat, didn't let him have his own food, and as if that were not enough, they thrust him into a pond. A fisherman pulled him out of there, stark naked. After that he had to enter service so he could buy himself some clothes. His brothers had taken his horse, his money, the psalm-singing bird, and had gone back home telling a big lie. But that pond was a magic pond and his two eyes grew back while he was in it. God will never abandon those who are true, He will help them, and so He didn't let him drown in the pond.

He said: "This is where I have been, how I got delayed, and this is how my brothers paid me back for my kindness."

"My sons," said the old king, "how did you dare do this to your own brother?

Well, son, if this is how they dealt with you, then I'll leave it to you to pronounce judgment on them. No matter how cruel the death you'll decide for them, you'll have my agreement. After what they have done to you, you must condemn them to what they deserve!"

"Father," he said, "I won't sentence them to death—they are my brothers and I don't have the heart to condemn them. Instead, give them their share and have them leave the country so I'll never hear of them again. But I won't put them to death!"

Right away the king ordered two fine horses with saddles brought up for them and gave them the gold he felt was their due. And in front of the assembled royalty he handed over to his youngest son the entire country, the crown, and his whole realm.

"From now on, my son, you'll be the ruler of this land."

He expelled his two other sons, made them leave the country. They weren't even allowed to stop on their way.

The young prince held a great wedding feast and they are alive to this day, if they haven't died.

# 15. Peasant Gagyi

AT 560 (*The Magic Ring*); MNK 560, with 26 close and 15 miscellaneous variants. Mrs. Palkó's text is closest to an early (1862) recording with the same title that hints at the hero's lowly origin. His name is a nickname, a mockery. *Gagyi* (from *gatya*=drawers, linen underwear) *gazda* (landed farmer) means: farmer who cannot afford wool trousers. It is possible that Aunt Zsuzsa's story originates from the same source as the 1862 version or was influenced by storybook reprints.

She heard the story from her brother János and son Mátyás. Her version is longer than the booktale, better structured, livelier, with original twists and turns. Her text lacks the integral introductory episode about the hero's generosity to animals who later provide him with the magic object and help when an impostor steals it. Instead, she starts with AT 1415 (*Lucky Hans*), to stress the hero's lowliness. He is a poor peasant, son of a widowed mother, and not very smart, deserving accidental luck. To provide for his eventual good fortune, Mrs. Palkó must introduce an episode of helpful animals at the point where the hero loses everything. Like the royalty of the tale world, the unsuspecting hero and his father-in-law are hunting in the deep forest. Three crows hear his complaints, but nothing is free: they demand payment for the rescue. The story-teller presents the negotiation with the crows and the promise to create a royal flower garden as a kingdom for the crows is fulfilled at the conclusion, along with the happy ending of the tale. Mrs. Palkó's heroes like to write letters (See also "Anna Mónár" [tale no. 24, above] and "The Twelve Robbers" [no. 19]), and the correspondence between Peasant Gagyi and his captive wife shows a remarkable variability in style, particularly regarding her illiteracy. Here, again, as in "I Don't Know" (no. 1) and "Death with the Yellow Legs" (no. 3), she amasses expressions that emphasize the spectacular wealth of Peasant Gagyi and to present the gradual role-reversal of king and the despised lowly hero.

The performance of this tale was enhanced by the presence of guests. On a January night in 1950, some 25 adults at the Fábián home hung on the lips of the narrator with intent attention, making encouraging, supportive, lighthearted, sometimes jocular comments. The openly sexual remarks—all from men—encouraged Aunt Zsuzsa to elaborate the idea of "illicit love" between the beggar and the princess. In many tales, princesses are stolen by monsters and dragons, beasts that refer to their human captives as wives without highlighting the aspect of sexual intercourse. But here, the disgusting old beggar changes identity by being bathed and dressed up; in fact, he becomes king incarnate. The tale situation here is evaluated from the more sober, practical view of villagers: the husband is gone for good, the wife is alone without a partner and a helper. Life must go on, there is nothing that would justify her faithfulness.

The snide remarks of commentators lead to the sexual overtones of the princess-impostor relationship. As an old widow—a devout, churchgoing woman—Aunt Zsuzsa never talks about things like that. She does not have one single dirty joke in her repertoire; she does not like to listen to them. She does not curse and does not use obscene words. I once saw her throw a young man out of her house when he showed up tipsy, directly from the pub, and began to tell a risqué story.

———

Once upon a time, beyond the seven seas and beyond their farthest shores *where the curly-tailed pigs snort*, there lived a man and a woman. They were very poor, and they had one little boy. The father died, and the boy remained with his mother. They were so poor that all they had was a wretched little cow. So wretched was the cow that every day they both had to pitch in to help it stand up, for by itself it couldn't get on its feet. One day the woman said to her son: "Son, your father is dead and this cow has completely deteriorated. You must watch over it, for it is all we have! It doesn't give milk any more, you see, and it won't regain its strength. Go, clean up the manure and scrub the cow! The muck is encrusted on it so thick that I don't dare let it out, for fear that someone will see it." She said: "No, son, this won't do. You'd better tidy up the cow a little, then take it by the rope, go into town and try to sell it. We are all in rags—I am even ashamed to have you go on the road."

"Well, you are right, mother. The children are always laughing at me, calling me 'Peasant Gagyi', because I haven't any drawers."

True, his skin was showing, front and back.

"You see, my son," she said, "that's why I am telling you to sell the cow. You must watch the money, bring it home and then the two of us will go shopping for clothes."

Well, the boy went out, scrubbed the cow, tied a rope to its horn and set forth with the cow in tow. As they were going towards the town, he met a guy who was on his way back, carrying some kind of leather on his shoulder.

He said: "Good day to you, fellow countryman."

"Good day to you, too!"

"Where are you taking this cow, son?"

"I am taking it into town, I'd like to sell it."

"What is the price of this cow?"

"Well, I think I should get at least 100 *forints* for it."

"Why not make an exchange? I'll give you this piece of leather and you give me the cow."

"Yes," he said, "but I need to buy clothes and boots for the money."

"Look, if you cure this leather, you can have boots made out of it, for yourself and for your mother. At least you won't have to pitch manure, you'll have less to do."

Peasant Gagyi thought for a while:

"All right," he said, "let's swap."

He exchanged the cow for the leather. He swung the hide on his shoulder and the man took the cow.

When he got home, the boy said to his mother: "Mother, I sold the cow."

"And what did you get for it?"

He said: "This piece of leather."

"Damn you! How could you let the cow go for this piece of nothing?"

"This isn't nothing. Once the leather is cured it'll be good for a pair of boots for me and for you," he said. "And we have less work, we don't have to feed the cow and clean out the manure. Isn't this better for us?"

"Get out of this house—I don't want to see you! Our cow wasn't worth much, and even that you squandered. And what now? We'll just stay naked? Go, anywhere you want—I don't need you here!"

Peasant Gagyi went out and took the piece of leather with him. He was greatly upset that his mother banished him from the house. He slammed the hide on the ground hard, he was so angry. All of a sudden, a little man, no taller than three hand-spans, sprang out and said:

"What do you command, Peasant Gagyi?"

"I command that by tomorrow morning there be such a big cow in the barn that its back touches the ceiling. It should be so fat that its flesh should quiver and it should have milk!"

All right. When they rose in the morning and he went out into the barn, he couldn't get over the cow that was in there. It barely fit.

He went back in the room and said: "Well, mother, go and milk the cow."

She said: "What cow? Are you the cow?"

"No," he said, "we have such a beautiful cow, you won't believe it!"

She said: "I don't know if I should go—I am not in the mood for jokes. I feel so desperate that I could leave here forever."

"Mother," he said, "don't be sad, I'm not joking. Take the pail and go milk the cow!"

"But what cow?"

She went out and looked. Indeed there was a cow, so large that she was afraid to sit beneath it. Its udders reached down to the ground.

**[Listener:] It must have given a lot of milk.**

The pail was filled with milk in no time.

She took it inside and said: "Peasant Gagyi, whose cow is this?"

"It is ours. Don't you believe that it is ours?"

She said: "All right, if it is ours, we'll have enough to eat and we'll even save some money to buy clothes."

"Well, I think so," he said.

Right away she put a big pot of milk on the stove. She boiled it but they had nothing else to eat along with it, not even bread. So they just drank the milk and what was left they let curdle to make butter. Soon they had cottage cheese, butter, and milk—

they had everything.

One day Peasant Gagyi set to thinking: If this hide brought me such a fine cow, why not ask for other things, too?

He took the piece of leather, hit the ground with it, and the little man the height of three hand-spans appeared:

"What do you command, Peasant Gagyi?"

"I command that a stack of chaff and a stack of bran be brought here to feed the cow. If I have no feed for it, it'll not give milk."

"Don't you bother," he said, "just leave it to me."

When he went out in the morning he found the cottage surrounded by stacks. Stacks of hay and straw of all kinds: of barley, oats, wheat, and rye—there were big stacks of each and plenty of husks.

"You needn't worry, mother, we have enough feed for the cow."

"I believe you, but the feed must be brought to the cow, it won't walk over to it by itself. And be careful not to let the cow thin down. The village would laugh at you if the fine animal we first had grew emaciated, just as the other one did."

He reflected for a while then he took the hide, threw it to the ground, and the little man the height of three hand-spans jumped out:

"What do you command, Peasant Gagyi?"

"I command that two horses be here by tomorrow morning, along with a wagon painted green. There should be a fine seat on it and a beautiful whip, its grip made of silver," he said, "and it should have *Beszterce harnesses*."

When they awoke in the morning and Peasant Gagyi went out, there were the two horses, so large that they barely had room in the stable. And there was a brand new, beautiful wagon, painted green. The harnesses on the horses were gleaming, sparkling. There was a fine seat in the wagon and a handsome whip with a diamond, no—what do you call it—silver grip. Well, that's all he wanted. He hitched the two horses to the shiny, green wagon, climbed into the seat and drove off. He drove on the road and the nice, rattling sound of the wagon brought everyone out of their houses to see who was coming. They looked and saw Peasant Gagyi speeding by. He had beautiful horses, they said. They thought he had gone into service somewhere to be driving such horses. He circled the village once, then went home.

"Mother," he said, "so many people were staring at me when they saw the nice green wagon and the two fine horses I was driving."

"Don't pay attention to them, my son," she said, "be glad you have them. But since you could order them, why don't you order some clothes, too, so we don't go around in tatters. You sit in your wagon in rags, son—I am ashamed of it."

He took the piece of leather and slammed it to the ground.

"What is your command, Peasant Gagyi?"

He said: "I command that I be brought five sets of clothes, complete with everything from shoes to caps. There should be clothes for every day and for Sunday" he said, "the kind I wouldn't be ashamed to wear walking into town, and the same for my mother."

When they rose in the morning there was a wardrobe in the house they had never seen before. It was filled with clothes, men's clothes, and white women's clothes. The wardrobe was packed.

"Now we are happy! I needn't be ashamed any longer—I can go anywhere."

One day Peasant Gagyi heard that an announcement had been posted that the king had a lovely daughter to give away. He who would have a bridge built to span the river—I don't know if it was the *Tisza*, or what the river was called—would receive her in marriage. Well, when Peasant Gagyi heard this, he went and told the king that he'd have the bridge built, if he gave him his daughter.

Said the king: "Get out of here, you shabby bum, get out! Aren't you ashamed to think that I'd let my daughter marry someone like you? Are you a match for my daughter? Out with you, or *I'll have your head impaled on a stake!*"

"Oh no, I am not going," he said. "Why did you post the announcement if you don't allow people to present themselves?" he said. "You declared that he who would have the bridge built would win your daughter. So I am undertaking to do it, but you must let me have your daughter."

"Go away! You had nothing, not even enough food to eat and you still don't have any." (They didn't know what he was able to do.) "And now you want my daughter? I say, get out!"

"Well, Your Majesty, whether you order me out or not, I am not going until you promise me your daughter."

"You dirty bum! Now that you have pushed me this far, you'd better have a golden bridge spanning from my castle to your castle by morning." (But he didn't know what castle Peasant Gagyi lived in.) "It must be of pure, shining gold," he said, "up to its girders on both sides, and the railings made of diamonds. If it isn't done," he said, "you'd better be prepared—I'll have your head *impaled on a stake*. And if it is, I won't say no. I won't say that you can't have my daughter."

Peasant Gagyi went home and pondered. He took out the piece of leather and smashed it to the ground.

"What do you command, Peasant Gagyi?"

"I command that by morning there should be a golden bridge reaching from my castle to the king's castle. A bridge of pure, shining gold, including its girders, and the railings on either side must be made of diamonds."

"Well," he said, "your most trifling worry should be bigger than this."

At sunrise Peasant Gagyi went out and there was the bridge. *His eyes nearly popped out*, it was so sparkling. And the king himself was astounded when he saw that the bridge was completed.

**[Listener:] By golly!**

"So, after all, he is not just some namby-pamby lad," he said, "he did what I ordered—he is not a nobody. But I won't give him my daughter yet—first I'll go see and inspect what his castle is like."

So he bade his daughter climb into the coach with him and they set out. When they were about midway on the bridge, they met Peasant Gagyi coming in his wagon from the opposite direction. He stopped when he saw the king and greeted him. But he didn't really know what greeting was appropriate for a king, so he just addressed him simply, the *Hungarian way*. The king acknowledged it:

"Where are you going, Peasant Gagyi?"

"To see you, Your Majesty."

"What for?"

"What for? To announce that the bridge is finished and to ask you whether you like it."

He said: "I like it, of course I like it."

"Well, for my part, I'd like it if you gave me your daughter."

"First I want to see, to look over your house," he said, "the house you live in. I want to know where I'd leave the daughter of a king. What do you think, I'd let her go just any place?"

"You may come."

So they went. Peasant Gagyi turned around, too, and they all went to the house. It was a little house, the smallest, poorest little house around. A narrow porch, a tiny room, that was all. The king's pigpen was better than that house.

He said: "Here is where you live, Peasant Gagyi?"

"Yes, here!"

"And I should let my daughter live in this house? But," he said, "if you follow my command and have a castle built like mine by morning, I won't deny you my daughter. Then I'll give her to you"—

**[Listener:] Was the daughter beautiful?**

(Of course she was beautiful!)

—"make sure that the castle is like mine."

"All right, Your Majesty."

Peasant Gagyi turned around and went home and the king went home, too. Peasant Gagyi took the hide, struck the ground with it and the little man the size of three hand-spans jumped out.

"What do you command, Peasant Gagyi?"

"I command that by morning a castle be here, at the head of the bridge, and that it *be suspended by three gold ropes*. The castle should have three hundred doors and one hundred and fifty windows. The hinges on the doors and windows should all be pure gold and the handles made of diamonds." He said: "*It should revolve on the spurs of a rooster* and the stairs should be pure gold, too."

"All right, Peasant Gagyi, it'll be done."

He rose in the morning. What he saw was not like the king's castle. Next to his, the king's castle was a wretched little cottage! Then Peasant Gagyi remembered that such a palace needed to have some things in it. Once again he took the hide and slammed it to the ground. Said the little man the size of three hand-spans:

"What do you command, Peasant Gagyi?"

"I command that whatever belongs in a king's house be brought here: furniture, beds, tables, in other words the finest fixtures in the world. The wardrobes should be filled with the best clothes and there should be pictures and ornaments embellishing the house. I am also telling you that the courtyard should be paved in marble and there should be a flower garden surrounding the castle; it should be without equal anywhere in the entire world. Flowers of all kinds should be blooming in it, flowers with exquisite fragrances, and at the very edge there should be rows of trees circling the whole garden. They should be fruit trees of different varieties and the finest there is."

He left, went to bed and when he got up, it was all there, and the fragrance of the flower garden enclosing the castle filled the air, far and wide.

**[Listener:] He was able to do it so fast?**

(It was finished overnight.)

He said: "Thank God, it is done."

The courtyard in the front was paved in marble, the stones one more beautiful than the other. He was so overjoyed, he didn't know what to do.

"Well, I'll see now if the king is still reluctant to give me his daughter."

Then he thought that he'd rather not meet the king until all was done according to his heart's desire. He took the piece of leather and hit the ground.

Said the little man: "What do you command, Peasant Gagyi?"

"I command that there should be a well in the middle of this courtyard. A well with a pump," he said, "and a lion standing on top. Out of the lion's mouth the water should flow into a golden trough!" he said. "In the corner of the courtyard there should be another well, where the cattle will come to drink. The troughs there should be made of cement and filled with plenty of water. Each trough should have its own pump supplying the water."

Well, this too was done. Then he slammed the leather to the ground once more:

"What do you command, Peasant Gagyi?"

"I command that all around the courtyard, on the perimeter, there should be silos. And there should be stables in front of them, for the horses, the colts, the mares, and the stallions, then for the oxen and the cows. There must be separate stables for each and the troughs in them, their sides and bottoms, must shine like mirrors. Behind the stables should be the silos so the different grains can be stored separately."

This was done, too. In the meantime the king grew alarmed for he could see from his castle the beautiful palace Peasant Gagyi had built.

He said, pounding his head: "Do you hear, my daughter? *If he asks for you once, I'll say yes a hundred times*. He is not just anybody. Look what he built, what a castle! Mine pales in comparison! Look, *three gold chains hook it up to the sky*. The castle is suspended on them."

**[Listener:] He enjoyed great wealth.**

"And look," he said, "it is *revolving on the spurs of a rooster*. It sparkles and glitters as it turns—you can see it from here. I don't dare go there, for he might say to me: 'You were too important—you didn't want to give me your daughter. I don't want her any more, now I can have anyone for the asking.'"

He was loath to go there for this reason. And all the while he was trembling, worrying whether Peasant Gagyi would come and ask for his daughter. But Peasant Gagyi didn't come, he wanted to tend to everything and acquire what he needed. His mother became such a lady that she walked around with gloves on her hands, a bracelet on her arm and gold rings on her fingers.

**[Listener:] Yet she was a poor woman.**

Well, Peasant Gagyi stood in his doorway and looked. He looked left and right and burst out laughing. He thought about his life and could hardly believe that this was his.

All of a sudden the king appeared, bringing his daughter.

He said: "Good day to you, my son!"

"Good day to you, too!"

"I have been expecting you, waiting for you a long time," he said, "but you didn't come. I don't know what kept you, was it your pride—or have you given up on my daughter, or what?"

"Well," he said, "I didn't come because I had no time. I was busy building."

"What you built is beautiful," he said. "How did you come by all that gold to have such a castle made?"

"That shouldn't concern you. It should suffice that I have it. This was your wish—it is now fulfilled. Do you like it, Great King?"

"I like it, I like it, my son. Anything more beautiful one couldn't imagine than what you built, or had built. But now you need a woman, or a queen. You have a castle, a fine place to live in, and you have everything else. What is still missing and what you should have is a queen."

"That will happen too. It'll happen soon," he said, "I am attending to it."

"Well," he said, "it's also my wish to give my daughter away in marriage."

This time he brought it up. He didn't wait for Peasant Gagyi to ask, he brought it up himself.

"Now then," he said, "would you give me your daughter, Great King?"

"I'll give her to you, sure I will. Of course, I will," he said. "*You need to ask only once and I'll say yes a hundred times*, for I see who you are."

Now he elevated him—he was no longer the dirty bum.

"Do what is necessary," he said, "so you can be wed as soon as possible!"

They did what was needed, designated the day of the wedding feast, and invited the guests. They came in coaches, in airplanes, and on motorcycles. They came as they could. *Gentlemen, kings, princes, barons, bare-assed farmworkers*—the king had assembled everyone. He ordered such a big wedding feast that the dancing and merry-making lasted for twenty-four days. There was great happiness. Then the feast was over. The old king went home and so did all the guests.

They had to rest. There were so many things, he had acquired so much that he didn't care about the piece of leather. He hung it up in a corner and left it there.

One day his father-in-law came over.

"Well, son, I came," he said. "I'd like to go hunting. I haven't been for a long time and I'd enjoy being in the forest."

"I'll go with you, father, sure I'll go. But please, take a seat first, let me offer you hospitality."

They sat down to eat and drink while the young bride busied herself around them, preparing provisions so they wouldn't go hungry. Then he had a steed brought up from the stable, fastened the saddle to its back and swung into it. His father-in-law mounted another horse and they set out. He took leave of his wife and they rode off.

Then, all of a sudden, a beggar appeared at the castle. Staff in hand and a knapsack on his back, he came and begged. The queen happened to be at the door. He greeted her and she acknowledged it.

"I ask you for some alms in the name of God. I am a poor man."

The young bride, the queen, ran and gave him fifty *forints* as a gift.

"Take it. I offer it to you in the name of God!"

She gave him a big, generous gift.

He said: "Your Majesty, I'd have another request if I may—perhaps you'd grant it."

"Well, if I can, why not?"

"Please give me a set of clothes. I am in tatters, you see. It is cold and I am freezing now that I have grown old."

Said the queen: "That you shouldn't ask for. How would my husband have them? He has clothes—but all are new, none are shabby. If he had something used, something old, I wouldn't deny you. I would give it to you in the name of God. The clothes he has are all brand new and without him I don't dare give you any of them," she said. "Why don't you come another time, when my husband is home? You'll get some from him, for he is not ungenerous."

Well the beggar thanked her for the alms and left. But once outside he turned around and said:

"I can't believe that an old pair of trousers couldn't be found in a royal household and that I have to leave here in rags."

Suddenly, the woman, the queen, remembered the hide and she felt sorry for the old man in tatters. She would have given him clothes, but she didn't feel free to do it.

She called out to him: "Come back, old man. Take this hide, I'll give it to you, you can cover yourself with it."

She didn't know what that piece of leather was. The woman had no idea where all the wealth had come from.

She said: "Here you are, you poor man. I'll give this to you. Put it on."

The man took it. In his misery he accepted it. The queen turned around and went inside. He started on his way and once outside the gate he stopped to look at the leather.

"Wasn't the queen ashamed to give me this? Couldn't she have found me some kind of coat, a *suba,* or anything other than this? She insulted me with this leather."

He took it and smashed it into the mud, hard. The little man the size of three hand-spans jumped out at once.

**[Listener:] He jumped out?**

(He did.)

He stood up and said: "What do you command? What do you command?"

"I command," he began, but got alarmed for a moment. He went back inside the gate and there he hit the ground with it again.

He said: "I command that this castle be surrounded by an ocean, an ocean so large that it couldn't be crossed any other way but by ship. It should be all around and enclose the castle completely. No one should be able to get in or out," he said.

No sooner had he pronounced the words than the ocean was there. The waves were breaking with such force that had a big log fallen in their way, they would have it carried away. Now what should he do? He couldn't get out either—since he was inside, he couldn't get out. He was frightened.

He went to the queen and said: "Your Majesty, I can't get out."

"Why? Are you ill?"

"No, I am not ill, but there is such a big sea outside, circling the entire castle, that I cannot get out. Not even by boat, the waves are as huge as in an ocean. One can only cross it by ship—there is no other way."

"How is that possible?" she said. "There is a flower garden around us. The castle is in the middle of the flower garden. Are you dreaming? What are you saying? Go," she said, "don't play tricks on me. I don't need your jokes."

**[Listener:] She didn't believe it?**

(No.)

"Come out," he said, " and see for yourself. Please come and look around."

The queen went out. She almost fell over when she saw that the beggar was right. There was an immense sea, with the waves swelling on it, something terrible.

"Oh, my God," she said, "how will my husband get home? How will he come home? How can he cross over? He cannot get here until they build a ship for him."

The young bride was upset—she wept, wringing her hands.

"Dear God, how will my husband come home?"

"Well, now, how would he come? Don't be sad, queen. I am here. I am here, in his place. You may be sure that your husband won't come back. Don't raise your hopes," he said, "that he'll make it home."

"Go away, you wretched old bum! Don't you speak this way to a queen!" she said. "Do you think I'd want a man like you? A beggar?"

"Look, think about it, the king won't come home," he said, "and you cannot live alone—you need someone. Let's get together. I'll do what a man has to do in the house and outside, and you'll have it easier."

The queen grew angry again.

"Stop aggravating and distressing me with your words. I have enough grief in my heart, I don't need any nuisance from you. If you entertain such thoughts, go to hell and not to the queen!"

The man grew silent for a while; then he said: "But I can't go away. I have to stay here."

"Then stay. Stay, but stop talking the way you do. It is not proper to speak to a queen in this manner."

A day or two passed.

"Your Majesty, think it over—let's join together. Your husband won't come home any more, so in the end you'll have to take up with me. The king has plenty of clothes, let me dress up and, you'll see, I'll turn into a handsome man. I won't look like a *peasant* once I am cleaned up."

Again she lashed out at the beggar, ordering him to shut up.

But time was passing, the days were going by. There was no sign of the king, so they got together. The man had noticed, however, that the hide had special qualities and sewed it on his body, onto his bare skin. He knew that whatever he commanded would be done on the spot, and realized that this is how the castle, the wealth and everything else had come to be. He sewed it onto his body so the queen wouldn't know. And he kept at the queen until finally she gave in and joined up with him.

She thought: I am waiting for my husband in vain, sooner or later I'll have to come together with him.

They came together.

Well, over there, the two kings ran out of food after a time, while they were hunting. They wanted to go home, but the news reached them that there was water everywhere. A huge ocean came to enclose the castle completely. No one could approach it, or get in. It was impossible to get into the castle. There was no ship, and no one could go by boat for waves as big as a house were welling up all over. Oh, was the king distressed! The old king just vanished—he left his son-in-law behind, but the young king remained there to ponder how he could get home. He had left his beautiful young wife at home and now he couldn't even get near her. His heart was filled with grief and he tormented himself, not knowing what to do. He had no food left. He shot some game, cooked it on a spit and ate it, but he had no bread.

He stood against a tree, resting on the butt of his gun. He was grieving and thinking of what he could do to get home.

Suddenly, three crows alighted in front of him. They scrabbled about in the muck and began cawing together. The king looked at them.

"Dear God, if only I could be a crow, if only I could fly! Maybe I could cross this ocean."

Then one of the crows spoke up: "Why are you grieving, King, Sir?"

"Don't even ask," he said, "you cannot help me in my distress anyway."

"Still, tell me, why are you grieving? Your sorrow is great, I can see."

"How could I not be grieving? When I left there was no trouble, and now such an immense ocean came to surround my castle, the water is all around in a circle, so that no people or animals can get even close to it."

**[Listener:] He didn't know about his wife's illicit dealings?**

(No, he didn't know about it.)

"Of course I am sad, there is a reason for it," he said, "but how could you help me? Is there a way you could help me?"

"Well," said the crow, "there may be a way, for I could fly across."

"Look," he said, "I'll write a letter and put it under your wing. If you can fly across, take it to my wife."

"I don't mind, I'll take it. Sure, I'll take it."

He wrote the letter and fastened it on the jackdaw's neck. It flew off with it and crossed the ocean. It entered the castle and when the queen saw the letter around its neck, she came running. The crow was so tame, it just stood there. The queen took the slip of paper and read her husband's handwriting.

He wrote: "Dear wife, there was a piece of leather on the porch, if you haven't removed it from there. See if you can find it but, whether you find it or not, send me a reply to let me know whether you have the leather or not."

So the jackdaw returned with a letter fastened to its neck. The king removed it and read what was written :

"Dear husband, the leather is here but I gave it to a beggar, not knowing what it was, and the beggar had asked for alms and clothes. I didn't dare to give him your clothes, for they are all brand new, and told him to come back when you are at home. He left in a fury because I wouldn't give him anything to wear. I felt sorry for him, for it was cold and I saw that he was shivering. Then I remembered the hide and told him to put it on his shoulders so he'd be protected from the wind. He took it. Now I don't see it anywhere. But the beggar is here—he wanted to leave but couldn't, there is an ocean all around. He wasn't able to go, he had to come back, and now he is here, in the castle. But I'll observe him and ask him where the leather is. If he has it, I'll write you so you'll know. It is too bad that you cannot come home—for me, too!"

Well the crow brought the letter and the king read it. It is all right as long as the man is there, for then we can find out where he put the hide. He wrote another letter:

"Wife, I am writing to say that when you get hold of the leather, if that person tells you where he put it, cut it up and sew it onto the body of the crow that brings you this note. There will be three crows going and you should sew a piece on each so you can send me the entire hide. And write me a letter to tell me how you are!"

As soon as she received the letter and read it, she began cajoling her whatchamacallit, her bedmate, into telling her where he had put the hide, the one she gave him.

"Why do you care since you gave it to me?" he said.

"Still," she said, "tell me, where is it?"

But since they slept together the young woman found out that he had wrapped himself in it. He had sewn his body into the leather.

**[Listener:] She embraced him and touched him.**

Right away she started in on him: "Look," she said, "do you know that ever since you came here, I haven't even had a drink with you? I say, let's go into the cellar and drink a glass of wine to my husband's health!"

"Let's go," he said, "I don't mind."

The man went along, happy, for he hadn't yet heard such talk from his wife. They sat down at the table and he said:

"Which is the strongest wine? Let's take some from that barrel."

He went, tapped the barrel, and drew some into a pitcher. They sat down at a table. In the center of the cellar there was a table with chairs around it. They poured wine and clinked their glasses.

"Let's drink to my man's health!"

The queen didn't drink, she just pretended to do so, and poured the wine out. It escaped the man's notice, he was so happy at the way the queen treated him. He emptied his glass.

"Now let's drink to my health," said the queen.

"Let's drink, I don't mind. God bless you!"

They finished the second glass, but the queen didn't drink, she just pretended to, and poured the wine into her bodice. The man emptied his glass. The wine was very strong. The beggar wasn't used to such potent wine.

He said: "Let's drink one to your health!"

They drank again and when they reached the bottom of the third glass the man keeled over.

**[Listener:] She succeeded!**

He slept like a log, he was so drunk. That was all the young bride needed, she took out a pocket knife and one by one cut off the layers of his clothing. She came upon the leather, sewn onto his bare skin. She cut off the lining and kept cutting and pulling until she had it all. Then she went upstairs.

The jackdaws had just arrived with the letter. She took the hide, held the bird down and sewed a section onto its body, leaving only the two wings free. She sewed the bird into the hide and did the same with the second and the third jackdaw. She divided the entire piece among the three birds and wrote a letter:

"Dear husband, I am sending you the leather as you requested. Please use every means you can to come home."

Well, the jackdaws left. They got back fast for they flew. They alighted in front of the king. He saw the leather and was so overjoyed that he didn't know what to do. He held the birds and removed the leather from their bodies.

One of the jackdaws said: "Great King, we brought what you wanted, but I won't let you have it until you promise that when you get back to your castle, to your flower garden, you'll make me king of the birds. I want you to authorize me to become king of the birds. If you don't, I'll fly away and you'll never see this hide again."

"Yes, of course, I promise! Not only do I promise but I'll act on it as soon as I get home, God willing. Come, we'll go together. And if, thanks to you, I get my flower garden back as it was, I'll install you. The other two will be alongside you: one will become a juror, the other a magistrate, or something. You'll have the most important positions in the castle," he said, "It is good that you brought me the hide."

Right away he cut the leather off their backs and pieced it together somehow, using twigs and thorns. He mounted his horse and rode off. The jackdaws followed him, cawing above his head all the way. When he reached the ocean he saw how immense it was—the waves swelled so high that they would have wrecked a ship. He took the leather, spread it out, and three little men appeared. Three of them came, as the young bride had cut the leather in three.

"What do you command, king?"

"I command that this ocean disappear from here and all should be restored to the way it was before, including the flower garden. The same flowers should be there, as fragrant as before. The fruit trees must be there, too, along with everything else. I don't want to see this ocean—it must dry up and the earth beneath it must be as smooth as it was before."

No sooner had he uttered the words than it happened. Swallowed by the earth, or what, the ocean just vanished. One could walk across with dry feet. The flower garden was back in its former place with beautiful flowers and paths between them. Overcome with joy, he didn't know what to do. He rode into the courtyard at a gallop. His wife came out running to meet him with open arms:

"Oh, my sweetheart, my lost husband," she said, "where were you all the time that I haven't seen you?"

"Well, where I was my life was rather pitiful, but thank God I am home now. It is only thanks to you that I was able to come. If you hadn't sent me the leather, I would have remained in misery. But I say thank God that I am home. Now where is that dogcatcher who sewed the leather on his body?"

She said: "He is asleep in the cellar."

**[Listener:] He was still asleep.**

(He was still sleeping.)

"Never mind," he said, "it is good that he is around—we'll take care of him."

He sent the jackdaws into the flower garden.

"Henceforth," he said, "from this day on, you'll be the kings of the birds—you'll be the greats among them. You'll be the greats of the flower garden! Oh yes, you'll be the rightful residents, the rulers of the whole garden."

All right. The birds flew into the garden, perched on a branch and looked around. They were hungry. Right away the king ordered two soldiers to go and get the man out of the cellar. They dragged him out at once, still asleep. They put him on a table outside and hacked him to pieces with an ax. Then they fed his flesh to the jackdaws, to the king of the birds. The birds had just arrived—they had to be treated to food.

"Eat amply, my guests!"

The jackdaws ate the man's flesh, there in the castle, in the flower garden. They hung it on the branches and pecked at it until it was all gone. Then the king and the queen exchanged wedding vows again and began a new life. They are alive to this day, if they haven't died. They lived and they died and for the listeners they . . .

**[Listener:] Tell us what they did. . . .**

# 16. The Golden Egg

AT 567(*The Magic Bird-Heart*) + 566 (*The Three Magic Objects and the Wonderful Friends*). MNK 566 (Fortunatus) lists 9 variants of this combination.

Aunt Zsuzsa learned this tale from young people in one of the neighboring villages in 1955, a year before she told it to me. Following her official recognition as a folk artist, she wanted to add to her repertoire. Wherever she went, she asked friends and relatives to tell or read tales to her. This one came from grandnieces in Mucsfa. The brief and original combination of the two tale types gives us an idea about Mrs. Palkó's style of adapting and internalizing plots. She does not change the content of the two stories—she structures and weaves them together into one, in such a way as to best express her opinion concerning the characters and their motivations. Her story is about money (gold in the hyperbolic language of the magic tale) and greed that has no class distinction. Neither rich nor poor is embarrassed to scramble for money in the most humiliating and disgusting way. In Mrs. Palkó's story the network of intrigue is enormous: only the poor woodcutter, the hardworking father who catches the bird, stays uninvolved. It all begins with the priest—the clerical lover as commonly featured in humorous folktales (AT 1725-1849). The flirtatious wife is illiterate like her husband; it is the priest who reads the inscription on the bird's wings and orders the woman to prepare him a meal; but folktale justice is served when the children, just back from school, unwittingly eat this magic meal. Realizing that they have eaten the precious bird, they run away, afraid of parental wrath. The two young heroes discover their luck later, when it turns out that the heart and the liver of the bird in their stomachs are inexhaustible sources of gold. From this point, as in other variants, only one brother's adventures are pursued; the other boy reenters the tale only during the reunification scene that provides the happy ending.

Enter the helper, offering shelter to the boy hero. But a sweet old woman like this is rare in magic tales, because she turns out to be a schemer. She steals the golden eggs from under the youngster's pillow, and denies room and board when the eggs stop appearing. The usual wedding party in the royal city ("capital city," in Aunt Zsuzsa's speech) is for having a good time. But the boy falls victim to his own openness and the greed of the newlywed princess and her cohorts: the queen and her cook, courtly ladies indeed. They drug the boy and she eats the heart he had vomited. His downfall is spectacular: he is left with nothing—no money, no food—out on the road. But as a "poor boy," he has the narrator's compassion: God leads him to the miraculous fruits that will avenge him and restore his luck. The three women are humiliated, transformed into donkeys with horns, tortured by forced labor and beaten, and the boy swallows the heart that the princess is forced to vomit. This ruthless punishment was narrated like a humoresque: the audience appreciated the account of how the doctor cured the sick women of their animal shapes; listeners laughed heartily as the enormous donkeys knocked down the ceiling in their fine room; folktale justice is served as the money returns to the brothers. After all, why did the princess steal? Her father the king had plenty, as he said himself when he hired the doctor to cure the donkeys: "if you could cure them, I'd give you so much money," he said, "that your children's children would eat it by the spoonful."

———

There was once a poor woodcutter. He went to the forest every day to cut wood. He and his wife had two children, two sons, who went to school. The boys already knew how to read and write, but their parents didn't. One day the man left to work in the forest and the woman stayed at home. The boys went to school and the woman received a priest who had begun to court her.

Well, the man was out in the forest, and as he was cutting wood, a bird took flight from a great big tree next to him. The bird flew off—he followed it with his eyes and saw how beautiful it was. He had never seen a bird like it. Each little feather on its body was of a different color.

"Oh," he said, "what kind of bird is this? It looks so beautiful! I have never seen one like it before. Surely, there is a nest in that tree, I'll climb up and look. There may be nestlings in it, young ones or eggs, I'll take them out."

He climbed up the tree and in the nest he found an egg, a golden egg it was. He removed it and put it in his pocket. When he came home he gave it to his wife for safekeeping. They all rejoiced for the egg was so beautiful, they had never seen one like it—it was pure gold. The next day the man went to the forest again to cut wood. He went to the same place as the day before, and once again the bird flew out of the nest. He watched it fly, it was a very beautiful bird. He climbed up to the nest and found another golden egg. The man thought to himself that instead of climbing the tree every time, he would come tomorrow, wait for the bird to return to the nest, and catch it. And that's how it was. He climbed up slowly, caught the bird in the nest and brought it down. He thought he would put it in a cage so it would lay eggs there and he wouldn't have to climb the tree any more. (Do you know this story?) Well, he took the bird home, put it in a cage, and they and the boys delighted in it. It was a great treasure.

Well, the man continued to go into the forest day after day, and the priest came to see the woman.

When he spotted the cage he said: "Where does this cage come from? And this beautiful bird, where did you find it?"

"My husband caught it in the forest."

He said: "Open the cage, let me look at it closely and see what it is like."

The priest took the bird out of the cage, examined it and noticed that there were golden letters on its left wing. He read them and they said that whoever kills this bird and eats its heart and liver will find a golden egg under his pillow in the morning. He looked at the bird's right wing. There, too, were letters. He read them. They said:

"whoever eats my heart and liver, will find a wallet full of money under his pillow." The man and the woman didn't know what the letters meant on the bird's wings; the boys knew, but they didn't tell their parents. (Like me, they didn't know how to read.)

Then the priest said: "Do you know what I want to say to you? Kill this bird and cook it for me for noon, tomorrow. When it's ready, call me and invite me over for the midday meal."

The woman thought about it for a while. She knew that the bird was very precious and wondered what her husband would say if he didn't find it? Still, she promised to do it. She was on good terms with the priest for he courted her, so she said she would kill it. The priest went home and asked her to tell him as soon as the dish was ready. So, the woman killed the bird and when it was cooked she ran to ask the priest to come for the midday meal.

Meanwhile the boys came home from school. Their mother wasn't there.

One asked the other: "What did mother make for dinner?"

They noticed that the bird wasn't in its cage.

"Oh, dear," they said, "the bird is gone, perhaps it flew away!"

They searched everywhere, looked in every room, but the bird was nowhere to be found. The boys were alarmed: "our mother left—she didn't lock the door—maybe someone stole the bird." This is what they thought. But since they were hungry, they began looking for something to eat. They looked in the pot and they looked in the oven, and there they found it. There was the bird, roasted pink.

"Oh," said one to the other, "you see, dear brother, our mother has killed the bird. How could she do it! But since she has done it, let's eat its heart and liver! You'll have the heart and I'll have the liver. Let's eat it!" he said.

So, they ate it but they gulped down the bird's little body as well. That's all they ate. Then they became worried about what their mother would say when she found that they had eaten the whole bird and left nothing for them.

Said the older boy to the younger: "Listen! We'd better run away, for mother will give us a good thrashing when she gets back," he said. "Let's run, let's get away before she comes home, for she'll beat us like a sack of corn."

The boys made off and soon the woman returned with the priest. He sat down at the table and the woman went to fetch the roast from the oven. There was nothing there. She felt very ashamed:

"Oh, forgive me, Reverend Father—the boys ate it!"

The priest became angry. He took the trouble to come, and it was for naught! He knew how special was the meat he had missed. The priest went home and the woman waited for the boys to come, to give them a beating, but they didn't show up. They ran and ran until they reached a big forest. They continued in the woods until they came to a crossroads and there they stopped. Said the older to the younger:

"Now let's separate. You go one way and I'll go the other."

One went right, the other left. The boy kept going in the forest until evening closed in. He wished he would come to the edge of the forest soon and find a village where he could spend the night. Well, he did get out of the woods and he found a small house, a little shack. A light was burning inside, so he entered. He said good evening and the old woman responded with a greeting.

"What has brought you here, son?"

"Well, dear auntie," he said, "I left to find my fortune but darkness closed in on me. Please be kind and give me shelter for the night."

"You may stay, son," she said, "but I am a poor woman, I don't have anything to offer you to eat."

"I don't need anything," he said, "just a place to lie down."

She threw a rag on the floor, made something resembling a small bed for him, and the boy lay down.

He said: "I'll be looking for something to do, I'll be looking for some work."

When the boy went out of the house, the woman quickly picked up the rags from the floor and found a golden egg. Oh, was she happy with the golden egg! She put it away.

"Listen, son, come back again this evening. You may spend the night here any time. I'll offer you shelter, with pleasure."

So the boy returned in the evening. This time the old woman gave him a better reception. She offered him food, made up his bed, and the boy went to sleep. The next morning the old woman found another golden egg and she put that away, too. On the third day the boy prepared to leave again.

On his way out he said to the woman: "Listen, old auntie, do you know what I have heard? It is posted in an announcement," he said, "that on Sunday the king is holding a big wedding feast. Rich or poor, everyone is welcome. Rich or poor, it won't make any difference."

"Why are you telling me this, son? Would you like to go?"

"I am going," said the boy, "but you may come, too. As an old woman you'll be well received, for sure."

"I wouldn't think of it," she said, "I am old, I don't care for big wedding feasts any more. I am telling you, son, don't you go either!"

"Why shouldn't I?"

"Well, because one must bring a present to a wedding; it is customary to give a present."

"I'll give one."

"And what will you give, son?"

"I'll give the bride a golden egg. She'll be pleased."

"All right, son," she said, "if you want to go, go."

When they woke the next morning, the lad got dressed, took a golden egg with him and left. As soon as he arrived he told the bride that he had brought her a golden egg. She was so happy—she had never seen such a beautiful golden egg before, she said. She accepted it and showed her mother and the old cook what a fine present she had received.

Said the cook: "We must call the boy and ask him where he found this egg."

He was invited to enter another room with the cook, the old queen, and the bride, and they asked him where he had found the golden egg. So the boy recounted to them that his father was a woodcutter, that he always went into the forest to cut wood and one day he saw a bird fly out of a nest and in that nest he found the egg. Twice he had found an egg there, but the third time he caught the bird and put it into a cage. The boy told them what had happened, that his mother killed the bird and cooked it for the midday meal. But first he told them about the letters on the bird's wings. They had read them and since their mother had killed the bird, they ate its heart and liver.

He said: "I ate the heart, so now every morning I find an egg under my pillow. My brother ate the liver and he gets a wallet full of money every morning."

That's all they needed to hear. They began offering him all sorts of fine drinks, and he wasn't used to them. He became drunk and fell asleep. Then he felt nauseous and began to vomit. He brought up the heart he had swallowed. When the bride saw this, she grabbed the heart, placed it in a dish, washed it and ate it. She washed it and ate it. When the poor boy woke up, the wedding feast was over. He returned to the old woman and bragged about the great celebration he had attended. But when the boy rose in the morning, the old woman found no egg. There was no egg. The next night he slept there again, and again there was no egg.

Said the old woman: "Son, you'd better move on—I won't keep you any longer— I am a poor woman. Look for work elsewhere!"

So the poor boy left. He was sad, not because the old woman had rejected him but because there were no more eggs. He knew then that they had made him drunk, that he had brought up the heart and they had taken it from him. In great sorrow he set out to look for his brother. Along the way he became hungry but had no food to eat. And he was very sad that they had stolen his treasure. Then, in the middle of the woods, he came to a road. He took it and suddenly he saw an apple tree on the side of the road. The apples on the tree were more beautiful than any he had ever seen, and their delicious fragrance filled the air far and wide. He thought that when he reached the tree, he would pick some of the apples—even if they belonged to the king he would pick them. As he approached, he saw that the apples were in such abundance as God had provided them; their color was brilliant—it was impossible to describe how beautiful they were.

If they are beautiful, they must be good, too—he thought, and picked one. He picked an apple and ate it. He took a bite and swallowed it. By the time he finished, he had turned into a donkey, so huge that maybe there wasn't another one like it in the whole world. The apple had made him into such an enormous donkey. He looked at himself:

"Dear God, I am transformed! The apple changed me by magic! I cannot go among people any more, from now on I must live my life in the forest."

Grieving, the donkey kept going, pressing ahead in the woods. Suddenly he caught sight of a pear tree on the side of the road. The pears were as beautiful as the apples. "It's all the same to me now—whatever else I could become, doesn't matter any more since I am an animal. I'll pick one."

He picked a pear, bit into it, and by the time he ate the whole pear, he had grown such big horns that it was terrible.

"Oh, Lord, it wasn't enough that I turned into a donkey, now I have horns, too. I have become a wonder!"

The poor donkey continued on his way, grief-stricken that he'd never recover his human form again. He saw a ditch and a stream; a clear, running stream. He thought he'd go and drink from it as he was very thirsty. He bent down and drank from the stream. And, listen! Miracle of miracles, he regained his human form. He became a beautiful lad, like a flower! More handsome than he has ever been.

"Oh, dear God, you have done it! You gave me back my own body! I know now what I'll do."

He walked until he came to a village and there he asked for a bottle. He put it in his pocket, returned to the stream and filled it with water. He put the bottle in his pocket and made his way back to the apple tree, but first to the pear tree—he reached that sooner. He filled one of his pockets with pears. Next he went to the apple tree and picked enough to stuff his other pocket full of apples. Then he headed straight for the *capital city*, the royal city, where the wedding feast had been held. He went to the market, took out the apples and began offering them for sale. The people came running in droves, they nearly crushed him. All asked where he had found the beautiful fruit, they had never seen such apples, they were so fragrant. They inquired about their cost, about the price of one apple, but he asked so much that no one was able to buy; he had set the price of the apples too high. Then the king's cook came along. She had heard about the beautiful apples offered for sale. She came over and asked how much did this apple cost, how much did he want for one. He named the price, and she got alarmed:

"Who can buy it for so much money? It is very expensive!"

He said: "It is, but it is worth it, for there is no better apple in the entire world."

She said: "I don't dare buy it, it costs too much. But wait, I'll go and ask Her Majesty the Queen whether I should spend all that money. It is very expensive."

"Well, go. You'll find the apples when you come back and you'll tell me then whether you want to buy them or not."

The cook went home and spoke to the queen: "Oh, Your Majesty the Queen, what apples I have seen! Apples like these don't exist anywhere else in the whole world! They are beautiful, the finest, I can't describe to you how beautiful they are, and how fragrant."

"Why didn't you buy them?"

She said: "He is asking so much for them that I didn't dare."

"How much is he asking? How expensive can they be?"

She told the queen.

"Go," she said, "buy them. We have the money, but we can't always get fruit of such quality."

So the cook went back and bought the apples. She bought the pears too, and took them home. Well, the queen didn't know what to do, which one to bite into, they were so beautiful, and they were good. The young woman who had just married also came in, and saw the fruit.

"Oh, mother," she said, "I'll die if I can't have one! They are splendid!"

"Go ahead, eat, my dears. I bought them to be eaten. She gave each an apple, they ate it and she, herself, ate one, too. As soon as they finished the apples, they turned into huge donkeys. The queen, the cook, and the young woman who was just married became three donkeys. They filled the room and were barely able to move around each other, so enormous were they. Then they started on the pears and ate them; they ate the pears. Now they grew horns, so tall that they knocked down the ceiling with them. The king knew nothing of all this—he wasn't present, he was in parliament.

Soon it was time for the midday meal and the king came home. He entered the room, the dining room—there wasn't anything there. Other times when he came home he found the table set, the meal ready, and now there was nothing. He asked the chambermaid, where were the queen and the cook, and was most astonished that there was no bustling about and no preparations to serve him dinner. Well, they were nowhere to be seen. The king entered the room where the donkeys were. When he saw them, when he saw that they could barely move past each other, he became frightened. Where did these donkeys come from? Who was the fool who let the donkeys into such a fine room? He kept looking for his wife but couldn't find her; neither could he find the cook, nor his daughter. The king became convinced that the three donkeys were his family members.

"Dear God," he said, "what could I do to have them regain their original form?"

Quickly, he summoned doctors from everywhere, one more learned than the other. The learned doctors came from all over, from other countries, too, but not one was able to help them. If only someone gave the donkeys back their former shape, he would pay any amount of money that person asked for. But no one succeeded.

Then the young man, who had the apples, heard that the queen, the cook, and the girl had turned into huge donkeys. He dressed in the attire of a doctor, to look like a doctor, and went to see the king. He announced himself:

"I heard, Your Majesty," he said, "what a wonder occurred in your castle, in your palace!"

"It's true," said the king, "a wonder like this perhaps hasn't happened anywhere else in the world."

"Couldn't the doctors find a way to help?"

He said: "I have searched everywhere, looked all over the world, but no one can help them."

"Your Majesty, maybe I can. I am a doctor, too."

"Well, if you could do something, if you could cure them, I'd give you so much money," he said, "that your children's children would eat it by the spoonful. I'd give you so much, if only you could help."

"Your Majesty," he said, "entrust them to me for one week. Let me take all three. I'll help them but only if you don't interfere. Just give me a cart," he said—(what do you call those wide carts, without sides?)—"a dray, give me a dray."

The king said: "You'll have it. I'll give you one."

He ordered it right away. The lad said he needed nothing else, just the dray. He harnessed the three donkeys—the king had ordered harnesses, too—hitched them to the cart and drove to the city. There he piled sacks of wheat and grain onto the dray, loading it as high as if it were a wagon full of hay. Then he took a big whip and began flogging the donkeys while he circled the city with them. This is how he made them suffer, driving them around for two days without letup. Then he pulled out the bottle of water to let them drink a little, but he gave it only to the queen, and the water restored her former shape at once.

He brought her home to the king and said: "Here, I cured one—this leaves two."

"Oh," said the king, "if only you could cure my dear daughter and my cook as well!"

The lad returned to the dray and this time he filled it with cement. He drove them all the time, with a load as heavy as for the three donkeys before, and he kept whipping them when they faltered. For two days he had them haul the cart around and around the city, giving them barely enough food to keep them from dropping dead. He gave them no water. After two days he let the cook drink from the bottle. She, too, became her former self again. He took her home to the king:

"Here you are. I cured the cook. Your beloved daughter will get well, too," he said, "but you have to wait a while longer."

He went back and packed the dray once more. He made the load as heavy as the first day and had the one donkey pull it. He gave the donkey not a bite to eat, no water, nothing. He tortured it until the evening of the second day, when it couldn't move any more. Then he took a pail, filled it with the contents of the toilet and put it before the donkey. The stench was terrible but the poor beast was so parched and famished that it swallowed it. The lad was the angriest with her, for it was she who ate the bird's heart. As soon as she ate from the pail, she felt nauseous and began to vomit. She brought up the heart and the lad took it. He placed it in clean water and washed it, changing the water maybe ten times, washing it clean, then he ate it. He ate the heart. Next, he let the donkey drink from the bottle and she regained her human form instantly. So he took the king's daughter back to the palace:

"Here she is, Your Majesty, I cured her."

The king gave the lad so much money in gold and silver that he could barely carry it. He had returned the dray, handed it over, too. What's more, the king enter-tained him lavishly, honored and thanked him for he was able to help when not one of the many doctors and wise men he had summoned could do anything. Then they took leave of one another and the lad went on his way.

He went until he found his brother. They fell into each other's arms and wept, for they hadn't seen one another in a long time. He told his brother how he had fared.

"So, you don't have any money?" asked the brother.

He said: "Sure, I do, the king gave me money."

But the brother had already bought a six-story house, he had so much money. And he had bought a big estate, he had become a very wealthy squire.

"Come, dear brother, come to the city where I live, we'll buy for you, too!"

So they went home together and acquired great wealth for the lad, an estate, a big house, three stories high—what was it like? I can't say, for I haven't seen it. Both lads took wives, turned into rich squires, such big landowners that no one was their equal—and they are still alive today, if they haven't died.

You see, everyone has to endure suffering in a tale.

# 17. Nine

AT 650 (*Strong John*); MNK 650 (*Strong John*) lists 24 tales as well as 35 other texts falling into eight distinctive type-combinations, A to H. Mrs Palkó's follows the outline of the main plot, lacking only the supernatural (mythic) origin of the strong servant. Hers is a realistic labor-contract story placed in the context of the irreconcilable differences between master and hired hand. Versions are particularly popular in East Europe where rudiments of a serf-based economy persisted longer than in West Europe. The master (king, landowner, judge, or priest) and the servant try to outwit—and eventually destroy—each other, but in the duel the servant is the winner.

Mrs. Palkó told this tale in 1950, in an afternoon visit at the house of the cobbler Cyril Sebestyén. She had heard it from Mrs. Fábián, her youngest daughter Erzsi, who read it from a book, probably the Benedek-edition that reprinted it from an 1862 collection. The hero's given name "Nine" (the boy who eats nine times as much as others) is quite common. In Aunt Zsuzsi's formulation there is a masterfully crafted dialogic relationship between the king and Nine. As things happen, the king, who hoped to hire a boy for nothing, becomes increasingly concerned with the high costs of feeding him, the damage he causes and his dangerous dealings with wild animals and devils. Nine actually does what he is told, no more nor less. He is a solid, honest, and loyal servant, eager to please. The tasks he is ordered to execute are absurd, hence his absurd acts and naively brutal display of physical strength. At the same time, the king is dishonest, pretending good will while trying, trick after trick, to destroy Nine instead of exploiting his abilities. That all this is a farce we learn from the easy and lighthearted resolution. All along, the king was afraid of the two slaps from the strong boy, and when the contract expires he appears a royal wimp. The princess aptly resolves the situation and they all live happily thereafter till death parts them.

———

In a land far, far away, *where the curly-tailed pigs play* and even beyond that, there was once a poor widow. She had a son, whose name was Nine. He was called Nine because he ate enough for nine men. The poor woman was worried—she had no husband and she was afraid that she wouldn't be able to fill the boy's stomach.

One day she said to him: "Son, you are hardy now, it's time you went somewhere and looked at least to earn your keep. I cannot make enough money to satisfy your hunger.

Said the boy: "I am not going; I am staying here. There is time for me to go later."

In her distress the poor woman went to see the king and said to him: "Great King, I have a son, his name is Nine. I am a poor widow and I cannot provide for him and for myself. Please let me bring him here so that you can place him in a job somewhere and find him a position. I don't mind if he gets no pay, he can do service for his keep."

"All right," he said, "bring the boy, poor woman, and we'll see what we can do with him." The poor woman went home, got her son and the next day returned to the king.

The king said to Nine: "Well, son, do you want to enter my service?"

Nine said: "Yes. And what do you pay?"

"Look, son," he said, "what should I pay you? How much do you want for a year?"

"I don't want anything else—just give me enough food to eat, as much as I need, and, when the year is over, allow me to slap you in the face, twice."

The king thought about it. He could tolerate being slapped twice, as long as he didn't have to pay. So they came to an agreement, the boy stayed, and his mother went home.

But the boy was really a lad. He was big enough to be considered a young man.

The king said to him: "Look son, I'll put you into the stable and give you four oxen to look after, and a wagon. You'll use them to go into the fields and into the woods, wherever there is work to be done. And it will be your job to feed and water them."

Well, they gave the boy enough to eat. Nine ate nine platefuls of soup and nine slices of bread. They thought he was famished and that once he'd had his fill, he would eat less. But he continued eating as much. He ate the shares of nine men.

One day the king gave an order: "Tomorrow morning, all of you farmhands will go and fetch some wood. The first to return from the forest will receive a set of clothes as a gift, with everything, from shoes to caps. Rise early, feed and water the animals and be ready to go by dawn!"

They went to bed and slept. The other farmhands got up at three o'clock, fed and watered the animals, but Nine slept on. He didn't get up. All the lads were ready with their oxen. They were fed, watered and scrubbed and just had to be hitched to the yoke. When that was done too, they set out. They left.

By the time Nine woke and got up they had finished milking the cows and had taken the milk into the kitchen to strain, nine big cans of it. While the farmhands were out straining milk, Nine drank all nine canfuls.   They asked him: "Nine, where is the milk? When we went out the cans were full and now they are all empty."

Nine said: "Where is it? I drank it. I am preparing to go to the forest—I was hungry."

Oh, did they get angry with him!

"Listen!" they said. "All the others have left and you just got up now? Have your oxen been fed and watered?"

"Well, they haven't eaten yet."

"The other hired hands are not obliged to feed and water your oxen. They left for the forest."

"I'll get there myself," he said. "I'll catch up with them."

He went and brought out the oxen from the stable and without feeding, watering or scrubbing them, he hitched them to the yoke. He took a long whip and drove them trotting out of the courtyard.

He left, but when he reached the forest the others had finished loading their wagons. They were ready to go home.

He said: "Well, well! Perhaps you are preparing to return?"

"For sure, we are. Didn't you hear the king last night? The first one home will get a set of clothes."

"Aren't you going to wait for me?"

"No," they said. "We got up at three o'clock and you stayed in bed. You were free to get up, too!"

When Nine heard this, he unhitched the oxen and let them roam free in the forest and forage for food. They were hungry and he thought that while he was loading his wagon they would eat their fill. Then he grabbed a tree and tore it out of the ground, roots and all. Not like the others, who cut the trees down with a saw and chopped them up, he pulled out the trees with their roots and threw them onto the road so the wagons couldn't pass. He hurled all the trees on the road. The drivers began to shout:

"Why did you block the road?"

"To make you wait for me!"

When he thought that he had torn out enough trees he loaded his wagon. He tossed them on with their roots and branches and made the pile as high as if it were a stack of cornstalks; one had to look up at it. Then he tied the trees down—so they wouldn't scatter—and ran after the oxen, ready to yoke them. He ran after them, but what he found was four wolves. They had torn the oxen to pieces and all that remained was their bones.

"Well, pals," he said to them, "what did you do here? You devoured my oxen? And how am I to take the wood home? Wait!"

He grabbed the four wolves and harnessed them to the wagon. He wanted to drive them, but the wolves couldn't manage the load, they couldn't lift the wood, or even budge the wagon.

Then he went back into the forest and continued walking until he caught two bears. He hitched them to the wagon and they started out, down the hill, at a trot. The others set forth, too, but they took the road, while the beasts dragged Nine through forests and fields and ditches—they went wherever they could. Nine was unable to control them.

"Just keep it up, if this is the way you like to go, it is all right, as long as you carry the wood," said Nine.

All of a sudden a devil appeared. He held a small stick in his hand and as the wagon was moving he kept pushing it between the spokes of the wheel.

Nine noticed it and said: "What are you doing there?"

He answered: "I am playing tricks, I am joking with you."

"You can joke all you like, but you must know that if you break the wheel, I'll have you grab the axle. You'll have to hold up the wagon if the wheel breaks."

The devil paid no attention to his warning, he continued shoving the stick between the spokes.

Suddenly, crash! The wheel broke. Nine didn't waste a moment, he jumped off the wagon and said:

"So, you are joking with me! What do you think, that I'll go back to fetch another wheel? Oh no, you come here and hold on to the axle until we get home!"

The devil had no choice but to do as he was told.

Well, they continued on their way. The beasts went like lightning, but when they came to a stream and had to cross over to the other side, they refused to get into the water. He unyoked them, put them on top of the wagon and tied them down so they wouldn't escape. Then he said to the devil:

"Now you hold on to the back while I hold the front while we'll carry the wagon across. We'll hitch up the beasts again on the other side."

So the devil held up the back, Nine the front, and the beasts were tied to the top of the big pile of wood on the wagon. When they crossed the stream, they stopped. Nine untied the beasts and harnessed them again. This time he hitched the two bears to the back and the four wolves to the front. They set forth but raced at such speed that all the devils of the world couldn't have pulled the wagon any faster.

Meanwhile the king grew impatient. The men were late returning from the forest much later than at other times. Not one of them had come back. He wondered what had happened to them.

He called one of his servants: "Go up to the tower, son, and look to see what is keeping them."

The lad came down and said to the king: "Your Majesty, they are coming, but I only see one wagon. It is not coming on the road, but through the fields and meadows, any which way. And it's not the oxen that are hitched to the wagon," he said, "but four wolves and two bears. It seems to me," he said, "that Nine is with them but the others are nowhere to be seen."

"Oh, God, I hope not!" said the king. "Go look again whether it is all wolves and bears pulling the wagon!"

The servant ran out, looked and rushed back:

"Well, Your Majesty, I wasn't lying. Nine is coming with four wolves and two bears. He is bringing such a big load of wood that it is terrible!

"Oh dear!" he said, "Go lock the gate, they mustn't be let in. I don't want those beasts to destroy us!"

The servant went, locked the gate and secured it well so they couldn't get in.

When Nine came to the gate, he wanted to open it. He couldn't, it was locked. He looked around but there was no one in the courtyard whom he could have asked to open it.

He said to the devil: "Look, I don't want to stand around here and wait. Take the back of the wagon, I'll take the front, and we'll lift it over to the other side!"

He unhitched the animals and tied them up outside, for he couldn't let them in.

"Now grab the wagon and let's heave it across," he said.

They threw it over with such force that the wagon collapsed and the wood on it broke into pieces. There was no need to chop it up. Next, Nine and the devil hurled the animals inside. There was a strong fence, they couldn't escape. Then he climbed over the gate and said to the devil:

"You are not needed any more, get lost!"

*The king nearly died, he was so desperate.* The bears were roaring, the wolves howling—he dared not go out. Then Nine took them, led them into a stable and shut the door.

The king asked him: "Nine, why are you so late? Your pals haven't come home yet, I haven't seen any one of them. You are the first."

"Well, I'll tell you," said Nine. "They left before me and had finished loading by the time I got there. They wouldn't help me," he said, "so I pulled out the trees by their roots and threw them on the road, making it impossible for them to pass and get home before me. Then," he said, "I ran after my oxen to yoke them, but the wolves had torn them to pieces. The others thought that since the beasts had devoured my oxen, I would have to stay there with my wagon. No, not me! I grabbed the wolves and two bears and hauled the wood home. I got delayed, too, because a devil came around and began playing tricks on me. He broke the spokes of the wagon wheel and I had to stop," he said. "But I got angry and made him hold up the wagon all the way home. We also had to cross a big stream. We unhitched the beasts, I put them on top of the wood pile and tied them down. The devil and I carried the wagon over to the other side—that delayed us, too. I thought the others would be back by now, but I see they are not," he said. "Yet we left at the same time."

Said the king: "And you, why didn't you come on the road?"

He answered: "Because my beasts didn't know that way."

When the king heard how strong Nine was, he became alarmed. He was ready to pay him for his service, provided he went away, so frightened was he. But he didn't show that he was afraid, or angry.

He said: "You are a good lad, son. You earned the set of clothes."

Right away they brought him the brand new clothes. Nine was happy. Then the others arrived, but they got nothing, because they were late.

The king kept pondering what he could do to get rid of Nine. One day he summoned him and said:

"Look, Nine, I want to have a well dug at the edge of the forest. I have hired the master workmen and you'll go with them. When you finish digging and reach the spring, you'll line the well with stones. But I say to you, you must watch over the workmen, be with them at all times, for you are the smartest among them. You should be the one to begin paving the well and laying the foundations."

Nine said: "All right, Your Majesty, it will be done as you wish."

They dug the well and came upon the spring. Water was flowing in abundance.

Nine asked: "Who among us will put in the foundation?"

The others said: "Nine, you are the strongest. You better go down!"

"I am not afraid," he said. "I'll go."

But they had agreed with the king that when Nine reached the bottom, they would drop a ten-ton rock on him, to kill him.

Well, Nine went into the well and they pushed the ten-ton rock down, thinking it would hit his head and he would die. But he noticed the whooshing sound of the falling rock. He looked up, saw the rock, caught it with one hand and hurled it out of the well. The workmen got so frightened that they nearly died. They feared that he would come up and kill them. But he didn't say a word. They worked until evening, finished the well and went home. The king called one of the master workmen to the side:

"Why didn't you do as you were told?"

"We did, but he threw the rock back out with such force that it whizzed far past our heads."

Then the king got even more alarmed. If Nine was so strong, and he were to slap him in the face twice when the year was up, he would die on the spot.

He summoned his advisers and began consulting with them about the best way to lose Nine.

The advisers told him: "King, we found the solution. Write a letter to the town magistrate and tell him that you are sending him the most notorious robber. You are handing him over and he'll know the rest, he'll know what to do."

So the king said to Nine: "Look, son, I am sending you to town hall to see the magistrate."

"All right, Your Majesty, but I'd like to know what for?"

"You see, son, the magistrate owes me a large sum of money," he said. "He knows how much, and I'll also tell him in my letter. You give him my message—that I need that money and would he please return it. You'll have to tell him verbally!" Then the king put the letter in an envelope:

"No one must open this, son. Hand it to the magistrate in person!"

The king thought that if Nine read the letter, he would know that he was being turned in.

So Nine went and knocked at the magistrate's door. He entered.

"Well, son," said the magistrate, "what do you wish?"

"If you please, Sir," he said, "the king sent me as his messenger to tell you that you owe him a sum of money; he needs it now—kindly return it. But I brought you a letter, too. I believe it is written there."

The magistrate read the letter and without a word placed it in his pocket. He pressed a button and right away four constables appeared. They grabbed Nine, put chains and a lock around his hands, and threw him into jail. Now Nine is taken care of, they thought. They had heard that he was the most notorious robber. They sentenced him on the spot to die on the gallows three days later. The king rejoiced that he was rid of Nine.

Well, the third day came. They beat the drums and let it be known that the most notorious robber would be hanged. Anyone who wanted to go to the hanging and see something amazing, could be there. They brought Nine out of the cell and were leading him to the gallows. A huge crowd had gathered to accompany him. They were taking him to the edge of the town. The hangman and the priest were walking with them.

When they came to the gallows the hangman said: "Now, son, which do you choose, the rope or the ax?" (which instrument for the execution.)

"First I want to know, why do you want to hang me or decapitate me?"

"Well, Son," he said, "I am not the one to hang you, it is the law. I was just given the order to execute you," he said, "but what you did, what crime you committed, I don't know."

"Well," said Nine, "if you take me for such a big criminal that I deserve to be hanged or beheaded, then I don't mind—go ahead, behead me!"

"So, son, put your head on the block!"

Said Nine: "I don't know how to place my head. Show me how, then I'll do it. This isn't something I have learned to do."

When the hangman lowered his head on the block, like so, Nine tore the ax from his hand and cut off his head.

"What do you think," he said, "that Nine can be beheaded so easily, without having committed a crime?"

The people got so frightened that they began to run, every single one of them including the magistrate. He ran so fast that his feet barely touched the ground. And Nine ran after them. Those that were able to get away were lucky, for the ones he caught he beat up, he beat one with the other. At least ten of them died, beaten to death. The magistrate ran home.

Nine followed him and said: "I saw you in the crowd, among those that condemned me. Why did you do it?"

"I didn't convict you, the law did."

"Well, I'll spare you so you can pay your debt, the loan you received. I was sent here to collect money, not to be hanged."

"What money?"

"The money you owe the king."

The magistrate thought to himself that Nine wasn't sent for that. They wanted to lose him for good. But he gave him the sum the king had asked for, just to have him leave as quickly as possible, just to be free of him.

It was the third day by the time Nine returned home. When the king saw him he began to shake—he almost keeled over.

"Here you are, Your Majesty, I brought your money," he said. "I hope you are not angry that I am so late?"

"Oh no! I am not angry."

"What weren't they going to do to me! But it is not so easy to do away with Nine! He has more sense than to surrender."

The king tried to placate him, so he wouldn't be upset.

During the night he came up with the idea that he would send Nine somewhere else. Maybe there he would perish.

He said: "Nine, take your beasts and go into the forest. I want you to gather all the bones you can find, put them in sacks, then go to the animal burial ground, get bones from there, too, and bring them home. Fill nine sacks—that will be sufficient."

Nine went to the forest. He collected plenty of bones. Then he went to the animal burial ground, filled up the nine sacks and took them home. He announced to the king that he had returned.

"Now, son," said the king, "I want you to go to the mill at the far end of town. That mill belongs to the devils. Tell them to grind these bones into the finest flour there is."

The king thought the devils would destroy Nine, for sure.

Nine hitched his beasts to the wagon—the four wolves and two bears—and set forth. The gate to the mill was open but one of the devils saw him approaching with the beasts and alerted the others.

"Oh dear," he said, "we must lock the gate! Nine is coming with four wolves and two bears!"

This devil, the gatekeeper, was the one who had to hold on to the axle of the wagon. He knew Nine—he locked the gate of the mill for that reason.

When Nine arrived he saw that the gate was locked, that he couldn't get in. He shouted for them to open it, but they were not about to comply. Instead, at least ten devils leaned against the gate to prevent him from coming through. Nine called out again, at least three times:

"Open up the gate!"

They yelled back: "Go away—we are not letting you in with your beasts! We are not milling!"

"You are not?" he said. He kicked the gate with such force that it flew open and the devils tumbled, head over heels, nearly breaking their necks. He went to the door of the mill and said:

"The king sent me to have these nine sacks of grain milled and if you don't give me the finest flour—just you wait, I am Nine, I'll teach you a lesson!"

Said the devils: "Look, Nine, we don't grind bones into flour. You might as well go back."

"You won't obey me?" he said. "If you don't make me flour right away, I'll put all of you under the millstone and grind you up!"

The devils were so scared that they produced the finest flour ever milled anywhere.

"Here, Nine, here is the flour. There is no charge, we don't want anything, just take it away!"

He loaded the sacks on the wagon and returned home. The king had such a fright when he saw him that king though he was, he made a big mess in his trousers.

And just then the year was over.

Nine said: "Your Majesty, the year is up."

Well, what was going to happen now? The king had a beautiful daughter and she feared for her father.

"Don't you remember, Your Majesty, that we had an agreement? When the year came to an end, you were going to let me slap you in the face, twice."

The king didn't know what to say, he was so alarmed.

But the princess spoke up: "Nine, don't hit my father. Slap me instead."

He said: "My agreement wasn't with you, but with your father, the king."

"Never mind," she said, "my father is old; I am young, slap me."

Said Nine: "I won't slap the daughter of the king. I'd rather you hit me."

"Will you let me?" asked the princess.

"I will."

The king's daughter raised her hand as if to slap Nine, but instead she threw her arms around him, hugged and kissed him.

She said: "Look, Nine, you are so brave. Don't threaten to slap my father in the face. I'd rather be yours. You'll be mine and I'll be yours until death do us part."

The king looked on, he watched his daughter. She'd have sooner become Nine's wife than let him slap her father.

Then Nine spoke: "King, will you permit me to take your daughter for my wife?"

"Sure, I will! How could I not give her to such a gallant man!"

Right away they announced the wedding and held a big feast that lasted forty-eight hours. They went on living and dying and dumping on the audience. So Nine became king. They are alive to this day, if they haven't died.

# 18. The Red-Bellied Serpent

AT 670 (*The Animal Languages*); MNK 670 (*The Shepherd Who Understands the Language of Animals*)—a fairly consistent tale, with 27 close and 3 deviant variants. Mrs. Palkó heard it from her brother János, but many people in the community know this tale; it belongs to the old stock of the Andrásfalva repertoire. The animal language episode, also found in "Prince Sándor and Prince Lajos" (tale no. 12, above) and "András Kerekes" (no. 13), is here embedded in an entirely different frame. It begins with the grateful snake episode that is completely missing from the two other tales. The idea that revealing the secret of animal speech will cause the bearer's death is an integral part of this tale and appears as early as the 1840s in a broadside illustration. The picture shows the shepherd at the table, lost in thought, his nagging wife standing in front, and next to her the stupid dog and the smart rooster. Only a part of the caption is legible: "Great is the sorrow and the crisis of conscience of the shepherd who understands the language of the animals, for he is to die if he betrays the secret; but as he cannot resist the insistent curiosity of his wife. . . ."

This is one of Aunt Zsuzsi's educational tales for young marriageable girls; it instructs them to respect and obey their husbands. Her real contribution to this tale is to place it into the context of the socioeconomic hierarchy of peasant society in her experience. The lowly shepherd boy is a good worker, herding the count's sheep, and a good man, but he is poor. This means that he owns nothing but his shepherd's crook, but—more than that—that he is an orphan, without parents or siblings. Even the head-shepherd snubs him when he asks for the hand of his daughter: "my daughter is not the same sort as you are," he says. But money buys everything: as soon as animal language leads him to hidden gold, the head-shepherd has a change of heart. "If he asks me once, I'll say yes a hundred times," the girl says. With money, it is easy to rise: buying the land and the castle of a count means becoming a count. The next step is to tame the girl and reach equilibrium.

Recorded in 1950, at the home of Mrs. Palkó. Two comments from the audience were also recorded. The first indicates that people agree with the storyteller's thoughts about class conflict. The second, by Mrs. Palkó's daughter Erzsi, adds an element that her mother forgot to mention.

---

Once upon a time, beyond the seven seas and beyond the glass mountains, there was a poor shepherd boy. He was so poor that all he had to his name was a shepherd's crook. One day he went to see a wealthy count and entered his service. He had some three hundred sheep to look after. They took him to the forest and showed him where he had to bring the sheep to pasture.

The squire said to him: "Son, you must come in every evening and give an account of the sheep, so I know that nothing is wrong with them."

Well the lad went out with the sheep, thinking all the while about the lovely daughter the bailiff had. He had seen the girl, taken a fancy to her and thought he would like to have her as his wife.

This is all to no avail—he thought to himself—since I am as poor as a church-mouse.

One evening he went in to give an account of the sheep, to report that nothing had happened to them, that they were all there. Once again he caught sight of the bailiff's daughter. He saw the girl and the girl saw him. They were looking at each other. Then the girl smiled at the lad.

He said to himself: She likes me. I'll try my luck and speak to her father.

The next evening he went to give an account of the sheep.

The bailiff said to him: "You are a good lad, son. Nothing has gone wrong with the sheep since you arrived."

Said the lad: "Bailiff, Sir, I'd say something to you if you wouldn't take it amiss."

He said: "Say it, son. What is on your mind?"

The lad answered: "What I'd like to say, bailiff, Sir, is that I wish to ask for your daughter's hand."

The bailiff burst out laughing: "Oh, son, don't waste time around her; it is no use. My daughter is not the same sort as you are. Go, son, look for someone your own kind if you want to marry!"

The lad felt ashamed. He turned around and left. He went back to the sheep to think, filled with sorrow. I should have known better—he thought—I am so poor, I won't find a girl for myself.

**[Listener:] Right, because he is not looking for someone of his own kind.**

One day, as he was leaning on his shepherd's crook, lost in thought, he heard a loud, piercing scream. He lifted his head, looked around, but couldn't see anyone or anything.

"Well, now," he said, "I'll herd the sheep together and go toward the sound. I want to see what is going on there." He ambled over and came upon a big fire and in the midst of the fire he saw a little red-bellied snake, writhing and shrieking. He was sorry for the snake so he went and cut off a nice long twig from the willow. He pushed it into the fire, and when the snake curled around it, he lifted it out.

Said the snake: "I thank you, young shepherd. You saved me from death. Now be so kind and take me to my father's castle, he will show you his gratitude for your good deed!"

He took the snake and put it in his bosom, on his bare skin. He asked the snake which was the way to his father's castle. The snake told him and they left.

They came to a barren plain in the midst of which was a big mountain and on the top of the mountain there was such a beautiful castle that he couldn't take his eyes off it.

He said: "Look, little snake, I see a castle over there."

"That is my father's castle, take me to it." And that is what happened. They came to the castle—he knocked at the door and a voice from inside beckoned him to enter. The young shepherd went in and, God Almighty, what a fright he had when he saw a terrible, huge snake sitting at the table! It was as wide as the hide of a belt and had a diamond crown on its head. It sat there, watching.

Then suddenly it called out: "What do you want?"

The young shepherd said: "Your Majesty, with your permission, I brought your son home."

He took the little snake from his bosom and held it up.

Said the snake: "Is it true that this man brought you home?"

"It is true. Not only did he bring me home, but he saved me from death. It is thanks to him," said the little snake, " that I am alive."

"Well, son, then come and sit beside me at the table and eat and drink as much as you can fit under your skin!"

Having feasted him, the king said: "What do you wish as a reward for having brought my son back?"

"Nothing else, Your Majesty, just teach me the language of animals."

**[Mrs. Palkó's daughter, Erzsi:] Oh, you left something out, mother! It was the littler snake who taught him.**

Said the king: "What good will it do to you to understand the language of animals? Wouldn't it serve you better if I gave you a plateful of gold?"

"Well, Your Majesty, I could use that too," he said, " but I'd rather learn the language of animals."

"Son," said the king, "I'll give you two platefuls of gold—it will be more valuable to you."

"Thank you, Your Majesty, but please teach me the language of animals instead!"

The snake answered: "All right, son, it is all the same to me. If that is your wish, I'll grant it."

The snake moved away from the table and breathed on the lad. That was all it did.

"You may leave now."

The lad thanked the snake for its gift and left.

He began thinking again how stupid it was of him not to want anything. Wouldn't he have been better off with two platefuls of gold? He said to himself: With two platefuls of gold I could have become a squire and could have had the bailiff's daughter. But now it is too late. This is the way it is.

He went back to the sheep. He found them as he had left them, in a cluster. He counted them, they were all there. He rested his back against a tree, leaned on his shepherd's crook and pondered. How could he have done such a thing? Fortune was within his reach and he rejected it.

Then a ram came over and rubbed against the tree where he was standing.

Said the ram: "Oh, if this young shepherd knew what is inside this tree, he would fell it immediately."

Said the lad: "I do understand the language of animals. Let me see what is in this tree."

He took his ax and began chopping away at it. When he was about midway through, gold started pouring out in abundance—so much gold that it lay in a big heap at the foot of the tree. Now what should he do? Where should he put all this gold? He had neither a satchel nor a sack. He pulled off his trousers, tied up the legs and filled them with the gold. Still there was a lot left. So he took off his *suba*, poured the gold into both sleeves and stuffed the remainder into his pockets.

What next? Where should he take this gold?

He had neither father, mother, relatives nor siblings. Where should he put it? He thought he would take it to the bailiff for safekeeping and ask for it when he needed it. That is what he did. When the bailiff saw all the gold the lad had brought, he was very astonished:

"Where did you find all this gold?"

He said: "You shouldn't concern yourself with that. It is mine, that is all. Be so kind and put it away and give it to me when I ask for it!"

From that moment on the bailiff was sorry that he had scolded the lad when he asked for his daughter's hand. Now he was ready to give her to him, if only he would ask, but the lad uttered not a word.

The bailiff said to him: "Son, you should take a wife, find yourself a good woman. You can buy a nice estate now with all that money—you won't even need the whole lot."

"That is my intention," he said.

"You may even become a count."

Well, the bailiff put away the lad's money. The lad kept what was in his pockets and went into town. He bought himself three sets of clothes, along with shoes and everything else that belonged to an outfit, and returned home. The bailiff waited impatiently for him to ask for his daughter.

"Here is my daughter," he said. "She is a good girl—you won't be sorry if you take her for your wife."

"I take her, for I love her."

The bailiff called his daughter and asked her: "What do you want, my daughter? Do you want to marry this lad?"

"Oh yes, I do! *If he asks me once, I'll say yes a hundred times.*"

Right away they went to the priest to register for marriage and agreed on the date of their wedding. Then the time came and they had their wedding feast.

"Now, son," said the bailiff, "you'll stay here until you find a castle or a count's estate that you can buy, together with the land, the livestock and everything. Then you can move away, but meanwhile remain with me!"

"All right, father," he said, "all right."

Then Sunday came and the young man said to his wife: "Wife, I'd like us to go into town for a stroll. I know many people there, and I'd like to show them the wife I have."

She said: "I don't mind, let's go."

Right away he brought out the donkeys he used to ride when he was herding sheep. There were two. He saddled one for his wife and one for himself. He took some money, they mounted the donkeys and left. They were chatting as the donkeys walked nicely side by side. Suddenly, who knows what crossed the young man's mind, but he spurred his donkey to move ahead by about ten steps. Then the one in the rear began to bray and the one in front answered back. The young man heard what they were saying to each other. He broke into laughter and laughed so hard that he nearly fell off the donkey. He halted to let the one in the rear catch up.

His wife said to him when she came close: "Tell me, dear husband, what made you laugh so heartily?"

Said the man: "Oh, wife, that, I am not allowed to tell you."

"Why not?"

"Because it is forbidden. If I tell you, I have to die."

"Oh no, you won't die," said the young bride. "Other people share more important secrets with their wives, yet no one has died so far."

"Well, other people can do as they wish, but I won't tell you, for I am not allowed."

"Then you don't love me. If you keep secrets from me, you don't love me."

"Of course I love you," he said. "No one can love his wife more than I love you. Still, I won't tell you."

"Well, if you don't, I am not going into town with you."

She turned her donkey around and set out for home. Then the young man turned around, too, and they both headed home. All along the way his wife kept pressing him to tell her what he was laughing at, what was it that made him laugh.

"Wife, don't waste your energy, for I can't tell you. You must understand this!"

They got back, dismounted, and the woman went inside, furious. The man tied up the donkeys in the stable and followed her in the house.

She said: "You should know that from now on I am not going anywhere with you—not to church, not into town, not anywhere, until you tell me what you were laughing at."

"Understand, woman, I am not free to tell you, for if I do, I'll die on the spot."

Said the woman: "Well, if you die, I'll bury you—tell me all the same. I don't mind, even if you die I want to know."

"All right, wife, if this is how you feel, I'll tell you. But first I want to go to town and buy a coffin. Meanwhile you prepare the bier."

So the man went into town, and the woman began setting up the bier. The man bought himself a fine coffin, all in glass, and a beautiful cross. When he got back the bier was ready and he placed the coffin on it.

"Is there warm water?"

"No, there isn't, but I'll heat some up right away."

Quickly the woman made a fire and heated the bathwater for her husband.

As soon as the water was warm, she brought in the basin and filled it. The man washed himself and she helped him.

"Now bring me my Sunday clothes and let me put them on."

The man got dressed.

"Well, will you tell me what you were laughing at?"

The man lay down in the coffin and clasped his hands, as if he were dead.

"Will you tell me now what you were laughing at?"

"I'll tell you," he said, "you won't have to ask me any more, for these will be my last words."

The woman left the door open. The man, the shepherd, had a little dog, whom he looked after and took along to herd the sheep. The little dog was so smart that he understood everything—the only thing he didn't know was how to talk. The door was open—the little dog came in and sat down at the foot of the bier in the middle of the room. He kept looking up at his master in the coffin and wept bitterly; like a human, he mourned his master.

Then a rooster came in.

Said the man on the bier: "Wife, cut a piece of bread for this little dog, you can see he is hungry."

Angry, she went and threw him half a piece of bread. But the dog didn't even look at the bread, let alone eat it. Then the rooster came and began clucking, as if calling the hens. Hearing the rooster the hens came flocking in and started picking at the bread.

Suddenly the dog spoke up and said to the rooster: "You heartless creature, how can you swallow this bread? How can you eat when you see that our dear master is lying on the bier, dying?"

Said the rooster: "Well, if he is lying there, he is crazy. I don't feel sorry for him since he is not using his head."

Said the dog: "What do you mean by not using his head?"

"I mean that I have many wives and I can give commands to all of them, as you can see. I have to cluck only once and they all come running. He only has one wife and he cannot teach her to obey. So let him die!"

The dying man heard this. He jumped up and began beating his wife, hitting her with the shepherd's crook, with all the strength he could muster.

"You still want me to tell you what I was laughing at, wife?"

She said: "Oh, dear husband, don't beat me to death! I'll never ask you again what you were laughing at, just spare my life!"

He said: "Don't you want me to tell you what made me laugh?"

He hit her again and again, on her back, on her head, until blood was running down her body.

Then he said: "Wife, I wasn't free to tell you then, but I can tell you now that the donkey I was riding called back to yours and said: 'you see, I left you behind, you can't keep up with me.' And your donkey answered: 'it is no shame that I am lagging behind you, for I am carrying three people while you are carrying only one.' This is what I was laughing at. This is what I didn't want to tell you."

From then on, from the time he beat her up, they didn't talk about it again. She never asked him what he was laughing at or what the animals were saying. She became so meek, she let her husband have his way and not once opposed his wishes. They lived as happily together as *two turtle doves* and are alive to this day, if they haven't died.

# 19. The Twelve Robbers

AT 706 (*The Maiden Without Hands*) + 451/I (*The Maiden Who Seeks Her Brothers*); MNK includes 11 close and 6 more distant type combinations. This was among Mrs. Palkó's favorite feminine tales—in it she could express not only the suffering of the heroine but also that of the king's mother. She succeeded not only in creating model characters but also in expressing her opinion about right and wrong behavior, choice of profession, choice of marriage partners, family relations, love and envy, torture and reconciliation. Above all, she succeeded in telling a suspenseful adventure story. She learned it from a Romanian girlfriend in Andrásfalva when they were both young. How much she changed the story one cannot tell, but the episode of the jealous sister-in-law who murders the dog, the horse, and her own child—as it appears in this telling, recorded from Mrs. Palkó in 1953—is known only in Romanian variants. It seems the unusual initial episode (the tale usually begins with the girl's mutilation by her lecherous father or other evil relative) is Mrs. Palkó's own invention. Beginning with episode I of AaTh 451, and turning the twelve raven-brothers into robbers, determines and complicates the story development and resolution. She maintains a feeling of ambiguity concerning the profession of the brothers, who live off crime, support parents with stolen money, and visit their transformed sister with criminal intent; they are not unredeemable because they are the heroine's brothers, her own blood. They were innocent in what they did to her—the sister-in-law is to be blamed. They are as innocent as the king, who was unaware of how the innkeeper's daughter manipulated the letters. The robbers are also forgiven for trying to rob their sister—they did not know it was her and, after all, this was their chosen profession.

The happy ending unites the entire family—including parents, brothers, and mother-in-law—in the castle of the glorious couple and son. Throughout the story, there is a bond of love between family members—they can hardly control their emotions. They keep kissing and hugging their beloved, and display their sorrow, grief, and helpless despair openly, by weeping uncontrollably. Yet the impostor, the innkeeper's daughter, and her entire family are destroyed with the utmost cruelty in medieval-style executions. The evil sister-in-law is simply forgotten in the course of events.

Aunt Zsuzsa elaborated this long tale with delight. She took her time to live through all the details, as she would customarily perform it at wakes or upon other occasions undisturbed by children's noise and people's comings and goings. The audience was relaxed, in no hurry. We were at the home of Cyrill Sebestyén, the cobbler. His wife Bori and two neighbor women joined me to hear the tale, which took hours to narrate. The guests sat spellbound, their eyes fixed on the lips of the narrator, waiting for the outcome. They kept urging her: "Go on, Aunt Zsuzsa, go on!" When she finally finished, they both jumped up, looking at the clock—and dashed out. They had left their children locked in their homes, without lunch, God knows what could have happened to them—they might have burned the house down. Later I asked these women: "This was the first time you heard this story?" "Oh, no," was their answer. "We've heard it many times."

This story is most remarkable in its use of extensive dialogue, self-characterizing deliberations, rhythmic repetition of formulas and episodes, and the retelling of the entire story at the end of the tale. Formulas are used to present situations and shape arguments, rendering the prose rhythmic, poetic.

The queen mother's voice is particularly poignant. She is sensible and reasonable as she argues in the interest of her son, who is too inexperienced to make responsible decisions. She sees the danger in marrying the disfigured girl who cannot be taken to parties to show off to other young couples; Mrs. Palkó cast the mother-in-law in the same formulaic role assumed by similar figures in "The Princess" (tale no. 6, above) and "The Serpent Prince" (no. 7). This mother is concerned with her son's future but fears that the poor girl will be hurt. When the substituted letters convince her that her fears have come true, she takes the side of the girl, the mother of her grandson. She puts up a desperate struggle and gives up only when peril threatens her son. Mrs. Palkó tells a traditional folktale, using all traditional tools; yet her own life experience fuels her representation. Another masterful segment is the letter substitution. There are 16 letters—eight real, eight phony—exchanged between the queen mother and her son. They push the story forward, each letter adding to the tension that ends with the expulsion of the heroine.

Repetition is the natural fuel energizing the story. In most cases, each heroic test is repeated three times: first, when the hero is advised by a helper; second, when the hero goes through with the task; and third, at the tale's end, when the hero makes a public statement and reveals his identity. There are other kinds of repetitions, but the most effective and dramatic is telling the story twice: first, as it happens; second, when the protagonist or his or her representative turns a gathering into a story-telling session and pretends to tell a fiction, but discloses his or her own life history, revealing the truth. This format has been used by many skilled community raconteurs, particularly when reciting AT 403, 407, 408, 706 and 707. Sometimes the tale ends with a realistic spinning bee, just like those familiar to Mrs. Palkó's audience, hosted in the royal palace by the false queen, where everyone, including the disguised heroine, has to tell a tale. In Mrs. Palkó's version of AT 408 (not included in this collection) it is at an embroidery party of court ladies that the princess reveals her identity. In "The Twelve Robbers" she has the heroine carefully prepare for an occasion to make her story public, so that truth can prevail. As elsewhere, Mrs. Palkó expresses her interest in the education of her heroes; the golden-haired child obtains the best schooling from his mother. He learns everything that happened in the family; he is prepared to be his mother's spokesman and tell it all.

The boy's retelling of his mother's story [pp. 241–47 below] is rendered in italics in order to simplify punctuation and to set the boy's narration apart from the rest of the story.

———

Once upon a time, in a land far away, beyond the seven seas and even beyond that, there was a simple farmer and his wife. They had twelve children. Twelve sons were born to them, but no daughter, not one.

When even the youngest had grown old enough to marry, the brothers agreed among themselves that they would become bandits. So much were they of one mind that not one of them spoke against it, that they better not do it—only the oldest said:

"We must ask father whether he permits it."

So, one day they went, stood in front of their father and told him that it was their wish, their intention to become bandits.

Their father said: "What do you want? Do you want to be hounded forever, always putting your life at stake? You'll never again be able to go among decent people," he said, "you'll have to camp in the dark forest, is that what you want? No, my sons, you won't get my consent to do this. If I was able to raise you, then you, too, can make a life for yourselves in this world, and be free. You don't have to become bandits and spend all your days locked up in prison."

"Father, you can say what you will, but this is what we chose for ourselves and this is what we'll do."

Their father saw that it was no use talking to them, that their mind was made up; so be it.

"Well, too bad, my sons, I brought you up and now you are abandoning me in my old age!"

"Don't be sad, father, we'll help. We'll provide for you in your old age, don't worry!"

It happened that at the time the woman was pregnant, expecting her thirteenth child.

"We only have one request, our father and mother," said the sons, "when, God willing, the hour comes for the child to be born—you know we were always hoping to have a sister—and if God gives you a daughter, tie a bundle of tow to the roof, so we can make it out with our telescope. If we see the bundle of tow displayed, we'll come home for the christening. But if it is a boy, put out a bunch of hay and then we won't come for the christening. He will join us later, when he is grown."

"All right, my sons," said the father.

They took leave of their father and mother and went into the deep, dark forest. There they set up camp, went robbing, and collected loot. They also acquired a little dog and trained him so that every month they could send money to their parents with him. They tied a bag around his neck, put the money in it, and the dog went to the parents. They took the money and sent the dog back.

Then, with God's help, the time came for the woman to deliver and she gave birth to a beautiful little girl. But they had forgotten what the sons had said, what sign they should display if a girl was born, and instead of a bundle of tow they put hay on the roof. So one morning the brother who was always keeping watch went in, dejected, and said:

"It 's no use—once again it is a boy, we don't have a sister."

"Well, if it is so, we won't go home," said the others. "When he is grown, he will come to us."

So one day passed after another, time went by, and soon the little girl was three years old. She was very clever and developed nicely, she grew smarter and smarter.

Every time the dog came with the money, she asked: "Mother, whose is this little dog? He is always coming to us."

Out of love the mother told her little girl: "He belongs to your brothers. You have twelve brothers, they are working in the forest and are sending us the money with the little dog."

But the little girl kept asking: "When are my brothers coming home?"

"They can't come home, my child, they have work to do there."

One beautiful summer day it was very warm and the little girl was playing in the sand in the courtyard when the dog came and brought the money. He paid no attention to her and she didn't bother with him, just looked at him and stayed outside. They removed the money from his neck, gave him something to eat and sent him back.

While the dog was inside, the little girl thought that she would go with him to see her brothers. So she stole out after him and followed him. But the dog, rather than going on the road, took to the fields. He didn't go straight on the path—still the little girl followed him all the way. Her mother knew nothing about this. When they were halfway there, the little girl grew tired and sat down on a furrow, but the little dog ran ahead. She sat there and broke into tears.

When the dog looked back he saw that the little girl was weeping. He turned around, sat down next to her and stayed there, without moving an inch forward or backward. The little girl cried and cried until she cried herself to sleep. And the dog didn't leave her, he kept watch over her. He didn't leave her side.

Meanwhile the bandits grew impatient. Where was the little dog? Other times he didn't stay away so long.

Their leader, the oldest brother, said: "One of you should go and see what is keeping the dog—whether he was caught, whether anything happened to him."

A lad took off who knew where to search for the dog; he knew the way the dog normally followed. Suddenly he caught sight of him. He came closer and saw that there was a beautiful little girl asleep and the dog was keeping watch over her. The lad was concerned not to rouse the little girl, so he waited for her to wake up. She awoke soon, looked around her and began to cry again.

The lad took her in his arms and asked her: "Where are you going, little girl? And who are you?"

"I am going to my brothers," she said.

"And where are your brothers?"

"In the forest."

"What are they doing there?"

"They are felling wood."

"And who do you belong to?"

"To my father and mother. I belong to my father and mother," she said.

"And what is your mother's name?"

"Mother."

"And your father's?"

"Father."

He was not able to get more out of her, she couldn't say her name.

"Now then," said the lad, "who told you that you have brothers in the forest?"

"I have, twelve of them."

"And who told you so?"

"My mother. My mother told me that my brothers were sending money; the little dog brought it, and now I am going with the dog to see them."

The lad knew right away that they had made a mistake when they put the hay on the roof. He kissed the little girl over and over again, held her tight, and took her with him. The other brothers came to meet him and asked him who was the little girl he was carrying.

"Ask her," he said, "she'll tell you. And if we think about it for a moment, we'll find she is our sister."

They all asked the little girl questions and she repeated the same answer, but the brothers became convinced that she was their sister.

"Well," they said, "if this is how it is, you won't go back, you'll stay here, with us."

The brothers loved her so much, they were so overjoyed at having her, that each of them, one after the other, took her in his arms and smothered her with kisses. And they were bringing her all sorts of things, since they were robbers. They procured the finest toys for her so she wouldn't feel sad and brought her dolls, one more beautiful than the other. The little girl never mentioned her mother or father, she was so contented with them. From the time she arrived one of the robbers always stayed with her at the camp. Meanwhile she was growing and became smarter by the day. They taught her how to read and write and bought her books of tales. She read them and then kept leafing through them, looking them over. Eventually she knew so much—having learned from the books—that she began asking her brothers why they didn't marry, why they didn't bring a woman to the house.

"Why aren't you bringing a woman here, dear brother," she said, "so I'd have someone to talk to?"

She was always reading, playing, doing whatever she liked, so her brother said to her:

"My dear little sister, it wouldn't be good for you to have a sister-in-law. She might scold you, even beat you."

"No, no, she wouldn't. We would get along well together," she answered.

She went on begging until her oldest brother felt sorry for her and brought a woman home. They loved each other and the woman didn't regret it. He was a handsome man, though he was a robber. But the first thing the robbers did whenever they came home was, one by one, to pick up the little girl and heap kisses on her. Only then did the brother turn to his wife. She began to feel jealous—the devil of jealousy settled in her heart. She thought to herself: I am his wife—no one should come before me!

She always felt left out.

One day she thought—an evil thought that rose from her heart—that she would do something to make her husband angry with the little girl and send her home. Then she wouldn't be around.

So she got to it and cut the little dog into pieces, the courier dog, the one that carried the money. She thought that he would be upset by this and send the little girl away.

But the little girl saw her killing the dog and cried: "Don't hurt the dog—he belongs to my brothers!"

"Listen," said the woman, "if you tell your brothers that I killed the dog, I'll cut you up, too, when they are gone! You say that you killed him!"

"I won't say anything," said the little girl.

When the brothers came home, they found the woman weeping.

"Oh dear," lamented the woman.

"Why are you crying, wife? What happened?"

"Something very bad happened."

"Tell me, what bad thing? Who hurt you? Why are you crying so?"

"No one hurt me, but the one you love so much, the one you always smother with kisses, killed that dear little dog."

The brothers asked: "Why did you kill him, sister? Did you do it?"

"I did."

"Why?"

"I wanted to. I wanted to."

They picked her up, kissed her over and over again, and said: "We must not harm the little girl because of the dog. We can always get a dog, but not a sister. We mustn't harm her."

The young bride was even more furious when she saw that the brothers didn't get angry. Meanwhile a child was born to her, too, and the brothers loved it as much as they loved their sister. Still the young woman was jealous that they always kissed the little girl first, before they kissed her.

Then the thought occurred to her that the brothers had a beautiful steed. They had several, but one of them was a particularly fine runner, their favorite. She cut its head off, slaughtered it, thinking that if they said nothing about the dog, they would surely be upset enough about this to send the little girl away. Once again she made the little girl swear that she would say she had killed the steed, and threatened that if she betrayed her she would cut her head off too, when the brothers were gone. In the evening the brothers came home and once again found the young bride weeping. They asked her what had happened—her husband and the others all asked what was the matter, why was she crying?

"There is plenty to cry about," she said, "since your good little sister, whom you love so dearly and whom you go on kissing, cut off the head of your finest steed, the best runner of all."

Said the brothers: "Well, if she did, she did. We can always buy another steed, but we can't find a sister growing on any tree."

They passed the little girl one to the other, kissing and hugging her—there was no anger whatever.

Suffice it to say that the young woman's heart was increasingly filled with a desire for revenge. She was forever thinking of what she could do to turn the brothers against the little girl. One day she set to it, heated the oven and put her own child on the peel, ready to shove it in and burn it. She thought that they loved this child very much, too—the father, as well as the others—so they would surely chase the little girl away.

And the little girl kept asking her: "Why are you heating the oven? What will you bake today, dear sister-in-law?"

When the oven was hot, the woman took her child and set it on the peel, preparing to push it through the door. The little girl's heart nearly broke:

"Oh dear, don't burn my little nephew, don't burn him, oh dear, dear!"

Said the woman: "Stop crying and tell them when they come home that you burned him! If you don't, I'll do the same with you!"

Well, the brothers came home. The little girl had cried all day, mourning the child. She was grief-stricken that the woman had burned him.

The woman clasped her hands over her head and wept and lamented. When the brothers arrived they got alarmed at seeing the young bride weep so bitterly. What could be wrong with her?

Her husband said: "Why are you weeping, wife? What happened to you? Every time I come home I find you crying."

"Don't ask me," she said, "don't ask me, any of you. All I want to say is that if you don't send the little girl away, I am leaving you. She is causing immense damage and it doesn't even occur to you that tomorrow it might be me she would roast, me she would kill, for you are so enchanted with her. You have spoiled her completely.

"What do you mean? What did she do?"

"She burned my beloved child! I heated the oven for baking and before I could notice it, she threw him in and burned him!"

Now the brothers were really angry, not only the father but every one of them. They went into the next room to discuss what to do with the little girl, for this they wouldn't tolerate. They didn't mind the dog, or the horse, but they were not about to put up with this! They began talking about the punishment she should receive. One said one thing, the other something else. One said they should light a pile of logs and when the fire was ablaze, they should throw her in; let her die the same death she had caused. Another said no, she should be hanged on a tree with a fire burning beneath her.

The third one said: "I think otherwise. We should make sure that she doesn't die quickly. She should suffer—suffer a long time."

Then the oldest brother, their leader, spoke: "The child was mine, my pain is the greatest. I say we should cut off her two arms from the shoulders, and her two legs, put her in a basket and take her into the forest, to the mountain. We must leave her on top of the highest mountain so she won't die quickly, but suffer in agony."

All of them agreed that this would be best. So they cut off her two legs, cut off her two arms, placed her in a basket, and two of them took her away.

They set her down at the top of the big mountain: "Here is where you'll stay!" and they left her there.

The girl wept bitterly. She remembered everything, how her brother had told her not to wish for a sister-in-law, for she might fare badly with her. And now she had to suffer all this pain, although she was innocent. If only she knew that she would die soon it would be easier to bear, but who knows how long she would have to endure the suffering? She kept looking up at the sky and praying to God that as they left her mutilated, He should take her to Him, not prolong her agony.

She had been on the mountaintop for three days, weeping and praying when the king came to hunt in the same forest where they had left her. He came with his soldiers right to the mountain where she was. There was a clearing where they set up camp, readied their guns and sat down for the midday meal. One of the soldiers kept watch, pacing back and forth around them.

Suddenly, as he was walking, the soldier heard someone cry. He listened.

"Dear God," he said, "this is the crying of some female."

He listened again and set out in the direction of the sound. He walked and crawled on all fours, until he finally reached the peak, and there he saw a beautiful girl sitting in a basket. She was so beautiful that he didn't know such beauty existed. But she had neither arms nor legs. The soldier got so frightened that he turned around, hurried back to the king and told him what he had seen. The king jumped to his feet, left his food and rushed to see if it was a ghost, or whatever else. He took two soldiers with him and climbed to the top of the mountain. It was true, there was a beautiful girl.

The king approached and asked her: "Who are you? Where are you from? And how did you get here?"

"Oh," she said, "I went strawberry picking and while I was picking, robbers attacked me and cut off my two arms and legs." She didn't betray her brothers.

The king took such a liking to the girl that he said: "Would you come with me?"

"Where to?" she asked.

"To me, to my royal palace. You'll stay there, with me."

"Oh, dear, how could I go?" she said, "I have neither feet nor hands!"

"I am not taking you to work, just to have you with me at the castle."

Right away the king ordered the soldiers to take the basket and carry it down.

Then he told one of the soldiers to go home at once, harness two horses to the carriage and come back immediately. In less than an hour the carriage was there. Gently, they took the basket and lifted it into the carriage. The king sat down next to the girl and they drove home.

He was the son of a king, not yet married, who became king when his father died. He brought the young girl home and placed her in a room. Then he called his mother to come in. His mother, the widowed queen, came at once.

"Look, mother, look what I brought!"

"Where did you find this poor girl, my son?"

He told her where he had found her.

"Why did you bring her, my dear son?" said the queen. "She is not able to do anything."

"I didn't bring her to work. Dear mother, permit me to take her for my wife."

"My son, what's gotten into you? It is out of the question, she is not suitable for you! Where she comes from, from what stock, wouldn't matter, but she has neither hands nor feet. Is this worthy of you? You could have the daughter of a king."

"Mother," said the king, "you can say what you wish. I see that she has neither hands nor feet, but I fancy her. Allow me to marry her, for if you don't, I'll go out into the wide world and leave you for good."

"Think it over, my son," she said, "you'll go to the park for a stroll, where every young married man takes his wife, and you won't be able to take yours. What will the people say when they learn what kind of woman you took for a wife? What will the country say?"

"Mother," he said, "I don't care about the country or the people. Allow me to marry her, or else I'll leave."

She thought it over. She'd rather give her consent than have her son leave for the wide world.

"All right, son," she said, "but don't regret it later!"

So the queen acquiesced.

"Son, take her for your wife but don't be sorry later! You are young, you don't think ahead, you'll be sorry, but then it will be too late."

"Never mind, mother."

Right away they took the girl into the bath, washed her and dressed her. Then they called a priest to the house and they exchanged wedding vows. So the girl without arms became queen. Her husband was very concerned about her—he loved her so much that he couldn't do enough for her.

Soon the young bride became heavy with child. The king was overjoyed. He wouldn't have let her go out of the palace, God knows, for anything in the whole world, so much did he love her.

This love didn't last long, however, for one day a courier came and brought a sealed letter to the king. The king took it, looked it over and, well, the message was that he mustn't delay, he must mobilize, for the *dog-headed Tatars* were about to attack. He should assemble his troops and go to war.

The king's heart nearly broke from sorrow. Not for having to go to war, but for his wife, for having to leave her. He put his arms around her and wept bitterly.

Then his mother came: "Why are you weeping, my son?"

"I have cause for weeping, dear mother. I have to go to war. What will become of my beloved wife?"

"Son, if this is what is troubling you, you mustn't worry—what am I here for? I'll look after her."

"Oh, mother," said the king, "if only you could promise that you'd watch over my wife, that nothing would happen to her!"

Said the queen: "Look, son—after you, my own child, she is my child, too. She is as close to my heart as you are. Don't worry, no harm will come to her, if only God would shield you from those wretched bullets!" The old queen tried to comfort her son.

Then it was time for the king to leave. He could barely bring himself to part from his wife. He kept begging his mother to take good care of her, to get a nurse for her who, under her supervision, would bathe her and feed her. And when her time will come to give birth, they should take pains to attend to her, for when God willing he returns, nothing will be forgotten.

So the king mobilized: the trumpets and horns began blaring—it was time to leave. The king took leave of his wife and they parted from each other in tears. He wrote to her, sent her a letter every day, telling her where they were and encouraging her not to worry for God would bring him home. He was always comforting her.

Well, be that as it may, there was an innkeeper in that town. And the innkeeper had a daughter who had high hopes that the king would take her for his wife. Who knows how, but she learned that the king had a wife. So she began thinking of how she could separate them from each other. She was beset by envy.

Then with God's help the time came and the little child was born. A boy with golden hair, so beautiful that *one could sooner look at the sun than at him,* so great was his beauty. The old queen loved him very much and was so overjoyed that she couldn't do enough for him. She thought she would gladden her son's heart by telling him how beautiful was his child. So the very same day she sat down and wrote him a letter.

She said: "My dear son, do not grieve, for happiness came to our palace. Happiness so great that it cannot be expressed in words. You have such a beautiful golden-haired son that *one can sooner look at the sun than at him.* And don't worry, your wife is well—she is being cared for, she is not in pain, and the doctors are at her side. So don't be concerned, and may God bring you home safely."

Suffice it to say that there was a postman in town who was delivering the mail. He was a drunkard, and when he was carrying the letters he never passed by the inn without entering for a glass or two. On that day, too, he went into the inn with the letters, and asked for a drink. The innkeeper's daughter, who took care of the drinks, brought it to him and said:

"Order some more, have another. One small drink is not enough for a man who is tired, who runs around so much. You need another."

He didn't have to be told twice. He asked for one more pint and gulped it down.

Then the innkeeper's daughter spoke again: "We have some good liquor, it just came in, we didn't have this kind before."

"Let me have a pint, let me see what it's like!"

She gave it to him. But the liquor was so strong that it was terrible. He emptied the glass and became drunk. So drunk that he fell asleep sitting on the chair. Then the innkeeper's daughter opened the case in which he carried the mail, found the letter the queen sent to her son, read it and threw it in the oven to burn.

Quickly she took a sheet of paper and wrote:

"Well, my dear son, you'll have a nice surprise when you come home! Your wife gave birth, but twin pups were born to her. Write to me and tell me what I should do. There is nothing but weeping and lamenting now in the palace. I can't help thinking of how I had begged you not to take her for your wife. What will happen when you come home and see this?"

The girl shoved the letter into the whatnot, roused the postman and said: "Get up and be on your way, or you'll be late! I have troubles enough without you!"

The son received the letter and read it.

"Mother you are asking what to do with her. All I have to say is that what was born, was born—and it is God's creature too. Take care of her until my return. When I am home we'll see what is to be done. Meanwhile do not harm the young, or their mother, and make sure that nothing happens to them."

So wrote the king to the widowed queen. When the postman came with the letter, he stopped at the tavern again. He never missed it for he was such a drunkard. And once again the innkeeper's daughter saw to it that he became intoxicated. She made him so drunk that he fell asleep. So, once again she took the letter and read what the king had written: "Though they are whelps, don't hurt them, look after them and after their mother."

The innkeeper's daughter became even more furious when she saw that the news hadn't aroused the king's anger. She threw that letter in the fire as well, and wrote another.

She wrote:

"Dear mother, summon two soldiers and have them take the basket with my wife back to where they found it. I don't want her any longer."

This is what she put in the letter. When the mother read it, she nearly *died of despair.*

"What got into my son?" she said. "How much he loved her and how often I told him, 'don't marry her, you'll live to regret it,' and he always answered 'No, never!'

And now this is what he writes to me? Now I shall not allow her to be taken away! What do you think? That I shall let this beloved child be taken from the palace? I would sooner die!"

In her answer to him she wrote:

"If you have no pity for your wife, think at least of your son!"

In short, whenever the postman was delivering letters, he always stopped in for a drink, and the innkeeper's daughter always made sure he became drunk. No one knew about this.

Again she threw the letter into the fire and wrote another:

"Dear son, tell me what I should do. The pups are whimpering so that I cannot close an eye. Who can stand this? I told you not to take her for your wife! And now you have a visitation from God, she bore you whelps."

Then she roused the postman and sent him on his way.

The king received the letter. Again all he heard was that the whelps were whimpering, that his mother couldn't stand it and he should tell her what to do.

He wrote back to her:

"Dear mother, suffer it for me; suffer it for me and wait for me to come home. Don't hurt the pups, or my wife; take good care of them!"

When the postman came he stopped at the inn, as always; the girl was waiting for him eagerly. She flattered him, kept smiling at him, cajoled him and made him drunk. Then she got hold of the letter once more, read it and threw it into the fire.

Instead she wrote:

"Dear mother, I told you before, don't complain to me—just think of what I have said. Have two soldiers take her away—I don't want her any more. Let them take her back, I said. I don't want to live with her."

When the queen received the letter she burst into tears.

"Dear God, how can I do such a thing?"

She was so sorry for her daughter-in-law and for the child, her heart nearly broke.

The old queen wrote yet again: "Dear son, don't break my heart completely, don't break the small part I have left. You didn't listen when you brought her home, but now I will oppose you. What do you think, have her taken away with her child? There is a God in Heaven!"

This time, too, the innkeeper's daughter got hold of the letter, read it and wrote another one: "Dear son, give me some other advice, or I don't know what will become of me. I must leave the palace for the pups are suckling so hard at their mother's breast that blood is oozing out of her. I must leave the palace unless you give me further advice and tell me what I should do with her."

She sent this letter and threw the other in the fire.

Her son read it and wrote back: "Dear mother, don't let her suckle them. She mustn't put them to her breast. Feed them a different way. She shouldn't give them her breast, she shouldn't have done it in the first place. But leave them alone until I return."

The innkeeper's daughter got the letter again, read what was in it and threw it in the fire. She sat down and wrote her own.

The son's letter had said: "Dear mother, don't write to me any more. I have understood everything and have asked you to endure it for me. I'll be home soon."

The innkeeper's daughter wrote instead: "If you write to me again, I'll never come home. I'll stand in the line of fire and face the bullets deliberately, so they'll hit me, if you don't take my wife back to where I found her. Or I'll go off into the wide world, for I no longer want her. And don't write me any more letters!"

This was the letter to his mother.

Well, when the old woman received the letter and read it, she felt as if the palace was collapsing around her, she wept so bitterly. She summoned two soldiers and told her daughter-in-law everything, for she didn't know about the letters until then.

She said to the soldiers: "Take this basket with the mother and child to the top of that big mountain and leave it there!"

The soldiers looked at each other. Yes, even they looked at each other:

"What does the king want? He is sending her back now, with the child? Why did he bring her home if he doesn't like her?"

Then the queen gently bathed the child, swaddled it and with a large kerchief tied it to his mother's bosom, as if she were carrying him. The kerchief held the child securely and she placed the mother's nipple in his mouth so he could suckle. She couldn't even do that herself for she had no arms—only the kerchief held the child. Then the soldiers drove them in a carriage to that same place, and left them there.

That is when she really began to cry—when the soldiers went and she was left alone with the child.

"Dear God, why do you punish me so when I sinned against no one, never wronged anyone?"

After three days she stopped having milk as she had nothing to eat. Even if there had been food, she wouldn't have been able to eat it without an arm. Blood came dripping out of her nipples. After being up there for three days she kept praying for Him to take the child, then her, or both of them together, but above all the child. She wept and wept and the child cried bitterly. She felt so sorry for him and as she tossed about straining to give the child her breast, he fell out. He had tried to reach the nipple, the kerchief loosened and he dropped out of it. The kerchief came apart and the little one slid down from her lap. He began rolling down the slope and she had to look on while her child went tumbling downhill. Her heart nearly broke but there was nothing she could do. When the child reached bottom, it was caught in a bush and cried there woefully. And she cried on top of the mountain; both mother and child continued to cry. She thought a wild beast would devour her son. If only it devoured her, too. As she was lamenting and grieving for her child, she saw an old man coming up the mountain.

Dear God Almighty, who is coming here? He walked by my child, didn't pick it up, yet he heard him cry—she thought to herself.

The old man reached the summit, walked up to her and said: "What are you doing here, my girl?"

"Don't even ask what I am doing. You see my child was attached to me—it got loose and rolled all the way down. Now it is crying there bitterly, and I cannot fetch it."

"Well, my dear little girl, I came here to ask you to have a look and see if there are any lice in my head."

"Dear grandpa," she said, "how can I? I have no hands. I can see with my eyes, but I have no hands."

"Do what you can. If there is no other way, do it with your shoulder," he said. "Just rub it, any way you can!"

Well, the poor woman began rubbing the man's head with her shoulder, the best she could. All of a sudden she had two hands. Her two hands grew back. While she rubbed him she got her two good hands back, as they were before they were cut off.

She looked up at the sky: "Oh, merciful, almighty God, look, I have two hands! You restored them to me!"

Then the old man said: "Go, fetch your child!"

"How can I go, dear grandpa, how can I, when I have no legs?"

"You have two hands, slide down the best you can. Use your two hands to help you along and pick up your child!"

She crawled out of the basket, planted her two hands on the ground and pushed herself forward. She began sliding down the slope and by the time she reached the bottom, she had two legs. Both her legs grew back, nice and healthy. She lifted up the child, she could do it now that she had two hands and two legs.

Then the old man came to her and she said to him: "Whom can I thank and how can I give thanks for this?"

"Thank the good Lord, he gave you back your two hands and two legs. Take your child, my dear girl, and go. There is a brook nearby, bathe him in it and bathe yourself too."

She went, found the brook and bathed the child and herself. She became so healthy, so beautiful, a hundred times more beautiful than before they cut her hands off.

Then the old man said to her: "Now go to the seashore, my girl. There is sand on the beach—lie down on it and rest. When you wake up, all that you'll see with your two eyes will be yours. But don't ever forget God as long as you live, for He'll always watch over you and protect you, whenever you ask Him and pray to Him!"

She thanked him for his good advice and his kindness, and went on her way. The sea was not far away; she found it easily, and there was nice, dry sand on its shore. She lay down on it with the child. She fell into such a deep sleep that only she knew— and God—how long she slept. And when she awoke, where did she find herself? In the sea there was an island and on the island stood an enormous castle. It had three hundred windows and one hundred and fifty doors, and even the handles were made of pure gold. *Three gold chains tied the castle to the sky and it revolved on the spurs of a rooster.* This is where she woke up. The castle spun around like the whirlwind and gold glistened on its corners. A gold staircase led up to it. And what an interior the castle had! No hand could describe its beauty, no mind could imagine such splendor!

She remembered what the old man had said, that what she saw with her own eyes when she woke up, would be hers. But then the castle was hers! So she took her child, went into the castle and looked at every nook and cranny. It was filled with things, one more beautiful than the other. Everything that belonged in a royal palace was there.

That was where she now lived with her child. And the child developed so well that soon it stood on its feet.

Before long his tongue came untied and he began to speak. He spoke like his mother, clearly. And she taught him how to read, write and count. His mind took it all in, and he knew more than a child who had gone through eight grades. He was very bright. His mother always talked to him about how she was born, and that she had twelve brothers who became bandits, robbers; how she had gone to visit them and that her sister-in-law had them cut off her two arms and legs. And the child wrote down all that his mother said. He wrote everything down, and then read his mother's life story over and over again. Meanwhile the child got to be about six years old, but he could have been older for he grew fast and his intelligence grew and developed as well. So, little by little, his mother related to him the course of her life and all that had happened to her.

The child asked: "Don't I have a father? Dear mother, have I no father?"

"I don't know, my son. If he is alive you have a father, but if he perished in the war, you don't have one."

So mother and child lived on there, they lived like Adam and Eve in paradise. They had everything. The fame of the castle spread far and wide and the robbers heard about it. But they didn't know who lived in the castle. They searched and pried until they found out that a widowed queen lived there. The brothers consulted and decided that they'd raid the castle and burglarize it.

They discussed it and agreed: "It would be good to raid it. We can clean it out, there is no man around in the castle."

So they took off. They didn't care when they got there, they were determined to go.

Meanwhile, as they were preparing the raid, the king came home from the war. Right away he went to see his mother and asked:

"Is my wife alive?"

Said the queen: "So you came back, my dear son?"

But the queen wept.

"I came back, mother," he said, "but is my wife alive?"

She answered: "I don't know if she is alive, or if the wild beast carried away even her bones."

"What are you saying?"

He ran into the room where his wife used to live. But she wasn't there.

"Mother, where is my wife?"

She said: "My dear son, have you lost your mind? What is wrong with you? Why do you ask me where your wife is? What did you write to me in your letter?"

The king stood aghast, his eyes fixed on his mother. What was she saying?

"I don't know, my son," she said, "whether it is I who lost my senses, or you."

"I don't know, but neither of us is speaking the right way. Mother, I can hardly wait for you to tell me, where is my wife?"

Said the queen: "She is where you sent her when you wrote. I had her taken to where you had found her."

"I wrote to you to have her taken back there?"

"Yes, you wrote it—I received your letters. And in how many letters did I tell you not to be heartless, for now I will not let the child go? What a beautiful child was born to you! A golden-haired, beautiful boy, *one could sooner look at the sun than at him.* And still you wrote that I should take her back to where you had found her, that you didn't want her anymore. In how many letters did I tell you what a beautiful boy you had, and every time you answered I should take her back to where you had found her, for you wouldn't ever want her again. And in your last letter you said that if I didn't have her taken away, you'd go out into the wide world, or you'd kill yourself. What was I to do? I had no choice but to send her back."

"And where is the child?"

"I sent it away, too. You wrote that I should do that, send her with everything she had."

"Well, mother, I don't understand how this could happen. You wrote to me not about a boy having been born, but about two whelps."

Then the old queen got alarmed, too.

"You wrote," he said, "that they chewed so hard at their mother's nipples that they nearly tore them off. And I answered that she should not put them to her breast and that in any case they should be left alone until my return."

Gradually it came to light who the letter carrier was. The old queen knew it, so they sent for him right away. They summoned him before the king, and the king asked him where he had gone when he was delivering the mail, who could have laid their hands on the case. Well, he had to say it, for he was dealing with the king. He told the truth:

"Your Royal Majesty, I'll tell it as it was and as it is. I am a man given to drinking, and I cannot pass by a tavern without stopping in. And every time I stopped in, the innkeeper's daughter made me drunk. She kept pouring me drinks until I was intoxicated. What she did with the letters then, I don't know, for I fell asleep and she roused me later."

Then the king knew what the innkeeper's daughter had done, but he couldn't utter another word about it. He turned around and said:

"I am going to look for my wife and will not rest until I find her. And if all I find is a small bone that belonged to her, I'll bring that home."

He wept so bitterly that his mother was unable to comfort him:

"My dear son, it is not my fault—I myself have cried enough."

The king left in deep sorrow. He went up to the mountain, but all he found there was naked earth. Then he descended from the top and wandered around. He didn't go home. Suddenly he saw that there was a golden bridge leading from the sea-shore to his castle, with railings made of diamonds. Alongside the bridge there was a footpath, bordered by two rows of trees. And on the trees all kinds of birds were chirping. Already the king's heart had been filled with sorrow, but now he was moved to tears by the song of the birds, by the beauty of their singing.

He thought to himself: Dear God, who built this bridge? When I went to war it wasn't here. I'll go until I come to the end of this road, to the head of this bridge, and see where it originates.

(Now let's leave the king, let him wander about!)

Meanwhile the robbers arrived. But they got there very early—it was daytime—and they were to work at night. So they lay down on the sand and waited for evening to close in. The golden bridge stretched across the sea from the palace and when dusk set in they took off, crossed over the golden bridge and went in. But when the robbers reached the palace, it was spinning around in circles so they couldn't just enter easily. Each of them had a hatchet, a small ax, and they began to confer on how best to use the axes. They were not dressed as robbers, they wore disguises, but under the disguises they carried knives and guns, *revolvers*. They said they should sink the ax into one of the steps, hold onto it and leap inside. So they cast their axes as the stairs were revolving and jumped in, one after the other. All twelve of them got into the palace.

When the twelve entered, the queen was chatting with her little son in one of the rooms, teaching him all manner of things. And she was telling him how, with the help of the old man, her two arms and two legs were restored. It was the good Lord who had given them back to her and it was He who had sent her this building.

"And, my little son, always pray, for only the good Lord is with us. Your father may have been shot in the war, he may have perished. There are my many brothers, but they are all my murderers—we have no one to trust but God."

This is what they were talking about.

"Come, my son, let's go into the room, you'll read to me there and I'll listen."

The child was able to read well already.

Then there was a knock at the door. The queen was frightened—who could come here at such an unusual time? Bowing and scraping, her twelve brothers entered, decked out in princely finery. She recognized them, but the robbers didn't know who she was. They bade her good evening and said "*I kiss your hand.*" They did kiss her

hand, for she was a queen. She graciously beckoned them to sit down in the uphol-
stered armchairs around the table. They asked her to forgive them for coming to visit
her at such an unusual hour.

The queen asked them: "Where do you come from?"

"We come from far away."

They mentioned a fictitious place from where they came, and didn't give their
real names.

"The fame of this palace reached us. We heard what a beautiful palace was built
here, so we came to see it."

The queen conversed with them politely: "I thank you for your visit."

She received them cordially, brought wine, and put all kinds of pastries and
delicacies on the table. They came from far away, they must be tired and hungry.

They began to talk and then, suddenly, someone knocked at the door. All said
"please, come in!"—and in came the king. His wife recognized him instantly, but he
didn't recognize her.

The queen looked at the child and started out the door. The child followed her.
They walked into another room, and she said to him with great joy:

"Now, my son, I'll tell you, the twelve gentlemen who came in before are your
twelve uncles and the one who just arrived is your father."

"What are you saying, mother? I do have a father?"

"Yes, my son, you do. The good Lord brought him home from the war. He came
looking for us, but he doesn't know who we are, he doesn't recognize us. Listen, my
son," she said, "I have told you my life story many times, and you read it often and
memorized it. Do you think you could recount it?"

Said the child: "Of course, I could, mother. I can tell every word of the story."

"My dear son," she said, "your twelve uncles came not to pay us a visit but to
burglarize us. And don't think that they usually go around dressed like gentlemen—
they are wearing disguises. But if you knew what was hidden beneath their disguises,
you would know who they really are, that they are robbers. Look, son, we don't need to
bring this to light now. We'll go back in—they'll be conversing with each other, and I'll
heap more food and drink on the table; and when they've loosened up from drinking,
and they're chatting, having a good time—then. . . . Now, my son, go into the room,
shake hands with every one and sit down with them at the table. And when you see
them eating and drinking heartily, thank the gentlemen, our guests, for their visit, thank
them first—and then say to them:

"'Gentlemen, dear guests, I would ask you, if you'd be so kind and tell me
something about the great, wide world, for you get around a lot, hear a lot and know a
lot.'

"Ask everyone to tell you a story. Say to them: 'each one of you tell a story.'
They'll agree, they'll be glad to do it, and then you tell them one, too. You say to them:
'I'd also like to tell a story, if you'd allow me.' Then, my son, begin describing my life

and how I came here, so they'll know who we are. They don't recognize us, yet they are my own brothers. They don't know us and your father doesn't know us either, yet he is my wedded husband. Can you tell the story?"

"For sure, I can, mother. Every word of it."

Then they went in and again took with them all kinds of drinks, a variety of wines, nothing but the finest, an assortment of pastries and meat dishes. The table was laden, full.

Well, the robbers had a lot to say—they were savvy. They asked the woman how old the child was when his father went to war—she had told them that she was a widowed queen. She answered that he was born after her husband had left. They were astonished at how big and intelligent the child was for his age. He was so beautiful that all of them just gazed at him. His hair fell to his shoulders in curls. He stood on a chair and listened to what was being said, watching each one of them attentively. He saw that they were enjoying themselves, eating, drinking, and talking to each other. They were waiting for the king to go so they would be alone. And the king was waiting for them to leave, but they just sat and continued chatting.

Then, suddenly, the child spoke up: "With your permission I would also have a few words to say."

Oh, they all agreed readily: "Go ahead, prince, say what you wish!"

"By your leave, gentlemen, our guests, I thank you for coming to visit us. It is rare that someone comes here with whom we can converse, so we are glad that now we are so numerous. I'd like to ask you gentlemen to be so kind and each one of you relate a story. I'd like to hear something about the big, wide world."

They all spoke at once: "We will, gladly, but then the prince must tell us a story, too."

"If you allow me, I will," he said. "But first I'd like to hear your stories."

Well, they began, each one told a story, (but not a long one like mine, their stories were shorter). Then the twelve brothers finished, they had lied all they could about what was going on in the world and said enough about themselves. The king was the last to tell a story. And then they all called on the boy, it was his turn.

"Now listen to me! But listen well, for this is a true story!"

With their mouths agape, they looked at the child, amazed at how he spoke.

(This story is told twice. He related the whole story from the beginning, word for word, the way I just told it. The brothers were all ears when they heard how angry the sister-in-law had become when they always kissed their sister and how she then decided to kill the dog. They couldn't believe that the child knew all this. This was about them— how the brothers didn't get upset; how the girl had to swear that she had killed the dog and still they didn't get angry. About how the sister-in-law had burned her own child and how the girl's heart nearly broke. So, word for word, the child related the whole story.)

The boy stood up and began:

There was once a well-to-do farmer and he had twelve sons. The twelve boys were born one after the other, there was no girl in between. They would have very much liked to have had at least one sister, and just then their mother was pregnant. She was expecting a little girl. Meanwhile, the brothers had agreed among themselves that they would become bandits but their father wouldn't give them his permission. Nevertheless, they persisted, until in the end they obtained their father's consent.

"Well, father, we are leaving," they said. "And when our mother has given birth, give us a signal! If it is a boy, tie a bunch of hay to a stake on the rooftop. We will see it through our glasses and know that it is a boy and then we won't come home for the christening, for when he is grown, he'll come to join us. But if it is a girl, put a bundle of tow on the roof, and we will come for the christening."

Suffice it to say that the parents forgot what the brothers had said and set out a bunch of hay, even though a lovely little girl was born. They put out hay, so the brothers didn't come home for the christening.

They went deep into the forest and set up camp. They had a little dog that they had trained, and with that dog the robbers sent money to their parents.

When the little girl grew bigger and saw that the dog came every month, bringing money in a bag tied to its neck, she asked her mother:

"Why is this dog always coming here?"

Her mother answered: "You have twelve brothers in the forest, they are sending the money.

She said: "What are they doing in the forest?"

"They are cutting wood, my child," said the mother.

"Why aren't they coming home?"

"They have no time, my girl, they are working."

One summer day the little girl was playing in the courtyard. She was about three years old. Suddenly the dog appeared and went into the house. They took the money from him and let him out. The little girl saw this and thought she would go with the dog. And so she went—the dog walked in front and she walked behind him. She was following the dog and when they had gone half the distance, the little girl got tired and began to cry. She sat down and the dog sat next to her until she was rested. Meanwhile the robbers began to wonder why the dog was so late, and their leader said:

"One of us should go find out what was keeping the dog."

A robber went and saw that there was a little girl asleep near the path, with the dog sitting at her side. He moved closer and saw what a pretty little girl she was.

He waited for her to wake up and said to her: "Who do you belong to, little girl?"

"To my father."

"And who is your mother?"

"Mother."

"Where are you going?"

"I am going into the forest, to my brothers."

*"To your brothers?"*

*"Yes, I have twelve brothers there—they are cutting wood."*

Then the robber knew that she was their own sister, that they had put hay instead of tow on the roof, so the brothers didn't go home. He lifted her into his arms and with great joy took her back to the camp."

(This is the story the boy told the brothers, there at the table.)

*Oh, how happy they all were when they found out that the little girl was their sister! They said: "We won't let her go home. We'll raise her."*

(How attentively the robbers listened! They knew the story was about them, but they wondered where the child could have heard it.)

*So they kept her there. They loved the little girl very much. One of them always stayed behind to watch over her. When they came home in the evening they always brought her something, toys and all kinds of things.*

*One day the little girl said: "Dear brother, why don't you bring a woman into the house? I would have a sister-in-law, someone to talk to."*

*"Let it be, little sister, it is better for you this way. If you had a sister-in-law, she might scold you—this way is better for you."*

*She said: "I wouldn't quarrel with her."*

*Well, one day the oldest brother brought a woman home. But when they returned at night, they continued paying attention to the little girl first, rather than to the young bride. They heaped kisses and love on her and turned to the young bride only afterwards. This made her feel very angry. Why did they love the little girl so? Why didn't they love her more? She decided that she would have the girl removed, taken out of her sight. So one day when the brothers were out robbing, she killed the trained messenger dog, cut off his head and made the little girl swear that she would say she had done it. When the robbers came home at night, they ran to the little girl.*

*Said the young woman: "You may go on kissing her, but she cut our dear dog's head off."*

*The robbers said: "Never mind, we can always get another dog but we can't find a sister growing on any tree. She is too dear to us, we'll get another dog."*

*The next day when the robbers left again, the young woman got to it and killed the best running horse they had.*

*She said to herself: If they didn't get angry about the dog, this will surely make them angry.*

*She said to the girl to tell her brothers that she had done it, or else she would kill her the same way. The robbers came home in the evening and they ran to the little girl to hug and kiss her.*

*"Oh, don't hug her and kiss her!"*

*"Why not? Did she do something again?"*

*"Oh, dear! Imagine, she killed the horse!"*

*"Let it be, we can always get a horse, but not another sister—she is dear to us."*

*The young woman grew even angrier. She now had her own child. She made up her mind to do something that would make the brothers furious, for sure. When they left, she fired up the oven and threw in her child.*

*The little girl cried out: "Don't burn my nephew!"*

*"I'll burn you too, if you don't say that you did it!"*

*At night when the robbers came home, they found the young woman weeping that her child was no more.*

*"Don't cry."*

*"How can I not cry when your sister burned up my beloved child!"*

*"What are you saying?"*

*"Well, I fired up the oven to bake bread and she threw in my child! I'll leave you if you don't take her away from here!"*

*Now the robbers were angry and began to consult.*

(The robbers looked at each other. How could the boy know all this? At the time they had no idea that their sister was innocent.)

*So they began to discuss what to do with her:*

*"Her hands should be cut off."*

*"No, she should be burned."*

*"No, she should be hanged."*

*"No, do you know what? We should cut off her two hands and her two legs and leave her on top of the mountain."*

*And that is what they did. They took her up on that big mountain and left her there. The poor girl cried her heart out, but she couldn't die, she had to endure her suffering.*

*Just then the king went hunting into that very forest. When they got there, they set up camp, the soldiers sat down and left one of them standing guard.*

(Now the king knew that the story was about his wife. He trembled, wondering how it would end, what had become of the woman.)

*The soldier who was standing guard suddenly heard a woman crying. He took off to see who it was. When he reached the top of the mountain, he found a beautiful girl in a basket, but she had neither arms nor legs. He turned around immediately and reported to the king what he saw.*

*The king went with two soldiers and asked the girl: "How did you get here? Who are you?"*

*She recounted to the king that she had gone to pick strawberries, that thieves had attacked her, asked her for money—but since she hadn't any, they cut off her two legs and two arms. She didn't betray her brothers, she didn't say that they had done this to her.*

(Hearing this, the brothers' hearts nearly broke, for now they realized that their sister was innocent when they left her to die. They could hardly wait for the end of the story to learn what had happened to the woman, where she was now.)

*Then the king said he would take her home with him, if she were willing.*

*"Sure, I'd go, but what can I do there? I have neither arms nor legs."*

*Right away the king ordered the soldiers to take the basket and bring it down. They brought it down from the top to where their camp was. Then he took the girl into his carriage and drove her to his palace. He placed her into a large room, had a nurse attend to her and said to his mother:*

"Mother, I want to take this woman for my wife."

*His mother didn't want to consent. But the prince threatened that if she refused, he would either kill himself or go so far away that no one would ever hear from him again.*

(Now the king's heart was touched, too. When he heard the story he knew that this part was about him.)

*Well, his mother agreed that he take the woman for his wife. Right away they called the priest and got married. They lived happily by the grace of God, for he loved her. Soon she became pregnant and then the king loved her even more, he was so happy.*

*One day a courier came and brought the king a sealed letter: if he wanted to save his country, he'd better mobilize immediately, for he was about to be attacked.*

*The king grew very worried. What would become of his wife when he left?*

*His mother said to him:* "Don't be sad, my son, for as long as I am alive, I'll look after her. She'll be as dear to me as you are."

"The son begged his mother repeatedly to take very good care of his child when it was born. Then he left and the woman stayed behind, her heart filled with sorrow. But her mother-in-law looked after her well, she couldn't have done better.

*Then the time came and she gave birth to her child. A beautiful, golden-haired boy was born to her. He couldn't have looked more beautiful in a painting. The old queen was overjoyed and wrote to her son at once:*

"God had blessed our palace. Your wife gave birth to a beautiful boy. His hair is pure gold. Don't worry, they are well and in good health. Take care of yourself and may God protect you from the bullets!"

*To make it short, the letter carrier was a drunkard. He never missed stopping at the tavern when he was delivering the mail. And the innkeeper's daughter was very jealous, she would have liked to become the king's son's wife. So she began thinking of all sorts of ways to lose the wife he had. When the letter carrier came in for a pint, she offered him more and more until he was completely drunk, keeled over and fell asleep. Then she searched through the letters and found the one the old queen sent to her son. She tore it up, threw it into the fire and wrote one herself:*

"My dear son, your wife gave birth. But her offspring is a whelp that whimpers day and night, robbing me of sleep."

*And her son answered:* "Let them be and take care of both of them until my return!"

*When the postman was to deliver this letter he again stopped at the tavern and the innkeeper's daughter once again got hold of it and wrote one instead:*

"Dear mother, send the woman back to where I found her. I don't want her any more."

*The old queen nearly died of despair. She couldn't imagine what had happened to her son. He loved his wife so, and now that she had a child he was sending her back? She didn't show the letter to the young woman but sat down right away and wrote back to her son:*

*"Dear son, what got into you? When I asked you not to take her for your wife, you said you would. Now that she has a child, I will not allow her to be taken away."*

*The tavern was on the postman's route so he stopped in every time. And the innkeeper's daughter again did what she did before.*

*She wrote another letter:*

*"Dear son, tell me what I should do. It keeps yelping and chewing its mother's nipples to pieces."*

*And the king wrote back:*

*"Dear mother, don't mind what it does. Feed it and take care of it but don't put it to the mother's breast!"*

*But the girl replaced the prince's letter and said:*

*"Dear mother, don't write to me any more! If you don't have her taken away, I'll go and never come home again!"*

*The queen got so alarmed that, weeping bitterly, she ordered two soldiers to take the woman back to the mountaintop, together with the child which was tied to her bosom. Her heart nearly broke, she felt so sorry for them. And the woman cried inconsolably. The child was suckling blood from her breast. She tried to rock him, but the kerchief which fastened him to her bosom loosened—he fell from her lap and rolled down the hill.*

*Then an old, white-haired man came. He passed by the child and went straight to the top of the hill where he found the poor woman weeping.*

*"What are you doing here, my girl?"*

*"What am I doing, dear grandpa? I am weeping for my child, I cannot go to fetch him for I have no legs."*

*"Well, my girl, have a quick look to see if there are any lice in my head!"*

*"How can I look? I have no hands."*

*"Do it with your shoulder. Anyway you can, just rub it."*

*The kindhearted girl felt sorry for the old man and rubbed her left shoulder against his head. And listen to the miracle! Both her hands grew back! She was overjoyed and thanked the Lord.*

*Said the old man: "Go, my girl, rise out of the basket and get your child."*

*"How can I when I have no legs?"*

*"As you can. Slide—you have two arms, lean on them!"*

*She began to slide and by the time she reached her child down in the valley, she had two good legs and the old man stood beside her.*

*"Now my girl, take your child, bring him to the brook over there, wash yourself and bathe him."*

*When she came to the brook, her child was chubby and healthy. She fell to her knees and thanked the good Lord.*

*Then the old man said to her: "Go forth, my girl. Soon you'll reach the seashore— sleep there for a while with your child, and when you wake, everything you see will be yours.*

*But don't ever forget God!"*

*Then the old man turned around and left. She came to the seashore and rested with her child. She fell into a deep sleep, as if she had died. When she woke up, she saw an island in the sea and on the island stood a castle, suspended on three gold chains. From then on things were right for them and the queen lived there with her small son. She raised the little boy.*

*After some time her twelve brothers came to burglarize her.*

(Now the robbers were really ashamed, for they knew for sure that the story was about them.)

*The king returned from the war, but his wife and child were nowhere to be found. Grief-stricken and weeping, he set out to look for them. He saw the bridge and thought that it wasn't there when he left for the war. Who could be living in the castle, who could have built it in such a short time? he wondered. It was all the same to him but he decided to find out.*

*The twelve brothers arrived at the castle in disguise first, then the king came. And now we are here together: you are my father, and you are my twelve uncles. You didn't recognize us, but now you know, I am the orphan boy!*

Then the king knew that the woman was his wife. It is impossible to describe the joy and happiness there was! The father took the child in his arms, then fainted. The brothers also knew that she was their sister. They fell to their knees before her, kissed her feet and asked her for forgiveness. The twelve brothers broke down in tears and begged her to forgive them. They didn't know what they had done for they had listened to the wife and they were not at fault.

"Oh, forgive us, we committed a terrible, heinous crime against you, who were innocent!"

They kissed her over and over again and asked for her pardon. They handed the boy one to the other, praised him for telling the story so well and heaped kisses on him. No one was able to sleep that night; they frolicked until morning. But the king had eyes only for his wife. He was overcome with tears when he heard the pain she had endured.

She said to her brothers: "I know, my dear brothers, that it isn't brotherly love that brought you here to visit me. You came to rob me—that was your intention. But now you know who I am."

They made merry until it was morning. Then the king said that he was leaving, for he had to complete a task he had set for himself. He summoned the innkeeper's daughter. He asked her who had authorized her to steal the letters, how did she dare do such a thing?

"Because I was hoping you would take me for your wife"—was the only answer she could give.

"You'll pay for this evil deed!"

They had her tied to the tail of a steed and dragged around the city twelve times until she was torn to smithereens. And they took the parts that fell off her body to the four corners of the city and shot them to pieces. This was her punishment. The king had them all put to death—her father, her mother, and the whole family.

Then they held a feast, a real one! They invited the priests and bishops and had a wedding celebration the fame of which spread to the far corners of the world. The king wept for joy, oh dear God, how happy he was! He didn't know whom to kiss more, his child or his wife. They brought the old queen to the palace and asked all the kings from surrounding lands to come. The young woman forgave her brothers—she harbored no anger against them—and invited her mother and father, so they were there, too.

This is the end of the story. They are still alive today if they are not dead, and *if you don't believe it, go find out for yourself.*

# 20. Fairy Ilona

AT 707 (*The Three Golden Sons*); MNK 707 (*The Golden-Haired Twins*) lists 28 close and 7 deviant variants. The type shows great flexibility and merges often with affinial tale types, particularly with episodes of 706. The structure of Mrs. Palkó's tale accords with three Hungarian variants and comes closest to a Székely text from 1907. This may suggest that it was a part of the old Andrásfalva stock, but the fact that she had heard it only recently from relatives, at a visit in Mucsfa, means that a storybook version had been in circulation. Mrs. Palkó loved her new acquisition and adapted it with delight to her repertoire, probably because of its close affinity to "The Twelve Robbers." By the time of the recital recorded here—a year and a half later, in 1956— she had completely adapted the extremely complex story by screening out unfamiliar elements and structuring it in her own manner, switching from one scene of simultaneous happenings to the other, and using her favorite formulas, sayings and commonplaces, internalizing the ordeal of the innocently suffering queen. There is only one episode she does not integrate: the turkey-herd girl is not rewarded for keeping the walled-in heroine alive.

When recorded, this story was still in the making, strongly influenced by the established form of "The Twelve Robbers." Comparing the exchange of letters between queen mother and king in "The Twelve Robbers" to the correspondence between cook and emperor in "Fairy Ilona" shows great similarity in content and style, but the "Fairy Ilona" exchange is less detailed. In general, the performance of "Fairy Ilona" is not as well balanced as older pieces in Mrs. Palkó's repertoire. Although her narration is captivating, some episodes are more elaborate than others. The theft of the horse, mirror, and military band is described in rather sketchy terms, while the trapping of Ilona at her vanity in the fabric store is featured with delicious humor and in generous detail, although the narrator makes a mistake. She forgets to mention Ilona's precious metal dresses.

Mrs. Palkó tells us that "if you like to listen to it, the whole story would have to be told again"—but then she gives a summary of Fairy Ilona's re-telling, reasserting that this beautiful story is "like 'The Twelve Robbers'—it has to be told twice." The distortions of this particular performance were caused by special circumstances. Mrs. Palkó was telling the story to her most devoted listener, Emma Sebestyén, who was familiar with her total repertoire and wanted to hear this new one. As it is obvious from her interjections, she discovered similarities between this and some other tales of Aunt Zsuzsa. Hearing this one for the first time, she listened with awe but she was also nervous because she had to fix dinner for her five children, back from school. She could not leave before she heard the end, but her body language and comments made Mrs. Palkó cut the end short.

———

Long, long ago, in a land far away, there was once a well-to-do farmer. He had three daughters.

One day their mother said to them: "My dear daughters, go and reap the hemp today!"

"All right, mother, we'll go."

So they went the next day. All three went and began to *harvest the hemp*, singing along while they worked. They sang songs as they gathered the hemp. Then the emperor's son happened to come by on horseback. The hemp field stretched all the way to the road, the *paved road*, and as they were not far from it, the emperor's son heard them singing. He reined in his horse, rode at a more leisurely pace, and listened to the songs. He came closer and closer in their direction, until he drew near them.

Said the oldest girl: "Look, the emperor's son is approaching! Oh, if only he took me for his wife," she said, "I'd spin so much yarn from one stalk of hemp, I'd weave so much cloth, that it would suffice for the emperor's whole army, and there would be some left over for me, I'd sew so many shirts."

Said the second girl: "But if he took me for his wife, I'd bake so much bread from the grain of one stalk of hemp, that it would satisfy the whole army, and there would be some left over for me."

Said the third, the youngest: "And if he'd ask my hand in marriage, I'd bear him such a beautiful golden-haired son that his equal hasn't yet been born in this world, he'd be so beautiful."

The emperor's son heard this. The girls went on with their work, and the emperor's son put the spur to his horse and rode off. He galloped away but was so agitated that he couldn't forget what the girls had said. He went home and couldn't sleep a wink all night—his mind was filled with the words of the youngest girl. He thought he'd return for a walk to the same place the next day, maybe he'd find the girls there, and this time he'd speak to them. But on the next day he took a carriage. When he arrived, he alighted and walked out to the girls in the hemp field. He greeted them and the girls reciprocated.

Said the emperor's son: "Tell me, which one of you said that if the emperor's son took her for his wife, she'd bear him such a beautiful golden-haired son, the likes of whom hadn't yet been born in this world?"

The girls became flustered. The two older ones pointed to the youngest: "it was she." She grew alarmed and turned as red as a beet in her embarrassment.

The prince said to her: "Repeat to me once more what you said yesterday!"

The girl said she was only joking, she meant it only in fun.

"Oh," she said, "I was only joking."

"We must turn the joke into reality," he said. "Get into my carriage—you are coming with me!"

Now the girl was really frightened. He helped her into the carriage and took her home.

He said to her: "Since you dared to say it, I'll take you for my wife."

It was no use for her to insist that she was only joking; he said the joke had to be made to come true.

So, he took the girl for his wife. They got married and *lived together like two turtle doves.* They loved each other. One day the woman, the young bride, felt that she was becoming a mother and told her husband. The emperor's son was so happy, he didn't know what to do so great was his joy, expecting to have two beautiful, golden-haired twin boys. He could hardly wait for the hour of birth to come.

But soon great sadness befell him for he received a sealed letter; a courier brought it and handed to him. He opened it and read that he was being summoned to war. He was to *mobilize* in haste and be on his way for the enemy was attacking the land. Oh, was the emperor's son distressed! What would become of his wife? With God's help the hour of birth would arrive and he wouldn't see those two lovely boys. But, after all, what could he do? He had to go. He entrusted his wife to the cook, for she had consoled him, told him not to worry.

"Don't grieve about leaving, Your Majesty," she said, "I am here, I'll look after her and attend to her, as if she were my own."

Well, the emperor's son impressed on the cook to take very good care of his wife, and when, God willing, the time came for her to give birth, to write to him immediately. She should write him a letter so he wouldn't worry.

"All right," she said, "just don't grieve, for I'll look after her so well that she won't *even lose a single hair from her head.* And I'll let you know right away when she has given birth."

So, the emperor's son left—the bugles had sounded. The army stood ready on the road, waiting for him. He took leave of his wife and departed, weeping bitterly. He never thought, never imagined that the cook would turn out to be his wife's greatest enemy. He didn't suspect it for he didn't know that the cook had a beautiful daughter, and she had always hoped that he would marry her.

**[Mrs. Adam Sebestyén:] This tale resembles "The Fawn."**

Three days after her husband's departure the young woman gave birth. Beautiful twins were born to her, but one was a girl, the other a boy. Both had golden hair and were so beautiful that they resembled angels from heaven rather than humans from this earth.

Well, their mother couldn't rejoice over them for long, for that night while she was asleep, the wicked cook took the two children from her and put two pups at her side in their place.

Then the cook called her husband and said to him: "Listen, I give you these two children—take them secretly to the forest, kill them and bring their eyes back to me! Take out their eyes and bring home so I'll be sure that you killed them. But no one must know about this!"

Then the cook sat down and wrote a letter to the emperor:

"Great Emperor," she said, "I should be writing to you about great joy, but an enormous disgrace befell your palace. Instead of giving birth to two golden-haired boys, your wife brought two pups into this world."

The emperor wrote back:

"Whether they are pups, or whatever else, never mind, let them be until I return."

(Well, let's leave them for now.) Meanwhile the man took the two children into the forest and set them down at the foot of a tree. They were truly beautiful children—he felt sorry for them.

He thought: Dear God, they are innocent, they didn't wrong me—why should I take their lives? Some day I may have to account for this.

So, he went ahead, made a small wooden crate and put the two children inside. He smeared the crate with tar, coated it all over, and lowered it into a stream flowing nearby. Then he let go of the crate, entrusting it to God. He thought maybe someone would come along to retrieve it—if not, God should take care of it. Then he caught sight of a nest on top of a tree with two young owls in it. He lifted them from the nest, removed their eyes, wrapped them in paper and took them home.

"Here you are, wife," he said, "it is done, I brought the proof to convince you. The proof is here that I killed them."

She didn't know what eyes they were.

"No one discovered the secret, I hope," she said, "and no one saw you!"

When the cook received the letter—she had taken it from the postman—she read what the emperor's son had written. He wrote that no matter what was born to his wife, it shouldn't be harmed.

So she sent him a reply:

"Great Emperor," she wrote, "it is unbearable—the pups are whimpering so that I cannot close an eye at night. Neither their mother nor I can find any sleep. Have some pity."

"I understand your suffering," he said. "I'll do what has to be done when I return home." This is what the emperor's son wrote back.

Then the cook sent another letter:

"Tell me what I should do, what should happen, for the pups are chewing at their mother's breast so hard that they are sucking blood, they are sucking her dry."

"Why did you let her put the pups to her breast?" he said, "why did you let her nurse them? They don't need so much milk, there are other ways of feeding them. But let them be until I come home!"

(Well, let's leave them now. Let's return to the children!) The stream carried the children farther and farther down to where a fisherman was fishing. He spotted the little crate on the water and wondered what it could be. He went out in his boat, caught the little crate and brought it to shore. When he tore it open he saw two beautiful children—maybe they even smiled at him.

"Dear God," he said, "you have sent them to me since I have no children! How happy my wife will be!"

They had been longing for God to give them at least one child—now he had sent them two. He took them home and told his wife what he had found. They kissed the children over and over again, the woman fixed some clothes for them right away, and dressed them. She cared for them as if she were their mother. And they grew and developed nicely, so beautifully that it was a delight.

Back home the emperor had returned from the war. As soon as he arrived he ran into the room to his wife.

"How are you, my dear wife? Where are your children?"

She broke into tears and told him what God had given her! She didn't know that her children were stolen from her.

Said the cook: "Your Imperial Majesty," she said, "how great a shame this queen brought on you! She may be called a queen, but she disgraced your palace! What will your friends say, and the other kings and emperors, when they hear of the offspring your wife bore you? How dishonored you'll be! I wouldn't keep her another hour!"

She kept at the emperor, kept talking to him until he said he would have his wife walled in, he wanted her no longer. The cook made him loathe her with all her talk of the shame she had brought on him, of how unfit she was for a nobleman and that she shouldn't be allowed to remain with him. He summoned two masons, had them cut an opening in one corner of the palace, wide enough for the woman, and ordered them to wall her in. But there was a girl who herded turkeys—she was devoted to the empress, and the empress was very fond of her, too. This young girl learned what they had planned to do and felt very sorry for the empress. Somehow, who knows how, she gained access to the gold in the palace and took a plateful. The emperor was away. As soon as he had given the order to wall in his wife, he left home. So the girl went to the masons and asked them if, in exchange for the gold, they'd make a secret little door, to let her bring food to the queen.

**[Listener:] They didn't want to give her anything to eat?**

(Well, he intended for her to perish there!)

"She was such a purehearted woman," she said, "so kind—I could die, I feel so sorry for her."

The mason accepted, he said he would do it—he'd make the wall in a way to let her hand in some food. He left a secret opening, only the good Lord and the girl knew about it.

"Be very careful," he said, "no one must know about it, for if they betray you, the emperor will have you die the most agonizing death."

And so the girl carried food secretly to the empress and kept her alive. (Now let's leave her and return to the children!)

The children were developing very nicely.

**[Listeners:] What happened next?**

(You'll see!)

**I've heard this story before!**

They grew taller and taller so that when they were four years old, they looked like they were six. Then the fisherman died and the children remained alone with their mother. She cared for them lovingly so they grew and flourished and were very beautiful; the woman didn't know what to do, she was so overjoyed with them. But grieving over her dead husband had made the woman sick and she, too, died. The two children became *orphans*. The little girl was very smart—she had watched her mother cook and bake and had learned how to do it. The boy took to the forest day after day; he had crafted a bow and arrow and went hunting all the time. He brought home birds, or a rabbit, and the girl prepared meals from what he brought. This is how they lived.

Once as he was strolling, roaming about, the boy wandered into the emperor's flower garden—he happened on it inadvertently. As boys would do, he peered into the garden for there were all sorts of game inside. He caught sight of a golden-haired rabbit and made up his mind that he would shoot it, if he couldn't catch it alive—he would shoot it if necessary, but he had to have it. From then on he visited the garden every day, kept watching for the rabbit and thinking about it. Then, one day, just as he began aiming his arrow to shoot, the king came out into the courtyard for a walk, and saw him. He called over to the boy:

"Halt! What do you want?"

The boy ran as if the devil were chasing him, he ran away so fast.

The emperor went inside and said to the cook: "I don't know who the boy is who is lurking around here," he said, "but he is a beautiful boy, with golden hair. He is forever aiming into the garden, I wonder what he is after. I have seen him twice," said the emperor, "but when I call him he runs like a shot, he vanishes."

Said the cook: "He ran away? Where did he run?"

He told her which direction the boy had taken. The next day the emperor went away, who knows where—he went somewhere. The cook packed a basket with food and fruit and headed to where the emperor said the boy had gone. She began tracking him and searched until she came upon the little shack where they lived. She went inside—only the little girl was at home.

The old woman entered and said: "Whom do you belong to, my little girl? Who are your father and mother? Are you alone?"

She said: "I am not alone, I am with my brother."

"Where is your brother?"

"He went hunting."

"And your parents?"

"Well," she said, "my father was a fisherman—they both died, first my father, then my mother. They died and now we are only two, my brother and I."

"Look, my girl," she said, "I brought you something to eat. Just tell your brother when he comes home that you saw in your dream that he must go and steal Fairy Ilona's horse. He is a hunter—it's proper for him to go on horseback and not on foot, and he can steal the horse. And if he asks you from whom you had heard this, just say that you saw it in your dream, that an old man came to you and told you that he must steal the horse, that he can do it. But don't betray me!" she said.

The woman thought that if the boy went there, Fairy Ilona would surely destroy him. For she began to doubt that her husband had killed the children and suspected that maybe it was the boy who had been lurking around the garden. He mustn't find out—not her husband, but the emperor—since it was her husband whom she had sent to kill them.

The boy came home, and by then the old woman had left. The girl told him what she had seen in her dream, that he must go and steal Fairy Ilona's horse, for when he went hunting it was fitting for him to be on horseback.

He said: "Did someone teach you this?"

"No, I saw it in my dream," she answered.

The very next morning the boy was off and on his way to Fairy Ilona. On the road he met a shepherd. He wished him a good day, and the shepherd in turn greeted him.

"Where are you going, son?"

He said: "I am on my way to Fairy Ilona," he said. "My sister saw in her dream that I should steal her horse."

"Oh, dear," he said, "you must be very careful, son. Ninety-nine lads have already left their heads there—you'll be the one hundredth, if she catches you. But listen to me, I'll teach you what to do. Go, but make haste, so you can get in while Ilona is asleep. If she is awake and catches you, she'll chop your head off!" He told the boy through which gate he should enter, for there were many, and in which stable he would find the horse.

The boy went and got the horse. He took it home, let it into the courtyard and went hunting. He didn't even give it any feed, so intent was he on going out to hunt. The young girl tended the horse.

The next day the old woman came again, and again brought some food. She said to the girl: "Look, my girl, tell your brother that in Fairy Ilona's room there is a mirror, he can steal it and he should do so. But don't betray me, say that you have seen it in your dream!"

When her brother returned from hunting she told him.

He said: "Isn't someone teaching you this?"

She said: "No, I have seen it in my dream."

The following day the boy set out once more and met with the shepherd. He told him where he was heading.

"Listen," he said, "be quick, you must get there before she rises. I'll tell you through which gate to enter and which door to open to reach that room."

The boy went and obtained the mirror, too. He succeeded. He brought it home but then he remembered the rabbit in the emperor's garden and rushed there once again. Just as he was aiming his arrow to shoot, the emperor called out:

"Come here, son, come to me! Don't be afraid, I won't harm you!"

But the boy panicked and ran. The emperor watched him but couldn't catch up with him.

The next day the boy went hunting again and the old woman came, as before. For the emperor kept repeating that he had seen the boy, that he had been around and the old woman was terrified that her secret would be revealed. Maybe her husband had deceived her and didn't kill the children, maybe this was the boy.

The old woman came and said: "Tell your brother, my girl, to go to Fairy Ilona and steal her military band. Have him bring the band home and you'll have a fine time when they play."

The boy went, the shepherd taught him once more how to accomplish it, and he got the band. Then, as soon as he took off to go hunting again, the old woman appeared:

"Look, my girl, look what I brought for you, and I'll bring much more, just tell your brother to go and steal Fairy Ilona herself, and take her for his wife!"

She thought that this time the lad wouldn't escape.

"But don't betray me, say that you have seen it in your dream!"

When the lad came home his sister told him what she had seen in her dream.

"My dear sister," he said, "hasn't someone taught you this?"

"Oh, no," she said, "I saw it in my dream."

So he set out the next day and met the shepherd.

"Where are you going, son?"

"Well, where am I going?" he said. "My sister saw in her dream that I can steal Fairy Ilona."

Said the shepherd: "Do you know with whom you are speaking?"

"Sure, I know," he said, "with a shepherd."

"No, son," he said, "you are wrong."

"Then, with whom am I speaking?" he asked.

He said: "You don't know?"

"How can I know? I know you as a shepherd."

"I am the Lord Jesus."

"That's not possible! Oh, don't tell me that! Our Lord Jesus is in Heaven, not tending the sheep."

"If you don't believe me, go and steal Fairy Ilona. If you don't believe me, go steal her!"

The boy left, but by the time he reached Fairy Ilona's palace, an immense sea came to surround it and he found no access. Such an immense, rolling sea that it was terrible. And there was no ship, no bridge, nor even a boat in sight, so he had to turn around. He went back to the shepherd.

"Well," he said, "you are back already?"

"Yes," he said.

"And you couldn't bring her?"

"No. I couldn't go in."

"Why not?"

"Listen, there is an immense sea all around—it encircles the palace, how could I get in? There are no ships!"

"Now do you believe who I am?"

"Yes, I do," he said, "I believe that you are the Lord Jesus."

"Then turn around and go back," he said. "Mount your horse and let it into the sea. Sit on its back and it will carry you across!"

"Oh, I can't do that," he said, "the horse will perish, it'll die on the spot. The waves are so high, it is frightening to watch them!"

"Don't worry, just let it into the water. And when you'll reach the other side, when you get to the shore, the horse will change into a store, a clothing store. This store will be so beautiful that its equal doesn't exist anywhere in the world and you'll be a salesman there, a storekeeper. You'll be selling the merchandise. In the morning," he said, "Fairy Ilona's maid will come out and see it. She'll go running to tell her mistress about the store that sprang up at the gate of the palace, wondering when it was built there and by whom. Would the mistress please go and look at it, she'll ask."

So Ilona went, and when she saw the store, it almost took her breath away, she was so astonished at how large it was and how it came to be there all of a sudden. She turned around, went back inside and put on nice clothes as she had decided to find out who was selling there. She opened the palace gate and *straightway* entered the store. Eyes couldn't behold the entire place—it was so big and there were so many beautiful garments in it, it was dazzling. But when she caught sight of the storekeeper, she forgot all about the clothes and *peed in her pants*. She couldn't take her eyes off him, he was so handsome, like no one else in the whole world, and she kept staring at him.

"Please," she said, "I'd like to buy your beautiful clothes."

"Choose what you wish, please," he said.

There were garments hanging all around.

"Dear me," she said, "I don't know which to choose."

(I forgot to say that the shepherd had given the lad a silver, a gold, and a diamond dress to take with him.)

Ilona went on picking and choosing among the clothes, looking at one after another. Then the storekeeper said that he also had ready-made dresses and brought them out; first the silver, then the gold and then the diamond dress. Ilona was to try them on in front of a mirror and see how they suited her.

"Well, it seems that you can't settle on any, maybe you don't like them."

"Oh, I do," said Ilona, "I do, but they are all so beautiful, I cannot choose among them."

"Please, My Lady, I have some dresses all made up, look at them, too!"

She said: "Show them to me!"

So he brought out the silver dress.

"Here you are," he said, "put it on, please. And here is a mirror. This mirror will let you look at the front and the back, so you can see how it fits!"

When Ilona saw the dress, she left all the others on the shelf. She put it on, stood in front of the mirror, looked at herself and said:

"It is very beautiful. It fits as if it had been made for me. I like it very much."

He said: "I have another, even more beautiful."

"Oh, please, let me see it!"

He brought out the gold dress and she put it on. It was even more exquisite.

Said the storekeeper: "You see, it looks like it was made for you." He praised it: "Oh, it is lovely!"

"I'll buy the two!"

"I have another, more beautiful still!" said the storekeeper.

"Oh, if you do have another, please show it to me," she said.

"I do," he said and brought out the diamond dress. She put that on, too. The dress was so dazzling that it blinded the eye. It was resplendent and she liked it very much. She looked at herself, turning this way and that, and suddenly she noticed that they were afloat on water. Looking out the window she saw that they were approaching the shore on the far side of the sea. The store had taken off with them and carried them along.

Fairy Ilona burst out laughing and said: "Listen, you stole my horse, you stole my mirror, you stole my military band, and now you stole me!"—but she said it laughingly. She wasn't upset at all for she was really smitten with the lad. As soon as they came ashore, the store changed back into a horse, and both found themselves astride its back, galloping away. It was a magic horse. This is how the lad succeeded in bringing Fairy Ilona home. He led her into their hovel, to his sister. They fell into each other's arms, weeping for joy, like little children, and kissed one another over and over again. Now the girl had a sister-in-law. The lad said nothing more to his sister, he just announced to her that henceforth she had a sister-in-law. He ushered her into the room, then bent down, grabbed his bow and arrow and made off to the emperor's flower garden to shoot the rabbit. As he was taking aim at the rabbit, the emperor saw him. He was on horseback, too, for he thought this way he could stop the lad from running away from him.

When the lad was about to shoot, he called over to him: "Son, wait a minute! I won't harm you, I just want to have a few words with you."

The lad leapt onto his horse, ready to make his escape, but the emperor, too, was on horseback. He jumped across the garden fence, caught up with the lad and said:

"What do you want, son?"

"I wanted to shoot that rabbit, but I am out of luck."

"Look, son, I'll give you that rabbit anyway, but I need to speak with you first. Whom do you belong to? Tell me, who is your father?"

"Well, Your Imperial Majesty, my father is dead—he was a fisherman. My father is dead and so is my mother—I am an *orphan*," he said.

"Now then, son," he said, "on Sunday night I am giving a ball—the guests have been invited, and I'd like you to be my guest, too. I'd be glad to have you."

"Thank you, Your Imperial Majesty, I'll talk it over at home and perhaps I'll come."

"That isn't a satisfactory answer," said the emperor, "I'd like to know."

"I'll come back tomorrow and tell you for sure," he said, "and I'll shoot that rabbit."

The lad went and told them at home that they were invited to the palace.

Fairy Ilona said: "And what did you say?"

He answered: "I said that first I'll ask them at home and then, when I go back there tomorrow, I'll give my reply."

"Look, I'll teach you what to do," said Ilona, "go there and if he invites you to the ball again, say: 'I'll come, Your Imperial Majesty, if you'll accept me with two others. Then I'll come with my wife and my sister.' If he says yes, I'll come, too, but we'll talk about it some more."

The next day the lad went and said to the emperor:

"Your Imperial Majesty, if you are kind enough to have me with two others, I'll come."

"Yes, of course. Of course, three of you may come!"

The lad was so beautiful that the emperor wished to be with him and look at him during the ball. He went home and told Ilona that they were welcome.

"Now listen to what I have to say," said Ilona. "The three of us will go, but you'll be mute. You mustn't say a word—no matter what they ask you, you are not to answer. By the time we get there the palace will be filled with guests—the kings, emperors, counts, princes, barons will all have assembled. You are expected to shake hands with them and announce your name, but say not one word. Later I'll tell them not to force you, not to torment you, for you are mute and I'll speak in your place. This is what they should be told."

Well, the day came—they washed, dressed up and groomed their hair. They put on beautiful clothes; the girl looked as lovely as Ilona—one couldn't tell them apart, she was just as exquisite—and they departed for the ball. The band played a march for them as they arrived, and the noble guests ran out to greet them. They shook hands and mentioned their names; the lad appeared only as a fisherman's son, he didn't give his father's name. The emperor came over to meet him, shook hands and thanked him for accepting his invitation. The lad said not a word, he just shook hands with the emperor but didn't speak. They were ushered inside and seated at a table among the kings.

Everyone stared at them, they were so beautiful. Then someone asked him where he came from. He didn't answer. Who was his father? He didn't answer. What was his name? He still didn't answer. Well, was he tongue-tied?—they asked. Was he mute? Said the emperor: "He isn't mute at all—I spoke with him yesterday. He has a clear, melodious voice."

Said the noblemen: "Then why isn't he saying anything now? Has he been struck dumb, or what?"

Fairy Ilona said: I beg Your Majesties, kings and emperors, do not torment my husband—it's no use, he is mute."

The emperor was astounded, the lad had spoken yesterday and now he was unable to utter a word.

"But," said Ilona, "if I may, I'll speak for him."

"Of course you may," they said, "we'll be glad to hear it, say anything you wish!"

"Well, with your permission I will," she said. "But first I'd like to say to you, Your Imperial Majesty"—and she pointed to the emperor—"please free the woman you had walled in, let her out and have her join us, then I'll speak."

They all became alarmed, and wondered who the woman was. "What woman?" they asked.

Said the emperor: "Oh, my God, this happened seven years ago—by now not even her dust remains."

Ilona said: "Just break down the wall and take her out!"

Right away they summoned the masons, opened up the wall and found the woman alive. The emperor had such a shock that he fainted, they had to revive him by sprinkling cold water on him. How could this happen? How could she still be alive after seven years? She was emaciated and as white as the wall. The emperor didn't know what to say, how to speak to her.

This must have been God's will; He brought her food—he thought.

Then the mason suggested they should call the turkey herd and ask her how the woman stayed alive. The girl told them how she had paid the mason to leave a secret opening in the wall so she could bring food to the woman; she had divided what she had and had shared it with her.

Then they took the woman to the bath, bathed her and dressed her like a queen, like an empress, and led her in to the guests. Whereupon Ilona asked the guests whether they would mind if she told them a story. They should each recount a story, then she would tell hers. But they wouldn't let the others speak, they wanted to hear her first.

(If you'd like to listen to it, the whole story would have to be told again, for Fairy Ilona stood up and began, as I have : "Long, long ago, in a land far away, there was once a farmer, who had three beautiful daughters." The entire story would have to be repeated: "and the girls went to gather hemp.") She began in the beginning, and the emperor's *eyes popped out* in astonishment at hearing that she knew everything and that the woman was innocent. So the truth became known and there was no end to the merry-making. But first the emperor had two steeds brought before him, the most untamed of all, and had the cook tied to the tail of one and her daughter to the other. He made the steeds circle the castle twelve times until their bodies were torn into shreds and scattered on the ground. This was their punishment. Then the emperor fell to his knees before his wife and asked her to forgive him for he didn't know the truth, and she, in her innocence, had to endure such great suffering. And so the ball turned into a wedding feast. They called a priest, a bishop, and exchanged marriage vows once again. From then on they lived a good life, and how happy was the emperor when he learned that the children were his!

(Well, this is a beautiful story. It is like "The Twelve Robbers," it has to be told twice.) Fairy Ilona had brought the truth to light for she had magic powers.

# 21. The Three Archangels

Motif A1331; MNK 794*: Benedek's storybook reprint of an 1872 text is the only other variant of this origin legend ever recorded. The narrator learned it from her brother János. The sensitivity to otherness in the multiethnic neighborhood of the Bucovina is shown in this biblical apocrypha: Hungarians and Romanians are gullible and open to bribery; only the Germans are disciplined to obey commands, irrespective of personal gain.

———

Well, the good Lord was really angry when Eva didn't obey him and committed the sin of taking an apple from the forbidden tree. The good Lord was very angry. He dispatched Archangel Gabriel to drive the pair out of paradise. When Adam saw him approaching, he said:

"Oh, Eva," he said, "Archangel Gabriel is coming. He is so irate, he'll chase us out of paradise, for sure. But don't worry, my dear, I'll deal with him. I'll offer him plenty of food and drink and I'll talk to him nicely so he'll have mercy on us and won't drive us out."

When Archangel Gabriel arrived, Adam came right away to welcome him. He greeted him politely, offered him fine fruit, an array of food and drink, and spoke nicely with him. Well, Archangel Gabriel didn't have the heart to expel them. He felt sorry for them.

"It would be a shame to chase out such generous people," he said.

He didn't do it. He returned and reported to the Lord:

"Almighty God, I couldn't bring myself to drive them out, they are such kind-hearted people."

Next, the Lord sent down Archangel Raphael, the Romanian angel. Gabriel was Hungarian. Adam treated him well, too, and spoke with him in the nicest way. Raphael felt very sorry for them; he didn't have the heart to drive them out either. He went back and announced to the Lord:

"Almighty God, I couldn't bring myself to chase them out, they are so kind, such good souls."

"Never mind," said the Lord, "I'll send down the German angel, Michael. I'll send Saint Michael."

Well, Archangel Michael descended next. Adam said to his wife:

"Oh, dear, Archangel Michael is coming. He is so angry! But don't you worry," he said, "I'll take good care of him, too. I'll speak with him politely and he'll let us stay."

When Archangel Michael arrived, Adam gave him a fine reception. He offered him hospitality and spoke to him in the most pleasant terms. But Michael opened the gates and said:

"*Marsch hinaus!*" [Out with you!]

They had to pick up and leave on the spot. The German angel drove them out, and this is how they left paradise. He had no pity, no matter how well he was treated.

# 22. The Smoking Kalfaktor

AT 812 (*The Devil's Riddle*); MNK 812 includes 16 variants. This religious tale, rooted in medieval legendry, is based on riddle-solving, a practice that played a part in the traditional Hungarian village wedding ritual. It was customary to question the meaning of numbers (Motif H543): the best man of the bride and the groom engaged in a playful bargaining for the bride. The nickname of the devil, *Smoking Kalfaktor* (a troublemaker, covered with smoke from heating the kettle of souls in hell), appears in other variants as well. Mrs. Palkó heard this tale from her father when she was very young. She narrated it at the home of her nephew, György Andrásfalvi, in 1948 when his wife Erzsi asked for it.

The atmosphere of this story is realistic. The narration closely resembles an account of a personal experience that took place in the village. It reflects the world view of poor Bucovina sharecroppers, their escape from misery into miraculous solutions through divine intervention, always a possibility in their belief—as if Mrs. Palkó had lived the life of the industrious poor orphan girl who made her living from weaving rugs for the wealthy, like so many women in fact did. Not love, but similar economic situations bring the heroine together with the servant of the magistrate. The narrative gives an account of what life was like in old Andrásfalva, how young people worked and courted, how they hunted game animals when they couldn't afford shotguns.

---

Long, long ago, beyond seven times seven lands, there was once a poor *orphan* girl. She lived alone in a small, smoky cottage at the end of the village. The girl was poor, her only wealth was in her two hands. She made beautiful things. She always worked for the city, for the ladies there, and she was even good at weaving and other crafts. Although she was poor, she had such fine clothes that the daughter of the wealthiest farmer looked no better. Well, she would have liked to get married—she could even have found a man to her liking. And, indeed, there was someone whom God intended for her—he was in service with the magistrate.

One day the magistrate said to him: "Son, it is time you took a wife, you are an orphan. Don't you have anybody? You have served long enough to become your own master! Or don't you know anyone? Look, son, at the end of the village there is an *orphan* girl, she is hard-working and very decent. No one could ever say anything bad about her, yet she is an orphan. Take her for your wife."

Said the young man: "Do you mean for me to go see her? I don't know her, how can I go see her?"

"Don't be shy. You must show courage if you want to get married!"

"Please come with me, Magistrate, Sir," the young man said. "Show me where she lives!"

The magistrate accompanied him to the gate: "Now go in and ask her if she would be your wife."

The young man went and knocked at the door.

The girl said: "Come in."

He entered. The girl was at her sewing machine, working.

The lad greeted her: "Good evening."

"Good evening," responded the girl. *"What are you doing here, where not even a bird can fly?"*

"Oh, that is not so," he said, "you live in the village, too. So I came, you see."

"Well, since you came, sit down, take a seat!" she said.

He sat down.

"I say, I wouldn't want to stay long. I'd just like to know if I can succeed in getting what I came for, or not."

"Well, what do you want?"

"I'd like to get married, if I found a girl who would be right for me."

"What sort of girl?" she asked. "There are fine girls who are also wealthy."

"No, that's not it. But she must have two able hands, and above all, she must be good—we can get by then, I am an orphan myself."

Said the girl: "Well, I have always clothed myself with the work of my two hands. I have no father, so I had to provide my own clothes, wood, and everything else, but thank God, I never lacked food."

"That's why I came, to ask you to be my wife, if you'd have me."

The girl answered: "I won't say anything until tomorrow. I have godfathers—I'll ask them for their advice, perhaps they know you. And you may come back tomorrow evening."

So the young man went home.

"Well, what did the girl say?" asked the magistrate.

"She said to wait until tomorrow night. She'll tell me then whether she'll marry me or not."

Right away the girl ran to her godfather to ask him, to tell him about the young man who came to call but whom she didn't know.

"I know him. He is the magistrate's servant. He is a hard-working lad, and don't worry, he doesn't drink or smoke, you'd be well suited to each other. You can marry him, my girl," he said.

The following evening the young man came, and the magistrate came with him. They entered and greeted her:

"We bid you a good evening!"

"Good evening," she responded.

"Well, what were your thoughts, what did you dream last night?" asked the lad. "What will it be? Aye or nay?"

She said: "Aye!"

"Good, then you'll marry me?"

"I will."

The magistrate put in a word, too: "Well, son, you are an *orphan*, she is an *orphan*, but you needn't worry, you'll manage to earn a living."

The very next day they went to the parish to register for marriage. The lad asked whether he could stay with her while the priest announced the banns three times.

"I don't want you to stay here. I kept my chastity until now and I don't want people to start gossiping about me."

The young man answered: "Don't worry, my dear. I'll sleep outside, but let me be here, so I can get things together; I'd like us to have a fine wedding feast."

When only a week was left before the wedding, the lad said: "My dear beloved, I'd better go hunting, maybe I can get some game for our wedding feast."

He took a stick with him—he didn't have a gun.

Said the girl: "Go, if you want to try your luck—I don't mind."

So the lad left early—it was still dark, and by daybreak he was in the forest. He walked to and fro in the woods all day long without hitting anything, not even a young rabbit. Evening closed in and he had nothing.

"Oh God—it is nightfall, I better go home! What will my sweetheart say when I come back empty-handed?"

He left the forest and began walking on the *paved road*. It was pitch dark; the darkness even swallowed the finger he attempted to push into it. His mind was filled with thoughts about how to face the girl at home since he wasn't bringing back anything. Suddenly, as he was thinking, the *smoking Kalfaktor* appeared on the road and said:

"What are you brooding over, young man? What is on your mind?"

He answered: "What is on my mind is that I have been roaming in the forest since morning and I haven't been able to hit anything! I am an *orphan* lad—I want to hold a wedding feast, but I don't have the means to do it. I thought I could at least bring home some game."

Said the Kalfaktor: "Now, pal, you mustn't worry. If you promise to answer all the questions I ask when I come to your house, I'll help you out."

Well, the poor lad was up against it, and, as they say, *a drowning man clutches at straws*, so he didn't think twice about what he was getting into.

He said: "I'll answer them."

"Then just go on home! Early in the morning come out into the courtyard and what you'll see will be yours."

The young man was happy and started on his way home; the smoking Kalfaktor vanished. As he was walking on the side of the road, he suddenly stumbled. He bent down to see what tripped him and found a gun on the ground, with a leather case alongside it. He picked it up but it was so dark he couldn't see it, he just felt it with his hands.

"Oh," he said, "this gun would have come in handy, but never mind, it's good to have it!"

There was also a flask filled with wine, half a cake and a roasted chicken.

"This is just what I need, I am hungry. I'll take it home and eat it with my sweetheart."

He went home.

The girl had been waiting for him already: "I thought you got lost, you are coming so late."

"I am bringing nothing else, only this case. Open it and take what is in it."

He suspended the gun on a nail. She took out the cake and the chicken and they ate and drank. Then they went to bed, the girl inside, the lad outside.

The lad rose in the morning very early, went out and looked around. There were nine pigs in the courtyard, so fat that they could hardly move. How did they get here? He remembered what the smoking Kalfaktor told him—that what he saw would be his.

"Come out, my dear Annuska, look at what we have!"

The girl went out and said: "Dear God Almighty, whose are they?"

"They are ours. Go to your godfather, call him over! Let him harness two horses and come here."

The girl ran to her godfather. As soon as he came, they loaded two pigs onto the wagon, took them to the market and sold them. Right away the lad had enough money to shop for the wedding, so they bought everything that was needed. Then they slaughtered two pigs for the feast, the cooks began preparing and baking, and they invited the guests. The wedding took place on a Sunday.

Well, time passed, soon the wedding feast was over. The young couple stayed at home, they were tired and could hardly wait to retire and rest. The guests had left.

Said the young man: "My dear, there is still plenty to do; we have to collect all the dishes, but let's leave everything, we have worked enough, we'll get up early in the morning. I'll help too, we'll wash the dishes, return those that don't belong to us and put away our own. Now let's retire and get some rest."

The girl made up the bed, the lad locked the gate and the doors, and they lay down. They continued talking for a while. When they were about to fall asleep, someone came in the door. And who was it? None other than a seven-year-old boy. He was so beautiful that his radiance filled the house with light. He bade them a good evening. They lay frightened in their bed.

"How did you come in, my boy?"

"Through the door."

Said the young bride: "Didn't you lock the door properly?"

The man answered his wife: "I am not drunk, I tested the door."

Then the boy spoke: "Dear uncle and aunt, I came to ask you to take me in for the night. Let me stay here—it is so dark outside and there are many dogs in the village, they'll devour me."

The young bride whispered to her husband: "Don't take him in, let him go somewhere else. The house is full of things, there is no room for a bed. The neighbors will accept him."

"My dear boy, I am sorry, we have no room, go elsewhere, go to the neighbors, they may give you shelter—there is no space here for you now."

"Dear uncle, I can hunker down in a corner—please let me stay!"

The young woman poked her husband: "Don't let him stay! Tell him to go somewhere else."

Said the boy: "Even where the broom is standing is room enough for me—allow me to take shelter there."

The man was sorry for the boy but the young bride kept poking her husband, urging him not to take in the boy.

The man got off the bed and made room for him: "Come, son, crawl in here!"

His wife became so angry that she turned against the wall.

Her husband said to her: "Why are you turning away?"

"Leave me alone! Why did you take him in? Don't you listen to me?"

Said the young man: "Oh, I felt sorry for him, you saw how he begged us to give him shelter. Don't be angry, turn toward me!"

But she said not one word, so he turned away from her. The woman faced the wall and the man the opposite way. They turned their backs to each other and after much grumbling fell asleep.

When they were in their deepest sleep, the *smoking Kalfaktor* appeared in the window and yelled: "Are you there, master?"

The man became very frightened, for he remembered that the *smoking Kalfaktor* had told him that he would have to answer his questions.

The boy jumped up and said: "I am here. What do you want?"

"Now," he said, "you must answer my questions."

The man listened in bed. He dared not utter a word.

Said the *smoking Kalfaktor*: "Tell me, what is one?"

"God is one," the boy replied.

"What is two?"

"Two are your eyes—they should both fall out."

"What is three?"

"Three windows are enough for a house."

"What is four?"

"Four wheels are sufficient for a wagon. A fifth is not needed."

"What is five?"

"Your five fingers should drop off, all five!"

"What is six?"

"He who has three plows and three oxen can work his land without another's help."

"What is seven?"

"He who has seven sons can go out and set up camp."

"What is eight?"

"He who has four sons and four daughters can break into dance without needing a stranger."

"What is nine?"

"He who has nine smoked pigs hanging to cure, can easily smear his lips with fat, or, for that matter, wipe the fat off."

"Well, you are lucky that you had the right answers," said the *smoking Kalfaktor.* "If you hadn't, I'd have taken you with me now to the bottom of hell. You and your wife, both of you."

Suddenly a strong wind started up; it was so fierce that they thought it would carry the roof away. The young man leaped out of bed.

"Oh dear, dear," lamented the young woman, "ask the boy to come back, let's put him to bed!"

Yes, but the boy was nowhere to be seen.

The man called out after him: "Where are you, son? Come back!"

"I am not coming back, uncle. I don't need your bed, I am not of this world. I live in Heaven—God sent me, I am His messenger. The good Lord didn't want you to be damned forever, so He sent me to answer the questions."

With those words the boy disappeared. Husband and wife regretted deeply that they didn't want to give him shelter, but it was too late. Then the young man told his wife what had happened to him and how the pigs were given to them.

This is the end. If they haven't died, they are alive to this day and they can be your guests tomorrow.

# 23. The Turk

AT 910B *(The Servant's Good Counsel)*; MNK lists 9 close and 11 deviant versions. This popular medieval exemplum appeared in Hungarian first in the *Gesta Romanorum* (1695) and soon became a standard piece in chapbook and oral narrative tradition. Mrs. Palkó heard it from her brother when he entertained fellow sharecroppers at a Moldavian camp. I recorded her version in 1953, at her home.

Mrs. Palkó's version is more complete than, and in many respects different from, others. She alone gives childlessness as the hero's reason for leaving home; she alone introduces the element of service in Turkey, which may have been borrowed from another ethnic group in the Bucovina. A contract for labor lasting until the worker's boots wear out appears in tales about service in hell (for example, AT 811) but does not fit this otherwise very rational story, entirely devoid of märchen magic. Priesthood as a career for poor orphan boys seems to be Mrs. Palkó's own addition; in her view a clerical career is equivalent to ascending the royal throne (see also "András Kerekes," tale no. 13, above). Mrs. Palkó is also responsible for reformulating this plot into an adventure novella; her creative use of Turkey as a foreign world contributes to the tension she develops preceding the swineherd's return to Hungary. Such elements as the "Turkish" guise of the hero, the rescue of the wrongly convicted travelers, the gun-trick (twelve-shooter, or six-shooter, in imitation of American Westerns), and the passport indicate an intermixture of traditional folk themes and elements of contemporary popular fiction. This tale does not fully fit the pattern of romantic tales (novella), but rather takes on a unique tone of good humored moralizing and admonition to exercise self-restraint, conveying simple, everyday wisdom to keep one out of trouble. Only Mrs. Palkó's version elaborates the three dangerous adventures of the Turk on his way home, increasing the tension as the tale approaches resolution—and its happy ending.

---

Once upon a time, beyond seven times seven lands and even farther, there was once a young couple. They had been married for three years and were still without child. They yearned for God to give them at least one, but it was no use—they had to accept that if God didn't wish to grant them a child, there was nothing they could do. This made the young man very sad.

He said to his wife: "Wife, if God doesn't give us an offspring, I'll leave you. I'll go off into the wide world."

"Oh, you wouldn't do that, you wouldn't leave me here, would you? We love each other and it is no fault of mine that God won't let us have a child."

"Look," he said, "I go out in the evening to have a good time, I go to the neighbors, and everywhere there are children. They rejoice in them, they play with them while I have no pleasure at all. So be prepared," he said, "come tomorrow, I am leaving."

The woman thought he was only joking, but sure enough, the next day he said:

"Wife, get me some provisions for the road. I am going."

"Well," she said, "if that's what you want, if you are not sorry to leave me, go. But you may want to come back some time, and there won't be anyone to come back to!"

They rose the next day. The woman baked and assembled some food. They were not well-to-do farmers, but whatever they had by the grace of God, she packed for him. He took leave of his wife and set out. The woman wept bitterly. She accompanied him to the gate, hoping that he would think better of it and turn around. But he did no such thing; he left. It was toward evening when he took off, an hour and a half or so to sundown. His wife retired to bed crying.

But then she thought about it, why should she go on crying? If her husband wasn't sorry for her, why should she feel sorry for him? She woke in the morning, but there was no sign of him, so she went over to the neighbor to complain that her husband had left her.

Suddenly she overheard people talking in the street, saying that the night before wolves had torn a man to pieces at the end of the village. They didn't know who he was, he was so torn up that they couldn't recognize him. Then the news spread in the village that a man had left his home; it must have been that man the wolves had torn apart. The woman wept bitterly—her heart nearly broke at the thought that she had driven her husband to his death, and that he knew what was facing him. Everyone was so convinced that it was he who was killed that they issued a death certificate for him. The poor woman was grief-stricken, she was in tears more often than not. The neighbors came to see her, they comforted her so that she wouldn't cry for the good Lord would help her somehow, and they'd stand by her, too. Whoever had a little more would share with her, she mustn't cry for she'll manage one way or another. So the woman stopped weeping—she couldn't make him come back to life anyway, she thought; shedding all those tears wouldn't achieve anything.

When about six weeks had passed from the time her husband had left, she realized that she was no longer by herself. She was expecting. Then she began to weep again.

"Dear God," she lamented, "this is why my husband went away, for this very reason. Had he known, he wouldn't have left me." But she didn't know it at the time either—the woman didn't know it herself. She went and told her neighbors about her condition, about the way she felt. They comforted her, said that she mustn't cry for God would be at her side.

(Now, let's leave the woman and let her carry her child in peace.)

When her husband left, the wolves didn't attack him—they tore another man to pieces. He went and went until he came to Turkey and there he continued until he reached the *capital city*. In the capital city he went straight to the prime minister and entered into his service; he made an agreement to work for him.

Said the prime minister: "What would you like, to be hired for months or for years?"

"For years, so I can earn a little more money," he answered.

"As for me," said the prime minister, "the only way I hire servants is that I give them a pair of boots, and they stay until the boots wear out. They report to me when they are torn, not before."

The poor man thought to himself: How long can a pair of boots last? Even if made of buffalo hide, they can't last more than three years. They get used all the time, they tear, they wear out.

"All right," he said, "I'll serve until the boots wear out. Then I'll come and report it to you."

So they agreed on the contract. Right away the prime minister had a pair of boots brought to him, with good, solid straps.

"Here, son, wear these. Let me know when they are torn, and then, if you wish, I'll pay you your dues and you may leave."

Right away he sat him down at a table and offered him food and drink—he treated him well. When they rose the next morning, the prime minister sent a soldier to hand the pigs over to him as he was to be the swineherd. They gave him three hundred pigs to look after; the soldier went with him to the forest and showed him the pasture where they had to be taken. And so he began *herding the pigs*. But he got himself a flute and as he walked alongside the pigs, he played it. He played the flute so beautifully that he had no equal anywhere. And he knew how to sing, too!

After herding the pigs for a week, he had them trained so that they marched home like soldiers, falling in line. And he played his flute along the way. People loved his playing so much that they leaned out their windows, even from the sixth floor, to watch him. And when he broke into song, they all gathered outside as if there were a funeral, just to listen to his singing.

He was happy taking care of the pigs for the food they gave him was very good. He ate the same as the prime minister, his meals were no different. And when he went out with the pigs, they packed ample provisions for him, roast chicken and pastries. He was in fine spirits for they treated him very well.

Five years had passed since he arrived and he hadn't even looked at his boots to see the condition they were in. He thought to himself: I'd better check to see if the boots are wearing out.

He looked but found them even shinier than when he put them on for the first time. They showed no signs of wear and tear, none at all. Well, never mind, he thought—it's better that I remain here longer anyway, I'll get a little more money.'

So he stayed another five years. Every evening he had to give an accounting of the pigs. Every evening when he came home, he had to report that nothing went wrong with the pigs, that they were all there.

When ten years had passed, he inspected the boots again. Not only were they not torn, they were even shinier than when he put them on for the first time.

What kind of hide is this? How can it last so long?—he thought. "Never mind, it is all right," he said, "I'll sit it out a few more years—maybe by then they'll be worn out."

Fifteen years passed and the boots were still not torn. He began to think:

Dear God, I left home fifteen years ago and I know nothing about my wife. Who knows what poverty she must be enduring? I'd like to go back now—but it is out of the question since the prime minister had told me that not until the boots wore out, could I say anything about returning home.

When nineteen years had passed, he became very sad for the boots were still not torn. He thought to himself:

They'll never tear.

He was no longer in a mood to play the flute, or sing. No one knew anything about him, only the people he passed on the road. And the villagers were wondering what had happened to him, why he stopped playing the flute, why he stopped singing.

One day a woman went out to the roadside when he came by, and said to him: "What is wrong with you that you don't sing your beautiful songs, or play the flute any more? Are you ill?"

"No, I am not ill."

"Then why are you so sad?"

"I can't tell you why."

"Still," she said, "I miss hearing those lovely songs. Maybe you aren't well, or aren't being treated well?"

"Oh, I am well. I didn't have it better in my mother's womb."

"Then tell me, what is wrong? What causes you to be so sad?"

"Look, don't ask. There is nothing you can do to help me in my troubles."

The woman said: "Please tell me, maybe I can. At least I can share your grief!"

"Look," he said, "it is now nineteen years that I have been in service with the prime minister. It is written in my contract that he'd give me a pair of boots and I wasn't to talk about leaving until the boots wore out. When they were torn I could report to him that I was ready to go. I have been wearing these boots for nineteen years and they are firmer than when I laced them up for the first time. I am grieving," he said, "for I have no news about my wife since I left, she may be bedridden for all I know. So it is time for me to go home. I am sad for I can't go while these boots last."

"Well, if this is all that is troubling you," she said, "I'll teach you what to do. Just don't give me away, or the prime minister will have me hanged."

"How could I give away someone who wishes me well? Not for anything would I betray a person who wants to help me!"

"Now then," she said, "when you come home in the evening and give your accounting of the pigs to the prime minister, don't say anything. Go in and have your dinner. After dinner, take off your boots, tie the straps together, go to the outhouse and lower them down to the bottom of the pit. When you can tell that they have reached the dirt, fasten the straps to a nail and leave them there. Then go inside, lie down in bed and in the morning check on the boots. If you find them with holes, don't say anything right away. Put them on as they are and go herd the pigs. When you come back at nightfall, report it to the prime minister. But don't you betray me for that would be the end of my life!"

He did as he was told. When he returned in the evening he went to see the prime minister and told him that all was well with the pigs—none got sick, or lost, they were all there.

"All right, son," he said, "have your supper and go rest!"

After his meal he did as the woman taught him. He took off his boots, tied the two straps together and lowered them down into the pit. When he felt that they reached the dirt at the bottom, he fastened the straps onto a nail.

As soon as he woke in the morning, he went to the outhouse and pulled up the boots. Dear God Almighty, not a scrap was left of their soles! The muck gobbled them up! He looked for some cardboard, stuffed it into the boots and put them on his feet. Then he went out with the pigs, and this time he played the flute with such fervor that the whole town was resounding. And coming back in the evening, he sang so heartily that even people living on the top floors leaned out their windows to watch him. Well, he went home and straight to the prime minister. He wished him a pleasant good evening.

"I am here, prime minister," he said, " and I can report that nothing went wrong— the pigs are fine, they are all here."

"All right, son"—he patted him on the back—"you are a good man."

"Prime Minister, Sir," he said, "there is something else I wish to tell you."

"Go ahead, son, what is on your mind?"

"Nothing much, Prime Minister, Sir— just that my boots wore out."

"That cannot be!" They had lasted for nearly twenty years, and the prime minister said they couldn't be worn out!

"Please, have a look, prime minister, Sir!"

He lifted one foot. Clearly the sole was gone, he was walking on cardboard. He lifted the other foot to show him—the same thing. There was nothing the prime minister could say.

"You are right, son, they are falling apart."

"They have been torn for a long time, Prime Minister, Sir. I have been walking around like this, on cardboard."

"Well now, son, what would you like to do? What is your wish?"

"I only wish to thank you, prime minister, Sir, for the kindness you have shown me," he said, "I appreciate it very much. I have completed my work, I don't know whether you were satisfied with it or not, but now I'd like to go home, for it is nearly twenty years that I haven't seen my wife. God knows how the poor woman is. I'd like to go and find out."

"All right, son," said the prime minister, "you may go. Come in tomorrow after eight o'clock and we'll settle our accounts."

(And now we'll leave him, let him rest for the night. There were troubles back home, I nearly forgot.)

When nine months had passed, the woman gave birth to twins, both of them boys. She nursed them for a year and then the state took them from her. She didn't want to let them go for she felt deeply sorry for them and she had been rejoicing so much in the two boys. But the state wouldn't let her keep them as the news had spread that she was living in great poverty and that her husband had died, so the state decided to raise them. They took the children away. Their mother grieved for them, it almost broke her heart. The state took care of their upbringing and schooling, and once they were gone, she never saw them again. The two boys became ordained priests. (And now we can leave them for a while!)

Over there, the man rose the next morning, went to the prime minister and greeted him politely.

"Well, son, you want to go home?"

"Yes, Sir, prime minister. I'd like to go home to see my family."

But the man didn't know what had happened at home.

"Now, son," said the prime minister, "I have kept it a secret all along but now I can tell you. I have grown so fond of you that there isn't another person alive who can be as fond of you as I am, for you have been my good and faithful servant. You never caused any trouble, always finished your work and if you weren't going home to see your wife, I wouldn't let you go. No, I wouldn't, not for half the world, so much do I like you and so pleased am I with you! But since you are going back to your wife, and you are right to want to do that, I agree to your leaving. And now tell me, how should I pay you?"

He ordered a soldier to bring in a bushelful of gold and spread it on the table:

"Tell me, son, should I give you this gold, or some good advice for the time you have served here?"

The man stopped and thought for a moment.

Dear God—he said to himself—the gold would come in handy at home, for I am a poor man, but I could use the good advice, too.

"Well, Prime Minister, Sir, if you please, the gold would be welcome, but so would be your advice."

The prime minister patted him on the back and said to him: "You are a good man, son, and you are a wise man. I give you this gold and I give you some good advice. And that isn't all."

He sent a soldier to a store to buy a set of new clothes for him. He had him outfitted from head to toe, and, in addition, got him a Sunday suit.

"Now, son," he said, "the soldier is back, what he brought is all yours. The prime minister doesn't let his servant go away in tatters."

"Thank you very much, Prime Minister, Sir!"

Then the prime minister had a beautiful steed brought out from the stable, the best running horse, all saddled up:

"Son," he said, "this is yours, too. The prime minister doesn't let his soldier leave on foot, since he has to go far. And now, listen, let me give you some good advice. Look son, I must tell you, you'll set forth from here now, but don't ever travel at night, only during the day. And be careful," he said, "as evening closes in, always ask for shelter. Be it in a village, or in a town, make sure that you find a place to stay, and then continue on your journey in the morning. I am also telling you that when you find a place and the master of the house isn't at home, only his wife, no matter how willing she is to take you in, don't accept it. Go somewhere else, where the man and the woman are both there! Do you understand me?"

"I do," he answered.

"This was my second advice, son. The third is," the prime minister continued, "that however angry you get with someone in the evening, don't take your revenge immediately; set it aside for the morning, and if you are still angry then, let it go until evening. Don't ever act in anger. Do you understand me?"

"I do," he said, "I do."

Then he sent a soldier once again to bring in another bushelful of gold, and said:

"Take this bushelful of gold to the baker and tell him that it is the prime minister's order that he mix it into the bread dough and bake it. But he must make sure that the gold doesn't melt inside, and the bread still becomes crusty."

It barely took fifteen minutes and they brought the bread. It was ready.

"Here, son, put this bread into your knapsack but don't cut it until a time when you feel such joy in your heart as you have never felt before. Then you may cut the bread but not before. And put the other bushel of gold under the pommel of your saddle. Wait a moment, son," he said, "I'd better give you a certificate. When you are home, you'll start going to the market." (A king ruled then too.) "The constables will begin investigating you because the world is treacherous. I'll give you a certificate that will let you go and shop anywhere, no one will bother you."

Then the prime minister went himself and brought out a *twelve-shot revolver*. (Do you know what that is? That's how the Székelys say it.)

"Look, son, you may need this. You never know whom you meet, it could be useful to you."

He thanked the prime minister politely.

"Well, son, are you satisfied with your wages?"

"Oh, Prime Minister, Sir, I'll never be able to thank you enough for all you gave me! I didn't expect this."

"You deserved it, son."

He fell to his knees and kissed the prime minister's feet and hands in gratitude for his kindness.

"I must tell you one more thing, son. *Don't ever leave the beaten track for the untrodden*. It could happen," he said, "that you'd come to a place where the road is curving and a path cuts across it. Just continue on the well traveled road. Never leave a beaten track for the untrodden. Do you understand me?"

"I do. Thank you, thank you very much."

Then he went out and took leave of the prime minister. Both were in tears—the prime minister wept, too. He leaped onto his horse and the prime minister kept his eyes on him, standing in the hallway, until he could no longer see him. And the town people whom he met on his way, all said farewell to him, weeping. Everyone loved the man. This is how he left.

He passed the *capital city* and proceeded on the open road. Suddenly he saw two people on horseback approaching from the East. There was a crossroads ahead. They rode so hard that their horses were foaming from the mouth.

Oh—he thought—how foolish they are! Why must they drive the beasts to exhaustion in this heat? Where are they rushing?

When he came to the crossroads, they got there, too. He was dressed handsomely in an officer's uniform. Well-built and corpulent, the man looked like an officer. They greeted him first, still from a distance, in Turkish, since they were in Turkey then. They bade him a good day and he responded.

He said to them: "What is your hurry? Why are you riding these beasts so hard? Don't you see how hot it is?"

"Well," one of them said, "we made haste, we saw you and wanted to meet you."

As they talked, this Turk noticed that they were not natives for their tongues tripped on the Turkish words, while he knew the language as if he had been born there.

"Who are you? Where do you come from?" he asked them.

"We come from such and such a town," they answered.

"And what nationality are you?"

"We are Hungarians. We have been in service here for ten years and now we are heading home."

"So," he said, "you are Hungarians?"

"Yes, we are."

"I am Hungarian too. Where are you from?"

"From Hungary," they answered.

"I am from Hungary too."

"Then let's go on together."

Well, the two riders were happy that they had found a companion. They could see that he was a tough, robust man. Letting their horses fall into a slow canter, the three men rode on side by side and continued to talk.

Then one of them said: "It would be good to look for shelter, comrade. Let's not travel by night!"

"I think so, too," said the Turk, "let's give ourselves and our horses a rest for the night."

They could see from afar that they were approaching a town.

Said the Turk: "Do you see that town? We'll ask for shelter there."

They spurred their horses into a trot and reached the city by sundown. They stopped at the first house, tethered their horses and all three walked in. There was a young woman inside, busy around the stove. They bade her a good evening and she in turn greeted them.

The Turk asked her: "Do you have a husband?"

"I do."

"Where is he?"

"In the forest, but he'll be home presently," she said. "Why are you looking for him?"

"We are seeking shelter for the night for three horses and three men, if that were possible," he said.

"Certainly, you may come in," responded the young woman. "I'll serve you a good supper, prepare you a good bed, and you may rest here until morning. There is a decent stable for the horses."

"But your husband isn't home," said the third man, "won't he be angry if you take us in?"

"Of course he won't be angry," she said, "we are of one mind."

"Well then," said the two men, "let's stay here!"

The third man said: "Let's go on to a place where the master of the house is at home."

Said the two men: "Why? She is sincere in offering us hospitality, a good bed and a good meal, what else do we need?"

"Listen," said the third man, "if you want to stay, stay, but I am going."

"Why? Can't you see that she is pleased to take us in?"

"Yes," he said, "but I am not staying." He rose, wished them a good night and left. He went perhaps as far as the third house. The light was on and a man was walking about in the courtyard, so he entered and bade him a good evening. The man responded with the same and asked:

"What do you wish?"

He told him he needed shelter for the night, for himself and his horse.

"Gladly," he said. "There is room for your horse and for you. Come in!"

So he went in. The master of the house took the reins of the horse, led it to the stable and gave it some hay.

"Later I'll give it fodder—meanwhile go into the room," he said.

"I won't go in yet," the man answered, "first I'll report to town hall—I am a traveler, so I'd better make myself known."

"All right," he said, "supper will be ready when you return—you'll have your meal and then you may retire to rest."

So he left. No one would have said that he wasn't Turkish and he didn't reveal that he was Hungarian. He came to the town hall and knocked at the door. He entered and saw that there were two constables, the magistrate and some important gentlemen inside. He greeted them and in turn they responded. He told them why he came, to report that he had just arrived in town. He was a stranger, he was looking for shelter and he was here to register.

They said to him: "Where do you come from? Where are your papers?"

He pulled out the certificate and showed it to them. They looked at each other— the gentlemen, the constables, all of them. Then they looked at the man, they looked him over from head to toe. Right away they offered him a chair, bade him sit down and tell them what life was like in the *capital city*. It was written in the certificate that he had stayed with the prime minister for twenty years, so they took him for an honorable man. They brought out a big box of Cuban cigars and he smoked one; he smoked like the Turks. Then they began to ask him questions and he answered intelligently. They offered him wine and showed him respect. They considered him to be an honest man for it was true, the law required strangers to make themselves known, in case something happened in town. He sat with them for a little while.

"I must leave now—I haven't fed my horse yet."

He shook hands with everyone and left. At the gate he stopped and reflected. He thought it would be a good idea to look in on his comrades, to see if the master of the house had returned. He remembered what the prime minister had told him, that he shouldn't stay in a place unless the master of the house was at home. He thought to himself that he would have a look to see if the master was there, if there was any trouble.

So he went there and slowly entered through the gate. The big lamp was still lit. He saw his two comrades sitting around a table and the young woman busying herself feverishly around the stove. They were talking pleasantly but the man, the master of the house, was not yet home. He thought he would go to the back and hide for a while to see what he would say when he came home and found that his wife had taken in the strangers without his knowledge. There was a shed at the rear of the house—the lamp cast a light on it. He went in and settled down by the window. Alongside it some harrows were leaning against the wall—he hid behind them so he couldn't be seen, in case someone came by. From there he kept listening, waiting to see what would happen next.

Suddenly he heard the gate opening. He thought it was the master of the house coming home. But no, it wasn't him, it was a young lad, a student. He, too, heard a lot of noise coming from the house, so he crawled in under the shed, but he didn't see the man hiding there. The lad peered through the window and saw that there were two strange men in the house, talking with the young woman. He listened for a little while, then he tapped on the window. The young woman noticed it and came out, leaving the two strangers inside. The lad bade her a good evening and the young woman bade him the same.

He said: "Who is inside?"

She answered: "Two strangers, travelers. They asked for shelter for the night and I took them in."

Said the student: "Why did you take them in?"

"I did it because I wanted to. Why? You don't like it?"

"Not very much," said the lad.

From behind the harrow in the shed, the man listened to what they were saying.

"Well," she said, "let it be, don't be angry—this could turn out to be an advantage for us."

Said the young man: "What do you mean? I don't understand what you are saying."

"I mean," she said, "that my husband will come home, I'll serve him his supper and I'll give them a good meal, too. Then I'll make up the beds so they can retire. My husband will also go to bed and when he is asleep, I'll take the knife used for slaughtering pigs, plunge it into his heart and kill him. Then I'll take the knife full of blood and hide it under the pillows of the strangers. Come morning," she said, "I'll go and report that I gave shelter to two strangers and they killed my husband."

The man listened to all this from behind the harrow.

"I'll ask the constables to come here, they'll investigate and will find the knife. The knife will be the proof that they had killed him—it will be discovered under their pillow."

The young fellow said: "If your plan works, it'll be very good."

"It'll work, you'll see."

Then the pair embraced and began kissing. The man, the Turk, looked on from behind the harrow, and he knew right away what was what. He remembered the words of the prime minister, the advice he had given him, and he could see the trouble that was brewing. He pulled out his pocket knife and while they were kissing and delighting in each other, he cut off the two corners of the young lad's jacket, and slid them into his pocket.

Soon the lad, the student, took leave of the young woman and left. Then the Turk came out from behind the harrow and left too. He went back to the house where his horse was stabled. He entered and said good evening. They were expecting him—supper was ready and they asked him to sit down at the table.

Said the master of the house: "Look, Sir, you needn't go out to the stable—I fed your horse. Have your meal and retire to rest!"

They treated him nicely, with respect. The man ate, went to bed and slept well until morning. He rose early and went to the stable to see his horse. He noticed that the manure was all cleared away and there was hay put in front of it. Then he walked out through the gate, looked around and saw a group of three or four men standing and talking here and another group of men and women assembled there. He greeted the neighbor:

"I bid you a good morning!"

"Good morning to you, too!"

"What is this early gathering about?" he asked. "Tell me something, what is the news?"

They said: "What? You haven't heard what happened last night?"

"How could I have heard when I never left my bed?"

"Haven't you heard," she said, "that next door a women took in two strangers, travelers, gave them a good meal and a good bed while her husband was in the forest, and when he came home, they killed the poor man in his bed during the night!"

"Oh, it's not possible that such a thing could have happened," he said.

"Yes, seriously. It is true. The constables came already and took the criminals away."

"Well, that's too bad, if it's so." He told his host what the talk was about outside, what the people were saying. "I don't believe it," he said, "I came with two travelers, they didn't look to me like they were murderers. But apparently the constables had already taken them to town hall."

Said the master of the house: "I am getting up and going to town hall to learn more. Come with me!"

"No, I won't go. I must attend to my horse," he said. "You go and tell me later what you heard."

So the master of the house left. When he returned he said:

"It's true, it's serious, they killed their host. Two constables took them, locked them up—and they have been condemned. They'll be hanged in three days: an eye for an eye."

Oh—thought the Turk—the prime minister was right. I had asked them to come with me but they liked it there. Now let them wriggle out of this, if they can.

He said to his host: "Well, in that case, I won't leave until their fate is decided, until they are hanged. I want to wait and see this through. But," he said, " I'd like to ask you to be so kind and let me bring over the two horses, my comrades' horses. I'll pay you for every bit of their fodder, for the stable, for everything, as long as you let me bring them here."

"Sure," he said, "I am accommodating, bring them over, there is room for them here, go ahead and fetch them!"

So he brought the horses and tended them as if they were his own.

Then the third day arrived. They beat the drums and announced that anyone who wanted to witness a hanging could come, two criminals would be hanged together.

Said the master of the house:

"Are you coming? Let's go early so we can hear the latest. I like to go to these events for people come from many parts to see such a wonder, and you hear something from here and something else from there. Come, let's go!"

Said the Turk: "Just go ahead, I'll follow you later. First I'll attend to the horses, feed them and water them, then I'll come too."

The master of the house left and he stayed behind. He fed and curried the horses and got dressed up.

Suddenly he heard that they were taking his comrades. The church bells were pealing, a priest was walking alongside them and the hangman was already there. A huge crowd was accompanying them through the town to the gallows at the other end. The people were running, pressing ahead. For a while he just watched, he didn't join them.

When they had gone past and when he thought they had reached the edge of the town, he leaped onto his horse. He took a different path and galloped through the fields as fast as he could. Leaving the town behind, the people came to the gallows and stopped there. A tremendous crowd had formed. The hangman stood in readiness to hoist them up. But it was forbidden to hang someone just on hearsay; the hangman had to first look towards the four points of the compass, to see whether anyone was coming to save the condemned. He wasn't allowed just to hang them.

Suddenly he caught sight of a horseman approaching from the east. He rode at a speed like, like, like lightning and he waved a white cloth in his hand. Upon seeing this, the hangman immediately called for a reprieve since a messenger was coming and he had to be heard. The crowd fell silent—people stood on their tiptoes to see who it was. Well, he arrived—his horse was covered with sweat, he had raced it so hard.

He called out: "Whom do you want to hang?"

"Two criminals, two murderers," they answered.

"How do you know that they are murderers?"

"We know, for we found the knife under their pillow," said the constables.

"You mustn't hang them," he said, "they don't deserve to be hanged."

"How do you know that?"

"I know. These men are innocent."

"How do you know that they are innocent?"

"I'll tell you, if you let me. Allow me to tell you!"

The young student was there and the wife, too.

"I'll tell you," he said, "but first grab that woman and the lad and tie them up."

They complied. "And who are you?"

"You know me, you know who I am. I announced myself at town hall."

He showed his certificate. Everyone said what a wise man he was having been in service with the prime minister for twenty years.

Said the magistrate: "It is true, I know this man, he came to report to me."

Then he told his story: "I traveled with them and I didn't know them to be treacherous men, or murderers," he said. "I told them not to stay there, but they liked the place. I left and went back later to see if the master of the house had returned, if there was any trouble because the woman had given them shelter without his knowledge. I waited, concealed in the shed, and what did I see?" (He also told them what advice he had received from the prime minister.) "Someone came in, but it wasn't the master of the house, it was the young lad. And," he said, "they embraced and the lad began to question the woman about the strangers to whom she had given shelter.

"'I took in two travelers. You don't like it?'

"He answered her: 'Not very much.'

"'Let it be, for this may yet turn to our advantage.'

"'What do you mean by that?' he said.

"'I mean,' said the woman, 'that when the strangers fall asleep and my husband is asleep, too, I'll take the knife used for slaughtering the pigs and stab him in the heart. Then I'll put the bloodied knife under the strangers' pillow and that will be the proof that they have killed my husband. Then the two of us can live together freely—not like now, in secret.'

"When I realized what was afoot, I immediately cut off the corners of the lad's jacket with my penknife and put them in my pocket. If you don't believe me, I show you the proof." He took them out of his pocket: "Here, see if they fit."

Right away the hangman seized the pair. The lad was hanged on the spot and the woman was taken away by the constables. Then they estimated the worth of their possessions and divided it up between the two travelers whom they had thought guilty, and gave a share to the Turk, who had enlightened them. So they let the three travelers go and locked the woman away forever. Rather than hang her, they locked her up for life.

This is how the two innocent men were freed. They returned to their lodgings, the Turk paid his host his due—even more, he doubled the amount coming to him for having kept the horses. Then they gathered their belongings and set forth.

The Turk said to them: "You see, comrades, I told you not to stay in a place where the master of the house was absent, but you liked it there. If I hadn't kept an eye on you, you would now be hanging from the gallows, innocent."

They kissed his hands and feet in gratitude for having saved their lives, and said to him:

"We want to give you the money we received, for you are the one who deserves it."

"I don't need that kind of money—I'd rather give you the share they awarded to me."

But they insisted and forced the money into his pocket:

"This is rightfully yours, you saved us from death!"

Well, they continued on their journey at a leisurely pace, ambling along. They came to a place where the highway curved around a mountain and a path led straight across.

The two comrades said: "Let's take this path and avoid the roundabout way. We can save time!"

"Not I, I am not going."

"You'll see," they said, "by the time you arrive, we'll have fed our horses, eaten and even had a rest. It will take you that long to get there."

"I don't mind," he said. "I won't *leave a beaten path for the untrodden*. If you want to go, go, but I am not going with you."

So they went and the Turk continued quietly on the main road.

They were still within earshot when he heard a lot of noise and shouting. Then he heard gunfire, so loud, that, that, that the crackling, pelting sound of bullets was all around, and there was screaming and yelling and everything.

He said to himself: They wouldn't listen to me, wouldn't obey, and now they are in trouble. I just saved them from death over there, and again they got into a fix. I told them to come the way I was going, but they didn't understand.

Still, he went after them to see what had gone wrong. He went into the forest and saw that they were surrounded by twelve robbers, who were shouting at them:

"Stop! Your money or your life!"

Poor horses, they were flecked with foam from being ridden so hard—and all the while the bandits were firing at them. When the Turk saw the distress his comrades were in, he took off in pursuit of the robbers who were chasing them. They were on horseback too. He pulled out his *twelve-shot revolver* and aimed with such precision that he cut all twelve of them down. They just rolled off their horses in a heap. Then he spurred his horse and galloped after his comrades, shouting:

"Stop, you two miserable fellows, stop!"

But they didn't stop—they thought the robbers were coming after them. They were so frightened that they didn't recognize who was calling them, they charged ahead. The Turk had a fine running horse—he urged it forward and got in front of them. Then they saw who he was.

"Halt!"

They came to a halt but all the color had drained from their faces.

Said the Turk: "I told you to come with me, didn't I? I told you not to *abandon the beaten path for the untrodden*, but you knew better. I just saved you from the jaws of death, didn't I, and you got yourselves into a mess again. Do you want me to beat you until I knock the wind out of you?"

"Oh," they said, "we do deserve a thrashing and we don't know how to thank you for your kindness. But let it go this time. From now on even if you tell us to go through fire, we'll do it."

Well, they got back to the main highway and stopped there for a while. They ate and the two comrades kept begging the Turk not to be angry with them: "We see that you are right. From now on we'll do as you say."

After eating and drinking their fill, they resumed their journey. They traveled so far that they were nearing Hungary. Then with God's help they made it into Hungary and there they halted.

The two comrades said to him: "It is too bad but we have to part for we are going west and you are going east."

"Well, if we have to part, let's part."

He drew the money out of his pocket:

"This is yours. Go, and may God be with you!"

"We don't want this! We don't want this!"

"It is yours"—he threw the money on the ground—"take it, I don't need it!"

So they took leave of one another. They went their way and the Turk headed home.

He reached his village and exclaimed: "Lord Jesus, blessed be Thy name, I lived to see my village once more!"

Evening was closing in—he looked for the street where he used to live and headed home. When he got there he saw that nothing was left of his garden.

"Oh, dear," he said, "my wife must have lived in great poverty—she even had to burn the garden." He tethered his horse to a tree and went to the window. The light was still on—it shone outside. He looked in and saw that the table was set, laden with so much food and drink that *its legs were bent from the weight of all the pastries.*

"What is going on here? Why these preparations?"

His wife in a big, white apron was busily carrying still more dishes to the table—roasts and chicken. Two young priests were seated at the table—his wife was serving them food and drink, and every time she filled their glasses she kissed them. This made him so angry that he reached for the revolver in his pocket. He wanted to shoot all three.

"What is this? My wife is carrying on a love affair with priests? Is this why I suffered and grieved for having left her?"

He held the revolver in his hand and then he remembered that the prime minister had said to set aside his anger of the evening until the next morning. He thought that so far everything the prime minister had told him came true. So he put the revolver back in his pocket and let his anger settle until morning. Instead of shooting, he turned around and went to the next house, where a well-to-do farmer lived. He knocked at the door and said good evening, but in Turkish. They welcomed him and he shook hands with the master of the house and with his wife.

He said in Turkish: "How are you? How is life treating you?"

Said the man in Hungarian: "I only know to speak Hungarian. I am Hungarian."

He greeted them in Turkish but they responded in Hungarian.

"Well," he said, "if you are Hungarian, I can speak Hungarian, too."

"God bless you, if you know Hungarian, for that is the only language I speak."

He looked like a Turkish officer—he wore a uniform.

"I'd like to ask the master of the house if he'd give me shelter for the night, and room for my horse in the stable."

"Certainly, *this is man's abode and God's resting place*, for a traveler. Please, come, make yourself comfortable and rest, I'll look after the horse. You are tired. Just remain seated!"

He went out, tethered the horse and gave it hay. Then he returned to the house.

"Where do you come from?"

"I come from far away. And I must apologize," he said, "that I came to you— that wasn't my intention. I wanted to ask for shelter next door, but I don't know how things are there."

"Very good, indeed," he said.

"*The table is laden so full that its legs are bent* and they are bringing still more food. I turned around and came here."

Said the master of the house: "Why? You could have gone in."

"Oh, no. *An uninvited guest should stay outside the door*, as the saying goes. So I came over here."

"Well, you didn't come to a bad place."

"I can't help thinking of that table groaning under the weight of food. What is going on there? A wedding, or christening?"

Said the woman, the mistress of the house: "Oh, well, there is such great joy in that house that it is indescribable. Do you know," she said, "that the poor widow has spent her life crying and grieving. The sun has set for her twenty years ago and hasn't risen until now. But today it rose brilliantly and is shining on her."

"Why, what happened? What do you mean?"

"I'll tell you, if you want to know. The woman has been widowed for twenty years—her husband was torn up by the wolves. After her husband had left out of sorrow for not having any children, she gave birth to twin boys. They didn't know that she was expecting, and then it was too late. Two sons were born to the poor woman and the state took them both a year later, after she finished nursing them. The state took them, had them educated, and the two boys became priests. Their mother hadn't seen them until today, when they came home. They'll be ordained tomorrow and will celebrate their first mass in their native village. They were born here, they'll be ordained here. Oh, how happy their mother is with them! If you'd see how she holds them pressed to her bosom, you'd know, Sir, how great her joy must be. She has been without her husband for twenty years and separated from her sons for nineteen. And now they'll say their first mass here, tomorrow."

The man's heart began to pound. Blessed be the prime minister who had given him advice that he should set aside the anger of the evening until the next morning, and the anger of the morning until the night.

He said: "I'd like to ask the mistress of the house to invite the woman to come here."

She answered: "We are godparents to her sons. We helped her in her misery, brought her food and showed her compassion. Others helped too and made sure that she had enough to eat—everyone was sorry for her."

"Well then," he said, "be so kind and ask the woman to come here so I can see her!"

The mistress of the house thought that he wanted to give her a present. So she went next door, put on a white apron and went in. All three rose from the table when they saw her enter.

Said the priests: "Dear godmother, you came over? Where is our godfather?"

"He'll come too, a little later."

"Why not now?"

"He can't now"—she said—"we have a guest, a gentleman, a stranger, who sent me to ask you, dear neighbor, to please come over. He wants to see you."

Said the young priests: "Who can he be? We don't know, but we'll go with you, mother."

So all three went over. They stepped in. The master of the house and the stranger rose from the table and shook hands with them. The woman, embarrassed, stood to the side, by the bed—she was shy.

Said the strange gentleman: "Why are you standing to the side?"

"I am all right here."

"I heard that you are widowed."

"Yes, I have been, for twenty years."

"How did your husband die? Of what illness?"

"The wolves tore him apart."

He said: "Could that be true? It is possible that it isn't so. Who saw it?"

"It is true," she said.

"What if I said that your husband is alive?"

The woman burst out laughing: "Oh, my husband has long been swallowed up by the earth. His body must have turned into dust by now."

"But if he were alive, what would you say? I say to you that he isn't dead."

She said: "Oh, I can't believe that. No one can make me believe it—I have a death certificate for him. How could my husband be alive?"

"Did your husband have some distinguishing mark?" he asked.

"Yes, he had," she said.

"What was it?"

"Under his left arm there was a mole."

Then the man unbuttoned his shirt and pulled it over his head:

"Was it like this?"

"Exactly—my husband had the very same mole."

"Now, wife, you may be certain that I am your husband. It was with me that you exchanged vows at the altar, it is me that you wed. They were wrong when they said that the wolves had devoured me—they didn't."

When the young priests heard that their father was alive, they fell over each other to embrace him. His wife, the priests, the master of the house, all wept for joy. Then they went back to the woman's house. They ate, drank and chatted until eleven o'clock, when the young priests said:

"We ate and drank and talked until now, but we can't go on for we are taking Holy Communion tomorrow."

They retired for the night and the next day the priests asked their father to be present when they celebrated mass that morning:

"When your first-born says mass, your younger son will preach the sermon, and when he says mass, I'll be the one to preach."

How proud and festive they all were when they went to church together! The man had to be held up on both sides—he fainted for joy.

When mass was over they held a big feast. They cut the bread, and the man felt such happiness as he had never felt before. He sliced the bread and all the gold poured out on the table. Oh, the jubilation that this brought about!

"Father, where did you get all this gold?"

He showed them the certificate—they read it and knew then where he had served.

He said: "I have once again as much."

He took the gold from under the pommel of his saddle. There was enough to go around in the whole village. Then he had a petition drawn up requesting the ministry to place one of the priests in their village and the other in the neighboring one, so he could see them every day when he went to church.

Thereafter they had a happy life. They grew rich and became counts. They had so much that they could share it with the poor. Then they made a garden, but not around the old house, for they bought another, several stories high.

*This is the end—run with it, and invite them to be your guests tomorrow!*

# 24. Anna Mónár

AT 956B (*The Clever Maiden Alone at Home Kills the Robbers*) + 954 (*The Forty Thieves*); MNK (*Daughter of the Miller*) lists nine variants. This combination of the main story with the last episode of the Aladdin type occurs in three other Hungarian versions. Mrs. Palkó heard it from her brother János.

This was the first tale Aunt Zsuzsi told me. She was not as relaxed as later, when she became used to my presence at the evening gatherings at her home. Her sentences were short and she did not elaborate episodes as much as she would later. But even in this unembellished telling, one can sense her skill in story construction, her ability to dramatize events. For example, she carefully sets the scene for the arrival of the robbers. The miller and his wife have already left for the party (the term "wedding," as used by Mrs. Palkó, is not necessarily a marriage feast, but merrymaking: dancing, singing, drinking, and eating), and the girl is left alone. She reads quietly, but in the way Aunt Zsuzsi describes the scene, one can feel the tension in the air, that something is bound to happen. With seemingly unimportant details she indicates that we are in the real world. She speaks about real people, real situations. The girl kills her attackers with a sword. But how come a miller keeps a sword in his home? This sounds incredible; Mrs. Palkó felt an explanation was needed. He served at the *huszárs* (light cavalry), the most respected branch of the military— who would not be proud and keep the sword to remember the glorious days of youth? Other highlights include the letter exchange between Anna and the robber-in-chief, the marriage proposal, the peculiar wedding party of the groom, and the old woman's self-sacrifice to save the girl. These frame and foreground the courage of the girl to show that she does not need help to take care of herself.

———

Once upon a time, beyond seven times seven lands, *beyond the clucking and pecking of nine turkeys and the paces of a hundred lice,* there was once an old miller who had a large mill. He amassed such riches with his mill that he had an enormous amount of money and land and vast herds of sheep and cattle. He was a very wealthy farmer. But they were only two, he and his wife—they had no children. So they were forever worrying about who would look after them in their old age.

One day he and his wife decided that they would adopt a little girl or a little boy, and soon they brought a little girl into their home.

Said the old miller: "Well, my girl, you came to my house and if you behave well, all this wealth will be yours. We'll raise you and marry you off."

The girl said: "All right, grandpa and mother."

This is what she called them. After only a few months, they grew very fond of the little girl for she was clever and most intelligent. They wouldn't have let her leave them for anything. She was growing up nicely.

One day the old miller said to her: "Listen, my girl, we have been invited to a *wedding* next Sunday. An uncle of mine is holding a big feast and has asked us to come. How should we do it? You wouldn't want to be there, for you are young, and it behooves us to go for he is my uncle; it would be a disgrace if we were absent."

She answered: "Don't worry, I'll stay home."

Someone had to be at home for the farmstead was large and they were uneasy about leaving it.

"All right then, we'll go, my little girl, but be on your guard, I beg you, for below us there are robbers in the forest and they often go plundering in the area. So I am cautioning you, try to finish the outside work before nightfall and then be sure to lock all the doors and gates so no one can enter. Once your work is done, there is no need for you to go out—just stay quietly indoors!"

So the old couple pulled themselves together, climbed into their carriage and left. The young girl stayed at home. When evening closed in, she lit two candles, placed them on the table, took her prayer book and read. All of a sudden, as she was reading, she heard the dog bark. "The dog is barking as if someone were walking about outside"—she said to herself —"but whoever it is, I won't let anyone come in."

Then, as she continued reading, she heard a knock. She said to herself: "Dear God, what could that knock be?"

There was a second knock, and a third. She put down her prayer book and listened for what would happen next. Soon the girl realized that the robbers were breaking into the foundation wall at the very place she was standing. She knew exactly what was going on. She understood what the robbers were up to, so she quickly moved away, stepped into the storeroom and there her eyes fell on a rusty sword hanging from a peg. The old miller had served with the *hussars* and brought the sword home as a souvenir. She lifted it off and set to sharpening it. When the edge was good and sharp, she went back into the room and stood facing the wall they were demolishing. They had broken in so far that even their whispers could be heard inside! Then, all at once, a hole appeared in the wall.

"Hey," she said to herself, "just come along—you are coming to the right place!"

When the hole was large enough to admit a man, the leader of the robbers said: "Now, who will be the first to go in?"

One of them said: "I'll go, the others can follow me."

Said the leader: "The first one in should unlock the door so we can enter, instead of having to crawl in through the hole!"

When the robber stuck his head in, the girl chopped it off, grabbed his two shoulders, yanked the body inside and shoved it to the side. Then came the second and the third robber and she cut off the head of each one. They called in again: "I said to unlock the door!"

The girl answered from the door in a deep voice:

"I can't—just come through here, one by one."

So eleven robbers came through and she cut the heads off all eleven, then pushed their bodies over to the side. When it was the turn of the twelfth, he stuck his two hands in first, found them soaked in blood and quickly withdrew his head. Still, the girl struck him and sliced off a piece of his scalp, but the wound she inflicted wasn't too deep.

"Just you wait, you beast, you destroyed my eleven brothers, you'll pay for this!" With those words he ran away, he ran back to the forest. Other robbers were camping out there, not only those eleven—maybe there were twice as many assembled in a den.

"Well, my comrades, I lost eleven of my strongest lads, but I will not rest until I have my revenge!"

That very night he sent the robbers to break into a pharmacy. They plundered it and brought back all sorts of medicines.

He said to them: "Listen to me. Take good care of my wound for I must get hold of that filthy girl *and, when I do, I'll kill her*."

"Oh, captain," said one of them, "you won't be able to put your hands on her easily; she is afraid of you so she is very careful."

He said: "If I can't do otherwise, I'll marry her and then I'll take my revenge."

And that's how it was.

One day he wrote a letter to the girl but he signed with a fictitious name, as if he were some young count. He wrote:

"My dear Anuska, I saw you once at the mill and since then I haven't been able to sleep or eat, all I do is think about you and about how I could make you my wife. I am writing this letter and sending you a photograph—if you fancy me answer quickly and tell me what you want! But don't break my heart, for I'd die for you!"

He posted the letter, and soon the girl had it in her hands. She opened it, it was from an unknown lad. The girl was surprised—who could he be, she wondered.

"My dear Anuska, send me your reply. If you write that you'll marry me, I'll be on my way to you immediately."

The girl received the letter and read it. She laughed and rushed in to the old folks to show them the kind of letter she got. The old man looked at it—he liked it too, for it was nicely written.

"Do you know him, my girl?"

"No, but he says he saw me at the mill."

The old man looked at the lad's picture and, well, he was taken with it.

"He is a fine, handsome young man. I don't know what his habits are, but he is a good-looking lad. What do you say, my girl?"

"I like him. If you give me permission, I'll take him for my husband. I'll marry him."

Right away she wrote him a letter that he may come, if he so wishes, and that she wanted her mother and father to meet him and see if they liked him or not.

By then his wound had healed but the area on his head remained bald. Still he was able to comb his hair every which way to cover it, so no one could tell that he had a bald spot.

He dressed up in his finest to look like a young count, and went to the girl's house. When he stepped into the room, the girl was alone.

"Well, my dear, beloved Annuska, I came," he said, "so we can talk to each other, not only in writing, but face to face. And now tell me, what do you want? Will you be my wife or not?"

"Wait," she said, "first you must speak with my father and mother. I'll marry you only if they give their permission."

They called in the old folks. The lad was in high spirits.

"Don't spurn this lucky chance. I believe you won't regret giving me your daughter."

"Well, son, I won't hold her back if she wants to go with you. She should marry whom she loves, for a girl must find a husband. But I have one condition: she must continue to live here; I won't let my daughter out of our house. I didn't raise her to have her leave us. Our son-in-law should move in, cultivate the land and manage the farm."

"I don't mind," said the lad, "I have a large farm too, the great estate of a count, but I'll lease it out. From time to time we'll go there to oversee it, but we'll settle down here."

Then they discussed when the wedding should be.

"I have to say that I can't come back to woo your daughter for I am not able to leave my farm until I hire some laborers. But you can make all the preparations and when I come, I'll bring my wedding party, and we'll get married."

And so the time came and on the day of the wedding the festivities began. They had invited the guests, as many as they wanted, and were now waiting for the bridegroom to arrive for the ceremony.

Suddenly the news spread that they were coming, twelve carriages were on their way. As the party approached, they could see that two men were sitting in each carriage and there wasn't a single woman with them. They were greatly astonished at this and wondered what customs prevailed in that village to leave the women behind. Then the party arrived.

"Are there no women coming?"

"This is how it is with us. When the bridegroom's party goes to the bride, women are not included, only men."

The wedding guests went out to greet them. They introduced themselves to each other, shook hands and prepared to go to the ceremony.

Then they went, the couple exchanged marriage vows, and by the time they returned the tables were set up. They sat down to eat and drink. When they had feasted enough, the bridegroom said:

"Well, my dear, we'll go now. I want to show my people the girl I took for my wife, for I, too, have many relatives."

But the old man said: "Just a minute. It was not part of our agreement that you'll take my daughter away."

"We'll come back," he said. "But I am asking you now, let me have the bride's dowry too, so I can show it off."

The old man became as gloomy as a rain-leaden sky.

"Don't you play tricks on me! I told you that I won't let my daughter leave this house. If you don't like it, don't bother. Don't take her for your wife!"

"But I told you," he said, "that we'll come back. First I take everything and then we'll bring it all back."

So they began loading the carts with bedding, furniture, thirty-three pairs of horses, oxen, cows, mares, calves, sheep, and swine.

"Well, now, I don't think you have to be ashamed when you arrive with this to introduce your bride."

They filled the twelve carts to capacity. The young couple climbed into the first vehicle, said farewell and took off. For a while they traveled on the main road, the imperial highway, but when the sun was about to set they turned off into the woods.

"My dear husband, why did you leave the main road?"

"Don't worry, my angel, we only have to travel half of the way through here."

But the girl became so agitated that she began to tremble at her husband's side. He noticed it:

"What's wrong, my angel? Are you perhaps afraid?"

"Yes, I am, for *I never leave the well-traveled road for the untrodden.* Why are you going through the woods?"

She became even more upset when she remembered that she had killed twelve robbers. Could it be that the one who had escaped was now plotting to avenge them?

Then they arrived at the robbers' den, and the girl knew right away in whose hands she had fallen.

"Don't be afraid, my angel," he said. He put his arms around her and led her through the door to an opening at the side of the mountain. He ushered her into a room. An old woman was there, a cook, who prepared their meals. She had been with them for twenty years.

"Well, old granny," he said, "I brought my bride home. I am entrusting her to you—watch over her and guard her with your life!"

He shut the door and the girl, the bride, remained inside with the old woman. The robbers assembled among the rocks and began discussing the most cruel death they could inflict on her.

Said the old woman to the bride: "My dear girl, whom did you marry? Don't you know that you wed the man whose scalp you had cut off? He took you for his wife not because he wanted you but so he could get his revenge. I feel sorry that you put your beautiful, young life at such risk."

The bride couldn't utter one word, she was so frightened.

(But let's leave her for now.) The old woman kept watch over her so she wouldn't run away. Meanwhile all the robbers had gathered to decide how to do away with the girl.

One of them said: "Let's cut off her two hands and two legs."

Another said: "Let's hang her from her tongue on a tree."

The third said: "Let's build a stake and burn her."

Still another said: "Let's skin her alive and cure her body with salt."

And another said: "Let's cut off her hands and gouge her eyes out."

One by one they gave their opinion but the leader only had one answer: "This is not enough."

Then he said: "Not this way. Let's call in the old woman—she has lived longer than we have—whatever she says, we should agree on."

He sent two robbers to guard the girl and asked the old woman to come in.

"Granny, we sent for you so you pronounce a sentence over her. What the brothers have suggested is not enough."

Said the old woman: "You know, sons, at the time you brought me into the forest I saw thorns, the same kind they used to crown Jesus king. Gather those thorns and beat her body with them, even her tongue. Then let her be for three days and when her wounds begin to fester, beat her again. And now go, all of you, don't delay and the more you bring back the better!"

Well, they accepted the old woman's sentence. The next day all the robbers left, only the old woman stayed behind with the bride. They told her that she would die the same death if the girl got away. Then they mounted their horses and rode off. The old woman ran inside:

"My dear girl, I feel so very sorry for you. My heart won't allow this to happen to you. I'll let you go and rather die myself, but I can't have you endure such agony. I am sorry for you. I am telling you, run as fast as you can and follow the trail on which you came. I know that I'll have to die in your place, but I don't mind—most of my life is behind me and it's no great loss if I perish, while you have just begun to live your life on this earth. I must also warn you to be careful as you are running for they have dogs that can track you down and lead the robbers to you. When you hear a dog barking, watch out, climb a tree—the one with the densest foliage—and be still; don't come down. If the dog doesn't signal to them, they won't find you."

The girl did as she was told. Suddenly she heard a dog barking.

"Dear God, where should I go?"

She looked around, saw a big sour-cherry tree and clambered up. But the dog stopped at the foot of the tree. Then the robbers came and they stopped while the dog kept barking. The girl nearly died of fear that they'd catch her. But fate had it that they didn't find her.

The leader of the robbers got angry—the dog couldn't be trusted. It ran ahead and they went chasing after it. Then they came back and once again the dog stopped at the tree. They looked and looked but couldn't see the girl. This made the leader really angry and he shot the dog. No more signals would be coming from it.

"Let's go back"—said the leader—"I'll get her sooner or later."

They returned home and sentenced the old woman to die. She had served them for a long time so they thought they'd rather build a stake and throw her in the fire. Still, they burned the old woman.

Now the girl didn't dare to come down from the tree. She thought a spy might have stayed behind, so she sat and waited for the sky to turn red on the horizon before starting to run again. But as she began to slide down, her skirt got caught and there she was, dangling suspended with her head down.

"Dear God, I was saved once and now I'll have to die here—either the robbers will come back after me, or I'll just expire."

But it was God's will that there should be a poor man living nearby, who on that day decided with his wife to go into the forest to gather wood. They took their wagon and thought that they'd load it to the top and then go home. As the woman was walking about, she caught sight of the girl dangling from the tree, upside down. She ran over to her, then she ran back to her husband and said:

"Do you know what I just saw? Robbers hung up a girl, let's go quickly and save her!"

They didn't know who she was. They stood on top of their wagon and pulled the girl down. She was half dead but blood was still pulsing in her veins. They placed her in the wagon and concealed her under some dry branches so the robbers wouldn't see her. They covered her up and took her home.

Said the man: "You know, woman, if the girl recovers we won't let her go. I'll run over to the old miller and ask him to call a doctor so she won't die."

And so it was. He went to the miller, who immediately harnessed two horses to the carriage. The doctor came at once, gave her an injection and the blue color began to fade on her face. But she didn't know anybody. The old miller came to see her and he didn't recognize his daughter either.

All of a sudden the girl began to speak. They asked her who she was.

"Father, don't you know me? I left your house only yesterday and you don't recognize me?"

"Dear God, what happened to you?"

"Oh, father, don't even ask. Do you know to whom you gave me in marriage?"

"To the one you chose."

"You gave me in marriage to the man I had wounded and he wanted to take his revenge."

Oh, the old man became alarmed, took the girl home and made her lie down. They doctored her until she recovered, and then she told them what had happened to her. When she finished, her father said:

"Let it be, my girl. From now on I won't let you go anywhere on your own. We'll watch over you and guard you with our lives!"

Well, the girl regained her health. They were not even sorry for the dowry the robber stole from them—they were just rejoicing that the girl had come back.

(Now let's leave her—she was in the good care of her father.) The robbers were furious.

"If I can put my hands on her again, I'll kill her!" the leader said.

He waited for a few weeks then he said to his companions: "Go into the forest and look for some hollowed-out trees. Cut down ten of them, saw off the hollowed trunks, and make them about two meters long."

They brought home eight of these trunks.

"We are done, captain."

"Now fit doors into them, so they can be locked from inside and can accommodate one lad each. Prepare yourselves—we are leaving tomorrow."

"Where to, captain?"

"You'll see where."

They woke the next morning and he said: "Get into the tree trunks and lock the doors."

They climbed into the carriages, one lad into the coach box, and they set forth. There were six carriages and each had three or four hollowed tree trunks. The leader put on a disguise to look like a merchant. They got into the carriages and drove off.

The road passed in front of the miller's gate. There was a lot of dust and it was blowing into their faces. They stopped toward evening—the captain jumped off the carriage and went to see the miller.

"I bid you a good day, Farmer Mónár!"

"A good day to you too, son!"

"I'd ask you, Farmer Mónár, to be kind enough to let us into your courtyard. Make room for the carriages and take us in, too!"

"Where are you traveling?" asked the miller.

Right away the robber named such and such a town, where a fair was being held and to which they were taking merchandise to be sold.

"What kind of merchandise? Why are you so worried about it?"

"We are taking honey to the fair. We heard that there were robbers camping out in the forest and we are afraid to stay on the roadside overnight, lest they steal it all. Be so kind and let us come in!"

The miller was a good-hearted man—he said: "You may come in."

They pulled the carriages in under the shed and asked the captain to allow them to go into the village to buy cigarettes and a few other things.

"Be back before dark," said the miller.

"Let's get into the tree trunks, and you'll have some supper too."

Now there were two lads in each tree trunk. The miller invited the merchant into the room, thinking that he was tired from the journey, and offered him wine. He told the girl to prepare a fine roast for the travelers.

Said the girl: "Yes, father."

She went, lit a fire in the kitchen and began cooking. No one knew who the strangers were.

Her father said: "Hurry up, the travelers are hungry."

She used up all the wood in the kitchen and ran to the shed to fetch some more.

The lads in the tree trunks heard her collecting the firewood and thought it was their captain walking about nearby.

One of them said: "Captain, captain!"

She answered, disguising her voice: "What do you want?"

"Think of us when you have supper!"

The young woman replied: "All right, I'll take care of you. It'll be ready soon."

She suspected that they were being duped, that these were the robbers, not the merchants they pretended to be. The girl thought right away that the man was her husband. She ran indoors. There was oil stored in the house—since they operated a mill they needed to have it on hand. She filled a large pot, put it on the stove and when it was boiling she poured the oil into a half-liter can and rushed out with it to the shed. Her father didn't know anything about it.

She said: "Quickly, open the door, I want to honor you with some wine. Supper will be ready soon."

She poured the oil over them and scalded them all so that they died on the spot. *Their eyes popped out.*

Then the young woman went inside. She walked into the kitchen and took out a large knife, the kind used for slaughtering pigs. She already knew that the merchant who was drinking with her father was her husband. She stepped into the room, stood behind him and thrust the knife into his back with such force that it pierced his chest. He died instantly.

The old man cried out: "What did you do, my girl, have you lost your mind? Oh dear, what did you do, my girl? You destroyed me and yourself! You murdered an innocent man—why did you do it?"

"No, father, I haven't lost my mind! You don't know with whom you were chatting. I knew what I was doing. These people are not merchants—he is the man I married—they came here to kill us and to plunder! Now come with me and see the honey they had in the tree trunks!"

They went out and she showed him: they were all dead.

Not only did the constables not punish the young woman, they rewarded her. That was the law then—nothing else needed to be done. "And you, Farmer Mónár, you had better sell your mill and leave, for you won't find peace here—who knows how many more robbers there are in the area. Go, cross the ocean into another land. You can live there like a gentleman with all that money, even if you cease farming."

And that is what happened. He sold his entire farm, bought a three-story house across the ocean and lived off the money he had. When the old couple died, the young woman married and from then on lived happily ever after.

# 25. The Wager of the Two Comrades

AT 1350 (*The Loving Wife*); MNK 1350 registers only one variant from 1904 and two from other Andrásfalva storytellers. Mrs. Palkó learned it from her brother János. It must have been shortly after the first World War; otherwise the couple and the buddy would not have been young. The mention of three thousand forints for funeral expenses indicates that Mrs. Palkó updated the story. The forint has been the currency of Hungary only since the Second World War and in 1950 (the time of my recording) 3,000 forints was the approximate cost of a village burial.

The plot of this story can be traced to a group of medieval literary anecdotes about the fickleness of women, similar to the libretto of Mozart's famous comic opera *Cosi Fan Tutte*. Mrs. Palkó's version employs the tricks of traditional folk jests. The story is masterfully structured, more like a theatrical comedy than a prose narrative. The narrator sets the stage by introducing the characters and the situation—the rest is the conversation of the actors. As events unfold in this three-actor drama, the emphasis is first on the change of heart of the young woman shocked by her husband's trick and then switches to the sly talk of the friend, persuading her to accept the tragic facts. To make it very clear that the buddy and the husband conspire to test the woman, the plot is told twice: first as it is proposed; second, when the husband goes through with it. As they tell and then act out their ploy, the arguments of the buddy seem so convincing and rational that the audience may well be convinced that there is nothing for the wife to do but accept the facts and find another husband to secure her meal ticket. But the corpse on the bier is a trickster, testing the limits of loyalty. Aunt Zsuzsi's personal opinion is expressed in the brief conclusion: the friend should not have subjected the young woman to such a cruel test; he spoiled a good marriage.

———

It happened in the war of nineteen fourteen. There was a couple, two young people, who loved each other very much; they lived such a good life together, like *two turtle doves*.

The man had a good friend, a buddy. They were so close that one never even had a drink of schnapps without the other. Then the war broke out and one man was taken by the army and the other stayed home. The young wife cried day and night—she didn't go anywhere, not to dances, not to weddings—she just stayed home, mourning her husband. The buddy's wife died during the war and he became a widower.

When a year had passed after the buddy's wife had died, the young woman's husband came home. Oh, were they happy when they saw each other again! She complained about how she had stayed home all the time, how she had gone nowhere, no matter how much they had called her, so sorry had she been for her husband. She didn't want to go out to have fun, she only went to church and there she always prayed for him. Her husband loved her dearly and found great joy in her, for there was much talk about women who had behaved badly during the war. But no one could say anything nasty about his woman. They had only good words for her, about how true and respectable she was. Oh, yes, the man always praised her; wherever he went he talked about his wife, about how honest his woman was, how the news about the ways of other women had traveled far, as far as the front, how they had gone carousing, but his woman had kept herself honorable.

One day the man and his buddy went to church together. He was a very pious man, he attended mass every day. When they came back from church, his comrade said to him:

"Let's go to the tavern and have a few drinks"—said the young man—"let's go, buddy. Thank God I have enough to pay, I won't be the worse for it."

So they went into the tavern and right away ordered drinks and two glasses. They toasted one another and talked.

Said the young man: "To your good health, comrade, and to the good health of my woman. I include her too, though she isn't here. God bless her for she is an honest woman."

His buddy said to him: "Don't trust the woman so much, my pal! It isn't good to trust a woman completely."

"You can't trust those you can't trust, but my woman you can."

"Well, pal, I wouldn't depend on it. I can't stand it that you praise her so much when other men have wives as pretty as yours."

"Comrade, this isn't a question of beauty but of honesty."

"Well, then," he said, "if you believe in the woman so much, let's make a bet!"

"And what should we bet on?"

"We should bet that when you die and while you are still laid out on the bier, your wife will already promise herself in marriage to someone else."

"Oh, my friend," he said, "it's better you don't waste too much effort on this. My woman made a vow that when I die she'll never get married again."

"So, let's bet, comrade, that she will," he said. "You'll still be on the bier and she'll already pledge herself to someone else."

"All right, but how will this be? Once I am dead, what will I know? She could pledge herself, but how would I know about it?"

"You would, my friend, just hear me out," he said. "When you go home now, make believe that you are very sick, ready to die. Just make believe that it is so, and this will really scare the wife. 'What happened to you?'—she'll say—'you were in good health when you left earlier'. And then you'll say to her: 'Don't ask so much, I am going to die, I feel it. There is nothing I need any more.'"

"And then she'll say: 'My dear mate, what's the matter? I'd better go and fetch some medicine, maybe you'll get better.'"

"'No, wife, no, don't go to the doctor. It's no use, I feel it.'"

"'Then I'll run for the priest so he can hear your confession. Look,' she'll say, 'here is some good tea, or coffee, or is there something else you'd want, my dear mate?'"

"'Don't offer me anything, just hurry up and prepare the bed so I can lie down; and take off my boots, I can't do it myself.'"

"Oh dear, how alarmed the wife will be! She'll be heartbroken at the thought of losing her beloved man. But she'll take off your boots and make your bed, as you had instructed her. You'll lie down and say to her:

"'Wife, instead of offering me food, run to my buddy and ask him to come at once so I can make a last will and testament. We have no children, so when I die and you are left alone, the relatives will take all we have to our name. Call my buddy, let him be my witness, for he has always been the most fair-minded with us.'"

"And then," he said, "while the wife comes looking for me, you pretend that you have died. The rest you can leave to me."

"All right then, what is the wager? Tell me!" the man said.

"If your wife doesn't pledge herself in marriage to someone else while you are lying on the bier, you'll know it, for you'll only pretend to be dead; then I'll leave my house barefooted, with only a shirt on my back and I'll give you everything I own, my land, my cattle and my houses, everything."

Said the young man: "Well, partner, in that case if you win, I'll also leave my house with only a shirt on my back and I'll hand over to you my land, my cattle—everything I own."

And so the wager was made; they shook on it and the innkeeper sealed it. The wager was made and the two men set out on their way home.

Meanwhile the young wife had been waiting for her husband, worried that he was late and wondering where he could be, as other times he'd be back from church sooner. She went out to the gate several times, looking to see whether he was on his way. The meal was prepared, ready for his return. But she looked in vain, he wasn't coming. She went out a second and a third time and finally she caught sight of him approaching ever so slowly; he seemed barely able to put one foot in front of the other.

Oh, my—thought the young woman—What's wrong with him? Usually he strides like a *hussar*. Perhaps he is drunk, but it's not his habit to get drunk; he must be sick.

She couldn't wait for him to reach the gate—she went ahead to meet him, maybe as far the third house on the road.

"Oh, dear, what's wrong with you?" she asked. "Why are you walking so slowly?"

"Let it be, woman, I'll tell you when we get home—if only I can make it, but I don't believe I can."

The young woman became alarmed: "What happened to you?"

They entered the house.

She said to him: "What can I bring you? Something to drink?"

"I don't need anything," he answered.

"Have a nice cup of coffee, or tea—I just made it. Which would you like?"

"Don't offer me any food or drink—just get my bed ready so I can lie down, and help me take off my boots."

The poor woman removed his boots but she was weeping so, she hardly knew what she was doing.

"Oh, my dear husband, please say where should I run, for the priest or for the doctor. Whom should I bring you first?"

"I don't need a priest, or a doctor, for I know that I must die now. Better make haste and get my buddy to come over."

"Oh dear, what good can he do? The doctor might help."

"Look, dear wife, I want to draw up a last will and have him be a witness."

"Oh my," cried the woman, "you want to leave me, you are not just joking with me, oh, my, my," she lamented.

"Dear wife," he said, "don't cry, go in a hurry, let me make a will while I am still able to speak. We have no children, so when I die the relatives could turn you out and take the farm and all our property from you."

The woman picked up and ran to the old friend's house, weeping bitterly all the way. As she opened the gate, she found herself face to face with him.

"What's the matter, neighbor? Why are you crying? What happened to you?"

"Oh, don't even ask, just come at once, please, my husband is calling you," she said.

"Why is he calling me? We came back from church together only a little while ago."

"Oh dear, maybe we won't get there in time to find him alive. He wants to leave a testament," she said, "he is calling you to be a witness, because you are the most fair-minded with us."

"My poor old pal, I can hardly believe it—we came home together, nothing was ailing him then."

"I am not waiting for you," said the young wife, "I must run home to see how he is."

The woman scurried home, entered the room and found her husband lying on his back, his eyes closed. She rushed over to his bed:

"My dear, beloved husband, open your eyes, your comrade is coming!"

He didn't respond.

"What has happened to you? You haven't passed away, have you?" wailed the woman. "Why aren't you talking?"

Well, the man didn't open his eyes. She felt his chest—he wasn't breathing.

"Oh, God, my beloved man is dead!"

Heartbroken, she wept and wept: "Why have you sent me away? Now I wasn't here when you died!"

Just then his comrade stepped in the door.

"Oh dear, dear, open your eyes, speak to your old pal! He liked you so much and now you won't even say a word to him."

The man walked up to the bed and said: "Well, what's the matter, buddy? Say something, why did you send for me? I came as you asked."

But he didn't answer. His comrade took his hand, felt his pulse and made a despondent gesture.

"What is it, neighbor? Could he be dead?" asked the woman.

"Well, yes, my dear. He won't speak to us in this world, that's for sure."

The woman threw herself on her husband, weeping, trying to rouse him, but to no avail.

Said the comrade: "Listen, neighbor, don't cry so much, he won't come to life any more. Once someone is dead, he is dead. Rather bring me a razor so I can shave him, and go, put on some water for he has to be bathed."

But the woman cried and cried—what was to become of her now? She wouldn't move from her husband's side.

"How could he leave me when we had enough to live on, enough work? Why did he choose to go to such a special place where I can't follow him?" She went on lamenting so loudly that her cries echoed throughout the house.

Then the man said: "Listen, neighbor, don't cry, you'd better hurry to dress the body while it's still warm; once it's stiff, we can't work with it. And see that the fire is lit and the water is heating so I can bathe him while you prepare the bier."

So the poor woman left the room to fetch the sheets and Sunday pillows from the chest, but she was weeping all the while. The man began shaving the body and the woman shouted at him that he shouldn't be so careless, he shouldn't pull her husband's beard.

"Oh, my dear," he said, "he can't feel pain any longer."

Then, as soon as the bier was set up and the dead man was bathed and dressed, they laid him out. But the woman kept lamenting:

"My beloved, beautiful husband, there wasn't another as beautiful in the whole world, and as kind. Not even once did he slap me, or I couldn't mourn him so," she said. "He never as much as scolded me."

After a while the comrade said: "Neighbor, listen, stop crying or I'll have to leave you. We must agree on what to do for the funeral, run to make sure the church bells will toll, find grave diggers and go into town to shop for what is needed for the wake. These are worries and all you do is weep and weep. And if I leave you, what will you do?"

"Oh, please, don't abandon me! Who else would help me?"

"That's just what I am saying. We have to alert the priest that your husband has died, have him sound the death knell, and who should take care of this but me? Let's decide who will go into town to do the shopping; we need a coffin, a shroud and candles. On whom could you rely to do this, whom could you trust with your money, if not me?"

"My husband said the same, that you are the most fair-minded with us," said the young woman.

"But listen, neighbor," said the man, "I'd like to have a word with you before anyone else gets here. I'd like to speak with you in private."

"So speak, friend, what would you like to say?"

"Well, neighbor, I want to say that we have known each other for a long time. We got along well when my woman was still alive. You know yourself that we wouldn't even have a glass of schnapps without one another," he said. "Already then I often thought, God, how fond I am of this neighbor. Though my woman was good, too, and beautiful and I loved her, I often thought that if it were God's will for my pal to die and my woman died too, I wouldn't want anyone else but you. No one knew this, I was just saying it to myself. And now, you see what has come to pass; my mate has died and so has yours. So I want to ask you to come and be my wife; it's a year now since I have become a widower. As if my heart had told me ahead of time that you'll be left alone, too. Why, you can't stay by yourself, you must marry again—the farm is large, it needs a man."

Said the woman: "Oh, dear neighbor, don't say such things—that I should marry again, that I should bury my beloved husband with the thought of getting married. Never, not me, for I couldn't ever find a man like mine was, as good as mine was. There isn't another one like him in this whole world."

"Oh, but there is," said the comrade. "My woman was good, too, but I had to forget her, for a dead person will never come to life again. And I am not saying that you should marry me right away. It's proper to mourn your husband, even for three months, good man that he was, and I'll wait for you," he said. "I just want to hear you say that you'll marry me, that you'll become my wife. My heart would then be so much more inclined to help you. You see, you need someone to do the shopping in town," he said, "someone to handle your money, someone you can trust, like me."

And he continued: "We must buy food, candles and a shroud for the funeral, we must do the shopping. You can give me as much as three thousand *forint*, you'd have nothing to fear, I wouldn't hide it, but," he said, "only if you tell me, even just with one word, that you'll be my wife and that, young as you are, you won't spend your life alone."

The woman thought for a while and then said: "Well, neighbor, I'll bear the burden for as long as I can bear it, but there will come a time when I'll be weaker and then I'll have to have someone at my side. Yes, I'll marry you," she said, "but not yet. For three months I'll mourn him."

"That's what I say, too," said the man.

So the solemn agreement was made, she pledged herself to him in marriage.

"Say, neighbor, you are sure that you'll marry me?" asked the man.

"Sure," she answered. "Once I have said it, I will."

"Well then, I must tell you something else, so you won't reproach me later that had you known, you wouldn't have made the promise."

"What do you want to say, neighbor? What's on your mind?"

"I'll tell you," he said, "my private parts are such that I wet the bed every night."

The woman was embarrassed hearing this from the man.

She said: "Don't worry, neighbor, it doesn't matter at all. My man even dropped a load in bed."

The dead man couldn't put up with this any longer. He sat up on the bier and said: "Drop a load in bed? When did I do that? How can you say such a thing?"

The comrade burst out laughing:

"You see, buddy," he said, "who was right?"

"How can you say that I dropped a load in bed? Not in my whole life, not even when I was drunk did I do that! I didn't even pee in bed! Is this how fair you are with me? You are accusing me of such things after my death?"

Said the comrade: "Buddy, stop fighting—God forbid there should be bad feelings. Just remember what I told you—that you mustn't ever trust a woman completely."

"Well, pal, how can one stand this?" said the dead man. "You see, wife, what you caused? Now we must move out of our house, we have nothing left to our name."

His friend said: "No, comrade, I don't want what is yours. Stay where you are. All I wanted was to show you that it isn't good to trust a woman totally and to let her know that you do. It'll spoil her."

So they remained, forgave each other, went on living together, but never again was their life as happy as before. They were forever making reproaches to one another. This is what the comrade brought about.

# 26. The Székely Bride

AT 1365F* + MNK 1164D** (*The Devil and the Székely Woman*), recorded in six variants. The storyteller heard it from the daughter of her sister in Mucsfa; I recorded it in 1959 at her home. The focal caricatured figure is a favorite among village women: a wife who is a Székely (like themselves), so stubborn and quarrelsome that she scares even the devil away. Only the hussar, the valiant cavalry man, can deal with her and take advantage of rescuing the devil from her. At this point, however, the educational tale for Székely girls is interrupted. Enter the hussar, bargaining with the devil: this episode is reminiscent of Mrs. Palkó's version of AT 332 (*Death With the Yellow Legs*), only here with a happy ending. The clever hussar, standard hero of Hungarian folktales, blackmails the devil-partner by threatening him with the Székely bride, whose whereabouts, by the way, have been totally forgotten. The girl—who started out as poor and eager to do housework to earn a dowry that would enable her to find a husband—destroys herself by her stubbornness. Mrs. Palkó's rhetorical question at the end—who knows what has happened to her?—means she really does not care for the foolish wife or her husband who "didn't have the good sense" to keep her alive. Finally, the hussar is the winner.

———

There was once a man and a woman and they had so many daughters that wherever they turned they stumbled over one of them. One day the youngest girl said to her father:

"Father, I'd like to go and enter into service somewhere," she said, "I have to earn some money to provide for my own clothing."

"Well, my girl, if that's what you want to do, go," he said.

So the girl left. She found a fine position where she was liked and where she, too, liked the master. They treated her well. One day while she was working there, a lad turned up, who knows from where, and fell in love with her.

He said to the girl: "I'd take you for my wife, if you'd marry me."

"I'll ask my father and mother and see what they have to say. If they give their permission," she said, "I'll marry you."

The girl went home and told her father that it was her wish to get married. Good fortune had come her way and she wasn't about to brush it aside. She wanted to marry the lad.

"Well, all right, my girl," he said.

So the pair went to the priest to register for marriage. Then they had their wedding and held a big feast.

A while later the young bride said to her husband: "Look, it would be nice to visit my father and mother, to see how they are doing."

For when she married, the girl had been taken from her home to the house of her husband.

He said: "I don't mind, let's go."

And so they set out. The young bride packed a loaf of bread, a jug of wine, and a flitch of bacon for the road and they departed. The man yoked two oxen and they left on a wagon. Soon they approached the girl's village. She said: "We'll be home shortly. We are coming to my village."

She looked into a courtyard and saw a stack of hay.

"Oh," she said, "look, what a huge stack of hay they have there!"

He said: "Wife, that's not hay, that's straw."

"That's hay, for sure," she said.

"It's not hay, it's straw."

They went on arguing until the woman grew so angry that she took the loaf of bread and flung it between the oxen with such force that it broke into pieces. This startled the oxen—they lunged forward and nearly tipped over the wagon as they charged ahead. They became wild.

Said the woman: "Say that it is hay!"

"Oh no! Why should I, when it is straw!"

Whereupon the young bride grew angry again, took the jug of wine and threw it between the oxen. This made them even wilder. She grabbed the flitch of bacon and threw that, too. She vented her fury on the oxen. Soon they reached the gate of the house. They opened it and drove in.

Said the young woman: "Say that it's hay!"

"Wife, stop being foolish. Of course I won't say hay when it's straw!"

Well, they entered the house. But the young bride's nose was so out of joint that she wouldn't say a word. Her father and mother were happy that the newlyweds had come to visit, and the neighbors and relatives had all gathered to welcome them. They were chatting and rejoicing with each other, but the woman was angry, in no mood to talk.

The man leaned over to her and said: "Don't show your anger here! Say something else, as it is fitting, don't be a fool!"

"Then say that it's hay."

"Oh no, I won't, since it's straw!"

Now the young bride became so furious that she fell ill. She developed a high fever, complained of a headache and pain all over her body. She was deathly ill.

Her mother said to her: "My dear girl, what is the matter with you? Why are you so sick?"

"I don't know, mother, when we arrived I wasn't feeling sick, but now I do," she said, "every part of my body is aching."

Her mother said: "Look, it's best for you to lie down."

They put her to bed, but to no avail.

The man came over and whispered to her: "Wife, come to your senses," he said, "stop this nervousness and say something different."

"Then say that it's hay!" she answered.

"Oh, no, why should I, when it's straw!" he said.

Well, now the woman became really ill. Her condition worsened, she even lost her speech.

Her mother said to her: "Oh, my dear daughter, we'd better call the priest so you can confess and not die without absolution. We'd better not have this on our conscience."

The woman didn't utter a word.

"Oh, dear God, she is dying!" said her mother.

She began crying, heartbroken. But the woman remained silent. She lost her speech. Her father ran to tell the priest and asked him to come and hear his daughter's confession for she was deathly ill. The priest came but the poor man had no notion of what had occurred between the couple. Well, she confessed. She did, or she didn't— only she knew—but she received Holy Communion. Then the priest left and the woman stayed at home. Her husband leaned over to her and whispered once again:

"Look, wife," he said, "you confessed, the poor priest took the trouble to come here, so be sensible and stop agitating. It's a shame, even a sin, it's not proper to be angry after confession."

"Then say that it's hay!"

"No, I won't, since it's straw," said the man.

Neither one of them had more sense than the other.

"Oh, no, I won't say it. How can I say that it's hay when it's straw?"

Well, the woman died. The priest had barely reached his home when they came running to tell him that the woman had passed away.

Said the priest: "I am glad that she had unburdened her soul; she had confessed and was prepared for death," he said. "We'll bury her, and may God let her rest in peace, now that she is dead. There is nothing more man can do."

The woman lay dead (like me, now) and the man went over to her again: "Look, wife," he said, "we had notified the priest that you have died and he already sounded the death knell. He'll be here shortly to bury you. Speak," he said, "say something different, talk to me in another way and forget all the nervousness."

"Then say that it's hay!"

"Well, I won't, since it's straw!"

Not even to keep her alive did the man say what she wanted to hear. He didn't have the good sense to agree with her that it was hay. For him it was straw, and that was that. Then the time came for the funeral and they went to fetch the priest. When he arrived the man leaned over his wife once more:

"Wife, listen to me," he whispered to her, "say something, or else the priest will take you away. He came to bury you and he is here now. They came with the banners," he said, "to take you to the cemetery! Say something different."

"Then say that it's hay!"

"No, I won't say it's hay when it's straw!"

So the priest completed the funeral rites, they placed the woman in the coffin, nailed it down and took her to the cemetery.

When they set the coffin down alongside the grave, the man bent over it: "Wife," he said, "there is still time, think it over. Once you are in the grave, you can't get out, they'll cover you with earth!"

"Then say that it's hay!"

"I won't say it, because it's straw," he said.

They lowered the coffin, covered it and filled up the pit. That's when it occurred to the woman that what she did was wrong, after all. But now it was too late, she would surely suffocate—if she didn't die another way, she would suffocate in the coffin since they had nailed it down.

Furious, she called out: "If only the devil would come and take me away!"

No sooner had she uttered those words than the devil was there.

"Here I am," he said, "why did you call me?"

She said: "Take me out of this grave."

He said: "Why did you call me? Why did you ask me to come?"

She said: "So you'd get me out of this grave."

Whereupon he said: "Well, come, get up on my back."

The young bride climbed up on the devil's back and he lifted her out. It took only a second and they were at the edge of the grave. Then she began goading the devil. She slapped his face, pummeled his head with her fists and tore at his hair; now she pulled his hair, now his ears—she battered him.

He said to her: "Woman, get off my back, I won't carry you any farther. I can stand it no longer—I am so exhausted that I can barely put one foot in front of the other."

But she didn't let up, she kept spurring him on, beating him, tearing at his hair and ears. She even bit him. So the devil had no choice but to continue with her. She was still beating him when they met a *hussar*. He was on horseback, coming from the opposite direction.

The devil said to him: "Listen, *hussar*, save me, free me from this young woman," he said, "I'll give you a whole country, if you save me from her clutches."

"For one country I won't do it," he said. "But if you give me three, I'll save you. You must give me three countries."

The devil thought about it and said: "All right, you can have three, as long as you free me from her."

So the *hussar* took the young woman off the devil's back and he said to him: "Look, man, I don't have any countries to give you. Instead, I'll go and inhabit three queens. I'll get inside the first queen and all you need to say is—'Go, pal!'—and I'll leave her. I'll leave as soon as you say it, but only then," he said. "And you must say it softly, so no one can hear it, only me, no one else."

The *hussar* said: "All right."

Well, they had come to an understanding. The devil crept inside the body of a queen and began to torment her. The king grew alarmed, he didn't know what had happened to his wife. He summoned doctors, God knows, from the whole wide world, the most learned and wise doctors, yet none could diagnose what was ailing the queen.

"Now," said the devil to the *hussar*, "you'll be a doctor, You'll become one, and you'll tell the king that you can cure the queen. All you have to say is—'Go, pal!'—and I'll leave her. Her health will be restored." And, he added: "I'll make a man out of you."

So they agreed that this was how it would be. The devil got inside one queen, began to torment her, and the king grew alarmed. Right away he summoned doctors from all over but not one was able to help her. Then the *hussar* went to see the king and said to him:

"Your Royal Highness, I'll cure the queen if you pay me."

"Sure, I'll pay you," he said, "cure her, if you can. And what do you want? How much are you asking?"

"I want a country," he answered.

"I'll give you one, with pleasure," said the king, "as long as you cure my wife."

Whereupon the *hussar* leaned over to what's his name, and whispered to him, "Go, pal!" The devil left the woman at once and she recovered. Then he got inside another queen and began to torment her. There, too, the king became so frightened, he didn't know what to do. He had doctors come from everywhere, but none could help. But the *hussar* went and cured her the same way. He said: "Go, pal!" The devil left the woman instantly and she became herself again. The *hussar* received a country and a sackful of gold. The previous king had also given him a sackful of gold for restoring the queen's health, so now he had two sacks of gold and the promise of two countries. Then the devil went to inhabit a third queen and began to torment her. No one could cure her either. But word had spread that there was a learned *hussar* around who could revive the dying, so they summoned him. He came and announced that he would help the queen but only if he received a country in return. He should be given a country and a sackful of gold. That's what he said.

"I'll give you what you want, gladly," said the king, "as long as you cure her."

Well, the *hussar* set about to cure her. He approached her and said: "Go, pal!" But this time the devil wouldn't leave. He felt comfortable inside the queen's body and refused to get out. No one knew this, only the *hussar* and the devil. No one else heard their conversation.

Said the *hussar*: "Aren't you leaving? Aren't you getting out, pal? Don't you want to go?"

"I am not leaving," said the devil. "I am happy here, I am staying. Be content with two countries and two sacks of gold. That's enough for you."

The *hussar* said: "I'll fetch the Székely bride! I'll bring her here this instant!"

The devil became so frightened that he left the queen and ran all the way to hell and there he descended to the very bottom, just to make sure that the Székely bride wouldn't find him. And so it was. What's his name, the devil, escaped her for he had left the queen. But he didn't stay put in hell—he jumped out of there, and didn't know where to hide for fear that the Székely bride would come after him and climb on his back again. Meanwhile, who knows what happened to the young bride. Did she go back to her husband or to her father? I don't know. She just disappeared and the devil was rid of her. He went back to hell. The husband is still alive somewhere, if he hasn't died. The *hussar* became an important man, with three countries and three sacks of gold to his name. That was enough for him to live on. This is the end of my story.

# 27. The Nagging Wives

This unique anecdote should be classified among tales of The Foolish Couple (AT 1400-1460). This is one of the many hilarious didactic stories for young girls and women that circulate mostly in women's work-circles. Mrs. Palkó's performance, recorded in 1955, provoked laughter among the women who had come with their small children and brought stools and distaffs so that they could sit and spin yarn while listening. Peels of laughter honored the rhythm of the recital of the two women's competition in showing their bare behinds to each other, each afraid to stop and thus to lose, with the anxious husband filling in for his wife in order to save the bread dough from spoiling. Mrs. Palkó's rhythmical dialogue develops gradually as the husband from time to time reports to his nagging wife how far he has progressed in preparing the bread. "Isn't that something?" Mrs. Palkó asked. "I told this to women but it was not for children to overhear. I would have spanked this woman who was stupid enough to show her behind. . . ."

———

Once there were two women. They were forever quarreling. Why they didn't get along, I couldn't say any more. They always stood there and squabbled in the street. They were neighbors. One day they went outside again and began to quarrel; they were on either side of the road but close to each other for the road was narrow. The dispute between them grew so ugly that they hurled the worst insults and filth at one another. The husband of one of the women was at home; he was inside the room. After a while he came out and said:

"Will you put an end to all this nastiness, or will you keep at it? Haven't you had enough of this bickering?"

The women didn't let up.

He said: "Come in, woman. You prepared the leaven, you should be kneading the dough now but you don't. Well, do you expect me to do it while you are standing there fighting? Come in!"

"Oh, no, I won't!"

The best was yet to come. The woman picked up her skirt, lifted it over her head, turned around and said:

"So there! This is the kind of woman you are!" and she showed everything she had. They didn't know what outrage to think of next—they turned up their skirts and pointed their behinds at each other. They both did the same. Then the man, the woman's husband, came out again and said:

"Come in, woman—I finished kneading the dough, it should be put into the pan, come in!"

She said: "I am not coming, because if I leave I will be stuck with the insult that I am like her behind. Let her go inside first!"

Said the man: "Come in, woman, the dough is getting runny and sour. Come in, the oven has to be lit!"

"Oh, no, I won't! I'll be stuck with the insult."

All the while she, too, was on all fours, showing her backside. Well, the man went in and put the dough in the pan. He did it to allow the women to finish with their business. But now the oven had to be lit, so he went out again. (He was as crazy as his wife!)

"Come in, the oven has to be lit, come in!"

"I won't come now, I don't want her insult to stick with me like a curse!"

Said the man: "Come in, woman, I'll take your place. I'll push down my trousers and I'll show her mine."

He said it softly so the other woman wouldn't hear: "I'll take your place, come in!"

He lowered his trousers and got down on all fours:

"Here, woman, look!"

She didn't notice that the two had switched—she thought it was still the woman showing her buttocks. She didn't know that the woman had gone inside to attend to her work and that the man had taken her place. When she looked back and saw, she began to clap:

"You are it! You are it! You are stuck with the insult, for you kept showing your arse until your guts popped out like a sausage. You see, it's your fault, you are saddled with it," she said. "Woman, your rectum has dropped down, you are it!"

Then the woman went inside and the man did too. They made peace with each other and there was no more quarreling. They are still alive today, if they haven't died.

It was the man's fault. Why didn't he grab the woman by the hair and pull her into the house? Why did he let them go on with their bickering?

# 28. Peti and Boris

AT 1408 (*The Man Who Does His Wife's Work*) + 1218 (*Numskull Sits on Eggs to Finish the Hatching*); MNK lists 12 variants. This is one of the most popular jocular tales known to women in Kakasd, and Mrs. Palkó is its master teller. Originally she learned it from Erzsi Matyi, wife of nephew György Andrásfalvi. Erzsi was recognized as a comic entertainer who liked to joke, sing mock-songs and mimic others at women's work-parties, but she stopped telling "Peti and Boris" because Aunt Zsuzsi's recital was so much better. She suggested that I ask for this tale. The house was full of neighbors and three folklore students were present at Aunt Zsuzsi's home at the time of the recording, the winter of 1949. She usually told her stories without body movement, but this time she acted out the stupid husband's role and squatted down on an imaginary nest and called "Krrrr, krrrr, krrrr" imitating the crowing hen, as if warming up the eggs with his bare bottom would restore the dead chicks.

During the 1970s and '80s, three more variants of this tale were collected in Kakasd from practicing women storytellers; all seem to have been influenced by Mrs. Palkó's story, but none approximated her mastery.

———

There was once a young couple. They had only one small son. They loved one another very much, but the man had a slight shortcoming—his wife couldn't do enough for him. He was never pleased with the amount of work she did. Yet they had decided in advance, once they had the little boy, and they had the farm, cattle, and poultry, that one of them had to stay at home while the other went to work in the field. So they agreed that the young woman would stay, since she had a small son, and there were the cows and plenty to do at home—a woman always has work to do in life. And the man would go to labor in the field. The poor woman worked hard, for a woman has a hundred chores around the house. When her husband came home, supper was always ready, there was fresh pastry and everything was done, the animals were fed and watered—still he was never satisfied. He was forever needling her that a woman had it easy at home in the nice shade while the poor man had to toil from morning to evening in the hot sun. He couldn't see that any work was accomplished at home.

The woman told him in vain: "Look, I have to run hither and yon, yet a woman's work isn't noticeable—only when it is neglected can it be seen. When it's done, her work doesn't show."

"Well, yes," he said, "but in the meantime you can lie down in the shade for a nice nap while the poor man goes on working in the field, with sweat dripping from his face."

"If this is how it is, then let me do your work in the field and you do mine at home. Tomorrow I'll go out and you stay here. But I am telling you, I better not find anything wrong when I come home. You must attend to everything the way I do. Feed and water the animals, milk the cow and bake the bread. I'll prepare the leaven and then you knead the dough and have the bread ready by the time I come home! You must milk the cow properly, make sure that the boy gets to eat and that the pigs, the chickens, and the ducks are fed. And you should know that two of the hens are brooding. One of them is ready to hatch the chicks, the other has only been sitting on the eggs for a week. Watch them— when they get off, give them somethng to eat and drink, then chase them back quickly and put them on their nests again, lest the eggs cool off. Look out for the chicks under the other hen. Take them out as soon as they hatch, or else they'll die! Then," she said, "mow some grass for the cow. If she doesn't get any, she won't give milk, she'll go dry. Next you must churn butter. Then the boy's clothes have to be washed; tomorrow is Sunday, he must have clean clothes. And you had better have a good meal waiting for me! I am telling you, you must attend to all this the way I do. You say that I have it easy at home in the shade, so now you'll know what a woman's work is like."

She put the hoe on her shoulder, packed some provisions for midday and left. She went to work in the field. The man watched and as soon as his wife was out of sight, he said:

"It's too soon to get up, I'll stay in bed a while longer, I'll rest a little more."

He lay down and fell sound asleep—it was ten o'clock when he woke again. By then the cow and her calf were mooing in the barn, the pigs were wrecking the sty, demanding to be fed—they squealed and made a tremendous racket—and the famished barnyard animals crowded at the gate. The little boy was awake and was crying.

"Oh dear, where should I begin? What should I do?"

He cut a slice of bread and gave it to the child to quiet him down and ran outside.

"What should I do first?" He rushed to the barn, put some hay before the cows, gave the pigs a little corn and then some swill. The cow had to be milked, but the little boy was sobbing for he wasn't used to being left sitting inside. His mother always gave him milk as soon as he woke up. Now there wasn't any, the man hadn't yet milked the cow so he had none to give. The boy kept crying. He grabbed the pail and ran to the barn to milk the cow and the boy went out after him. He was still little, very young; he had just learned to walk. As he stepped out, holding the slice of bread in his hand, the dog came along and tried to snatch it away from him. But he bit the little boy's finger and he started to scream. The man had nearly finished milking the cow— he was about to collect the last drops— when he heard the boy wailing. He thought that maybe the dog had jumped on the child, that he must have been frightened to be screaming so loud. Quickly he set the pail down near the cow's rump and ran to see what was wrong with the boy. He found him bleeding and became alarmed.

"Dear God, what happened to him?"

As he came near, he saw that the dog had almost bitten off the boy's finger and had taken the bread from him.

"Oh, dear God, the trouble I'm in for having taken it easy, for resting a while longer and going back to bed! If I had risen early, I could have attended to everything properly, but I wasted my time sleeping and now I am late."

Well, he bandaged the boy's hand and rushed back to the barn for the pail so he could give him some milk. Meanwhile, however, the cow had stepped into the pail, tipped it over, and all the milk had spilled.

"Dear God, what am I to do now? The milk is gone, what can I give my little one?"

The boy didn't stop crying, asking for the milk. He was used to having fresh milk every morning.

"Quiet, my son," he said, "I'll churn the butter and spread it for you on a slice of bread." Then he remembered that the woman had told him to knead the dough, that he had to bake bread. He could see that he had to get to the kneading first, to allow time for the dough to rise. He ran to do it:

"Dear God," he said, "by the time I am done kneading, I'll be late with the butter."

He took the tub and strapped it onto his back. He thought that while he kneaded the dough he would be moving and the butter would churn on his back. This way he could accomplish the two tasks together. He secured the tub on his back and began kneading. But he still had to heat the oven.

He said to himself: I'll finish kneading, then I'll heat the oven.

Well, as he was working the dough, bent over, the milk spilled out from the churn onto his neck. It spilled all over him; he was covered with sour cream from head to toe. Now this too was wasted. What could he do?

"I'll go and knead the dough, at least we'll have some bread."

When he finished kneading, he remembered that he still had to mow. But he had no time. And he forgot all about the brooding hen and the chicks about to hatch. She must have crushed them in the meantime. He ran to the hen and there were the chicks, all of them lying dead on top of the eggs, the hen had tread on them. He looked for the other hen, it was out of the nest, the eggs were cold, who knows when she left them. He had neglected to attend to it, to give the hen feed and water and set it back on the nest. So once again there was damage, the eggs were lost, for once they cool off, the chicks perish. Now where should he run next? What more should he do? Evening was closing in, he had raced to and fro and he hadn't eaten yet, he had found no time to eat.

Well, what could he do now? He had kneaded the dough but it had to be warmed up since the oven wasn't lit yet; the milk was spilled and the chicks were dead.

So he said: "I am not going out to mow—evening has set in and I still have to milk the cow and prepare supper. She told me I should have supper ready for her when she comes home for she always had a warm meal waiting for me, and she said I must do the same. I haven't any time left for mowing."

Their house had a thatched roof and there was some grass, some wheat, or something, growing on it. He thought he would take the cow up to the top and let it graze there for he wasn't going to mow any hay. He brought the cow out of the barn, tied a rope to its neck and began pulling it up on the roof. But the rope broke and the cow fell back down; it fell just as the woman entered through the gate. It was evening and she was returning home.

"What are you doing, you fool? What are you doing?" she said. "Where are you pulling that cow?"

"I wanted it to eat the grass on the roof."

"Oh you, poor idiot, you, where did you get the idea to hoist a cow up on top of the roof? There is hay, good alfalfa and everything in the garden, it just has to be cut. Didn't you ever see me, a woman, mowing hay for the cow? Don't you know how to mow?"

"I had no time. There wasn't enough time," he said. "I thought there would be plenty of feed for the cow on the roof."

They called the neighbors, lifted the cow back on its feet and tethered it to the stall in the barn.

"Well," she said, "I hope supper is ready at least!"

"Oh no, it's not—I haven't even lit the stove."

"And the bread? Is it baked?"

"Oh no, it's not. I forgot all about it. I kneaded the dough, but then I forgot it. It's there, in the back."

She went to see—the dough had spread all over.

"Oh dear, dear," she said, "how much damage you caused here today! And this little boy, maybe he hasn't eaten anything all day."

"Well," he said, "I put a slice of bread into his hand, but the dog bit his finger and took the bread away."

"How could that happen?" she asked, "You gave him some bread and let him go out to the dog?"

"I didn't let him. I went to milk the cow and before I finished, he ran out after me and the dog bit his hand."

"Now you see what you are like?" she said. "All along you have been saying that a woman didn't have much to do at home, that she could sleep in the shade, that she had it easy while you were hoeing under the hot sun. I'd be glad to go out into the field every day—I'd rather go there than work at home. I have ten times as much to do here as you have out there, and still you are never satisfied with what is done around the house. Tell me," she said, "what happened with the chicks?"

"Oh, dear," he said, "I don't even dare to tell you, wife—the hen crushed them all. As they hatched she tread on them, for I forgot to remove them. She tread on them and they all died."

"And the other hen?"

"The other hen left the nest and I don't know whether it went back or not," he said. "I looked once and it wasn't there yet."

"You know, you should be hanged, you deserve nothing better! You should hang from a tree, from the gallows, the kind of man you are!"

"Oh, my dear wife!"

"Is supper ready?"

"Don't ask—I haven't even started the fire."

"Get out of my sight, I don't want to see you!"

The man disappeared in haste and went to sit on the eggs. The hen wasn't there so he sat on the eggs, stark naked. He took off his trousers and sat on the eggs, naked, to warm them up.

Then the woman called out: "Where are you? Where are you? Have you cut the wood? Is there any firewood?"

The man didn't answer. Where could he be? Maybe he hanged himself somewhere. She went looking for him and found him under the bed, sitting on the eggs in the basket.

"Oh dear, what on earth are you doing there? Why are you sitting on the eggs?"

"Krrrrrr!" he growled.

"Get out of there! Get off that nest, shame on you!"

"Krrrrrr!"

"Come on— get out of there!" The woman went for the broom. "You'll see, I'll chase you out of there the way they chase the hens out," she said, "but I'll use the broomstick on you, not the brush!"

Well, by the time she got back with the broom to drive her husband off the nest, he had emerged, but all the eggs were broken where he had been sitting, and his behind was covered with them. Now he was soiled not only by the milk that had spilled down his neck but he had egg smeared all over himself. What was he to do? How could he face his wife? There was a bucket filled with water near the well. Someone had drawn it up. He went and used it to wash, so his wife wouldn't see the eggs on him. They were running down his legs, and they were those smelly eggs, the kind that were about to be hatched. As he was washing, the ravenous pigs broke out of the sty, attracted by the odor of milk and eggs. They rushed at him and chewed everything off his body. They devoured what they could and he was left diminished for they bit off his equipment, too. He began to scream at the top of his lungs:

"Don't leave me, don't leave me, for I'll die! I'll die of the pain!"

"So die!" said the woman. "A man like you deserves to die! You never gave any credit to a woman. No matter how much I worked, you were never satisfied. You wretch, you, you, you, I don't even know what to call you," she said, "you sluggard! You had yourself in mind when you said that a woman had it easy, for she could stretch out in the shade and sleep. Not I, I never slept, there was no time for that!"

In short, he didn't accomplish anything and what he did was useless. All he caused was damage. This is the end of the story, but they are alive to this day if they haven't died.

# 29. Könyvenke

AT 1450 (*Clever Elsie*) + 1384 (*Husband Hunts Three Persons as Stupid as His Wife*) + 1245 (*Sunlight Carried in a Bag into the Windowless House*) + MNK 1284A* (*The Chicken-Raising Woman*) + MNK 1294C* (*The Stuck Child*) + AT 1288 (*Numskulls Do Not Find Their Own Legs*) + MNK 1250C* (*Measuring the Well*); an extremely popular chain-tale that links up a variety of numskull anecdotes as its episodes. Storytellers improvise easily by selecting from a wide variety of materials that could stand by themselves. MNK lists 18 variants, of which four contain indigenous Hungarian incidents; one of these is the invention of the storyteller.

"Könyvenke" is also a spinning-room tale, told by women to women in Kakasd. It is so popular that anyone would be able to tell a couple of episodes from it. Pointing to her grandchild, Mrs. Palkó said, "Heard it from my mother when I was a little girl, like this one." This performance was recorded in 1950, during a session in which many educational stories for women were exchanged. Mrs. Palkó deviates from the most common form of the tale, which opens as the family awaits the arrival of the daughter's bridegroom; the daughter is sent to the cellar to fetch wine for the wedding party, but cries uncontrollably as she imagines that a horrible fate may someday befall her child in the cellar; she is joined by her two younger sisters and mother—all crying in the cellar as they hear the bride's tale of fear. The groom then goes looking for other fools. Skipping this introductory story, Aunt Zsuzsa adds a new element. The man earns money for teaching fools common sense. Upon returning, he can reward his home fools with a thousand forints.

The word *Könyvenke* has no lexical meaning; it may be a distortion from the title of a famous booktale, *Kelemenke ködmönkéje* ("The Little Sheepskin Smock" or "Little Clemens"), or "Who inherits the little smock?" It may come also from the distortion of the word *könyv* ("book"; diminutive, *könyvecski;* speakers of the Székely dialect use diminutives very frequently). "Speckled Jesus" (*tarka Jézus*) is the dialect term for speckled magpie.

---

There was once a woman and a man and they had a daughter. One Sunday the man and his daughter went to church and the old woman stayed home. When they were coming back, they could hear that the woman was crying inside the house. They could hear it from the road. The girl ran in and said:

"Dear mother, why are you crying so bitterly? Why are you crying?"

She said: "How can I help it, my dear girl? When I sat down here by the stove

323

to pray, I looked up to the rafters and caught sight of that big block of salt there. Then I thought that if you get married and you have a boy and name him Könyvenke, and you put him down on the table to swaddle him, that block of salt could fall down on the boy," she said, "and Könyvenke would die; then who would inherit the little book?"

The girl began to cry too—they were both wailing so loud that the sound echoed throughout the house.

Then the man came home and he said: "What is this? What is going on here? What has happened to you? Why are you crying your hearts out?"

"How can we help it?" said the woman. "Look here, listen to me. If our daughter gets married and she has a boy and she puts the boy down on the table to swaddle him, and that big block of salt drops on him, Könyvenke will die and then who will inherit the little book?"

"Well," the man said to them, "I don't know if there are two other fools in this world who would be your equals! I am going now, and I'll keep on going until I find two fools like you. Is this a reason to cry?"

The man pulled himself together and set out for the wide world, in search of the fools. As he traveled he saw a man in an attic, under the roof. It was customary for houses to have windows in the back, so this house had one too, but it had no other windows, nor doors. He saw a man dipping a sieve into the air and drawing it in under the roof. Hey—he thought—what is this man doing with an empty sieve, what is he scooping out of the air?'

He came closer and greeted him: "Good day to you!"

The man reciprocated.

"What are you doing with that sieve? What are you scooping out of the air?"

He answered: "What am I scooping? I finished this house two years ago and it's so dark inside that I can't see, so I am bringing in the light with this sieve."

"Well," said the man, "I have found a match for one of them, for my wife; I have to look for one more, for my daughter!"

He said: "Do you have an ax, good man?"

"I do."

"Let me have it."

He took the ax, cut out three windows and a door, and right away it became as light inside the house as outside.

"You see, good man," he said, "you could have been doing that for a hundred years, even a thousand, and you wouldn't have had any light in the house."

The man thanked him for cutting the windows and he continued on his journey. As he went, he came to a house and there he saw a woman in the courtyard, beating a hen with a broom.

He said to her: "Auntie, what's all the fuss about? Why are you beating the hen?"

The woman kept striking the hen.

She said: "I have to, she has some thirty chicks and she won't nurse them. The poor chicks are crying but she won't let them suckle. The little ones are crying, that's why I am beating her."

The man said: "That's not the way to do it, auntie, there is no need to beat the hen. Do you have some cornmeal?" he asked.

"Yes, I have," the woman answered.

"Well, if you have," he said, "then bring me a plateful, and some water!"

The woman brought out the plate, he mixed the meal with the water and scattered it on the ground. Immediately the chicks came running, along with the hen, and they ate their fill. When they had enough, the hen settled down nicely and all the chicks crawled under her wings.

"You see," he said, "they are nursing now—this is how you must do it from now on."

The poor woman gave him a hundred *forints* for having taught her what to do.

Well, the man went on and next he saw a boy who had stuck his hand in between two stakes and caught it there. He wanted to pick a flower and his hand got caught. He saw the boy screaming his lungs out and a woman running to him with a knife.

The man said: "What is going on here? What happened? What is wrong with the boy, why is he screaming so?"

Said the woman: "He poked his hand through the fence and it got stuck. He can't pull it out, so I am bringing the knife to cut his hand off."

"Oh, don't you do that, auntie, don't cut off his hand! Wait a moment, you'll see, he'll withdraw it right away."

He went, broke off a rod and struck the boy's hand very hard. The boy yanked his hand out from between the stakes, as if it had never been caught there.

"You see," he said, "this is the remedy, not the knife—you would have deprived him of his hand! Oh dear," he said, "when I set out, I had in mind looking for two fools, finding pairs to mine, but I already came upon at least four or five."

Well, the woman gave him three hundred *forints* for freeing the boy's hand and saving it, so it didn't need to be cut off.

The man continued on his way. Suddenly he saw a group of women in a ditch—there could have been maybe ten of them sitting on the edge with their legs tangled. They were squabbling and making a lot of noise.

He said: "What's the matter with you, women? Why are you quarreling?"

They were even scratching each other's faces.

Said the women: "How can we not quarrel—when we sat down here to chat, our legs got tangled and now we can't find our own."

"How is that?" he said. "Your legs got tangled and you can't make out which are your own?"

"How can we help it, when one says 'this is mine', and the other says 'this is mine'? So we started to fight."

"Wait a moment, I'll sort it out," he said.

He was still holding the rod with which he had hit the boy's hand. He struck the women's legs hard, very hard, and each pulled her own back at once.

"God bless you for this good deed, dear man," they said. "We wanted to go out into the forest for our men had gone there in the morning to catch the speckled Jesus. We heard that they caught him, that they got the speckled Jesus," one of them said, "and we wanted to see him."

"Well, then go, and let me come along, I'd like to see him, too."

So they went and found the tree from which the men had sought to pluck the speckled Jesus. But instead of one of them climbing up to get him, they had all gathered—one of them stood at the foot of the tree, another mounted on his head and a third mounted on the head of the second. They continued climbing, one on top of the other, until one of them reached the top and called out:

"I've got him! I caught the speckled Jesus!"

But it wasn't Jesus he caught—it was a magpie. The man at the bottom wanted to see it and slipped out from under the others. They fell to the ground, one broke his leg, the other his neck, yet another his arm—all the men were crippled.

Said the man: "What are you doing here? Couldn't you have brought a ladder? One of you would have gone up to get it and then the rest of you could have seen it. Who ever heard of mounting on each other's heads?"

"Well, good man, why didn't you come sooner? You could have taught us and we wouldn't have done it this way."

"Oh, dear," he said, "I have seen plenty of fools, plenty of idiots—I am not going one step further; I have had it with them!"

The poor man turned around and headed home.

"Well, wife," he said when he arrived, "I thought that you two were the only fools around, and I have found enough for a whole village."

Then he told his family what he had seen. But he returned home with a thousand *forints*; he had earned the money along the way.

This is the end of the story, and they are alive to this day, if they haven't died.

# 30. The Uncouth Girl

AT 1450**** (*Puella Pedens*) + MNK 1471C* (*Girl Cooks Stuffed Cabbage with Urine*); MNK lists 5 variants. Mrs. Palkó learned this tale in Andrásfalva from a woman she could not remember. No wonder: it belongs to the most popular educational tales recited at informal get-togethers.

In traditional peasant terms, a girl's bad reputation may cost her her expected career: marriage to a nice young man with whom she will succeed in establishing a family and attaining wealth and respectability. The girl must be industrious and thrifty, clean, and well-mannered, experienced in household chores—accomplished in her share of the responsibilities that help marriage partners achieve success. Thus, teaching appropriate female roles is the purpose of the many tales that mock the unacceptable behavior of girls and young wives. Mrs. Palkó was a master of such anecdotes.

I recorded "The Uncouth Girl" in 1956 at the home of Mrs. Gertrud Szakács, one of the recognized entertainers of Kakasd. She and Mrs. Palkó competed with each other in telling stories about girls who cannot spin, girls who burn their dirty clothes because they cannot do the laundry, and girls who cannot talk and dress properly. This tale is told also by others in the community—women and men—but no one can provoke as much laughter as Aunt Zsuzsa.

Underlying this story is the social custom that precedes marriage. Székelys maintain strong family ties: to marry an outsider is the topic of tragic ballads, horror tales, and legends. In this case, parental agreement is sought. In a ritual encounter, the two families examine each other; the boy's parents casually visit and look around to get an impression of the girl's worth. The prospective in-laws are addressed respectfully by first name—"Aunt" Margit (Margaret) and "Uncle" Józsi (Joe)—by the young man at his first visit. When the real encounter occurs, with every indication that it is not going to work, the young couple and the parents shake hands at the beginning of the house visit: this is a receiving ritual. Then, the guests are invited to take a seat. The family is aware that the parents of the young man will look around to see if the girl fits their expectation of a daughter-in-law, so they do the best to display a spotlessly clean home. After the guests are seated, they are treated to brandy sweetened with sugar. The meal, indeed, is a display of the skills of the prospective bride. The menu prepared by the uncouth girl—meat (chicken) soup, roast meat, and the stuffed cabbage (*galuska* in Székely dialect) is traditional for festive occasions in Hungarian peasant homes.

The closing formula is one of the many traditional rhymes Mrs. Palkó employed; she used this one to tease her listeners.

---

Once there was a woman who had a daughter. The girl was pretty, she was upstanding, but very lazy. She was also sleepy, she liked to sleep a lot. But this wouldn't have mattered so much—what mattered was that she farted, she farted like a draft-horse.

Her mother often said to her: "Watch your arse, my girl. When you go dancing, when you are with young people, be careful, you'll bring shame on yourself if you fart," she said, "you'll become the laughingstock of everyone there. Think about it!"

It was no use. The girl was accustomed to letting go when she had the urge. The whole village looked down on her, no one invited her to dance, even the girls shunned her for fear that she would fart when she was in their company and others would think that one of them did it. It happened, as it did to that other girl, that a lad from a neighboring village noticed that no one took a turn with her, so he asked her for a dance. And he began inquiring whether she had a suitor. She hadn't had one until now, she said.

"Well, if I came to your house, would you accept me?"

"Sure, I would," she said.

"Then I'll come this evening. I'd like to speak to your father and mother and ask them whether they'd let you go to another village, for maybe they wouldn't."

"Oh," she said, "my parents won't mind if I live in another village when I marry."

"Then I'll be there tonight, for sure," he said.

The girl rushed home and said to her mother: "Mother, we'd better tidy up the house—a suitor is coming this evening."

"You are telling me to tidy up? You are a girl, this is your job!"

The girl straightened the bed, cleaned the lamp and swept everywhere. Soon the young man arrived. He knocked at the door. But her mother had told her beforehand: "Watch your rear-end, don't let it erupt!"

Well, the lad walked in and bade them good evening. The girl offered him a chair and they began to talk. The girl was very talkative, she loved to chat. Then the lad asked her whether she'd spoken to her mother, whether her mother would let her marry someone from another village.

"She said she didn't mind—if I love you I may go with you."

So the lad started in on the subject: "Look, Aunt Margit and Uncle Józsi"—he called them by their names— "I'd like to ask for your daughter's hand, if you'd be kind enough to let her marry me. I live in another village but she won't be badly off for I only have my mother and father and I am their only son."

Said the girl's mother: "Son, if you love each other, I don't mind, I'll let her go. She has a nice trousseau—we have some property, and we haven't any other children either; she is our only one."

Meanwhile the girl left the room ten times to break wind outside so as not to let it happen in front of the lad. Well, her mother and father gave her permission to leave their house.

Said the lad: "I must tell you that I won't be able to come here every day. I'll be back a week from Saturday and then we'll go to the priest to register for marriage. There are a few things I must attend to until then, and settle matters with my mother and father."

They answered: "All right, son, that's fine, as long as it is certain. But don't deceive us!"

"Quite certain, you may expect me," he said. "Perhaps my parents will come that Saturday evening, too. We'll register and on Sunday the priest will publish the banns. Maybe they'll come to look around and attend Mass."

The young man rose from his seat and shook hands with the old folks and with the girl:

"We are agreed," he said, "I'll be here Saturday evening."

The girl saw him out, they talked a little while longer, then the lad left. The girl went inside and her mother said to her:

"My dear girl, you didn't let a fart while you were talking, did you?"

"No, mother, I didn't," she said, "I held it back, but I am so swollen that I'll burst!"

"Well, my dear girl," said the mother, "you must break the habit. Maybe you can stop farting so much."

Soon it was Saturday.

The woman said: "Now, my daughter, make a little effort! We must clean the house and dust everywhere. His parents will come to look around and they'll know you by the work you have done here."

And that's what they did. They whitewashed the ceiling, they laundered and in the afternoon they began baking. They baked small pastries with honey, then killed chickens and ducks and cooked a good soup for Sunday. They bought brandy and sweetened a bottleful with sugar. And they prepared a large pot of cabbage stuffed with rice and meat for the suitors. By evening everything was done and the woman said:

"Well, my dear daughter, your father and I are going over to the neighbors for a little diversion and you'll stay home. Watch the stuffed cabbage, don't let it burn! Stay here and be careful, don't let the flames get too high for the broth will boil away. If you see that it does, add some more water. And watch it, don't fall asleep! Don't let the lad find you sleeping!"

"I won't sleep," she said, "I'll wait for him."

"If you fall asleep you'll fart, and if he happens to come in, he'll hear it. He'll be so disgusted that he'll refuse to have anything to do with you."

Well, the girl sat down by the stove and watched over the stuffed cabbage. It was past eight o'clock and the lad hadn't turned up. She said to herself: it is eight o'clock and he isn't here yet. Maybe he won't come any more. Why should I suffer here, by the stove? I'll go and lie down.

So she did. She had lit the lamp and let it shine, and put the dumplings on the fire. She fell asleep in no time for she was very sleepy. She liked to sleep even in daytime.

The girl was fast asleep when the lad arrived and knocked at the door. No one answered. He peered in through the window and saw that the girl was sleeping and no one else was inside. So he let himself in quietly and looked at the girl. She was in such a profound sleep that saliva was dribbling from her mouth, so soundly asleep was she. He didn't wake her—instead he crawled under the bed. About a quarter of an hour later the girl woke up, opened her eyes and looked around. There was no one in the room. Well! She stretched her arms and legs and let such a fart that the bed-slats rattled.

She said: "And this is for the one I was expecting and who never showed up!"

Then she turned in her bed and let another one—crack!

"This, too, is for the one I was expecting and who didn't come!"

Suddenly she remembered that her mother had told her she should watch the stuffed cabbage so it wouldn't burn. She jumped off the bed and ran to the pot to see if any broth was left in it. The juices had boiled away and the cabbage was becoming charred. But as she made for the pot, she let as many farts as she took steps.

"Oh, dear, what will my mother say when she comes home! The cabbage is beginning to smell—it must be burning for all the liquid is gone."

She ran to the water bucket to pour some into the pot, but it was empty—there wasn't a drop of water in it.

"Darn! I had the time to fetch water but now, in this darkness, I am afraid to go out to the well."

She looked out the window.

"I won't go out, it's too dark, I won't go out. Come what may, and I don't care what mother will say, I'll do something else."

She went over to the stove, squatted down over the pot and peed into it, so there would be liquid on the cabbage. All along the lad had been watching her from under the bed.

"Well, now," she said, "mother will never know whether this is water or urine."

She went back into bed, lay down, and—bang, bang—she farted so loudly that the room was resounding! When the lad was sure that she was asleep, hearing her snore, he crawled out from under the bed and left.

Soon, the girl's mother came home and said: "Are you sleeping, my girl?"

She said: "Yes, I am. What else should I do? I haven't been in bed very long."

"Has the lad been here?"

"No, he hasn't," she said. "Why should I wait up, if he doesn't show up?"

"Someone must have bad-mouthed you before him, for sure," she said. "He must have heard about your ways. And how is the cabbage doing?"

"It's cooking."

"Did you add some water?"

"Yes, I did."

The mother looked at it—there was little liquid in the pot.

"It isn't quite cooked yet."

"I would have needed more water but there wasn't any in the bucket and I didn't dare to go out; I was afraid."

"Oh, my dear girl, you were afraid to go out on our property?"

So the lad had left. The next morning they saw him in church along with his parents, who had arrived the night before but had stayed elsewhere. When they came out of church, they took the mother and father by the arm:

"Please, come to us, come for the midday meal!"

The lad's parents were a little hesitant, and the girl's mother and father didn't know how the lad had fared.

They insisted: "Come, have a meal with us, please come!"

Well, the lad wouldn't go—he stayed behind, but the parents went.

The girl's father ran back to him: "Come, son! Don't you want to come? Come, we were expecting you last night."

Well, the lad agreed to go along, too. He went and they shook hands. They sat down at the table and had food and drink placed before them. There was good soup, they ate it; then the meat was brought out and next the stuffed cabbage. The lad took some soup and ate the meat but he wouldn't touch the stuffed cabbage. They urged him to have it—it was very good, they said—he should sample it.

The lad said: "Thank you very much for your kindness, but I had enough."

"Why? You haven't even tasted it."

"I wouldn't want to. In all my years I haven't ever eaten stuffed cabbage cooked in urine."

"What do you mean?" asked the mother and father.

"I mean that's what the girl did last night."

He told them from beginning to end what had happened the evening before.

"It wasn't enough that she filled the room with farts," he said, "that wouldn't have mattered so much. But then I saw her jumping out of bed, worried that the stuffed cabbage would burn. She looked at the pot and saw that there wasn't any liquid in it. Then she ran to the bucket and found that it had not even a drop of water. 'Oh, dear,' she said, 'I could have gone to fetch water while it was still daylight, but now I won't go out in the dark.' She stood on the stove, crouched over the pot, and peed into it. 'So there,' she said, 'mother won't know anyway whether it's water or urine.' And this is what I should eat? Listen! I thank you for your hospitality but I wouldn't have your daughter for anything! You can keep her!"

And so the girl stayed behind, grieving, and the lad went on his way, happy. He wasn't at all sad—he rejoiced that he came to know her in time. Then her mother took her to task. "Listen, you! Didn't I tell you not to lie down and fall asleep, lest he come and find you sleeping? And, didn't I tell you to watch yourself and not break wind while the lad is here, to control your arse a little? But that wasn't enough—you peed into the pot and had your mother and father eat the dumplings cooked in urine! Is this what I taught you?"

She gave her a proper thrashing.

"You chased that nice lad away, he wouldn't have anything to do with you either. You'll never find a husband!"

And that's how matters remained. The girl is still a maiden today, if she hasn't married, or died. *The story is over, go run with it. They lived and they died and they all dumped on the audience.*

# 31. The Dumb Girl

MNK 1471A*1 (*The Speechless Girl*) lists 2 variants; another didactic tale for girls. This girl fails because she does not know how to be social, how to behave in the company of a young man, and how to talk properly. She is being advised and warned by her mother but she does not know how to conceal her shortcomings at the crucial moment: the visit of a suitor. This text not only reveals the norms of good behavior in Kakasd but also Mrs. Palkó's well tuned sense of humor, her ability to make her audience laugh. Her dialogues are lively, particularly as the mother tries to teach her daughter how to talk to a young man. Also, in the speech of the girl, her desperate eagerness is shown. She overdoes it, tries to find a topic to talk about; she is loud and fast, says more than she should, and the more she tries the more mistakes she makes. Mrs. Palkó felt the spanking justified, as did the other women present spinning. Recorded in 1950.

———

There was once a woman and a man and they had a daughter. She was pretty, she was decent, she just wasn't very talkative. When they asked her something she answered, but she never started a conversation, she didn't like to do that—she was always quiet.

One day her mother said to her: "Why aren't you talking, my girl? It isn't very nice that you keep silent so much—people might think that you don't know how to talk. Don't you see, when the girls, your friends, come to visit, they banter, they chat and you don't say anything, as if you were dumb. You won't ever find a husband this way," she said, "for the news got around that you are tongue-tied."

Well, Sunday came and there was a dance. The girl dressed up and went along, but the village lads were not too inclined to take a turn with her for she never said a word. They didn't care for her. But there were young men from the neighboring community who invited her to dance and one of them asked her where she lived. The girl told him where her house was.

Said the lad: "I'd like to come to your place."

The girl was happy for no young man had yet come calling and now, God willing, it might happen.

"You may come."

"So," he said, "when you are ready to go home, tell me and I'll go with you."

The girl thought she'd better go ahead to warn her mother that a suitor was coming.

When the lad wasn't looking, she ran home and said to her mother:

"Mother, I found such a handsome young man that there isn't another one like him here, in the entire village. He said he'd come here tonight."

"All right, my girl," she said, "just pay attention and be sure to chat with him. Don't be so dumb!"

"Well, mother, I came to tell you, so you can teach me how to converse with a young man."

Her mother said: "Listen, my girl, when he arrives and greets us, receive him the way we do. Offer him a chair right away and say: 'please sit down, I know you are tired.' Then sit down next to him," she said, "and ask him some questions: 'Why did you come to this village? Are you looking for a girl from here, or why? Have you had a sweetheart before?' Speak quietly so we, the old folks, don't hear you and the lad won't be embarrassed. This is how one chats with a young man, my girl. Then when he leaves, follow him, see him out. And if he asks you whether you want him to come courting, say that if his intentions are honorable he may come, but if all he wants is to make fun of you, if he just wants to come for a while and leave you, then he'd better stay away. This is how, this is the way one talks with a young man," she said. "If he wants to kiss you, kiss him back, show him that you fancy him, too. This is how one talks with a young man."

Well, supper was ready—they ate in a hurry lest the lad catch them in the midst of their meal. The girl washed the dishes quickly and tidied up.

Then there was a knock at the door.

The girl called out instantly: "Come in!"

The lad entered, said good evening, and they, in turn, greeted him. The girl rushed to get a chair and offered it to him:

"Come, sit down, you must be tired!"

He said: "Oh, I am not so tired—I never get tired from dancing."

Said the girl: "I didn't get tired either—I was there, too."

Well, the lad sat down; the girl pulled up a chair and sat down beside him.

"Tell me, how did you come in?"

The young man answered: "Through the gate, how else? I couldn't climb over it."

"But through which gate, the big one or the little one?"

Said the lad: "I wasn't riding in a carriage, I didn't need to come through the big gate, the little one was wide enough for me."

"Did you look in the corner of the gate?"

"Why should I have done that? I just came through, on my way in."

"I am asking because I want to know if you saw the big pile of shit I left there."

Said the lad: "Well, instead of leaving it there, why didn't you gobble it up? I didn't ask you to tell me about that."

The girl's mother was so ashamed hearing her daughter speak this way that she left the house. And the young man leaped up from the chair at once:

"Don't worry, I won't come to see you again, or even your gate. If this is how outspoken you are, you might as well stay by yourself!"

The lad thought the girl spoke to him out of mischief; he didn't know that she had no brains.

When he left, the girl's mother came back in:

"Listen, you! What did you say to the young man? Is this a way to make conversation? This isn't what I have taught you!"

The girl didn't have to wait for the lad to kiss her—he didn't pause at the gate to talk with her. He went as fast as he could and he may still be going.

"You see, my girl," she said, "how you embarrassed that young man. He'll never set foot in here!" She gave her daughter a good thrashing and so did her father.

The girl remains an old maid to this day, unless she has found a fool who asked her to be his wife.

# 32. The Two Brothers

AT1536A *(The Woman in the Chest)*; MNK lists 13 variants. The core element that unites the variants of this widespread international tale is the wandering corpse, fearsome to the believer and comical to the doubter, which has been developed variously in a variety of moral stories, tailored to fit diverse social situations. Mrs. Palkó learned it from her brother János. It must have been in the local tradition long before she told it in 1950; I have heard it from three other narrators later, in the 1980s.

The main problem of the Kakasd version is social injustice, unequal distribution of goods—a relevant issue in Hungarian peasant society. Families were torn apart over the division of inheritance, lawsuits consumed fortunes and ended in bankruptcy. Land distribution among the Bucovina settlers in Kakasd also caused family feuds. This story is not fueled by the moral of the magic tale, which rewards virtue and punishes vice. It is the rich and the poor, the lucky and the unlucky who oppose each other. The children of the wealthy farmer deserve equal shares, no matter how lazy the younger brother, and how hard working the older. As a matter of fact, the younger brother is a potential folktale hero: out of luck, out of wits, poor, rejected by his parents—a ne'er-do-well, driven to gambling and drinking. The description of his pitiful condition sets the stage for the tale justice. The older brother can take care of himself: he has everything. He is the model of frugality, fitting the image of traditional peasants who work with their wives in the field to set an example for their hired men.

As the action begins, we see the younger brother working hard for his brother—he does not fit his initial character anymore. But so humiliated, and with so little, the younger man cannot better himself. As a last resort, he uses his wits: he assumes the role of a trickster, to correct the injustice committed by his parents in turning his sibling relationship into a landlord-servant relationship. Mrs. Palkó knew similar cases, fracturing the strong kinship ties of Bucovina Székelys; she spoke from personal experience when she featured the outburst of the younger brother upon seeing the loaded pantry of his older brother: is this fair? The sly trick that forces justice to prevail draws upon the local belief that people who died with unfinished business will return to the living (see also "The Count and János, the Coachman," above). In "The Two Brothers," Mrs. Palkó rises above her devout, religious worldview and makes the younger brother provide for divine justice, driving his superstitious brother to despair.

Mrs. Palkó describes the wealthy brother's inheritance sometimes as 80 acres large, sometimes as 60—the brother's wife is also said to have brought 60 acres into the marriage. The narrator probably forgot what she said first; her intent was to say that the older brother owned lots of arable land compared to the two acres his younger brother inherited.

———

*There was once a willow tree, right here, on Kopovics Mountain. The willow tree had ninety-nine branches and on the ninety-nine branches sat ninety-nine crows—and if you don't listen to this story, they'll peck your eyes out!*

There was once a well-to-do farmer who had eighty acres of land but only two sons. One of them was very industrious and upstanding—he enjoyed working and managing the farm, but the younger one was a loafer, a ne'er-do-well, who had taken to drinking and playing cards. That's all he ever did. He picked the house clean and depleted their wealth. His father noticed it and one day said to him:

"Son, what will become of you if you don't want to work? Don't you see that everything rests on your brother's shoulders—the stable, the fields—he is always working inside and outside, and you don't want to touch a thing. You just drift and bum around. And I see," he said, "that the flour is dwindling in the sacks and the grain is running low in the attic, all because you are lazing about."

The son answered: "This suits me. I am the younger one, I should be treated with consideration."

"That's fine, my son, but you could also show some consideration for your brother. Make a little effort! He has too much to cope with."

There were stables with cattle, horses, and mares, and there were sheep and cows. The farm was very large so the son thought it could be run like a count's.

Once again the father said to him: "Son, I see that you are not improving, you are becoming worse by the day, all you do is squander a lot of money. I can't condone such behavior. You'll come to regret it for I'll leave everything to your brother and you can go for all I care!"

This made the young man hold his tongue, but he couldn't shed his bad habits. He kept the wrong company and continued his riotous living. He hired musicians, arranged one ball after another, spent heaps of money in the tavern, and lost a great deal playing cards.

Well, the father knew that he was a spendthrift. He was no longer to be his son if all he did was throw money away.

One day he said to him: "Look, son, I give you two acres of land, a wagon with two horses, a cow, a good, fat pig, and you can go and be on your own. I'll even build you a house on the two acres. You may do with it as you please, but if you get into trouble, it will be your lookout. I won't argue with you any more and I'll leave everything else to your brother."

"All right, father, but then I'll take a wife."

"Do that, I don't care, whether you take the daughter of a count or a Gypsy for your wife, it's your business."

So, he had the house built and let his son go. He gave him two horses and a wagon, a milking cow and fat pig for slaughter. All was well, so far.

But the father's farm was so large that herds of pigs and sheep were driven out to pasture. He was a very wealthy man, like a count. His older son worked like a beast, day in and day out.

He said to him: "Son, you are not getting ahead in spite of all your efforts. You ought to take a wife," he said, "a woman could give you a hand and you'd have it easier. Your mother is old, she can't work any more, she could use the help too."

So the son got married. He wed a girl who had sixty acres. She was an only child and had a very rich father. He gave her sixty acres of land and now the farm became even larger. It was a handsome estate, fit for a count. He managed it well, worked hard, hired laborers, and cultivated the land. Nothing was left unattended, he took care of everything. Well, he was a wealthy man.

One day his younger brother said to him: "You could hire me as a day laborer. I can't eke out a living from the two acres, it's not enough. I'll come to work for you and you pay me as you would a stranger."

"I won't pay you the same as I would a stranger. I'll pay you the regular wages and then once again as much," answered the brother, "I see that you are not as well off as I am and I feel sorry for you."

So he went to work there every day and when he returned home, he always carried bagfuls of wheat flour, slabs of bacon, and links of sausages with him.

"Here, take this for your wife. She should have good things to eat, too, while you work here."

And so it went every day. Then the father fell ill and died. He died and the older brother was left alone with his mother. But before he died the father said:

"I entrust you with your mother, my son. Take good care of her and when she dies give her a decent burial!"

"All right, father."

"But don't give anything more to your brother, not an inch, not a foot of land, he doesn't deserve it."

So, the three of them went on living together, the young woman with her husband and the mother. They had a good life and managed the farm well.

One day the younger brother said to his wife: "Well, wife, I won't go along with this any more."

"Go along with what?"

"Working for my brother every day. His father was my father too, not only his, and she is my mother, just as she is his. And I should go on working for him as a day laborer, for wages? It hurts me deeply," he said, "that they made him into a count and paid me off with two acres of land. This is not justice."

"If this is what your father decided, it has to be so. It is stamped and sealed, the property has been divided. You got what he thought you deserved. This is what he gave you, and there is nothing you can do about it."

"But I will do something about it."

One day the older brother said to his wife: "Tomorrow we'll both go out into the field to hoe."

Meanwhile the mother had died, too. She died and he gave her a fine funeral.

He said: "Look, a lot of time has passed since my mother died, since we had her buried and did what was needed. Now the weeds have grown so tall in our cornfield that they are choking the crop. Let's leave everything and go hoeing tomorrow morning."

"I don't mind," she said, "I like to hoe."

So they left, locked the door, and went out to the field. But the younger brother knew where they kept the key. He went there, walked into the pantry and looked around. He saw a roomful of lard, sausages, and ham hanging from the ceiling and bags of wheat flour and bread set out on a bench. And there were at least ten containers filled with fat, lined up in a row.

He said: "Is this fair? Here it is packed to overflowing with all manner of things and I should work as a day laborer to provide for our bare necessities? This must change."

He went and dug up his mother from the grave and at nightfall took her home. The young couple had not yet returned from the field, so he took the mother in the pantry and sat the dead body down beside the door. He placed a container of fat in front of her and put a wooden spoon in her hand. He stuck it between her stiff fingers and lifted it up to her mouth. But he dipped the spoon in the fat first, before bringing it to her mouth, to make it appear that she was eating. He sprinkled wheat flour on his mother's apron then he emptied the bag, leaving a handful at the bottom, and took the rest of the flour home. He also left a spoonful of fat in the container. The container was large, it could have easily held thirty kilos and it was full to the brim. He poured out all the fat and took it with him. When he thought that he had taken enough of everything he left his mother there.

Soon the couple came home. The young woman ran to milk the cows. She made haste, finished milking and carried the full buckets inside, into the pantry, where she kept them. She walked in with the milk and, dear God Almighty, she saw the mother sitting there with the container of fat and eating from it. There was flour strewn about and one bag stood empty, she had eaten it. The young woman rushed to the stable screaming and lamenting.

"What is the matter with you, my dear?"

"Oh my," she said, "your mother came home!"

"Well, where is she, if she came home? She is dead!"

"She is there, in the pantry. There is a container of fat in front of her," she said, "she is eating from it. And the flour is gone from one bag, she only left a little at the bottom."

"Go on, you must have been dreaming! What's wrong with you? What got into you?"

The young man went inside and found that it was really so. He had such a fright that he backed out the door. Seeing his mother gave the young man a shock.

"But she is dead, how is it that she came home?"

He ran to his younger brother who looked very alarmed:

"What happened to you, brother? Why are you beside yourself?"

"How can I not be? Listen, mother came home from the cemetery!"

"We had buried her, for sure."

"She came back from there, from her grave."

"Well, where is she?"

"I'll tell you. She is sitting in the pantry," he said. "She ate a whole containerful of fat—there is barely any left at the bottom—and she emptied a bag of flour and ate that. I haven't yet looked whether she touched anything else. Come with me, I am frightened!"

"All right," said the younger brother. Both went into the pantry and looked around. Well, at least two sausages and two hams were missing as well.

"How could she eat so much? I never heard of the dead eating! She ate like a bird when she was alive. She used to take only a tiny amount, and I would encourage her to have more for one can't live on so little food. What is the matter with her that she consumed all that now?"

"What is the matter with her?" said the younger brother. "This isn't good, to be sure. No it isn't, now I say so myself, it isn't good. Something, or someone, made her come home."

Said the older brother: "Dear brother, take her back and bury her! Bury her once more! I'll give you two acres of land, so you'll have four, just bury her, or *I'll die of despair!*"

"Well," he said, "since she acted this way, I'll take her and bury her. But you must give me what you promised."

"Oh, I wouldn't go back on my word! I'll give you the land with pleasure, just bury her!"

So the younger brother took his mother and placed her in the coffin. But he didn't fill the grave, he left it as it was dug up, he covered the opening only with branches. Then he went home:

"You can stop being afraid of her now, brother."

"Oh, dear Jesus, protect me!"

The very next day he had the surveyor come and measure two acres of land.

"Here you are, dear brother, henceforth you will have the four acres to get by on. May God grant my mother her rest and may she never come home again. May God rest her soul!"

Well, the following day passed and nothing happened. But on the third day the younger brother was at it again. On the third day he took his mother out of the coffin, brought her home and sat her down once more among the bags of flour. He emptied another container of fat, left a small amount at the bottom and smeared some on his mother's mouth and apron. Then he put the wooden spoon into her hand again, as if she were eating, and sprinkled flour all around her.

When the couple came home in the evening and the young woman went into the pantry to fetch the meat she would cook for the next day's meal, she saw the mother sitting there again. She ran out, screaming:

"Oh dear, come quickly! Your mother is back. Come and see, she ate another containerful of fat and a bag of flour is missing! I haven't even looked at the meat yet, whether it is all there, or whether she took some of that too."

Her husband went in and they inspected everything. Some of the sausages were gone and so were buckets of milk and a container of fat. No matter how much one has, if one keeps taking, without adding, the supplies become depleted.

Said the young man: "If this goes on much longer with my mother, we'll be reduced to begging. How can she eat so much? I gave her quite a fine funeral and we had a feast at her wake. In the name of God, I even had masses said for her. What else does she want? Why does she keep coming back?"

He went to his brother and said: "Bury her, my dear brother, for my heart is breaking, I am so afraid. And my wife can't sleep at night," he said, "she wakes up screaming, she is so terrified."

"All right, I'll bury her."

"I'll give you another two acres of land, dear brother, just bury her!"

And that's how it happened. He buried her again, placed her in the coffin and once again he covered the grave only with branches. The following day his brother had two acres of land measured out for him:

"Now you own not two, but six acres of land."

Well, for the next two or three days no miracles occurred. Then he went at it anew and outdid himself.

The older brother bred colts. One of them stood out and was so well trained with offerings of sugar, that it followed him everywhere to get it. He always carried sugar in his hand for the colt, whether it was standing in the stable, going through its paces in the courtyard or grazing, and the colt got used to it. It became so attached to the man that when he went into the field the colt went after him; when he went into the stable, it went after him there. It kept following him for the sugar, so when they went out hoeing, the colt trotted along with them.

"We'd better go hoeing tomorrow," he said to his wife, "there is still a little left to do, but we can finish it comfortably. It is time we got through with the work in the field."

The younger brother noticed them going out to hoe, so he dug up his mother again and brought her home. The people were all in the field, no one could see him. In any case the house was set apart from the village so he took her out of the grave in daylight, bundled her up in a blanket and carried her home. Then he let the colt out of the stable and tied the mother onto its back. He secured her with a wire by winding it around her waist then around the colt's tail, and bringing the wire forward from below, he looped it around the mother's head, so she wouldn't sway back and forth on her mount. He had even put a saddle on the colt and sat his mother onto it, with her legs hanging down. Next he placed the wooden spoon in her hand and let the colt out the gate. As soon as it was outside, the colt knew where the fields were.

The eighty acres they owned formed a single piece, bunched together neatly in a bundle, as it were. Well, the colt knew exactly where the fields lay, where its master would be, so it ran there straightway to find him.

The man was hoeing and after a while when he grew tired he straightened out, leaned on the hoe and looked around. Suddenly he caught sight of the colt running toward him at breakneck speed. The colt was in good spirits for it was always kept in the stable and now that they had let it out, it skipped and pranced as if it were about to jump off this world. The mother was seated on its back. The young man saw her at once:

"Oh, look, my dear wife," he said, "my mother mounted the colt and came after me! Look, how she is threatening me with the wooden spoon!"

The mother held the spoon in her hand and it wavered as the colt pranced, so the son thought she was threatening him.

"Dear God, where can I go? Where can I hide? Who knows what she'll do when she gets here! She'll stamp the soul out of our bodies, or she'll do something else. She is warning us in a way that we'll never forget," he said. "Tell me, where can I run?"

The young woman answered: "Run, anywhere you can, but I can't run. The strength drained out of my legs, I can't do it. Run if you can, but I am not up to it."

The young man looked about to see if anyone was coming their way. The colt was in high spirits—instead of running straight to its master, it galloped to the middle of the field, made a wide turn and only then came prancing up to him. It was feeling frisky and couldn't get enough of running. Meanwhile the man pulled himself together, picked up the hoe and scurried home, as fast as his legs would carry him. He was afraid so he looked back to see whether the colt was following him. When he saw that it had turned in the middle of the field and was coming toward him, he became frightened out of his wits. He ran even faster, made a big mess in his pants, then tripped in his trousers and fell down. He didn't know how to collect himself rapidly enough so the colt wouldn't catch up with him. He jumped up and took off, but he fell at least ten more times before reaching his home. However, instead of going inside, he ran to his brother but no sooner had he closed the gate behind him, than the colt was already there. When he got to the house, he knocked the door down—he didn't take the time to open it, just kicked it in, and he came crashing to the floor, door and all. The brother bolted outside and acted as if he didn't know what had happened:

"What is it, my dear brother? What is the matter? What happened to you? Is someone chasing you, or what?"

He could barely utter a word: "Lock the door, please!"

"How can I? You knocked it down!"

"Then lock the door to the room! Don't let her in, or I'll die on the spot!"

"Let in, whom? Who is pursuing you? Who is after you?"

"Well, my mother mounted the colt and came out to me in the field. And how she threatened me, how angry she was! I don't know why. Dear brother, why do you think she is not leaving me alone?"

He said: "I know why. You see, brother, I didn't want to say anything until now, but I know why mother cannot rest in peace. I know why she cannot rest and why she keeps coming back to you."

"Then tell me why. I'll do anything she wishes as long as she stops returning home. I am terrified of her!"

"Look here. I was our father and mother's son too, the same as you. It would have been right, and God would have ordained it so, that they leave their wealth to both of us, for I was their son just as you were. But, you see, they disposed of me by giving me two acres of land, while they gave you sixty acres. He left me two horses and a cow, while he left you a stable full of cattle and how many mares, draft-horses, oxen, cows, sheep, and pigs! You got everything and I got shortchanged and dismissed. She cannot rest for she hadn't divided the wealth fairly. That's why she is not at peace. Father is resting, you see, and God is punishing our mother. Look," he said, "if you were to divide the wealth evenly between us, mother wouldn't come back any more, for I believe this is why she cannot find peace."

"I'll do it. Tomorrow I'll have the imperial land-surveyor come and I'll ask him to divide the land in two. We'll share the cattle and everything, we'll share even the spoons so I am not left with a single piece more than you. We'll divide all there is nicely, as becomes two brothers, and maybe mother will give up visiting me."

And so it happened. The following day he had the land-surveyor divide the land in the middle.

He said: "One half is mine, the other half is yours."

He returned home and they divided the horses, the mares, the oxen, the cows, the pigs, and the sheep. They even divided the chickens.

So the younger brother went, buried the mother, and covered up the grave. From then on she never returned to the house, she left them in peace.

This is the end of my fable—*run along with it, and tomorrow let them be guests at your table.*

# 33. The Gypsy King

AT 1640 *(The Brave Tailor)*; MNK lists 21 variants. Mrs. Palkó's version contains one single episode (motif K1951.2; AT 1640/V) of this extremely popular international tale. There is only one Hungarian text, told by a Transylvanian Gypsy, that contains the tricks of the Gypsy king (Kovács 1944 II.176-79).

The story belongs to the old Andrásfalva repertoire but it seems to have been latent for some time. Aunt Zsuzsi told it to me in 1959, as she had heard it recently from her son Jóska. József Palkó, himself a good storyteller, informed me that he heard this tale from his grandfather when he was a child, but could only remember this much. The fragment skips the main theme—sham hero wins princess and kingdom by accidentally winning contests—and frames the story of the "Runaway cavalry-hero," placing a Gypsy hero in the center.

Gypsies constitute an ethnic/racial subculture in Hungary. Originally from Northern India, they began to arrive in Hungary in the fourteenth century. Their social and cultural distinctiveness prevented their blending into the mainstream; they often appear as the dupes and numskulls in folktales and anecdotes.

In Mrs. Palkó's story the king is a coward who yields to the insistence of the Gypsy lad, and allows him to take his place because he is afraid of going to war. Here again, the narrator expresses her respect for education. For choosing kingship as career model, it is not enough to don the king's costume: one has to be educated to reach that rank—unless one is prepared to go to war.

Here, as in other folktales, the medieval image of war is presented: the king is up front, leading his army. The two armies meet at the battlefield with their kings in the lead and fight head against head, until only a few of the defeated remain "to tell the tale" (see also "I Don't Know," tale no. 1, above). But the young Gypsy doesn't care; he is too stupid to realize the danger and he desperately wants to see how it feels to be king. As the army is outfitted and follows the king's movements, the soldiers seem to be well disciplined. There is respect and awe for the army: when each soldier snatches a pair of *bocskor*, the vendors don't dare protest. But the Gypsy emerges as a hero for the peace-minded Kakasd audience, remembering their own war-torn motherland. The enemy is defeated without firing a shot, fleeing their proverbial nemesis, the dog-headed Tatars (who also appear in "I Don't Know" and "The Twelve Robbers," tales no. 1 and 19, above)—but this time the Tatars are present only in the imagination, as part of the Gypsy King's ruse. Some of the elements of this satire—stealing *bocskors*, mooning (as in "The Nagging Wives," no. 27 above)—seem to be original inventions.

Mrs. Palkó wasn't sure that I knew what a *bocskor* was, so she interrupted her story to ask me. I did not like her distracting her audience to ask a question from me, the only outsider. But it was a gesture of concern and courtesy: she believed the *bocskor* to be a specific Székely footwear. Actually, it is a commonly known light, heelless sandal, cut from one piece of leather to cover both the sole and top of the foot, and fastened with a string.

————

Once upon a time, far beyond seven times seven lands, there was once a big, adolescent lad, a strapping Gypsy lad, who very much wanted to become king. He was forever sending messages to the king that he wanted to be king himself, that he should let him be a king, too.

Well, what could the king say? He just laughed and chuckled at the foolish ideas of the Gypsy lad. It's not so easy to be king. One doesn't just become king without any schooling! It's not enough to don royal garments and declare that "I am king." He just laughed and chuckled at the thought.

But the Gypsy lad went on sending messages to the king day after day that he would like to become king himself. For however short a time, but he would like to be king, if only to know that he had been king once.

Well, time passed and one day a ruler, an enemy, declared war on the king. He declared war and told him to be prepared, to call up his soldiers and *mobilize* for he was about to be attacked. War was imminent. The king became very distressed but then he remembered the Gypsy lad. He summoned him and said:

"Young man, you'd like to be king?"

"I'd have wanted to be, for quite some time," he answered.

"Well, listen, now I am willing to let you become king. I'll agree to it," he said.

"All right then," said the lad, "With your permission I accept."

"Do you know that you'll have to go to war?" asked the king, "for war has been declared on us."

Now the Gypsy lad became alarmed. He began to think.

The king said: "You can only become king if you are prepared to go to war. And do you know that the king has to be up front in the line of fire? It's not for the army but for the king to be in the lead."

This made the gypsy lad think again. How should he respond?

"Well, I don't mind, Your Royal Highness," he said, "even if I have to go to war; I'll go, as long as I can be king."

"Now then," he said, "here is your chance to be king."

He outfitted the lad, gave him clothes and everything else. Then he sent a message to the army and alerted them that they had to go to war. He *mobilized* the troops.

Soon the army stood ready on the road in front of the royal palace. Only the king was missing. They were waiting for him to come. The *sound of rolling drums and blaring horns* filled the air. The troops stood there, waiting for the king. Well, the Gypsy lad put on the royal attire and mounted the beautiful horse they gave him.

He said: "Great king, I have a request to make of you."

"Tell me, what is your wish, what do you desire?"

"The only wish I have" he said, "is that you should give orders to the troops, for they know you, not me, to be their king. I may be king, but they don't know me, they recognize you as their king. They won't heed my word," he said. "So, I am asking you to order them to do everything I do. What I do, they should do, too. Nothing else, just have them do what I do."

"All right, that's not a great deal to ask," he said.

He spoke to the soldiers: "Listen," he said, "you must look upon this man as you look upon me. He is your king now, your leader. You must obey him and heed every word he says. Since he is king, you must regard him as if he were me. Consider him the same way you'd consider me."

The soldiers accepted and agreed to abide by the king's orders.

Well, they departed. They set forth and they went on and on, through forests and fields, cities and villages until they found themselves . . . yes, in the midst of woods again. The gypsy lad broke off a green, leafy twig from a tree and tucked it in his cap. When the soldiers saw this, each one took a green twig and also stuck it in his cap. Then they mounted their horses and continued on their way. They rode until they came to a large body of water. There was no bridge, no plank for a walkway, and the stream was so wide and deep that the horses couldn't be let into it. The gypsy king pondered for a while. How should they get across? He walked up and down on the bank, thinking, looking, but to no avail—he didn't see anything resembling a bridge, or a walkway, leading to the other side.

Suddenly, who knows what crossed the king's mind, he pulled the green twig from his cap and threw it into the water. The soldiers saw this, and since they had been ordered to do everything the king did and to obey him, each removed the green twig from his cap. He didn't have to say that they should throw them into the water, they pulled the twigs out of their caps and tossed them in. All those green twigs formed a bridge, and on that bridge they crossed over with their horses to the other side. They went across the water. The mass of twigs made a bridge. Well, they reached the opposite shore and continued on their way forward. They came to a big city and within it to a market, where lace-up moccasins, *bocskors,* were being sold. (Do you know what a "bocskor" is? Romanians wear them.) They were selling them in the open market, displayed on tables. (I know how they were selling the *bocskors,* there were oceans of them in Bucovina!) The Gypsy lad saw them and since he was a Gypsy and he loved *bocskors,* he snatched a pair, tag and all, and tucked it under his arm. Seeing this, every one of the soldiers also took one. The *bocskors,* cut and set out in pairs, were lined up on the table nicely, in rows, like books. So each soldier took a pair. The king took one and they did, too, and tucked it under their arm. No one dared to say a word. Jews were selling the *bocskors* but they dared not speak up—after all it was the army. One doesn't pick a fight with the military.

Well, they continued on their way. They went on and on and on, advancing, until they reached another stream. That stream, too, was so wide that it was impossible to cross for there was no bridge. So the gypsy took the *bocskors* from under his arm and threw them in the water. Then the soldiers grabbed the *bocskors* from under their arms and threw them all in. Once again a bridge was formed by the huge number of *bocskors* and they crossed over. As soon as they were on the other side of the river they saw big billows of smoke; the air was so thick with haze that it obscured their vision.

The king said to the lads: "Do you see all that smoke up ahead?"

They said: "Yes, we do."

"And do you know what it is?"

"Some kind of fog," they answered.

"That's not fog, it's dust," he said, "that's where the enemy is. They are coming toward us. Their horses are raising dust," he said, "that's what you see."

The soldiers were startled; they were frightened, to be sure! But they moved on, they didn't stop, they rode ahead to face their opponent. Then the fog lifted. The sun rose in the sky and in the daylight the enemy troops came into full view. All the mist, all the dust had settled. The army facing them edged closer until the soldiers could see each other clearly. Then both armies stopped. The two enemies eyed one another—they glared at each other.

Suddenly, someone from the ranks of the enemy standing opposite them, spoke up:

"Listen," he said, "do you know this army?"

They said: "How could we know it when we haven't had to face it until now? We see this army for the first time, so how could we know it?"

"Have a good look at it," he said, "for these are the *dog-headed Tatars*," said the other, from among the enemy who had come to attack them.

"It's you who had better have a look," the man answered, "for these here are the one-eyed, *dog-headed Tatars*. It's not wise to cross swords with them," he said.

Now why did he say that? Because the Gypsy king had raised himself on his horse, stood on all fours and pointed his arse, his buttocks, at the opposing army. Then all the soldiers turned around on the backs of their horses, dropped their drawers, the trousers they were wearing and stuck out their bare buttocks for the enemy to see.

He said: "Do you know what sort of soldiers these are?"

"How should we know?" they answered.

He said: "These are the one-eyed Tatars. Have a good look at them! They have only one eye, and what a long nose and what a pair of lips they have," he said, "they are man-eaters!" [Mrs. Palkó laughs]. The king had said this. Not the gypsy, he and his army were busy showing their bottoms to the whatnot, the enemy. It was the other king.

Said the enemy soldier: "I only heard about them," he said. "I heard that these one-eyed, *dog-headed Tatars* ate human flesh, they lived on human flesh. It's not good to get into a fight with them. Oh dear," he said, "we'd better turn around and go home. I won't tangle with them, they are the worst. They are evil men!"

And so the enemy turned on its heels and ran away, *not a single soldier remained to tell the tale.*

The Gypsy king, too, turned his horse around and rode off. He went home.

The king said to him: "What happened, is the war over?"

He said: "Yes, it's over."

"Why? Is there no one with whom to do battle?"

He said: "Not a soul is left on the front, they all ran away."

"Did you fire your guns?"

"I didn't hear any shooting," he said, "they ran without us firing a shot."

"How did that happen? What sort of a war did you wage that ended without shooting?" the king asked.

So he recounted what he did. The king shook hands with him, patted him on the back and said to him:

"You are a good man, and you are smart," he said, "to have brought the war to an end without a single bullet."

And so he received permission to remain king, and he continued to take delight in it. After all, he had saved the ruler from the war, for if he had gone, he would have never done the same, and he might have perished along with his entire army. In this manner the war had ended without any fighting.

They are still alive today, if they haven't died.

# 34. Gábor Német

A new folktale type, which follows the conventional line of construction and ideology of magic tales, yet is transposed into an industrial environment. As a career story, it recounts a peasant have-not's ascent to the industrial working class and on to the top: factory ownership in the spirit of the folktale. From the identification of the village, Gálfalva in Transylvania, and from the fact that the actors are given full names, we might presume a popular literary model. In its current form, however, it is a genuine, typically Bucovina Székely construction. Mrs. Palkó learned it from Márton László but she often heard it also from her father, and her brother, János. She liked this story very much and told it repeatedly to neighbors, as on that evening in 1950, the same year that I recorded it from two other women of her generation.

Notably, the spirit of the peasant-tale completely absorbs elements of urban-industrial life. The subject is a worker's ascent; its goal, a poor laborer's empowerment; ideologically, however, the tale fulfills social justice according to old-fashioned patriarchal peasant standards. The story of the factory worker is argued in terms of peasant norms and values. This kind of blend of the rural-agricultural and urban-industrial could not have taken place in Hungary, where farm mechanization was introduced forcibly by the new political system following World War II, transforming peasant life and screening out interest in, and occasions to tell, traditional tales. It seems that stories like that of Gábor Német had their roots in the first encounter of agricultural laborers—in this case, migrant sharecroppers of Andrásfalva—with industrial work in the backward conditions of the Bucovina. This tale became popular among the poor of Andrásfalva, in the neighborhood of the village where seasonal laborers lived during the winter, spending seven months of the year on large estates. This is where Mrs. Palkó's father, brother, Márton László and other prominent storytellers entertained their fellow workers.

The content, viewpoint, commonplaces of Aunt Zsuzsa's version exploit traditional formulas. The pattern of the hero's voyage to the city (from Gálfalva to Budapest)—arrival, job seeking, conversation with the guard, his hiring by the factory owner, the test, the first meal after being hired—strongly resembles the voyage of any adventure-seeking folktale protagonist. The description of the opulence of the factory and the wealth of the owner resembles also the metaphoric wealth of tale kings. The factory owner is the king and the patriarch, generous to his employees. He adopts the hero, becomes his loving father, makes him his heir, conferring royal power on him. Mrs. Palkó's creativity is at its best in this tale, polished by frequent recital. She understands people, their weaknesses and strengths; she is able to describe individuals who characterize themselves as they converse. One can visualize the opposition between the magistrate and his wife, and the hostility of his sisters, that contextualize Gábor's humiliation and departure. The girl has no power, she has to give in. There is no way out, only two alternatives: love or money, happiness or power.

As in so many of Mrs. Palkó's other tales, the hero of "Gábor Német" is an impoverished young man. Poverty in her Székely terms means that he has not inherited land and must make a marginal living by daily hard work; that he is an orphan, alone, without the support of a caring family, parents and siblings. There is no one to pity him, comfort him, serve him a warm meal, and wash his laundry; he cannot even get married. On the other side, the girl is surrounded by a wealthy extended family, dominated by a proud and strong willed father. (The stereotypical wealthy farmer is often depicted as a corpulent, mustachioed man in boots, puffing on his long-stemmed pipe, and when he is nervous, he chews it.) The poor boy came from a good family, had good schooling, and a good trade, but his parents died, and without wealth, his courting the farmer's daughter was socially unacceptable. He was badmouthed for daring to visit the girl in the spinnery. Evidently, in this social hierarchy, lone individuals are ineffective; only the family support system can make them succeed. When Gábor made his fabulous career, it was time to find a wife, as his adoptive father told him. The family has to continue and the son's duty is to occupy the place of the father, nurture him as long as he lives, and then give him a proper burial and pay for masses for his soul's well-being in heaven. Mrs. Palkó explains cheerfully the Galambos family's visit at the factory, where Gábor is now the boss, and the story achieves a perfect recon-ciliation and happy end. But she points out that the magnanimous and forgiving Gábor is now on a higher plane than the daughter of the magistrate. Any royal princess would be happy to become his wife. Juliska's status-equivalent would be a count, not a king: it is Gábor's turn to stoop down to her.

––––––

Once upon a time, in a land far away, beyond the seven seas and beyond the glass mountain, in Gálfalva, there was once a man by the name of András Német. He had a son called Gábor. They were so poor that they did not even have a foot of land, only a tiny parcel on which their small house stood. They were poor but they worked hard and earned their daily bread with their labor. The boy, Gábor, went to school. When he completed the eighth grade, they apprenticed him to a carpenter to learn the trade and the old folks struggled along as best they could.

In their village there was a magistrate. His name was Bálint Galambos. He was such a wealthy farmer that he had a hundred acres of land and only one daughter, whose name was Juliska. The girl was very, very beautiful; her mother and father were truly proud of her.

(Well, let's leave the magistrate now.)

Meanwhile, Gábor's father and mother died and he remained all alone. He had finished his training but didn't have the means to buy the wood-working tools he needed. So he wasn't able to work at home and instead went to the city to serve as an apprentice. There he received a salary. He was a very, very upstanding lad, had learned his trade well and did nice work—he was liked everywhere.

One day he was back at his house; he had buried his mother just a few days before. He was very sad, wondering what would become of him, who would cook for him when he returned home, who would offer him clean clothes, now that he had no one, only the good Lord above him. He was feeling so despondent, he even wept in his sorrow, yet he was a stouthearted fellow. Lost in his thoughts, he was sitting there on a chair brooding when someone knocked at the door.

Gábor said: "Come in!"

And whom does he see? In comes Bálint Galambos's daughter, Juliska.

"Good day to you, Gábor!"

"Welcome, Juliska," he answered.

"How are you, Gábor? How are you doing, all by yourself?"

"Well, you can imagine, Juliska, how I am doing, without a father and a mother. I come home and all I see is four walls."

"That's why I came, Gábor," she said, "to cheer you up. I often think about you at home, how lonely you must be and how time must weigh on you now."

"Well, that's true, Juliska. If only I had a sister who could do my laundry and have a warm meal waiting for me when I come home. But I have no one, only the good Lord above me."

"Oh, I feel for you, Gábor," she said. "I am sorry for you, and I say to you, Gábor, you should take a wife!"

Gábor said: "But Juliska, what have I to offer a wife? This pitiful home? I have nothing, so who would want me? No one, for I am a poor lad."

"Look, Gábor, don't grieve, you have two able hands and you can make a living. Get married, take a wife and you'll have it much easier!"

"Now tell me, Juliska," he said, "whom should I take for a wife? Who would have me, poor as I am?"

Said the girl: "I'll tell you, Gábor. Come to see me in the *spinning-room* and I'll marry you, for you may not believe me, but I love you very much."

Gábor answered: "Don't say that, Juliska. Your father thinks the world of you, and he is right. You are his only daughter and you are wealthy. What would he do if I set foot in your house? He wouldn't even let me say why I came, he would chase me out immediately."

The girl said: "Gábor, don't be concerned about anyone—just come to our house and if my father says something, let him say it. But be sure to come," she said, "for I'll marry you, I want no one else!"

She kept prodding him until the lad agreed to go to her house that evening. Well, he promised and Juliska, happy, covered him with kisses.

"Don't be sad, don't be sad any more!" she tried to comfort him.

Gábor got ready, he combed his hair. He was a very handsome lad, only poor. He went to the house and stopped in front of the door. He hesitated—should he go in or not? The magistrate was so wise and so proud that when he met a poor man he didn't even greet him, nor did he return the other's greeting. Then how could he appear before the magistrate's eyes? Still, he remembered how Juliska begged him to come, how she said she loved him.

"I'll go in, come what may."

First he looked in the window and saw that the magistrate was sitting at the table, alone, smoking a long-stemmed pipe. Juliska and her mother were bustling about in the house.

"Oh, well," he said, "I'll go in after all. There are no strangers present and even if he berates me, if he insults me, no one will hear it."

He knocked at the door.

"Come in," said the magistrate.

Gábor entered: "Good day to you, Mr. Magistrate!"

"Good day," he muttered under his breath, reluctantly.

But Juliska called out loud and clear: "Greetings, Gábor, you came to see us?"

"Yes, I did."

"Well, since you came, I'll bring you a chair, sit down," said Juliska. She stood beside him and asked:

"What do you do, Gábor, now that you are all alone at home?"

The father just listened.

"What do I do? Time hangs a little heavy on my hands, but there is nothing I can do about it."

"Don't be sad, Gábor, you'll take a wife and things will be much better."

Suddenly the magistrate spoke up; he began to grumble sitting at the table:

"Why did you come here?" he said. "What exactly do you want?"

"Well, Mr. Magistrate, I came so that somehow these difficult days would go by more easily. How can they pass, if I don't go anywhere?"

"And you found no other place, you had to come to us? Or, are you perhaps interested in my daughter?"

The lad said not a word.

"Shame on you to show your face in this house! You wouldn't mind having a girl with a hundred acres, would you? Do you see the door through which you entered?" he asked. "Open it and get out!"

Gábor didn't know what to say. He was embarrassed to go and he was embarrassed to stay, for the magistrate continued railing at him.

"Such a wretch, a beggar, a filthy bum, and he dares to come after my daughter!"

Said the girl: "Dear father, don't show contempt for the son of any man. He may be poor," she said, "but he didn't come to us to ask even for a handful of flour, or a glass of milk. He managed without us until now—he didn't die. He may be poor, but he is an honest lad, he has two able hands and he earns his livelihood."

When the magistrate heard that the girl took the lad's side, he became really angry:

"Get out of here, you tramp, you good-for-nothing, you louse—get out of here, or I'll take the gun and blow your brains out!"

Now the woman spoke up.

She said: "What do you want, old man? Do you want to do to your daughter what my parents did to me? Do you want to find someone for her to love, as my father did for me? He made me marry you for your wealth, when I didn't love you even one little bit; they forced me to do it for money! I never loved you and I don't love you today!"

The old magistrate was so angry that the pipe began to tremble in his mouth. He chewed on the pipe stem in his fury.

Said the woman: "I won't permit you to choose someone for her, she should marry whom she loves! I never loved you, I don't love you today! I could never go to a dance with you and have fun, I never found any pleasure in the large farm for I couldn't stand you! This is what you want to happen to your daughter?"

Then someone knocked at the door and they fell silent. They stopped quarreling. The magistrate's two sisters came in, a younger sister and an older sister. They said good evening and the magistrate greeted them. The woman jumped up right away:

"Please, sit down, take a seat!"

But the older sister didn't even bother to sit down, she went straight to Gábor and looked him in the eye:

"Who are you? Are you perhaps Gábor?" she asked.

"I am," he answered.

"So you came to the *spinning room*! Do you by chance fancy Juliska, the magistrate's daughter?" she said. "And you think you are the sort of lad she deserves? Don't even bother to come here any more, son. You'd better leave the way you came, she won't ever be yours!"

Then the other woman went and sat down next to Juliska. The two women sat on either side of her and began whispering into her ears:

"Are you out of your mind? Why did you let this beggar come here? He is not suitable for you, you could have a young man from the city, a real gentleman, any one of them would take you with pleasure. And how many sons of farmers have come here already to court you? You wanted none of them, and now you want to go with this lousy bum, this nobody?"

They continued to fill Juliska's head with such talk until she finally turned to Gábor:

"Gábor, you'd better go home. Don't come here again, not tomorrow, or the day after, and don't even think about me any more," she said, "*I'm not cut from the same cloth as you!* And I don't want to hang a beggar's sack around my neck. The truth is my father won't let me go with you anyway, and I thought it over, too, I am not the right one for you."

Gábor said: "Well, thank you, Juliska, I didn't expect this of you. I had no intentions at all, and never even dreamed of thinking about you in this manner. You visited me, you encouraged me to come to you. Thank you very much, my dear Juliska, for this pleasant parting of our ways! You'll see, God will make it possible for me to find a suitable mate. I am not worried that this won't happen. It's true, I am poor, but I am hard-working—and with God's help, I'll get by—I don't need your father's hundred acres of land."

Deeply ashamed, Gábor went home. He sat down and thought about how scornfully the magistrate had dismissed him—even the girl had treated him with disdain. That night he didn't sleep a wink, he simply couldn't. He decided that since the people for whom he worked owed him money, he would go to the city in the morning to collect it, then he would pick up and leave the village, and no one would ever hear from him again.

When the day broke, that's just what he did. He washed, combed his hair, dressed neatly and went into the city, to the people who owed him wages, and asked to be paid. He slipped the money in his pocket and went home. Then he packed his everyday clothes in a bundle, put the bundle on his back, locked the door with a key and left. On his way he met children in the street who were going to school. They began to call out to him:

"What's going on, Gábor? Were you at the *spinning-room* last night? Have you perhaps set your eyes on Bálint Galambos's daughter? Weren't you ashamed to go there, knowing she had a hundred acres of land? You'd fancy her, wouldn't you? But she couldn't care less about you!"

When he heard that even the schoolchildren knew of his whereabouts the night before, he became so furious, so bitter that he decided to keep going until he found a suitable position and would never think of *Gálfalva* again.

And so he went all the way to *Pest*, to *Budapest*, and there he began to enquire where the furniture factory was located. People explained to him where he should go, they even took him to the gate of the factory and said:

"This is the furniture factory."

He went up to the gate—a guard was standing there. He spoke to him, shook hands with him, and told him what he wanted. He wanted to go into the factory; he was looking for work, he would like to work there.

Said the guard: "Go in, my friend, there is another guard inside, he'll take you to the gate of the other factory, where you have to enter."

So he went in, found the other guard and told him that he was looking for work, having just completed his apprenticeship; he was a good worker and he'd like to find a job.

"Well," he said, "I'd like to speak to the owner of the factory, but I don't know him."

Said the gate-keeper, the doorman: "Wait here, my friend, wait, he'll be out in a moment, he just arrived at the factory. I'll show you who he is and then you go talk to him."

Soon the owner of the factory appeared.

"There he is, go, speak to him!"

Unhesitating, he walked up to him and greeted him politely.

The owner responded: "Well, son," he said, "what's on your mind, what do you want?"

"If you please," he answered, "I am looking for work. I'd like to work here as a carpenter."

"What do they call you? What's your name?" he asked.

"My father was András Német; I am his son, Gábor Német."

"How old are you?"

He told him his age.

"Do you have a certificate, showing that you completed your apprenticeship?"

"I have."

"Well, let me see it."

Gábor gave him the certificate. The owner looked at it.

"Come to the office with me!"

He led him into the office, offered him a chair, and bade him sit down at the table. Gábor laid out his credentials, certificates and various papers from school. All had only praise and good things to say about the lad. The owner of the factory looked them over:

"I see that you are very able," he said, "you'll stay here."

Right away he ordered food and drink to be brought for Gábor and then he said he would show him his place of work. When Gábor had finished eating, the owner of the factory asked him questions, whether he owned any property and so on. He told him how poor they had been; still his father had him trained as a craftsman and now he'd like to earn his own livelihood. The factory owner liked what he heard.

"Come, my son, don't worry—if you like to work, there is plenty to do here."

So, he took him into the factory. When Gábor saw how many people worked there, he felt overwhelmed—there could have been more than two hundred and fifty. He showed Gábor his work-bench.

"Look, son," he said, "this work-bench is yours and the wood-working tools here belong to it. They are for you to use."

In this factory they produced only fine things, beautiful wardrobes, sofas, the best of everything. It was amazing to see how the people worked. They didn't even lift their heads, so absorbed were they in what they were doing. While the owner of the factory was talking to Gábor, in came a schoolboy.

"Please, Sir," he said, "I need a ruler."

"All right, son."

Right away he turned to Gábor:

"Well, son, this will be your first job, make a ruler for this schoolboy."

Gábor took a strip of wood, cut it with a saw, screwed it into the vise and began planing it. In ten minutes it was ready. The owner of the factory watched how Gábor set about his work. He did such a fine job that the owner was really pleased. He handed the ruler to the boy and said to Gábor:

"Now, son, you can start on the rest of the work!"

All the necessary material was there, so he added: "You'll make a wardrobe first."

He showed him a sample, he showed him what the wardrobe should look like. Gábor set to it, he worked so fast that he completed one piece after another. While the others worked on one piece, he always finished two or three. Not only was he fast, his work was beautiful and good.

One day, when he had been there for a year, the owner of the factory called him into his room:

"Well, son," he said, "I am very pleased with your work. From now on you won't touch the planer, although I see you handle it well. I'll appoint you supervisor over the others. That will be your task, to supervise.

He took such a liking to the young man that he shared his meals with him during the entire year; Gábor ate what he ate.

Then he moved him from that position, he was no longer to be a supervisor, but a cashier; he was to pay the workers.

"Son," he said, "I trust you. I see you have a good mind, you'll pay the workers, you'll be the cashier. But I am telling you, my son, pay everyone fairly, not a single penny should be withheld from the workers!"

He spent a year in this position, too. Then the owner called him in once more and said:

"Gábor, my son, do you know what came to my mind? I like all your work—you are fair, you are kind and you are intelligent. So I thought," he said, "since I am growing weaker in body and mind and since I have no children, if you accept, I'll hand the factory over to you and have you manage it for a year. You deserve it, you see, you have the ability to be at the helm. It'll mean less worry for me, but I'll always be here to give you advice."

And that's how it was.

Gábor managed the factory for a year and not a single mistake was made. The workers produced fine work and he knew what to do with the finished product, what material was needed—he knew everything as if he had been born to it.

"Well, son," said the owner, "a year has passed since you have been managing the factory, and now I'd like to transfer it to you altogether. I want you to become the master here during my lifetime and to be in charge not only of this factory but of my mansion and of everything there is here. I have grown old," he said, "and I have had many people work for me but I have never yet been as pleased with anyone as I am with you. Come with me, my son," he said, "let me show you everything!"

First he took him through the factory where he had been working. Then they continued and came to a glass factory. Beyond the glass factory there were iron works and beyond was a textile mill, and so on. There were so many factories that it was terrible; he grew tired just walking through them.

"Look, my son, all this is yours. Come, now I'll show you the warehouses!"

He took him to the place where the furniture was stored, the finished pieces, those they had crafted.

"You see, my son," he said, "this is all yours. All you have to do is sell it, convert it to money."

Then he took him to the glass factory. What beautiful glasses, pitchers, and plates were there, only the finest!

"You see, my son, this is yours, too."

Next they went to the warehouse where the enamel-ware was kept, where the pots and pans were made. It, too, was full of finished products.

"You see, my son, this is yours, too. All this can be sold."

Then he took him to the warehouse where the iron goods were stored, all sorts of locks, hinges, and God knows what else.

"You see, my son, this is yours, too."

Then he led him to the next place which was full of the finest luxury cars.

"You see, my son, this is yours, too."

Then he walked with him to yet another warehouse where the big trucks were stored.

"You see, my son, this is yours, too."

Then they went to the coal depot:

"Well, son, this too is yours."

Then he showed him the freightcars, the small wagons, that carried the finished goods out of the factory:

"Look, son, this too, is yours."

Then he went with him to the clothing warehouse, where the garments were kept, men's suits, finished and unfinished. The warehouse was full, one couldn't move in it.

"You see, this is yours, too. The factory workers buy their clothes here."

He said to him: "I showed you everything here, now you must see the granaries."

He showed them to Gábor. One was filled with wheat, the other with rye, barley, and oats.

"You see, my son, these are all yours. And now let's go to the stables."

They went into a stable and, dear God, what a stable it was! It had two rows of stalls and two rows of mangers throughout. And the mangers where the horses were feeding were made of mirrors—their bottoms and sides were all mirrors. And the horses were so fat they nearly burst, so fat were they.

"Sir, why are the mangers here all made of mirrors?"

Said the owner of the factory: "They are made of mirrors, my son, so the horses can see themselves, they feed better that way. When they see another horse reach for the food, they'll hurry and eat more. They'll have a greater appetite, that's why they are so fat."

Next they went to the mares, there again the mangers were made of mirrors. Then they went over to the colts.

"These are all yours, my son."

And, finally, to the oxen and to the calves, all in their separate barns.

"Well, my son," he said, "all these are yours."

Then he had the notary come and he signed over to the lad everything he owned, his entire fortune.

"Look, son," he said, "while I am alive, I'll be at your side. But from now on I won't have the burden on my mind, the worries, I am leaving them to you. But be good, my son, *don't be harsh to the workers* and don't withhold anything from their wages—*pay them honestly what is owed to them, so you'll be loved by all, not cursed.*"

Gábor answered that it would be so.

"And when I die, don't forget me," he said, "have Masses said in my memory and pray for me."

Gábor promised to do so—even if he hadn't asked, he would have thought of it himself, he said.

"I have one more request, my son, one more thing to say to you. It is my wish that you should marry while I am still alive so that I can see the woman you'll get for your wife and how you'll live together," he said. "Look, son, you can have whomever you fancy, you mustn't fear that someone might reject you. You can even ask the king's daughter and she'd be happy to accept. Anyone would marry you. But, my son," he said, "I still want to show you my cellar." In that cellar were twelve cash-boxes. "You see, my son, this one has the bundles of millions—it is filled with them; that one holds the fifty-thousand notes; the next, the one hundreds; then the fifties, and so on." The twelve cash-boxes were filled with bank notes. Elsewhere stood barrels brimming with gold and silver coins, and God knows what else was stored in those rows of barrels.

"These are all yours, you'll pay the workers out of them. But be careful," he said, "so you won't be cheated. Don't take what belongs to others, but don't let anyone take what is yours!"

Then he said: "My son, choose someone you like and take her for your wife."

Gábor said: "How should I address you? 'Father'—or the way I did until now? I believe you deserve to be called my father. I want to say that there is someone I have chosen, if she hasn't married in the meantime, if she is still a maiden."

"Who is it?" he asked.

"In Gálfalva, the daughter of Bálint Galambos, Juliska."

He said: "Well, my son, if you love her, if you choose her, propose to her and take her for your wife. I have no objections."

"Then I'll write to her quickly to find out whether she is still a maiden."

So he sat down on the spot, took a pencil and paper and wrote her a beautiful letter, if she was alive and not married, she should answer him. Better still—she should come and bring her mother and father. "For I believe" he added "he will no longer sling mud at me when he sees my present situation."

When Juliska received the letter and learned that he was alive, her heart nearly stopped beating, she was so overjoyed. She had had many suitors, one more desirable than the other, but she didn't want any of them—she kept grieving for Gábor. And in her sorrow she became so emaciated that she was only skin and bones.

Said the woman to her husband: "What do you think, Bálint? Should we let her go?"

"I don't care what she does. All along you have been quarreling with me, saying that it was my fault our daughter grew so thin for she loved Gábor deeply and I had denied her. Now go ahead, do what you want."

"It's not like that," said the woman, "now it's quite different. Gábor writes that we should go, too, so we can see what his situation is. If we let her go, then we should go with her."

She added: "We have enough money for the train and it would be worthwhile to see Pest and look around."

So the three left together. When they arrived in Pest they inquired about the factory, but they thought that Gábor was there only as a worker. Some policemen showed them the way and the gate through which they had to enter. There was a guard at the gate then, too, and they asked him whether they could go in.

He asked them: "Why do you want to go in? What do you want?"

They said: "We'd like to know whether Gábor Német is in this factory."

"Gábor Német?" asked the guard.

"Yes, we came to see him, we'd like to speak to him."

"Oh," said the guard, "Gábor Német is the boss here. He became so important that I'm not sure whether you can speak to him or not, he has risen to such a high position."

"What do you mean?" they said. "Are you joking with us?"

"I am not joking," he said, "he is the boss of this factory. You may go—there is another gate-keeper inside, he'll help you."

So they entered, found the other guard and asked him if they were allowed in to speak to Gábor Német.

"Wait," he said, "let me telephone inside. They'll tell me whether you may be admitted or not." He telephoned, then spoke again:

"And what do you want? He is not referred to as Gábor Német, but as the owner of the factory. He is now addressed as 'Sir.'"

Bálint still couldn't believe it. Then the message came back over the telephone that they should be permitted to enter.

So they went in, but Gábor didn't come out right away to meet them. He remained in his room and the old factory owner came to greet them instead. He asked them what they wished, why they had come.

They answered: "We'd like to speak to Gábor Német."

"Gábor is now an important gentleman," he said, "but I'll ask him to see you and find out what you wish."

The old man knew well who they were. Meanwhile Gábor got dressed inside, then came out to them. He had turned into such a fine looking man, he was so, so, so beautiful that it was impossible to describe how beautiful he was; he wore gold rings, encrusted with diamonds, on all of his fingers.

When he stepped forward and shook hands with them and when the girl saw Gábor, *she wet her pants*, so overcome was she with love and joy at seeing what a splendid man Gábor had become.

"Well, my dear Juliska," he said, "I couldn't believe that you were still a maiden. But you waited for me—and although today I could find someone more suitable than you—for your father had hammered it into my head enough that *you were not cut from the same cloth as I*—today I could say the same. While it is still true that not only the wealthiest landowner, but the son of a minister would ask you to be his wife because you have a hundred acres of land, I can tell you that even the king's daughter would marry me gladly, if I proposed to her now. But I remembered that you were not ashamed to come to me and comfort me when I was all alone, grieving and mourning, and you said that you had loved me since we were in school together. I remembered all that. I am not taking you for my wife for your hundred acres, or for your father's honor, but because I feel sorry for you. I have no need of him even if he had another hundred acres of land. Look, my dear, what you see here around you, all the factories, the warehouses, the stables, the beautiful mansion, all this belongs to me."

For the time being he didn't even mention what was inside.

"Still, I don't think of myself as lofty and choose you for my wife. Yet what is your fortune today compared to mine? Your father has held you high," he said, "as high as the stars, with his hundred acres! But we'll forget that now," he said. "Your father and mother may return home, if they wish, or if they prefer to sell their possessions and live near you in the same city, they are welcome here—but you are mine!"

Then he asked the old factory owner for his opinion, whether he would give him permission to wed the girl.

"I told you already, my son, you may choose whomever you love, I don't mind."

So they got married right away. The old folks went back home, sold their holdings and came to live in Budapest with their daughter. The young couple lived together like *two turtle doves*, so beautifully. The old factory owner died soon thereafter. Gábor had him buried with great pomp and had a Mass said for him and his wife every single day. This he never forgot.

They are alive to this day, if they haven't died.

# 35. Margit

This narrative mirrors the bleak and hopeless conditions of Bukovina agricultural laborers prior to World War II. It may originate from pious reading materials dispensed by the Roman Catholic Church, but it is more likely that true conditions inspired it. During years of drought and economic depression, masses of farmworkers lost their jobs and means of existence.

Mrs. Palkó referred to Márton László as her source for this tale, although she herself lived through similar hardships. Her recital expresses her heartfelt compassion; nevertheless, her narrator's tone here, dealing with everyday events and common people, is very different from that of her consciously crafted, aesthetically pleasing traditional tales.

In this story, tragedy visits a good family. Many children means God's blessing in Bukovina Székely terms; six to eight children in a family is normal, and ten is no rarity. Margit had pride, but she should not have bragged—she brought the wrath of a cruel society upon her family. The wealthy can save provisions for hard times, but what do the poor do in a hostile world where no one helps? God gave too much rain in the spring, and Whitsun (50 days after Easter) was too late to begin plowing, to promise a harvest. Let the family starve to death? The poor man cannot live with his conscience for stealing; he repents, sells his winter coat to buy enough bread to stuff the mouths of the crying children for two days.

Aunt Zsuzsi's "happy ending" is that the man confessed his sin to the priest and was forgiven, not that the family was saved from starvation. As long as the sack of bread lasted, "they remained alive," she said, "but God only knows what became of them once they had no bread left." Tape recorded in 1950.

---

Once upon a time, beyond seven times seven lands, there was a poor man who had a beautiful wife. They were a young couple but by the time they were married for seven years they had thirteen children. Twins were born to them every year and they were all diminutive, tiny.

The poor man went to work every day. He provided for his family with the labor of his two hands. Well, the poor man went off to work and the woman stayed home. It was a hot summer day. She gathered her children and took them out to the side of the road under the windows, and settled down with them. Two were nursing at her breasts and the others played around her.

Soon an old woman came down the road toward her. She knew Margit.

"Good day to you," she said.

"Good day to you, too," responded Margit.

"Tell me, Margit, are all these children yours?"

"Sure they are," she said. "I have three boys and ten girls; three boys and ten girls."

Said the old woman: "Oh, Margit, that's too many!"

"Too many for you, but not for me. For me they are not too many," she answered.

Said the old woman: "Really, Margit, for you they are not too many?"

She said: "Really not, for God gave them all to me."

The old woman said: "But, my God, how do you provide for them? You are poor, you have no land or anything else."

The woman said: "What we have is hand-to-mouth, but we eat every day. There is just enough to go around."

"Margit, how can you support all these children?"

She said: "I am not worried—we have two pairs of able hands, my husband is hard-working, he brings money home every night, that's how I provide for them. My husband loves his children. When he comes home, he picks them up one by one and smothers them with kisses. He kisses me too, and then I know what he wants."

"All right, Margit, you speak with pride, but just wait and see. Go on spending and spending, I only hope you won't come to regret it!"

With those words the old woman left, very angry. Margit picked up her children and went inside. She wouldn't sit in front of the gate any more, she thought, for she could see how annoyed the woman was. Even if she felt some gleeful pleasure, she wouldn't sit outside the gate again. When her husband came home in the evening, she complained to him:

"Listen to what happened to me!"

"What happened?"

"I sat by the gate with my children when an old woman came by. She greeted me and I responded. Then she said: 'Tell me, Margit, are all these children yours?'

"'Sure they are,' I said, 'they are all mine.'

"'Oh, my dear Margit, so many children in such a short time!' she said.

"'Too many for some, but not for me, God gave them all to me.' Then I said that I had a good husband, who brought money home every night, who loved his children and kissed them one by one and kissed me too, and then I knew what he wanted.

"'Well,' said the old woman, 'just go on spending and spending, Margit, but don't regret it later!' Then the old woman left and I came back inside, but all day long I couldn't forget the words she had dropped into my lap."

"Don't worry, wife, as long as God grants me good health, I'll provide for them."

Well, that winter they managed somehow but in the spring it started to rain and rain and rain. It rained incessantly so it was impossible to plow and sow. They became very alarmed. Around Whitsun the rain stopped and the soil was dry enough for them to begin plowing. But by then it was late. They planted potatoes and corn and those who had some, sowed barley, but everyone was late. Thereupon followed such a drought that everything burned up, it was so severe. With no rain, and all the drought, the soil became parched; nothing grew, nothing of what was planted. Everything withered.

That summer there was no crop. Such misery set in that the poor died of starvation. The rich farmers got by, for they had crop stored away and, in addition, they had cattle. Once they used up their grain, they took the cattle to another region and sold it. They may have had to pay a lot, but they could buy food and had enough to eat.

But Margit's family had nothing, no money saved, no grain stored. They hadn't the means to do it. The children were famished—they hadn't had a morsel to eat in three days. *They wailed and shrieked like organ pipes*, so hungry were they, and there wasn't anything in the house to offer them.

Said the man: "Do you know what, wife? I'll go over to those wealthy people for whom I had worked," he said, "maybe they'll have pity on me. One of them may give me a piece of bread, the other something else and we'll plug the mouths of all our hungry children."

He brought out a sack and left. He started at one end of the village and went into every house. And every single person said the same: "why should I give you anything? You didn't have to have so many children; this wasn't necessary. You could have avoided it. And Margit was so haughty when someone suggested that you had too many children."

"Well, if they are not too many for you," said the old woman, "then provide for them now." And no one in the whole village gave him even one slice of bread. All said they shouldn't have had so many children. The old woman had bad-mouthed Margit to everyone for having said that she didn't believe she had too many children, that she had a hard-working husband who provided for them. So now no one had pity on her.

The poor man went home in great sorrow. The children were screaming and wailing, begging for food—his heart nearly broke, he was so sorry for them. The woman had grown weak, she hadn't eaten for many days. She was so weak, she was barely able to speak.

"Well, there is nothing else I can do," said the man, "I'll go into town, maybe I'll get work there, cutting wood for the rich folk."

He used to go to work there, he used to get work cutting wood. So he went into the town this time again. He started at one end and finished at another. Everywhere he was told that they couldn't use a laborer, that food was scarce and the money that would pay for labor was now needed to buy food. They didn't need workers—what had to be done they did themselves and they were not hiring anyone by the day.

So, he didn't receive a penny there either. Sick at heart he walked by the rows of stores, and strolling along he wondered what he should do. How could he go home to face all those crying children?

He thought to himself: There is nothing else for me to do—I'll go to the end of the world, but not home! I'll go away forever, but I won't go home! My heart would break if they died of hunger before my very eyes.

As he battled with his conscience and racked his brains in front of a store, he looked up and saw a sign. The writing on the sign said, in red letters and even gold letters, that here resides the finest, most learned, master gold clock- and watch-maker.

He thought to himself: If he is working with gold clocks and watches, he is playing with money. I'll go in—who knows, perhaps he'll give me a little money, since he is handling gold, so I can buy at least one loaf of bread to take home.

He entered into the store and said: "Good day to you!"

"Good day," answered the watchmaker.

He was busy working on some watches. The walls all around were covered with clocks. The big ones were on top, beneath them were the smaller ones, then came the smallest and at the bottom were the pocket watches. All were made of gold. Their glitter was dazzling. When the man stepped in, the watchmaker, who was working with an apprentice, turned to him and said:

"What can I do for you?"

Said the man: "For me? Nothing." He felt ashamed to ask for a hand-out, he was bashful. Embarrassed, he didn't dare to ask. Instead he said: "I came to you because I have an American gold watch, it is broken and needs repair. Could you take care of it?"

He answered: "All right, why don't you bring it in ? Or do you have it with you? If you bring it, I'll inspect it and if it can be repaired, I'll find a way to do it, just bring it in!"

The man moved away and stood against the wall. The watchmaker had his back turned to him as they spoke:

"When will you bring it?"

"Tomorrow," he answered.

Meanwhile he secretly lifted a pocket-watch off the wall and slipped it into his pocket. A small pocket watch it was.

"Fine, then I'll bring it tomorrow, if you can fix it."

"Well, I'll look it over," he said, "and I'll repair it."

So the poor man left but he was so frightened that he didn't know what to do, lest they discover the missing watch and have the constables arrest him. Then his family would die of hunger, for sure. He started running but feared that someone would notice that he had stolen something. He continued walking briskly, in one street and out the other, so that he couldn't be trailed, in case someone wanted to follow him. Meandering through the town he came to the other end and there he saw a blue sign, saying "bakery."

"Oh," he said, "I'll go into this bakery, pawn the gold watch and buy some bread."

He entered: "Good day to you!"

The baker responded: "Good day!"

Said the man: "Look, master baker, I came to you for I have a gold watch which I'd like to leave as security for some bread, and if you wait a few days I'll be back to redeem the gold."

The baker took the gold watch, looked at it and saw that it was an expensive one.

"I'll give you bread in exchange," he said.

Said the man: "But I must tell you right away, don't sell it to anyone, for I'll redeem it myself."

He filled the sack he had brought with him to the top. Well! He put it on his shoulders and set out for home.

When he got there he found them all so weak, they couldn't cry or speak any more. The poor little, innocent children were already in the grip of death. The woman was better able to withstand hunger but the children couldn't bear it. Their father went up to them:

"Here, my dear children, I brought you some bread."

He pulled out a pocket knife and sliced the bread into a big heap on the table. The children grabbed what they could—he barely managed to keep up with the slicing. They ate and ate until finally they had their fill. There was enough bread left for the next day.

Said the woman: "Where did you get bread, my dear husband?"

"Well, God helped me, but in the end I don't know if he will punish me for it. Do you know what, wife? Find me my winter coat, I'll take it to the market in the morning and sell it."

"Oh, no you won't," she said, "you won't sell it! You would be left without anything to protect you, to put over your shoulders when frost sets in! What are you thinking? That's all you have, and you want to sell it?"

"I do, wife. Who knows what will happen by autumn. I may be dead of hunger. I don't know whether I'll live that long or not. I'll sell the coat now because I must."

"Why? What do you want?"

"Look," he said, "I stole something and it weighs on my heart. I never took anything that belonged to someone else, not even a needle. I never touched as much as a needle that wasn't mine, and now what have I sunk to! I stole a gold watch and I will not carry the burden on my soul to the hereafter. I want to redeem it. I'll sell my winter coat, redeem the watch and return it."

The woman had no choice—she gave him the coat and the man took it into town, to the market. It was a fine coat, it caught everyone's eye. They bought it for little money for when a man is in dire straits he has to accept half-price for what he sells. He sold the coat and went back to the baker. He said to him:

"Do you have my gold watch, master baker? Let me have it, please, I brought money." He paid for the bread, redeemed the gold watch and had enough left from the price of the coat to get another sackful of bread.

He said: "Master baker, would you be kind enough to let me leave the sack until I return?"

"Why not? There is room here. But where are you going?"

"I am going to church. I heard the bells toll as I came here," he said, "I'll attend Mass."

"Go ahead," said the baker, "you can leave the bread, you'll find it here."

The poor man left and went to church. Other people were on their way, too—he wasn't late. He went in and attended the Mass. Then the priest stepped into the confessional and began hearing confession. When Mass was over the people streamed out and those who wanted to go to confession remained. He walked over to the priest, to the confessional, and whispered that he wanted to confess.

"All right," said the priest, "kneel down!"

"But I don't want to confess here. I am a little deaf and I wouldn't like other people to know my sins."

The priest said: "Then come to the sacristy, I'll hear your confession there."

"No, that's no good either," he said, "for the boys are coming in and out. My sin is so great that I don't want anyone to be a party to it."

"Well, what should we do? Come to the rectory!"

There he was willing to go. The priest walked over to the rectory—the poor man followed him and confessed. He confessed that he had committed a great sin, he had stolen something. He also told the priest what drove him to stealing.

He said: "Never in my life have I stolen anything from anyone, not a blade of straw, and now I had to steal a gold watch to save my children from dying of starvation. But," he said, "Father, I redeemed the watch from the baker and now I'd like to return it, but I am afraid to do it."

"Return it, good man, go ahead, return it! Don't let it weigh on your soul! You admitted it, you paid for it, so give it back. And now you may partake of Holy Communion. You did the right thing to have confessed it, so you don't carry the sin on your conscience."

Well, they went, the poor man received Holy Communion, and when they came out of the church, he said to the priest:

"Father, please return the watch for me. I don't dare to go there. If he is a treacherous man, he'll hand me over to the constables. Even if I return it, he may still deliver me to the constables and they'd lock me up. What would happen to my family then?"

"All right, I'll do it. I'd be glad to take the watch back—just tell me from which shop you took it."

He said: "It's written above the door that here resides the finest gold watchmaker."

"I know where it is. I'll take the watch and you just stay put here until I return."

"I'll stay, I promise," he said.

So the priest went and found the sign above the door. There was the shop. He heard such a racket and screaming from inside that it was terrible. What was going on? Should he go in or not? He saw that someone was being pummeled and beaten. He looked again, what was going on? Then he entered and saw that two constables and the watchmaker were hitting the young apprentice so hard that the blows resounded. Blood was streaming from the boy's nose and mouth.

The priest entered and said: "What are you doing? What is going on here?"

"Listen, Father! So far nothing has ever disappeared from this shop and now a gold watch is gone from the wall. No one else could have taken it but he, that's why I am beating him," he said. "He is denying it, he says he didn't do it. The constables came to interrogate him but he wouldn't confess—the questioning was to no avail. His mother came and brought him a change of clothes. She is here, waiting. When she saw me beating the boy, she started blustering that I'd better stop, that her son wasn't the kind to steal, she knows that because she has raised him—she said. She didn't teach him to steal, she taught him just the opposite, and the boy shouldn't be beaten for he is inno-cent. Someone else may have done it, but not her son. If he had stolen the watch, he would have said so by now, with all that thrashing."

Then, to make matters worse, the constable attacked the woman and slapped her in the face. She deserved it, not the boy, he said, if she had no husband to teach him. There was no mercy.

"Now," said the priest, "stop beating the boy, for I say that he is not at fault. He is innocent."

"So who could have done it?" asked the watchmaker. "You were not here to take it."

"But I brought the watch back. Here it is," said the priest, "the boy is innocent."

"How could you have the watch? You were never here before!"

"Well, listen to how it happened. It's thanks to an honest confession that the watch turned up. Someone was here yesterday," he said, "who claimed to have an Ameri-can gold watch that needed repair. Do you remember?"

"Sure, I remember," he answered.

"That poor man stole the watch. But he is not to blame for he did it out of necessity. He has so many children," he said, "thirteen small children and they had not a bite to eat for five days. They were wailing and shrieking of hunger, like organ pipes. What could he do? He went all over town looking for work but he couldn't find any. He had to steal. Today he came, he had sold his winter coat and redeemed the watch. He came to me, confessed and sent the watch back with me. He was afraid to return it himself lest he be arrested by the constables."

Well, the watchmaker took the gold watch, and the constables said that the poor man should be left alone. He did the right thing by returning the watch; he was an honest man to have sent it back. So the poor man was forgiven, yet he wasn't even present. The priest went home to the rectory and told him that he could go now, there wouldn't be any trouble.

"I returned the watch, but that poor boy received quite a thrashing. They suspected him of stealing it. Still, in the end it all got sorted out."

The poor man went home with the sack of bread and while it lasted they remained alive, but God only knows what became of them once they had none left.

They are alive to this day, if they haven't died.

# Glossary

## Terms, Special Meanings, Concepts, and References

Bloodstopping with vinegar: common home remedy (as in tale no. 8).

*Bocskor:* light heel-less footwear, cut from one piece of leather, like a moccasin, fastened with a leather string.

Call to arms: in Mrs. Palkó's tales, declarations of war, troop mobilizations, and military recruiting mix medieval, feudal, and modern village communication concepts with the latest technology. The king receives a war declaration from the enemy by telephone, telegram, or letter; then, "the bugles are sounded," "trumpets and horns begin blaring," "drums are rolling," and the soldiers, headed by the king, line up in their uniforms to go to the battlefield and meet the enemy face to face.

Capital city: the town where the king has his residence.

Child: always means a male child.

Cleaning the lamp: as in tale no. 30 refers to a petroleum lamp.

Corpus Christi flower carpet: in preparation for the Mass at the feast of Corpus Christi, villagers strew flowers along the route of the procession to the church. Mrs. Palkó noted the similarity of this ritual decoration to the "flower carpet" created by I Don't Know in destroying the royal garden (tale no. 1).

Dowry: trousseau, including clothing, linen, and woolen goods, that girls prepare for themselves. It is their responsibility to grow the hemp, prepare the linen and the sheep's wool yarn, spin and weave, sew, and embroider. The dowry is essential for the household of a newlywed couple.

Execution: in magic tales, antagonists are punished according to the most cruel methods, many of which mirror actual medieval practices: impalement, burning at the stake, breaking at the wheel, burying or walling-in alive, or dragging the condemned, tied to the tails of horses, to death. Mrs. Palkó, compassionate as she is with innocent victims of murderous attacks, likes to set an example by having villains annihilated publicly. After the execution, the remains of the evil perpetrator (and all members of his or her family) are cut into four pieces, nailed to the four city gates (east, west, north, and south), and then shot down from the gates, burned to ashes, and thrown into the wind to be dispersed.

Forint: name of the Hungarian currency since 1948.

Glass mountain: a folktale image, a hard and slick, sparkling, crystaline mountain that cannot be scaled or penetrated, only flown over on the back of a magic horse. It is also a marker between this world and the world of the magic tale, mentioned in opening formulas (as in tales no. 7, 8, 18). It also appears in impossible tasks, as when the prince must jump over the mountain to catch the apple which the princess has thrown.

Godparents: the system of godparenthood contributes significantly to the welfare of Bukovina-Székely society. At baptism, godparents—a primary couple and often several secondary and honorary couples—make the pledge to take responsibility for their godchildren if the parents cannot. Families are large: within three generations, as many as 150 to 250 blood and affiliate relatives share or cross godparentship with each other. An average couple baptizes sixty to one hundred children: a huge undertaking and an enormous responsibility, but one that offers security in a society where no health, disability, retirement, or death benefits are offered.

Hemp gathering: "Fairy Ilona" (no. 20), Mrs. Palkó's version of AT 707 (*The Three Golden Sons*), begins with three village girls gathering hemp from the waterhole for the yarn they are going to process and spin. Their minds are on their future: marriage, which will follow once they have assembled their dowries. Nice, dutiful, domestic girls think big: the handsome prince is a bachelor, what would they do for him if he came forward as a prospective suitor? Of course, they are just dreaming, half-joking when the prince overhears them.

The Hungarian Way (*magyarosan*): Peasant Gagyi (tale no. 15) is an unpretentious self-made man. Even after becoming a wealthy farmer, he likes to express himself in plain words, *magyarosan*, the Hungarian way.

Hussar (Hungarian *huszár*), "strides like a hussar": a soldier in the light cavalry. The hussar division of the Hungarian army distinguished itself during the warfare against the Ottoman Turks, who occupied Hungary from 1526 to 1669. Later in the seventeenth, and also in the eighteenth, centuries, hussar companies served as complements to the heavy cavalry of European forces. The hussar is a stock character in Hungarian folktales and legends.

King: the image of the king in Hungarian folktales is feudal and patriarchal. He is an absolute ruler, a powerful landowner and farmer who hires his servants and supervises their work but socializes only with his equals: the royalty of neighboring countries. As a loving and righteous father of his subjects, he rewards and punishes; but he is also an old man, dependent on the help and loyalty of his children. The king's image has military overtones: his attire is like that of a high-ranking eighteenth-century army officer, full of glitter, bright colors—gold, red, and blue—shiny boots and spurs, a *csákó* (shako: a cylindrical, shielded tall soldier's cap, worn by hussars until the end of World War I), and a sword. His entourage is also military. All males in his household—boys, envoys, footmen, attendants, guards, house servants—are also soldiers. The visual image of royalty has been influenced by fairytale storybook illustrations since the second half of the nineteenth century.

Kissing hands: respectful greeting of older relatives, social superiors and women; common as a Hungarian greeting custom.

Opening and closing formulas: complex folktales in European tradition consist of three parts. The main story is told by storytellers as fiction; therefore, to lead the audience from everyday reality into a fantasy world, an introductory story (opening formula) is told. After the main story comes to its end, a concluding third story (closing formula) is told, to lead the audience back to the real world. The opening and closing formulas, framing the narrative, are short, humorous, rhythmic, often rhymed, resembling a lying tale, full of absurdities, teasing and provoking the audience, using rough language. From the "Once upon a time, there was . . ." to the "They lived happy ever after," there is a great wealth of international tale formulas available to storytellers who use them as their taste and wit dictate. Mrs. Palkó is not consistent in applying formulas like some of the great male storytellers are. Sometimes she begins without a formulaic introduction; other times she starts with the plain, conventional "Once upon a time" and ends with "they are still alive if they have not died"; and sometimes she makes quite original choices. In the opening cadence, the distance between this world and the tale world is stressed. "Beyond seven-times seven lands," "beyond the seven seas"; "beyond the glass mountains, and even farther"; "Where the curly tailed pig snorts," or "plays" or "digs"; and "beyond the clucking and pecking of nine turkeys and the paces of a hundred lice." The distance may be only a put on, a joke, because the cited Mountain of Kopovics (tale no. 32) is clearly visible from Andrásfalva. It is the place where evil spirits take people who are out on the streets during the forbidden hours, between midnight and one o'clock. There is the "willow tree with ninety-nine branches, sitting on each ninety-nine crows" that warn the audience to cooperate: "If you don't listen to this story, they will peck your eyes out." The closing formula is even more personal: "Here is the end, run along—tomorrow they will be your guests"; "Tomorrow they'll be Lajos's guests"; "They live or they die, they all dump on the audience"; and "If you don't believe it, go find out for yourself."

Orphan: the lowly hero and heroine has no family and no property, is completely left to his or her wits and hard work to survive. The term "orphan" is often used by Mrs. Palkó to refer to a young person with one living parent.

Oven: a white-washed baking oven in village homes is surrounded by a bench-like wooden apron upon which family members sit or rest and sleep after working hours. The dry steam of the straw- and cow manure-heated oven was believed to heal common colds and body aches.

Paved Road: highway. "Imperial highway" (where the Emperor travels).

Peasant (also "looks like a peasant"; "I won't look like a peasant once I am cleaned up": "coarse, peasant-like appearance"): the false queen who substitutes for the banished heroine, looks sunburnt, coarse, rough, uncouth, compared to the pale, golden haired princess (see, for example, tales no. 6 and 15).

Pigs marching: swineherding is one of the preferred occupations of lowly tale heroes. While the pigs are grazing, the swineherd plays the flute, teaches the pigs how to walk the military way, and how to dance to the tune—a common feature in tales (for example, tales no. 14 and 22).

"Praise the Lord!" "For ever, Amen!": traditional formal greeting exchanged between a Roman Catholic priest and his parishioners.

Ranks, occupations, and classes: Folktale society is hierarchical. At the bottom layer are poor peasants, with little or no land or property, owning too little to make a living. There are also herdsmen, and fishermen. Craftsmen include millers, wheelwrights, smiths, carpenters, and cabinetmakers, who may become prosperous if they are hard working and ambitious, but who are vulnerable to economic disasters. Also in economic trouble are wealthy farmers who inherited land but went bankrupt because of crop failure and too many children. The innkeeper, the traveling salesman, the discharged soldier are marginal transients, so is the Gypsy, more miserable even than a poor peasant. Above peasant society is the nobility, born with title, inherited land and power: the county squires, counts, barons, princes—and the king at the top. High rank can be won by the poor folktale hero: he can buy a farm, a flower garden, and a luxurious castle if he comes into the possession of money; he can become a count by acquiring the estate of a count; he may even become a king. But he can easily lose a kingdom if beaten by an enemy, by intrigue or mismanagement. There is a special career model in the folktales of the Székelys: that of the priest. Any gifted poor child can become a priest by going through school; the hero can rise in rank from parish priesthood to bishophood or even the papacy, as in "András Kerekes" (tale no. 13).

Revolver, six- and twelve-shooters: common in adventure tales, perhaps inspired by Western novels (see, for example, "The Turk" [tale no. 23]).

Revolving castle: A wandering tale hero often encounters a magic advisor living in a hut that revolves on the foot of a duck, a chicken, chicadee, or turkey. The dwelling stops revolving to allow the boy to enter and receive advice. But at the end of the long quest, there is a gold castle, suspended from the sky by gold chains, that revolves speedily on a rooster's spurred heel that is impossible to stop. Only the hero knows how to throw his ax so that he can make his entry and accomplish his goal: capturing the elusive fairy, disenchanting the princess, rescuing the king's stolen daughter, or liberating his bride lost by deceit. This motif, known in Hungarian folk tradition, has been traced to the ancient shamanistic world view of the Uralic and Altaic people, and has also been found in the tales of Hungary's East European neighbors (see, for example, tales no. 14, 15, and 19).

Schooling: Illiterate Zsuzsanna Palkó had great respect for education. From early childhood, her heroes excelled in learning. They loved to go to school, they respected their teachers and learned how to read and write, how to converse politely with adults; they particularly liked history and could tell stories and give witty speeches. The forsaken queen in "The Twelve Robbers" (tale no. 19) gave a superb education to her golden-haired son, preparing him to become her spokesman. Some of the heroes were sent away for higher education and acquired wisdom from wise men, priests or wealthy sponsors.

Shako: *csákó* ( see King).

Spinning, spinnery, spinning-room: traditional women's work and workplaces, sites of traditional courtship and entertainment activities. Until the first decades of the twentieth century, village women gathered according to age and neigborhood groups to spin their yarn from hemp. During the winter months this dull, manual work provided occasions for get-togethers, singing, dancing, play-party games, and storytelling. Welcomed as visitors, husbands and boyfriends dropped in during the evening hours to participate in the merrymaking (see, for example, tales no. 4 and 34).

Suba (Hungarian, *Shuba*): long fur cloak for men, made from the long-haired Hungarian sheep. With the fur inside, plain subas were made of five to seven skins; the fancier, embroidered holiday wear required 12 to 24 skins (tale no. 15).

Smoking Kalfakter: the devil, a troublemaker darkened by the fire in hell (tale no. 22).

Tatár, Dog-Headed: Folk memory of the devastating twelfth-century invasion of Tatár hordes was reinforced by seventeenth- and eighteenth-century border raids that resulted in a cycle of local legends about Dog-Headed Tatárs. Historians are uncertain whether "dog-headed" means that the nomadic Tatár warriors' skulls were ritually deformed, or that their chiefs wore totemic dog-skull insignia, or that the adjective developed from a nickname characterizing a horrific and absurd archenemy as the reality-based legend character assumed the fantasy image of a folktale monster (see, for example, tales no. 1, 8, and 33).

Wedding: not necessarily a marriage ceremony but a party, an entertainment for married couples, as for the parents of Anna Mónár (tale no. 24).

# PROPER NAMES

Belzebub: Beelzebub, the name of a Phoenician god, became another name for Satan in the Old Testament. In Hungarian tales about the stupid devil (AT1000-1199), the most common given names are *Belzebub, Lucifer, Plutó, and Drumó.*

Beszterce harness: Beszterce is a Transylvanian town famous for its saddlery makers.

Budapest: the capital of Hungary, created in 1896 from the unification of two older towns, Buda on the west, and Pest on the east bank of the river Duna (Danube).

Bálint: Valentine (tale no. 34).

Gábor: Gabriel (no. 34).

András Kerekes: Andrew Wheelwright (no. 13).

Anna Mónár (Molnár), nickname Annuska: Ann Miller, the miller's daughter (no. 24).

Erzsi: Lizzie.

Fairy Ilona: Fairy Helen, a standard Hungarian folktale character. (*Tündérszép' Ilona* is a proverbial reference to fairylike beauty.)

Peasant Gagyi: from *gatya* (underdrawers); a nickname referring to poverty; a man who wears white linen drawers but does not have wool trousers.

Gálfalva: village in Transylvania.

János (diminutives Jánoska, Jancsi): John, Johnny, common name of folktale heroes.

Józsi Halász: Joe the fisherman.

Juliska: diminutive for Julia.

Kopovics Mountain: a Carpathian peak neighboring Andrásfalva (tale no. 32).

Mátyás, Matyi: Matthew, Matt.

Peti and Boris: Pete and Barb.

Sándor: Alexander.

Székely: the Hungarian ethnic subculture of southern Transylvania and its exile settlements in the Bucovina, Moldavia, and Serbia.

Tisza: the second longest river in Hungary (tale no. 15).

Zsuzska: Susie.

## SAYINGS AND FORMULAIC SPEECH

Mrs. Palkó's poetic märchen language is both deeply traditional and uniquely her own. Certain phrases and images that she employs spring from the common vocabulary of Hungarian folktales. Other figures of speech are known especially as the property of the Székelys, who possess a nationwide reputation for poetic and archaic speech. Noted for the beauty of their dialect and their witty use of language, Székelys regularly place first in national oratory competitions.

In addition to more widely-known expressions, Mrs. Palkó employs a number of phrases and images that are unique to her tales. Each item in the list that follows ends with a reference indicating whether it is a widespread Hungarian folktale phrase, a phrase used especially by Székelys, or Mrs. Palkó's personal formula.

"One does not have to light a candle; her beauty illuminates the room"—describing a tale heroine. [Mrs. Palkó's phrase]

"What are you doing in this Godforsaken place where not even a bird can fly?" asks the supernatural helper when the hero arrives. [Hungarian]

"Steep as the Calvary." The Calvary is a cultic site in Roman Catholic settlements, on a hill above the village, where the Stations of the Cross lead. [Mrs. Palkó]

"As many children as there are holes in a sieve and one more"—describing the poor family that has too many children. [Hungarian]

"We don't come into this world together and we don't leave it together"—says the princess consoling her father who cannot stop mourning for his wife. [Mrs. Palkó]

To die of despair; "I nearly died of despair"; "I could die, fall into despair"—to suffer a heart attack; "my heart broke"; "I could drop dead from shock"; "I could die of fright." [Székely]

"The drowning man clutches at straws," a desperate person would do anything to improve his or her situation. [Hungarian]

"He should eat what I eat, and drink what I drink, and not a single hair should be missing from his coat"—before departing, the king gives special orders on the special treatment of an enchanted prince. [Mrs. Palkó]

"When it wants hay, give it oats; when it wants oats, give it water, but never give it what it asks for"—a villain's command for cruel treatment. [Mrs. Palkó]

"The devil of envy had taken hold of his heart"—the guardian of the hero decides to mistreat his or her ward. [Mrs. Palkó]

"We will run wherever our eyes will lead us"—the tale hero describes his aimless wandering in the magic forest. [Mrs. Palkó]

"Grapes were in such abundance that they were sinking to the ground"—description of a rich vineyard. [Mrs. Palkó]

"Not a single hair should be missing from her head"—the prince asks another to care for his wife while he is at war. [Mrs. Palkó]

"Don't let the breezes or anything harmful touch you." [Mrs. Palkó]

"Her heart nearly burst from happiness." [Mrs. Palkó]

"Hip-hop, take me where I want to be"; "One, two, three, take me where I want to be"— magic command to supernatural helpers or animated objects. [Hungarian and international]

"The legs of the table bent from the weight of the food"; "The table was so laden that its legs were bent from the weight of the food"—a plentiful feast [Mrs. Palkó]

"This is man's abode, and God's resting place"; "God's is the shelter, and man's resting place"—magic helper offers hospitality when the hero on his quest asks for a night's shelter. [Hungarian]

"I need to go out"; "let's go out to pee"; "I'm scared to go out in the dark"—"to go out" to the outhouse, often a euphemism. The trip outside is sometimes used to allow a secret communication, as in "The Fawn" (no. 8) when the sister asks her brother to accompany her outside so that she can tell him the secret that their life is in danger. [Hungarian]

"Only a handful of soldiers remained to tell the tale"—according to folk tradition, the winner of a battle leaves a few soldiers as eyewitnesses, so that they can report the defeat to their people. [Hungarian]

"Screamed so hard that her eyes were popping out"; "her eyes popped out and her mouth fell open"; "one could barely look at it, for one's eye would pop out"; "his eyes nearly popped out"—descriptions of eyes popping out from the effects of staring (sometimes attached to descriptions of mouths dropping open from amazement) as if emotional impulses would make eyes come out of their sockets. [Székely]

"Poor as a church mouse"; "they were as poor as church mice"— meaning that there is no food in church for mice to eat. [Hungarian and international]

"To throw [or turn] somersaults in anger"—the devil or other evil spirit does so and usually bursts and dies. [Hungarian]

"Could look sooner at the sun than at her"; "look at the sun, not her"; "one could sooner look at the sun, so great was his beauty" —common description of the beauty of folktale figures; to look at the sun is dangerous to the eyesight, but the beauty of the princess or the gold-haired children is even more radiant. [Hungarian]

"You are mine and I am yours and nothing but death can part us." "You are mine and I am yours, only the shovel and the spade should separate us"—only death (as represented by gravedigging tools) should part us. In folktales narrated by others, the saying is often extended to say "only the shovel and the spade and the church bell will separate us." [Hungarian]

"I never leave the well-trodden road for the untrodden"; "don't ever leave the beaten track for the untrodden"—don't risk doing something unusual or unknown; follow others and stay safe. This saying is common not only in folktale narration, but in day-to-day proverbial speech. [Hungarian]

"They lived like two turtle doves"—doves, always found in pairs, are universal folk models of conjugal love. [Hungarian and international]

"An uninvited guest should stay outside the door, as the saying goes"—common saying and practice. The unwelcome suitor finds his coat on the porch when he leaves, a sign that the family wants him to leave the girl alone. [Székely]

"Wet her pants"—she was so infatuated with him that she could not hold her water: a common saying in everyday speech. Mrs. Palkó uses it for humorous effect in her folktales. [Mrs. Palkó]

"I'll see whether you are worth your keep or only half"; "I'll see if what you eat is half or fully wasted"—the employer says to the new swineherd. [Székely]

# Index of Tale Types and Motifs

The first table below lists Zsuzsanna Palkó's folktales according to the international classification developed by Antti Aarne and Stith Thompson in *The Types of the Folktale*, Folklore Fellows Communications, no. 184 (Helsinki: Suomalainen Tiedeakatemia, 1961). Entries followed by [MNK] are special Hungarian types or subtypes, listed according to supplemental numbers derived from the Hungarian Folktale Catalogue, *Magyar Népmesekatalógus*, edited by Agnes Kovács (in nine volumes, Budapest: MTA Néprajzi Kutatócsoport, 1981-1992).

      To aid readers interested in further exploring these tales and their social contexts, the third column below lists the number assigned each tale in Linda Dégh's *Folktales and Society* (Bloomington: Indiana University Press, 1989), which discusses all 75 of Mrs. Palkó's tales as well as tales by other narrators in Kakasd.

## Tale Types

| Type number and Title in Aarne and Thompson's *Types of the Folktale* | | Mrs. Palkó's tales' corresponding numbers and titles | Number in *Folktales and Society* |
|---|---|---|---|
| 302. | *The Ogre's Heart in the Egg.* | 10. The Sky-High Tree. | 12. |
| 314. | *The Youth Transformed to a Horse.* | 1. I Don't Know. | 3. |
| 317. | *The Stretching Tree.* | 10. The Sky-High Tree. | 23. |
| 326. | *The Youth Who Wanted To Learn What Fear Is.* | 5. The Count and János, the Coachman. | 12. |
| 328. | *The Boy Steals the Giant's Treasure.* | 2. Zsuzska and the Devil. | 6. |
| 332. | *Godfather Death.* | 3. Death with the Yellow Legs. | 7. |
| 403A. | *The Black and the White Bride.* | 6. The Princess. | 16. |
| 407B. | *The Devil's [Dead Man's] Mistress.* | 4. The Glass Coffin. | 9. |
| 425A. | *The Monster [Animal] as Bridegroom [Cupid and Psyche].* | 7. The Serpent Prince. | 20. |
| 450. | *Little Brother and Little Sister.* | 8. The Fawn. | 21. |
| 465C. | *A Journey to the Other World.* | 9. Józsi the Fisherman. | 22. |
| 451I. | *The Maiden Who Seeks Her Brothers.* | 19. The Twelve Robbers. | 35. |
| 465C. | [MNK] *The Fish Maiden.* | 9. Józsi the Fisherman. | 22. |
| 468. | *The Princess of the Sky-Tree.* | 10. The Sky-High Tree. | 23. |
| 500B*. | [MNK] *The Psalm-Singing Bird.* | 14. The Psalm-Singing Bird. | 29. |

# Motifs

Here follows a list of some of the more important motifs found in Zsuzsanna Palkó's tales, listed according to the classificatory system developed in Stith Thompson's *Motif-Index of Folk-Literature* (6 vols.; Bloomington:Indiana University Press, 1955-1958).

| | | | |
|---|---|---|---|
| A1331. | Paradise lost. | 21. The Three Archangels | 39. |
| D1454.4.1. | Tears of gold. | 6. The Princess. | 16. |
| E371. | Return from dead to reveal hidden treasure. | 5. The Count and János, the Coachman. | 12. |
| E415. | The dead cannot rest until certain job is completed. | 5. The Count and János, the Coachman. | 12. |
| E463. | Living man in dead man's shroud. | 5. The Count and János, the Coachman. | 12. |
| G36. | Taste of human flesh leads to habitual cannibalism. | 8. The Fawn. | 21. |
| G61. | Relative's flesh eaten unwittingly. | 8. The Fawn. | 21. |
| H543. | Escape from devil by answering his riddles. | 22. The Smoking Kalfaktor. | 40. |
| H1556.1. | Test of fidelity by feigning death. | 25. The Wager of the Two Comrades. | 48. |
| K1951.2. | Runaway cavalry hero. | 33. The Gypsy King. | 59. |
| M225. | The Gouging of Eyes for Food. | 14. The Psalm-Singing Bird. | 29. |
| R131. | Exposed or abandoned child rescued. | 13. András Kerekes. | 28. |
| T231.3. | Faithless widow ready to marry messenger who brings news of husband's death. | 25. The Wager of the Two Comrades. | 48. |
| T671. | Adoption by suckling. | 13. András Kerekes. | 28. |